E. B. W. Phelps

Annals of the Church of Christ

With a Glance at the Churches in America

E. B. W. Phelps

Annals of the Church of Christ
With a Glance at the Churches in America

ISBN/EAN: 9783337004668

Printed in Europe, USA, Canada, Australia, Japan

Cover: Foto ©Lupo / pixelio.de

More available books at **www.hansebooks.com**

ANNALS

OF THE

CHURCH OF CHRIST

FROM THE BEGINNING TO THE PRESENT TIME

WITH A GLANCE AT THE

CHURCHES IN AMERICA

BY

Mrs. E. B. W. Phelps

CINCINNATI
THE J. F. SHUMATE COMPANY
1885

THIS VOLUME

OF

"𝔖𝔨𝔢𝔱𝔠𝔥𝔢𝔰 𝔬𝔣 ℭ𝔥𝔲𝔯𝔠𝔥 𝔍𝔦𝔰𝔱𝔬𝔯𝔶"

IS AFFECTIONATELY DEDICATED

TO

HON. ISAAC M. JORDAN.

Clifton, July 5, 1885.

"Glorious things of thee are spoken,
   Zion, city of our God;
He whose word can not be broken,
   Formed thee for his own abode;
On the Rock of Ages founded,
   What can shake thy sure repose?
With salvation's walls surrounded,
   Thou mayst smile at all thy foes."

PREFACE.

The author of the Annals or Sketches of the Church has through a long life felt a deep and abiding interest in all that concerns the history of the people of God whom we call the Holy Catholic Church. A few moments of leisure taken from each day of a busy life, has for a decade of years been employed in the collection of *facts* relating to the Church. The period of time that our record embraces, *begins* when the disciples bade adieu to their Lord on Mount Olivet, and continues to trace the outline of remarkable or interesting epochs to the present hour. It is a popular history for young and old, and is abridged chiefly from the works of Dean Milman. We are also indebted to the histories of Mosheim and Gibbon and to the later ecclesiastical literature of Southey, Schaff, Froude, Green, etc. We know that many noble church histories are in existence, but they are very elaborate and are but little read except by students of divinity. Our book is succinct and simple, but contains many interesting facts that intelligent Christians ought to know. We have tried to state the facts that have been handed down to us from age to age, without garbling. When the Roman soldiers looked upon the coat of our crucified Lord, they said, "Let us not rend it;" so would *we* present, without the touch of passion or prejudice, the varied events we have contemplated. But alas the tissue of Church history, is not a seamless robe, without spot or wrinkle: it is full of incongruities. Clouds and shadows intervene, but there is a light shining through the mist, that reveals a "little flock" who have, in every age, served God acceptably. With a heart full of love, we have found it difficult to portray dispassionately all the aspects of this many-sided subject. We have tried to educe the truth by looking at the *Past* in the light of the *Present*. Though the manners and sentiments of the human actors, in the last eighteen centuries, have undergone many changes, yet they have contended in every age with like passions and with similar motives as ourselves. May the readers of the following pages derive as much interest in reading them as the author has experienced in collating them.

> " Dim as the borrowed beams of moon and stars
> To lonely, weary, wandering travelers,
> Is *reason* to the soul. And as on high,
> Those rolling fires *discover* but the sky,
> Not light us here ; so reason's glimmering ray,
> Was lent not to *assure* our doubtful way,
> But guide us upward to a better day."
>
> —Mrs. E. W. B. Phelps.

Clifton, Cincinnati, Ohio, February 1, 1880.

INTRODUCTION.

"The gates of Hell shall never prevail against it."

Nearly nineteen centuries have passed away since Jesus, the Divine Founder of our religion, uttered this saying, with regard to the Church. These words were addressed to Peter and to the rest of the disciples, when He was alone with them. These men were timid and doubting, unlearned in the wisdom of the world. Our Lord lived not in an age of darkness and ignorance, but in the famous Augustan age, renowned for learning and letters. But, he was the carpenter's son from an unimportant city of Galilee, and his disciples, men of humble occupation, fishermen and tax-gatherers. How knoweth this man letters? was the question asked by one, who knew his humble origin, and yet heard Him speak "as never man spake." Humble and apparently helpless as these disciples of Jesus were, they did batter down the strongholds of Pagan superstion; they did overcome Jewish prejudice, and they subdued spiritual wickedness in high places. Before that generation had passed away, disciples of the crucified one were found among the members of Cæsar's household. These things were accomplished not with human weapons, but with the sword of the Spirit, the Word of God. The stone that the prophet saw, centuries before our Lord came into this world, cut out of a mountain, without hands, has filled the earth.

"It is not assumed that the Church is a perfect institution, represented as it is by fallible, erring men, but it is "the pillar and ground of Truth," overlaid with many of the devices of man. In the wear and tear of ages "The City of God" has been soiled and defaced by pride and ambition—the citizens of the new Jerusalem, like those of the old, have not all been true or obedient to the commands of their founder, but have sometimes aspired to be lords over God's heritage, and have starved and misled the flock they were commanded to feed and guide. It is granted that in the successive ages of its long life, the light of the Gospel has sometimes shone feebly. It shone as the sun shines through a mist, but it was still the glorious light of God, behind a cloud. "The influx of wealth when the church was about three centuries old; the barbarism of the dark ages; the intellectualism that preferred *debate* to brotherhood, and some grievous errors in matters of faith, have *infected* the Church, and cast shadows upon the Tabernacle of God; yet the Shechinah is the light of Heaven, and can never be extinguished."

"The Church," says Macaulay, "has often been compared by divines to the Ark, but never was the resemblance more perfect than during that evil time when she rode alone through darkness and tempest on the deluge, beneath which all the great works of power and wisdom lay entombed, bearing within her that (apparently) feeble germ from which a second and more glorious civilization was to spring." The Church is the Ark of the Covenant, as it has brought down to us unimpaired, not tables of stone, but the Oracles of God as revealed to us in the New Testament. It is painful to read many chapters in the history of the *Visible* Church, but it must be borne in mind that in the middle ages there was a world within the Church, and all the righteous acts committed in Christendom have been charged to *it* by succeeding generations. The Popes and other prelates, by unjust usurpations and unrighteous persecution, believing that orthodoxy and not Christian love was the test of discipleship, have inflicted grievous wounds upon Christ's body—the Church. But it must be acknowledged that the power of the Pope in the dark times of war and violence was often exerted as a defense and protection to the people against the tyranny of despots not so powerful as themselves. The history of the invisible church has never been written. How many millions of private Christians have been united to Christ, as the branches abide in the vine, rich clusters of beauty and fragrance, but whose names have never been inscribed on any page in this world's history. In that day when small and great stand before God, their names shall be written in the Lamb's Book of Life. How would the love and devotion to the cause of truth, that burned in so many hearts from the time of John Wycliffe to the Reformation, have been made known to the world, except by the persecutions that then arose? We should never have heard of the humble Monk, who assisted the great Luther, in the Augustinian Convent, in comprehending the great doctrine of justification by Faith, when reading together the New Testament. These things convince us that amid all the darkness and corruption of the Middle Ages there was still a little flock within the visible Church, who cried day and night "to him who sitteth upon the throne."

It is not only within the Church that the moral power of Christianity is felt, but the influence of its spirit has moulded the thoughts and opinions of the whole civilized world—"the leaven of Christianity has silently worked upon masses of men, breaking down its great social evils." There are many, alas, who "live without God in the world," trusting to their own strength, and refusing to recognize the good that is in them as the result of a Christian education, or the reflected Christian influence of those about them. The author of *Ecce Homo* has well replied to those who say that "The Church" is a failure. *Ecce Homo*. "If the object of civil society be the security of life and property, and increase of prosperity through the division of labor, civil society is not a success. Men are robbed and murdered; whole classes live in pauperism, insecurity, slavery. A sufficient reason for dissatisfaction, a good ground for complaint—but not a sufficient reason for dissolving civil society and relapsing into the normal state." In like manner if the Church fails to do her whole duty, let us strive to quicken her energies, to rouse her sense of responsibility, through all her ramifications, for we can ill afford to sever the strongest and most sacred tie that binds men to each other. How would the moral pulse of this great world stand still, if the prayers of unnumbered hearts did not daily ascend like incense to the skies, and if the life-giving truths that issue from all the pulpits in the land did not give strength to the weak, direction to the strong, and comfort and rest to the weary! To whom should we have recourse in all our mental and spiritual conflicts, but to those whom Christ has appointed to teach all nations? Who shall strike the rock in the parched wilderness of this world, causing waters of refreshment to flow, or who shall feed the hungry soul, if the manna of the Word of God, dispensed by the Church, be withdrawn?

When our short life is ebbing, who shall cheerfully point to a better inheritance on high, if the voice of the preacher be hushed? The promise of Christ is with his people: "Wherever two or three are gathered together in my name, there am I in the midst of them." The promise of Christ is with his faithful ministers, the successors of those who gazed upon their Lord, as he ascended from the Mount of Olives: "Lo I am with you alway, even unto the end of the world."

> " The church must stand acknowledged,
> While the world shall stand,
> The most effectual guard,
> Support and ornament of virtue's cause."

ANNALS OF THE CHURCH OF CHRIST.

CHAPTER I.

"When Thou hadst overcome the sharpness of death, Thou didst open the kingdom of heaven to all believers."

The first Church of Christ was assembled in an upper room at Jerusalem; perhaps it was an upper room in the Temple, but the exact location is not important. The disciples of Jesus were there; their names were about an hundred and twenty. Peter, and James, and John were there, and Andrew, and Philip; Thomas, Bartholomew or Nathanael, Matthew, and James the son of Alpheus, and Simon Zelotes, and Judas the brother of James. The women were there, who had ministered to the Lord of their substance; they who had stood by His cross, and who had visited His sepulchre. These, with Mary the mother of Jesus, had now assembled with "His brethren" with one accord in prayer and supplication. The last words that our Lord had uttered in their hearing were still sounding in their ears, like heavenly music. The words were new, but they were spoken with authority: "Go ye into all the world, and preach the gospel to every creature; baptizing them in the name of the Father, and of the Son, and of the Holy Ghost; teaching them to observe all things whatsoever I have commanded you; and lo, I am with you alway, even unto the end of the world." He commanded that repentance and remission of sins should be preached in His name among *all* nations, *beginning* at Jerusalem.

How full of solemn grandeur must have been the feelings of this little company of believers, as they remembered the parting words of their Lord and Master! The command to preach, and baptize, and organize, was doubtless intended specially for the eleven apostles; but the words that *follow* were intended for all and every one in that company, and for all believers in every age and nation. "Ye shall be *witnesses* unto me, both in Jerusalem, and in all Judea, and in Samaria, and in the uttermost parts of the earth." The Master had left them, "a cloud had received Him out of their sight;" yet they were full of courage. Peter, who had been so timid, now *stood up* in the midst of the disciples and, after comforting them with the fulfillment of prophecy, declared that one must be ordained in the place of Judas, to be a witness with them of the resurrection of their Lord. Matthias was appointed, and numbered with the eleven apostles.

Ten days after this time, when the day of Pentecost had fully come, *they* were, with all, with one accord in one place. They were baptized with the Holy Ghost, and began to speak with other tongues as the Spirit gave them utterance. This great miracle was quickly noised abroad, and a vast multitude was gathered — "devout men out of every nation under heaven" were then dwelling at Jerusalem. All were amazed at this wonderful gift of tongues, and some *doubted* as to the source of the inspiration. Some unbelieving mockers cried out: "These men are filled with new wine." Peter lifted up his voice and addressed the assembly, explaining to them that this outpouring of the Spirit was in fulfillment of prophecy. He called upon them to repent of their sins, and to be baptized, every one in the name of Jesus Christ, for the remission of sins, and they should receive the gift of the Holy Ghost. So effective was this sermon of Peter, together with the influence of the miracle, that three thousand on the same day were added to the band of Christian believers. About this time Peter and John, who continued to observe the regular hours of Jewish worship, went up to the Temple to pray. They there, at the gate of the Temple, performed in the name of Jesus a great miracle, which attracted much attention. It excited much jealousy in the high-priest Annas, and in all the hierarchy who were at Jerusalem. This miracle of Peter and John is recorded in the third chapter of the Acts. The apostles were required to stand before a council composed of rulers, elders, and scribes, to give an account of "the good deed done to the impotent man." Peter then proclaimed boldly that the miracle was performed by the power of Jesus Christ, whom *they* had crucified and slain — declaring that: "This is the *stone* which was set at naught by *you builders*, which is become the head of the corner; neither is there salvation in any other; for there is none other name under heaven given among men whereby we must be saved." The boldness of Peter and John, and their unlearned simplicity, greatly surprised the Jewish council. They, after they had held a conference together, called in the "unlearned, ignorant men," and commanded them not to speak at all, or teach in the name of Jesus. Peter and John replied to the proud rulers as men must reply who knew in their inmost hearts that they had a commission to execute, given them by their Lord and Master. The apostles returned to their company, and reported all that the chief priests and elders had said unto them. They lifted their voices in joyful accord to God, saying: "Why do the heathen rage, and the people imagine a vain thing?" The apostles continued to preach and work many signs and wonders, and the *people* magnified them, but the high-priest and many of the Sadducees were filled with indignation, "and laid their hands on the apostles and put them in the common prison." But the angel of the Lord opened the prison doors, and "commanded them to stand and speak in the Temple, all the words of this life."

The high-priest and the senate of the children of Israel were anxious and excited when they heard that the apostles had escaped from prison, and were standing in the Temple, teaching the people. Then went the captain with the officers, to bring the apostles (without violence, for they feared the people) before the council. "Did we not strictly command you," said the high-priest, "not to teach or preach in this name? Ye have filled Jerusalem with your doctrine, and intend to bring this man's blood upon us." Then Peter and the *other* apostles replied: "We must obey God rather than man." The violence of this council was restrained by Gamaliel, a wise man among them, held in much reputation. His words were: "Refrain from these men and let them alone, for if this work or this counsel be of men, it will come to naught; but if it be of God, ye can not overthrow it; lest haply ye be found even to fight against God." And to him they agreed; and they departed from the presence of the council, rejoicing that they were counted worthy to suffer *shame* for *His* name. And daily in the Temple and in every house, they ceased not to teach and preach Jesus Christ. Gamaliel seems to have been one of those wise, good men, of whom in every age there have been a few representatives, who despise a persecuting spirit, and who fearlessly stand up for truth or an inquiry into truth, though surrounded by a greater number of seditious opposers.

The number of the disciples at this time was greatly multiplied. The apostles, wishing to give their whole time to prayer and the ministry of the Word, determined to appoint seven additional officers in the Church, called deacons. These men seem primarily to have been appointed to superintend the bodily as well as the spiritual wants of the great influx of disciples. They were dedicated to their work in the most solemn manner; they were set before the apostles, and when they prayed they laid their hands on them. Two of these deacons became very celebrated afterwards, in the history of the Church. Stephen was the first Christian martyr. He was drawn into controversy with the Alexandrian Jews, Cyrenians, Libertines, and others, and as they could not resist the power and energy by which he spoke, they were greatly *enraged*, and suborned men to bring charges of blasphemy against him, and accused him of an intention to change the customs which Moses had delivered. While he was making his defense before the "men, brethren, and fathers," and was declaring his faith in all the interesting points of Jewish history, when he quoted the words of Moses to the unbelievers in his days, calling them "stiff-necked and uncircumcised in heart and ears," believing that Stephen made the application of Moses' words to them, they were cut to the heart, and gnashed on *him* with their teeth. They did not permit him to continue his narration. And when Stephen, lookingly steadfastly upward, said: "I see the heavens opened, and the Son of man standing on the right hand of God," they rushed on him with great violence, cast him out of the city, and stoned him. He calling upon God and saying, "Lord Jesus, receive my spirit," kneeled down and cried with a loud voice, "Lord, lay not this sin to their charge." How cruel and dreadful is fanaticism! Many of these Jews doubtless thought they were obeying the law, as recorded in the 13th chapter of Deuteronomy. The clothes of the *witnesses* of this martyrdom were laid down at the feet of a young man named "Saul." The Jewish law required the presence of two or three witnesses, to testify as to the cause of blood-shedding.

The most dreadful crimes have sometimes been perpetrated according to the forms of law. Law, it has been said, is the voice of God, but it has not always been so administered as to protect and defend the rights of the innocent from the infuriated passions of bad men. Religion, heaven-born as she is, awakens and rouses the deepest and strongest passions of the heart, and if not kept in subjection to the "Law of Love," as revealed in the New Testament, has produced and will produce the most direful consequences.

The deacon Philip went to the city of Samaria, and preached Christ unto them. In this city, Philip had great success, notwithstanding the presence of Simon, a sorcerer. When the apostles, who were at Jerusalem, heard that Samaria had received the Word of God, and that they had been baptized in the name of Jesus Christ, *they* (the apostles) sent down unto them Peter and John. These now *laid their hands* on the converts, that they might receive the Holy Ghost. Philip also made another convert of rank and importance, an officer who held a high station with the queen of the Ethiopians. The persecution after the martyrdom of Stephen was very favorable to the progress of Christianity. The disciples were scattered abroad throughout the regions of Judea and Samaria, except the apostles. They seem to have remained at their post in Jerusalem. The death of Stephen seems to be connected with the conversion of St. Paul. Saul, breathing threatenings and slaughter against the disciples of the Lord, went to the high-priest for letters to Damascus, that he might seize any Christians, men or women, that he might bring them *bound* to Jerusalem. And as he journeyed and came near to Damascus, there occurred the remark-. able conversion which changed a fierce persecutor into the most zealous of all the Christian teachers. It was the privilege of this great man to hear the voice of his Lord and Master; to hear the words of reproof in a loving voice, which bade him arise, to go to Damascus, not to persecute, but to receive the initiatory rite of baptism into the fold he had so lately threatened and despised. He is received and greeted as a brother by Ananias at Damascus, who had been instructed by a vision not to doubt the new disciple. Saul was probably deeply touched by what he witnessed at the martyrdom of Stephen; but, as is sometimes the case, his fury was increased and maddened by the *doubts* that now entered his mind. "To propagate Christianity in the enlightened West, where its most permanent conquests were to be made, to emancipate it from the trammels of Judaism, a man was wanting of comprehensive views, of higher education and more liberal accomplishments. Such an instrument was found in Saul of Tarsus. Born in the Grecian city of Tarsus, yet a Roman citizen, his Judaism was in no degree weakened by his Grecian culture. Saul stood on the confines of both religions, qualified beyond all men to develop a system which should unite Jew and Gentile under a more harmonious and comprehensive faith." Above all, his extraordinary, unprecedented conversion gave him a zeal which seemed to eclipse the rest of the apostles.

Part of the three years which elapsed between the conversion of Paul and his first visit to Jerusalem, was passed in Arabia. He had narrowly escaped the fury of his brethren at Damascus, who sought his death. He passed, it is supposed, more than a year in Arabia, in exile, employing himself, probably, in instructing the Jews, who were scattered in great numbers in Arabia. Though he had sacrificed much favor with his countrymen in becoming a Christian, he was at first coldly received by the Christians at Jerusalem; even the apostles stood aloof. Ananias, enlightened by a vision, had convinced the Christians of Damascus of Paul's sincerity, and by their loving zeal he had been delivered from the fury of the Damascene Jews. Barnabas, a convert of Cyprus, introduced Paul to the apostles at Jerusalem, declaring to them his marvelous conversion, while journeying to Damascus as a persecutor, and how he had preached boldly at Damascus in the name of the Lord Jesus. And Paul was with them, coming in and out at Jerusalem, speaking boldly in the name of Jesus and disputing with the Grecians, whose wrath was kindled against him. The brethren then brought Paul down to Cæsarea, and from thence to Tarsus. The Christians at this time, just previous to the accession of Herod Agrippa, enjoyed peace about *three years*. The time was zealously employed in disseminating the gospel in every part of Judea. The peace enjoyed by the Christians at this time is attributed to the fact of the anxiety of the Jews about the independence of their religion. The frantic Caligula, emperor of Rome, insisted that his statue should be placed in the Temple at Jerusalem. The Jews, filled with horror at such a demand, refused to sow, or reap, or attend to their accustomed duties, unless the emperor should desist from so sacrilegious an attempt. It required all the moderation and conciliation of Petronius, the Roman governor, to quiet the Jewish people. By well-timed delays, in postponing, by various expedients, the desecration of the holy house, the foolish, profane desire of the emperor was not executed. He died! *

During this time the apostle Peter passed *through all quarters*, preaching and working miracles at Lydda and Joppa. While at Joppa, he was summoned to Cæsarea to visit Cornelius, a Roman centurion. It was on this occasion that Peter declared that the partition-

---
* Caligula.

wall between Jew and Gentile was broken down, in these words: "Of a truth I perceive that God is no respecter of persons, but in *every nation* he that feareth God and worketh righteousness is accepted with Him." Peter's sermon on this occasion was accompanied by the gift of the Holy Ghost, and they of the circumcision who came with Peter were astonished, that upon the Gentiles was poured out the gift of the Holy Ghost.

CHAPTER II.

When the apostles and brethren who were in Judea heard that the Gentiles had received the word of God, they contended with Peter, saying, "Thou wentest in unto men uncircumcised and did eat with them." But when Peter rehearsed the matter relating to *Cornelius*, from the beginning, they glorified God, saying, "Then hath God also to the Gentiles granted repentance unto life." Jewish prejudices were beginning to yield. The first step towards abrogating the differences between Jew and Gentile was taken by Peter. Paul, assisted by Barnabas, was the most active apostle in emancipating the Jewish converts from the inveterate prejudices of their old religion. Samaria had already received the new religion to some extent, but it seems the conflict in that city was with Orientalism rather than Judaism. Christianity, aspiring to the moral conquest of the world had to contend with three antagonists: Judaism, Orientalism and Paganism. The conversion of Cornelius, recorded in the 10th chapter of the Acts, took place before the persecution of Herod Agrippa. Herod affected the *splendor* of his grandfather, Herod the Great, but unlike him he made the strictest profession of Judaism. He determined to suppress Christianity by vigorous means. James, the brother of St. John, was the first victim. At this time the power of life and death was restored for a short time to the Jews.

Peter was imprisoned. Prayer was made without ceasing for him. The same night, as we learn from the 12th chapter of the Acts, when Herod would have brought Peter forth, he was miraculously delivered from the prison. He at first thought "he saw a vision, and wist not that it was true." When Peter was come to himself, he said, Now I know of a surety that God hath sent his angel and delivered me from Herod and the expectation of the Jews. Then Peter went to the house of Mary, the mother of John, whose surname was Mark, where many were gathered together praying. Christianity had now been preached at Phenice, Cyprus and Antioch. A great number believed and turned to the Lord. When the church at Jerusalem heard of the conversions at Antioch they sent forth Barnabas that he should go thither. Barnabas was glad when he saw the grace of God at Antioch. He went to Tarsus to seek Saul, that he might assist him in the work of teaching at Antioch. For a whole year Barnabas and Saul assembled themselves with the church and "taught much people." The disciples were called Christians first in Antioch. A famine prevailed about this time, A. D. 43, in Judea. The disciples determined to send relief to their brethren in Judea by the hands of Barnabas and Saul. Claudius Cæsar was then Emperor of Rome.

In the terrific and repulsive circumstances of Herod's death, shortly after the deliverance of Peter, the Jewish historian, Josephus, and the writer of the Acts, agree. Christianity as yet was but an expanded Judaism; it was preached by Jews, it was addressed to Jews. The son of Herod, being a minor, could not succeed his father, therefore a Roman prefect assumed the provincial government of Judea. The Sanhedrim had not now the power to take violent measures against the

Christians. After the mission of Paul and Barnabas to Jerusalem, about the time of the Herodian persecution, these two distinguished teachers were invested with the divine sanction in the apostolic office. By fasting and praying and laying on of hands, these men were prepared for their work. They went to Selencia and to Cyprus and when they were at Salamis they preached the Word of God in the synagogues of the Jews. They visited Paphos and Perga in Pamphylia, also Antioch in Pisidia. In this city the ruler of the synagogue, after the reading of the Law and the Prophets invited Paul to make an exhortation to the people. After giving them the principal points in the Jewish history, Paul declared to them the birth, death and resurrection of Jesus and explained to them the prophecies of David with regard to Jesus. "Be it known to you therefore, men and brethren, that through this man is preached unto you *the forgiveness of* sins, and by Him all that believe are justified without the Law of Moses. And when the Jews were gone out from this assembly, the Gentiles besought that these words might be preached to them the next Sabbath. And the next Sabbath day, came together almost the whole city, to hear the Word of God. But when the Jews saw the multitudes, they were moved with envy, and spake against the things spoken by Paul, contradicting and blaspheming. Then Paul and Barnabas waxed bold and said, It was necessary that the Word of God should first be spoken to you; but seeing ye put it from you and hold yourselves unworthy of everlasting life, lo, we turn to the Gentiles." And the *word* of the Lord was published throughout *all* that region. But the Jews stirred up the devout and honorable women, and the chief men of the city raised a persecution against Paul and Barnabas and expelled them from their coasts. Then they went to Iconium, into the synagogue of the Jews, and a great *multitude* both of Jews and Greeks believed. But this city afterwards became divided in sentiment, and when an assault was about to be made the Apostles fled to Derbe and Lystra, cities of Lycaonia. There they preached the gospel and performed a miracle on a lame man, and when the people saw what Paul had done they lifted up their voices in the barbarous dialect of their country saying, "The gods have come down to us in the likeness of men." And they called Barnabas Jupiter, and Paul Mercurius, because he was the chief speaker. Then the Priest of Jupiter brought oxen and garlands and would have done sacrifice unto them, which when Paul and Barnabas heard, they rent their clothes and ran in among them, crying our, "Sirs, why do ye these things? We are *men* of like passions with you, and preach unto you, that ye should turn from these vanities to the living God, which made heaven and earth and all things therein." With these words they scarcely restrained the people from doing sacrifice unto them. Lystra and Derbe were cities in the center of a Pagan population. Christianity came now for the first time in direct collision with Paganism. Jews, however, came thither from Antioch and Iconium and instituted a persecution against the Apostles; they stoned Paul, and drew him out of the city, believing him to be dead; but as the disciples gathered around him Paul rose up and came into the city. The next day the Apostles went to Derbe, and taught many. They returned also to Lystra, to Iconium and to Antioch, confirming the souls of the disciples. They ordained *elders or presbyters in every church, commending them to the Lord in whom they believed. After these things they returned to Antioch (in Syria) and rehearsed to the church what God had done, and how God had opened the door of faith to the Gentiles. And there they abode a long time. About this time Paul and Barnabas met certain Judaizing teachers saying, "Except ye be circumcised ye can not be saved." It was determined at Antioch that Paul and Barnabas should go up to Jerusalem unto the Apostles and elders about this question of circumcision. The church *brought them on* their way; they passed through Phenice and Samaria declaring the conversion of the Gentiles, and they caused great joy to all the brethren. And the apostles and elders came together to consider this question, whether it was needful to keep the Law of Moses as regarded circumcision. And when there was much disputation Peter rose up, arguing against the yoke of circumcision, as regarded the Gentiles. Then the multitude kept silence, listening to Barnabas and Saul, who recounted what God had wrought for the Gentiles by them. Then James after some words of instruction and referring to the words of Simon, declared his sentence—"My sentence is that we trouble not them, which from among the Gentiles are turned to God. But that we write unto them, that they abstain from pollution of idols, from fornication, from things strangled and from blood." Then pleased it the Apostles and elders with the whole church to send to Antioch chosen men of their own company, with Paul and Barnabas, Judas and Silas, chief men among the

---

* Bishops, Elders or Presbyters are names, applied to the *same* office while the *Apostles* lived.

brethren. And they wrote letters by them after this manner: "The Apostles and elders and brethren send greeting unto the brethren of Antioch, of Syria and Cilicia—Forasmuch as certain which went out from us have troubled you with *words*, it has seemed good to us, being *assembled* with one accord, to send to you our beloved Barnabas and Paul, who have hazarded their lives for the Lord Jesus; also Judas and Silas, who will tell you the same things. We desire to lay upon you no greater burdens than these necessary things, abstinence from meats offered to idols, from blood and from fornication. "When they were dismissed they came to Antioch and delivered the epistle to the multitude. Judas and Silas were permitted to return unto the Apostles Paul and Barnabas, but Silas was pleased to abide there still. When Paul and Barnabas revisited the cities where they had made many converts, Barnabas desired to take John Mark, but Paul chose Silas, so that they separated, Barnabas going to Cyprus with Mark, and Paul with Silas to Syria and Cilicia. When Paul returned to Lystra he found there a disciple, Timotheus, or Timothy, afterward so celebrated on account of the two epistles written to him by Paul, when he was bishop (as tradition says) of Ephesus. As they passed through the cities they delivered to the brethren copies of the *decrees* they had received from the Apostles and Elders at Jerusalem. And the churches were established in the faith and increased in number daily. After passing through Phrygia and Galatia, Paul passed from Troas over into Macedonia, a vision having appeared to him in the night, saying "Come over to Macedonia and help us." He went to Philippi, one of the chief cities of Macedonia. He met by the river side, Lydia, a seller of purple, who became a disciple, (she was of the city of Thyatira), she was baptized with her household, and she persuaded Paul to abide in her house. About this time Paul and Silas were taken by certain men, and brought to the magistrates of Philippi who were incensed against Paul and Silas because they had exorcised from a damsel, a spirit of divination. This girl had brought money to her masters by soothsaying. Paul and Silas were beaten and then thrust into the jail at Philippi, and their feet made fast in the stocks. At midnight Paul and Silas sung praises unto God, and the prisoners heard them. Suddenly an earthquake shook the prison, and all the doors were opened. The keeper awaking, fearing that the prisoners had fled, drew his sword and would have killed himself, but Paul ciied to him, "Do thyself no harm, we are all here." Then the jailer called for a light, and came trembling, falling down before Paul and Silas, saying, "Sirs, what must I do to be saved?" and they said: "Believe on the Lord Jesus Christ, and thou shalt be saved and thy house." And they spoke unto him, and unto all that were in his house. And the jailer washed the stripes of Paul and Silas the same hour of the night, and they were baptized, he and all his, straightway—and he set meat before them. The magistrates became alarmed when they heard that the men whom they had imprisoned were Romans, and they came to them giving them liberty and beseeching them to leave the city. They left the prison and entered into the house of Lydia, and after comforting the brethren they departed from the city of Philippi. They passed through Amphipolis and Apollonia and came to Thessalonica.

In this city there was a synagogue of the Jews; and after the manner of Paul, he reasoned with them three Sabbath days, out of the Scriptures, alleging that Jesus was Christ and that he must needs have suffered and risen from the dead. A great multitude of the Greeks believed, and many of the devout women. But the unbelieving Jews stirred up an uproar among the people, saying, "*These* who have turned the world upside down have come hither also, doing contrary to the decrees of Cæsar saying: There is another king, one Jesus."

The brethren then sent away Paul and Silas to Berea. The people of Berea were more noble than those of Thessalonica, inasmuch as they daily searched the Scriptures whether these things were so. But a disturbance occurring in Berea, Paul was sent away by the brethren; but Silas and Timothy abode there still. Paul went to Athens and preached on Mars' Hill. Paul was invited by the philosophers of the Epicureans and Stoics to come to the Areopagus and speak of the new doctrine. Paul made an eloquent speech to them, which is found in the 17th chapter of the Acts, quoting from their own poets to strengthen his argument for the living God, and reproving them for their superstition. When he spoke of "the resurrection of the dead," some mocked —but some converts were made. From Athens, Paul proceeded to Corinth. This city had now recovered all its wealth and splendor. It had been destroyed by Mummius a Roman consul, 146 B. C. Julius Cæsar planted a colony there. It then arose like a phœnix from its ashes. It formed a connecting link between Italy, Northern Greece and Asia. It was a rich central commercial mart. An unusual number of Jews had at this time congregated in Corinth, in consequence of an edict of Claudius expelling the Jews from Rome. Suetonius the historian attributes this edict to the mutual hostility of the Christians and Jews. Christianity must, therefore, have made considerable progress in Rome. With two of the exiles Paul now made his abode and pursued with them the same occupation. The Jews, even *the most learned*, usually applied themselves to some art or trade. Paul was a *tent-maker*. At Corinth, for the first time, the Christians seemed to have a separate school of instruction. They seceded from the synagogue, and Crispus, one of the chief rulers, joined with them. Silas and Timothy came over to help Paul. At length Paul declared to those Jews who opposed him and blasphemed, his determination to devote himself to the Gentiles. Many of the Corinthians, hearing the arguments of Paul, believed and were baptized. Paul had while in Corinth an encouraging vision. "For I am with thee; I have much people in this city." 'Strengthened by *impressions* like these, Paul remained a year and six months in Corinth. But Gallio, the Roman deputy "cared for none of these things," and gave no heed to the complaints of the Jews against the Christians. From Corinth Paul went to Ephesus, previously visiting the churches at Cæsarea and Antioch. Paul seems to have remained in Ephesus and in the neighboring country for the space of *two years*, so that all they which dwelt in Asia, heard the word of the Lord Jesus, both Jews and Greeks. Paul met in Ephesus some of the disciples of John the Baptist. These he fully instructed in the doctrines of Christianity. The most eminent of these disciples was Apollos, who being an eloquent man became very conspicuous as a teacher—

the other disciples formed the nucleus of a Christian community at Ephesus. Many of the Jewish exorcists dwelling at Ephesus came and confessed and showed their deeds, and burned their books which had been of great pecuniary value to them. But there was a common article of trade at Ephesus, that was not so easily surrendered; this was a shrine of silver made for the temple of Diana. The sale of these shrines and other works of art had gradually diminished, and at the instigation of Demetrius, one of the chief artisans of these shrines, a great popular tumult was excited. This man addressed the multitude, saying, "Ye see and hear that not alone at Ephesus, but through all Asia, this Paul hath turned away much people, saying that they be no gods which are made with hands. So that not only our craft is in danger to be set at naught; but also that the great goddess Diana should be despised and her magnificence destroyed, whom *all* Asia (a part of Asia Minor) and all the world worshipeth." When the people heard these things they cried out, "Great is Diana of the Ephesians." The city was filled with confusion. Some of the chief men who were friends of Paul would not suffer him to adventure himself among them.

CHAPTER III.

PAUL'S TRAVELS.

The town clerk of Ephesus finally appeased them by consenting to their belief, that the image of Diana had fallen down from Jupiter; "seeing that this thing cannot be disputed, ye ought to be quiet." He then reminded them that they were in danger (as Roman citizens) (Acts xix. 35) of being called to account for this day's uproar. He told them—as we would tell the rebellious to-day—that the *law* was open; all their evils would be redressed in a lawful assembly, "seeing that these men are not robbers of your temples or blasphemers of your goddess." The temple of Ephesus was one of the wonders of the world. Paul soon afterward withdrew from the excited city and pursued his former line of travel through Macedonia and Greece. The exiles from Rome had quietly passed back to their usual residences in the metropolis. In writing his epistle to the Romans, Paul evidently addresses those, with whom he is personally acquainted. As he had not yet been to Italy, he had doubtless formed these acquaintances at Corinth. He abode three months in Greece, after leaving Macedonia. He then returned to Philippi, in Macedonia, where he took shipping and sailed over the Ægean to Troas. While Paul was preaching at Troas, the night being far spent, one of his hearers, Eutychus, fell down while asleep, from the third loft. Paul soon restored him. From Troas to Assos Paul went afoot, but the ship took him in and came to Mitylene. While at Mitylene, Paul sent to Ephesus for the *elders* of the Church. After giving the Elders many exhortations, how they should behave to the flock of God over which the Holy Ghost had made them overseers, he took a solemn leave of them, telling them to remember the words of the Lord Jesus: "It is more blessed to give than to receive." And he kneeled down and prayed with them all, and they fell on Paul's neck, and wept sore, *sorrowing* for the words which he spoke, that they would see his face no more." And they accompanied him to the ship. Paul continued his travels to Coos and to Rhodes and to Patara, then taking another ship, sailed to Tyre, where they remained seven days. They found disciples at Tyre; when they parted from these friends, they with their wives and children kneeled upon the shore with Paul and prayed. Then they came to Ptolemais and then to Cæsarea. In this city they abode at the house of Philip the Evangelist. Here the disciples besought Paul not to go to Jerusalem. But Paul was determined to go, "and after these days we took up our carriages and went up to Jerusalem." Some of the disciples from Cæsarea went also, together with an old disciple from Cyprus, with whom we should lodge. We were received gladly at Jerusalem, and the day after Paul went in with us unto *James*, and the Elders all were present. Paul declared to them *what* God had wrought for the Gentiles by his ministry. And they glorified the Lord. And when we had saluted them— they said to Paul, "Thou seest, brother, how many thousands of the Jews there are which believe, and they are all zealous of the law: but they are informed of thee, that thou teachest all the Jews, that are among the

Gentiles, to forsake Moses, saying that they ought not to circumcise their children. What is it therefore?" Paul had gone to Jerusalem to keep the feast of Pentecost, the birthday of the Law. Understanding the violence of his enemies at Jerusalem, he determined to comply with the laws of prudence, and on the advice of his friends he went with four persons into the Temple who had taken upon them a vow, that he might evince a personal reverence for the religion of his ancestors. He was recognized, however, by his enemies, who made a sudden outcry and charged him with having introduced into the temple Trophimus, a convert, who had come with him from Ephesus. He was charged with having conversed with this uncircumcised stranger within the three pillars or palisades, which in the three languages of that time, Hebrew, Greek and Latin, forbade the entrance of any who were not of pure Jewish descent. They drew Paul violently out of the temple into the court of the Gentiles; they were about to kill him, when the chief captain heard of it; he ran with the soldiers and centurions and commanded him to be bound with two chains, and carried into the castle. He was borne by the soldiers, to rescue him from the violence of the people. The captain, Lysias, supposed him to be an insurgent chieftain who might create a dangerous riot. He demanded of Paul who he was, and what he intended to do. Then Paul said, "May I speak unto thee?" Lysias said, "Canst thou speak Greek?" Paul said, "I am a Jew of Tarsus, a city of Cilicia, a citizen of no mean city, and beseech thee to suffer me to speak unto the people." Paul stood on the stairs and beckoned with the hand unto the people. A great silence now ensued and Paul spake to the people in the Hebrew tongue. He addresses them as "Men, brethren, and fathers," telling them that he had been brought up in Jerusalem at the feet of Gamaliel, their celebrated teacher. He then tells them of his remarkable conversion to Christianity while journeying from Jerusalem to Damascus—as recorded in the 22d chapter of the Acts. In order to prove his sincerity, that he had been a zealous Jew, he tells them that he was present at the martyrdom of Stephen and held the clothes of those who stoned him. He tells them of his baptism, and of a *trance* in the temple at Jerusalem when the voice of the Lord, who had appeared to him in the way said to him: "Depart; I will send thee far hence unto the Gentiles." They heard him until the word "Gentiles" was uttered. They then *lifted up* their voices and cried, "Away with such a fellow from the earth." The chief captain had him brought into the castle, that he should be examined—he probably understanding nothing of the address that Paul had uttered and wishing to discover the cause of the violent agitation of the people. And as they were about to bind him with thongs, Paul said, "Is it lawful for you to scourge a man that is a Roman and uncondemned?" When the centurion heard that, he said to the chief captain, "Take heed, what thou doest, this man is a Roman." Then the captain said, "Tell me, art thou a Roman?" He said, "Yea." The captain said, "With a great sum obtained I this freedom." And Paul said, "But I was *free-born*." Paul was loosed from his bonds, and on the morrow he was set before the chief priests and the council. As Paul was speaking, Ananias the High Priest, commanded him to be smitten on the mouth. Then Paul said, "God shall smite *thee*, thou whited wall;

for sittest thou to judge me after the law, and commandest me to be smitten contrary to law?" And some said, "Revilest thou God's High Priest?" "I wist not, brethren, that he was the High Priest; for it is written, 'Thou shalt not revile the ruler of thy people.'" When Paul perceived that there was a mixed council of Pharisees and Sadducees, he cried out that he was a Pharisee and the son of a Pharisee, "and for the hope and resurrection of the dead I am called in question." The chief captain seeing the tumult, brought him by force out of their hands to the castle. A conspiracy was formed against the life of Paul, the plot was discovered, and Paul was conveyed to Cæsarea under a strong guard. The captain wrote a letter to the governor of Cæsarea: "Claudius Lysias, unto the most excellent governor Felix, This man was taken of the Jews and would have been killed, but I came with an army and rescued him, having learned that he was a Roman. When I inquired into the cause, I perceived it to be questions of their law, but to have nothing laid to his charge, worthy of death or of bonds." When they came to Cæsarea and delivered the epistle of Lysias to Felix, he asked of what province he was. When he heard that he was of Cilicia, "I will hear thee," he said, "when thy accusers have come." And he was placed in Herod's judgment hall. After a few days, Ananias with elders and a certain orator came down to set forth their charges against Paul. Tertullus, the orator, called him a pestilent fellow and a mover of sedition. Then Paul was invited by the governor to make his defense. Paul spoke of the resurrection and explained to Felix why he had gone up to Jerusalem. Felix having married a Jewess, had some knowledge of the questions that Paul discussed; he had, too, been a judge of the Jewish nation for many years. Felix postponed a decision until Lysias came down; he commanded a centurion to keep Paul and give him liberty. Felix with his wife Drusilla afterwards sent for Paul, and heard him concerning his faith in Christ. And as Paul reasoned of righteousness, temperance, and *judgment* to come, Felix trembled, and said, "Go thy way this time; when I have a convenient season I will call for thee." After two years, Porcius Festus came in Felix's room, and Felix, willing to show the Jews a pleasure, left Paul *bound*. While Festus was at Jerusalem, the High Priest and the chief of the Jews, besought Festus that he should send Paul to Jerusalem to be *judged*, but Festus answered that Paul should be kept at Cæsarea, and that he would shortly depart thither. "Let them therefore, said he, which among you are able, go down with me and accuse this man if there be any wickedness in him." Paul was a few days after summoned to the judgment-seat of Festus at Cæsarea. The Jews which came down from Jerusalem laid many grievous complaints against him which they could not prove. Then Festus said, "Wilt thou go up to Jerusalem and *there* be judged of these things before me?" Then said Paul, "I stand at Cæsar's judgment-seat. To the Jews I have done nothing wrong, as thou very well knowest. If I be an offender or have done anything worthy of death, I refuse not to die; but if there be none of these things whereof these accuse me, *no man* may deliver me unto them. I appeal unto Cæsar." Festus, unlike Felix, seems to have been ignorant of the Jewish religion; the questions discussed between Paul and the Jews were incomprehensible to him. Festus tells Agrippa that the Jews had certain questions against Paul of their own superstition and of one Jesus, which was dead, whom Paul affirmed to be alive. Agrippa's curiosity is awakened, and he desires to hear Paul. On the morrow, Agrippa came, and Bernice, with great pomp to the place of hearing. Agrippa had just come from Rome to Cæsarea with his sister; he had succeeded to a part of his father's dominions. He was in possession of the Asmonean palace at Jerusalem, and had the right of appointing the High Priest. The Roman governor seems to have consulted Agrippa, as a man of moderation and knowledge of the Roman law. "I have brought this man before thee, O King Agrippa, that after examination had, I might have somewhat to write. For it seemeth to me unreasonable to send a prisoner (to Rome), and not withal to signify the crimes laid against him."

The 26th chapter of the Acts contains the eloquent speech and defense of Paul before Agrippa. As Paul proceeded with passionate eloquence, Festus cried out, "Paul, thou art beside thyself; much learning doth make thee mad." But Paul said, "I am not mad, but speak forth the words of truth and soberness. The king knoweth of these things, before whom I speak freely. For I am persuaded that none of these things were hidden from him, for this thing was not done in a corner." Then Agrippa said unto Paul, "Almost thou persuadest me to be a Christian." Then said Agrippa unto Festus, "This man might have been set *at liberty* had he not appealed to Cesar." In the 27th chapter is related Paul's journey to Rome. He and other prisoners were put under the care of a centurion. After a shipwreck and many dangers, they arrive at

Rome. During Paul's journey he had a vision at night, which assured him that notwithstanding the wreck of the ship, all that sailed with him should arrive in safety. Christian brethren from Rome met him before he reached the city. The centurion delivered the other prisoners to the captain of the guard, but Paul was suffered to dwell by himself with a soldier that kept him, and after three days Paul called the chief of the Jews together, and explained to them his cause and why he had appealed to Cæsar. They replied to him, "We desire to hear what thou thinkest: for as concerning this sect we know that everywhere it is spoken against." And he appointed a day; there came many to him, unto his lodging, to whom he explained the kingdom of God, persuading them concerning Jesus both out of the Law of Moses and out of the Prophets, from morning until evening. And some believed the things which were spoken and some believed not. And Paul dwelt two whole years in his own hired house, and received all that came unto him, preaching the kingdom of God, and teaching those things which concern the Lord Jesus Christ, with all confidence, no man forbidding him.

END OF THE SCRIPTURE NARRATIVE.

CHAPTER· IV.

PAUL'S WRITINGS.

St. Paul wrote thirteen Epistles.* The Epistle to the Romans† is the first in order, as published in our Bibles. This Epistle was written from Corinth, during his *second* residence in that city. Paul had never been at Rome, when he wrote the Epistle to the Romans. During his first visit to Corinth, Paul had formed an intimate connection with Roman Christians, resident at Corinth and at Cenchrea, its port; these had been banished by Claudius from Rome, together with many Jews. The greater part of the Christian exiles seem to have taken refuge with Aquila and Priscilla. Paul was in Corinth "a year and six months," testifying in the synagogue every Sabbath, that Jesus was Christ. When Claudius was dead, the Jews and Christians naturally crept back to their old homes. The Christians from Corinth would convey to their brethren at Rome the more perfect knowledge of Christianity taught them by Paul, during their banishment at Corinth. In writing to these Roman Christians afterwards,

---

*We have said Paul wrote thirteen Epistles. Some learned men now think that the Epistle to the Hebrews was not written by Paul. Some attribute the Epistle to the Hebrews to Apollos.

†Paul's Epistle to the Romans, says Luther, is the masterpiece of the New Testament. Coleridge says, the Epistle to the Romans is the most profound work in existence. Justification by Faith is the subject of this Epistle.

he says to them, "Your faith is spoken of throughout the world." The *history* of the Roman community, says Milman, is remarkable. It grew up in silence, founded by some unknown teachers, probably by those "strangers from Rome" who were in Jerusalem on the day of Pentecost, at the first publication of Christianity by the Apostles. During the reign of Claudius Christianity had made such progress as to excite tumults and dissensions among the Jewish population of Rome; the attention of the government was attracted and both parties expelled from the city. The foundation of the Christian Church at Rome by either Peter or Paul is utterly irreconcilable with history. The first chapter of the Epistle to the Romans proves conclusively that the foundation of this church was long previous to his (Paul's) visit to the Western metropolis. Paul's Epistle to the Galatians was written, it is supposed, during his first visit to Ephesus. Galatia had derived its name from the settlement of the Gauls in this country. There were, probably, great numbers of Jews in this district. It is very evident from what we have seen of the question agitated at the first council of Jerusalem, that there was a conflict among the early Christians with regard to Judaism, or the ceremonial rites prescribed by the Law of Moses. Was the cumbrous *framework* of Mosaic observances still to be observed by the Christian Church? Many of the Gentile converts were ready to submit to the faith of Christ, with its exquisite morality; but could they submit to the unmeaning regulations of diet, dress and manners required by the Jewish ritual? Christianity had now advanced beyond the Jewish population, and these questions were strongly agitated. To meet these difficulties, St. Paul seems to have written the celebrated Epistle to the *Romans*, also his Epistle to the Galatians. St. Paul teaches in these Epistles that the *ceremonial* Law of Moses was annulled, that it was a temporary institution, designed during a *barbarous age* to keep alive the principles of true religion. It is certain that the first generation of Christians had passed away before many Jewish converts to Christianity had emancipated themselves from the yoke of Jewish observances. For a time it is believed that *two Sabbaths* were kept. As Christianity advanced, taking in a larger proportion of the Gentiles than of those of Jewish descent, the synagogue and church became more distinct. *Judaism gradually* died away within the Christian pale. A *latent* Judaism has at certain periods *lurked* within the Church and manifested itself. At Corinth St. Paul wrote the Epistles to the Thessalonians. St. Paul is said to have written, when he lived at Rome in his own hired house, the Epistle to the Ephesians, one to the Colossians, and to the Philippians. He also wrote two letters to Timothy, who is regarded as the first Bishop of Ephesus The first of these letters to Timothy was written from Laodicea, the second from Rome, when Paul was brought before Nero a second time. The Epistle to Titus was written from Nicopolis. The two Epistles to the Corinthians were written from Philippi in Macedonia. At the end of the two years' sojourn of Paul in Rome, he is supposed to have left the city for a time. The year after his departure is noted as the beginning of the Neronian persecution in the *Annals* of *Rome*. The Christians were accused of burning the city, and were subjected to terrible tortures. New *punishments* were invented. Some of the Christians, of whom the world was not worthy, were sewed up in skins of beasts and covered with melted pitch and burned by a slow fire. These horrible details of the Neronian persecution are mentioned by the *historians* of that day. Tacitus says, Nero, in order to divert a suspicion from himself, resolved to substitute in his place some *fictitious* criminals. With this view he inflicted horrible tortures on those men who, under the appellation of Christians, were already branded with infamy. "These derived their *name* from Christ, who in the reign of Tiberius, suffered death under Pilate the Procurator," A. D. 66. Tradition assigns to the last year of Nero the martyrdom of St. Peter and St. Paul.* The martyrdom of Peter rests altogether upon unauthoritative testimony, *that* of St. Paul upon the authentic record of the second Epistle to Timothy, when St. Paul says, "I am ready to be offered and the time of my departure is at hand." When Paul wrote this, it is said that the government of Rome had been entrusted to Helias, a freedman of Nero. The tradition is that Paul, as a Roman citizen, was beheaded, not by the order of Nero, but by the sentence of the Governor. When Rome was burned, all the monuments of Grecian art and of Roman bravery were involved in one common destruction—the trophies of the Punic and Gallic wars, the most holy temples, the most splendid palaces. The gardens and circus of Nero, on the Vatican, were polluted, says Gibbon, with the blood of the first Christians. Near the same spot a Christian Temple now stands, which far surpasses

---

*Tradition says that the soldiers and executioners who carried him to his execution, were converted by him; but this may be *romance.*

the ancient glories of the capitol. The fame of St. Peter has eclipsed that of St. Paul in the Eternal City. The most splendid temple erected by Christian zeal bears the name of St. Peter. It is most remarkable that in no part of the Scripture record, is there any personal history of St. Peter as connected with the Western Churches. *Until* the conversion of St. Paul, St. Peter was the most eminent and prominent of the teachers of the Gospel of Christ. He was the chief speaker on the day of Pentecost; he first opened the door of admission to Cornelius, and proclaimed that the partition wall was broken down between Jew and Gentile. Peter wrote two Epistles—they are written apparently from Babylonia. "The church which is at Babylon saluteth you." Lightfoot, learned in Jewish antiquities, maintains that Peter lived and died in Babylonia. It is certain that large numbers of Jews lived in Babylonia, and it is believed that, as the Apostle of the circumcision, he went thither to preach the Gospel to the Jews in that region. There is no record or contemporary evidence that Peter ever was at Rome. But it is confidently believed that there were two parties, both at Rome and Corinth. The Petrine party was a Judaizing church, and the Pauline a Hellenistic church. Irenæus, Dionysius and Epiphanius maintain the *tradition* that Peter had a *residence* at Rome and that he suffered martyrdom there by crucifixion.

Palestine seems to have been assigned to James the Just, he who gave his sentence at the council of Jerusalem to abolish circumcision. Paul escaped the vengeance of the Sanhedrim, but they wreaked their vengeance on one far less obnoxious to the Jews generally. The head of the Christian community at Jerusalem was

James. On the death of Festus, the Roman governor, and before the arrival of Albinus as governor, Annas, a fierce Sadducaic, High Priest, seized the opportunity of the suspension of the Roman Power, to reassert the power of the Sanhedrim over life and death. Many were executed by Annas, by stoning, and James, the head of the community, commonly called the Bishop of *Jerusalem* (the mother church), suffered martyrdom. Tradition says James was thrown from the walls of the temple. This persecution of Annas rests on the authority of Josephus, who says Annas put them to death on account of their religion. Who but Christians could have been obnoxious to capital punishment? The power to persecute by the Jewish hierarchy was now drawing to a close. The time was come when all the righteous blood that had been shed by the rebellious and fanatical Jewish leaders should be avenged on that generation.

Titus, the son of Vespasian, was making ready, in marshalling his hosts, to attack the sacred city, over whose calamities the Saviour of the world had wept. In the year 70, dating from the birth of Jesus, Jerusalem was trodden under foot by the Roman armies, under the command of Titus, the eldest son of Vespasian, then the reigning Emperor of Rome and of the civilized world. The beautiful temple, built by the *returning* captives from Babylon in 530 B. C., and afterwards richly embellished by Herod the Great, was leveled with the ground. A burning taper in the hands of a reckless Roman soldier, accomplished the prediction of our Lord. The Christians at Jerusalem removed to Pella, a neighboring city, so soon as the fated city became "encompassed with armies." They were therefore not involved in the miseries of the siege.

Many Jews, it is said, of wealth and distinction, also fled to the same locality. Domitian succceded to his brother Titus after a short reign. A proconsul of Asia, during the reign of this tyrant, banished St. John, the beloved disciple, to the Isle of Patmos. In this island tradition places his writing the Apocalypse, as well as his own word: "I John, who also am your brother and companion in tribulation and in the kingdom and patience of Jesus Christ, was in the Isle that is called Patmos, for the Word of God, and for the testimony of Jesus Christ." John returned to Ephesus, and probably ended his days in that populous and commercial city. Ephesus was the scene of the first collision between Orientalism and Christianity. Ephesus was the *third capital* of Christianity. In this city the Gospel of St. John was written. This Gospel was not written, says Milman, against any peculiar sect or individual, but to arrest the spirit of Orientalism. "Ephesus," says Farrar, "witnessed the full development and the final amalgamation of its elements in the work of John, the Apostle of Love." Christianity was born at Jerusalem in the cradle of Judaism; it was the mother Church. *Antioch* was the beginning of the Christian Church of the Gentiles. When John wrote his Gospel a spirit of Orientalism seemed to threaten the beautiful simplicity of Christianity. While St. John appropriates the term Logos or *Word* of God to the divine authority of Christianity, and even adopts some of the imagery from the hypothesis of conflicting light and darkness, he entirely rejects the speculati on of the Gnostics on the formation of the world. Though in the writings of John (Milman, our author, continues), there is something of a mystic tone when he speaks of the union of the soul with the

Deity; it is a *union* made by the aspiration of the pious heart and by the union of pure and holy love with the Deity. It requires not, as the Gnostics do, abstraction from matter, but from sin, from hatred and from all fierce and corrupting passions.

The Church that Paul founded at Ephesus (of which Timothy is reputed to be the successor of St. Paul as Bishop) became a Christian metropolis of a line of Bishops, and *there*, four centuries afterward, was held a great Ecumenical Council, which deposed Nestorius, the Patriarch of Constantinople. But now for centuries its candlestick has been removed.

It has been asserted that St. John wrote his Gospel to refute the heresies of Cerinthus, a famous Gnostic of Ephesus. It is very certain from the contents of the Gospel itself, that it was written to supply several interesting incidents in the life of Christ omitted by the other three Evangelists, and to give to his disciples in every age, those last words of comfort and instruction of the Master, as contained in the 14th, 15th and 16th chapters of St. John's Gospel. The conflict with Gnosticism seems to have commenced before the death of St. John. Simon Magus, mentioned in the Acts in a conflict with St. Peter, was an Orientalist or Gnostic, calling himself "the Power of God." It is not within the scope of our ability or purpose, in this abridged history of the Church, to enter into the depths of the shadowy and fanciful doctrines of the Gnostics. They called themselves Christians, yet they did not *limit* their creed to the teachings of our Lord as contained in the four Gospels, and in the Epistles of his Apostles: but they *multiplied books*, in which they sought to adapt their respective tenets to the teaching of Christ—not regarding or fearing the denunciation of the Apocalypse: "If any man, shall *add* unto these things, God shall add unto him the plagues that are written in this book: "and if any man shall take away from the words of the book of this prophecy, God shall take away his part out of the Book of Life." They, the Gnostics, were divided by their differing opinions into many sects. They flourished for the most part in the second century, but were partially suppressed in the third century. The most formidable sect of the Gnostics in the latter part of their history, were the Manicheans. They were found chiefly in Egypt and in Asia, and sometimes distributed in the Western Provinces. They blended with the faith of Christ some tenets of oriental philosophy, together with the religion of Zoroaster. They rejected the Old Testament. They dwelt on the malignity of matter, the existence of two principles, and a mysterious hierarchy in the invisible world. They regarded Christ as an emanation from God, but relieved Christ from the degradation of a human birth, by supposing that the *Christ* descended on the Man Jesus at his baptism; and from the ignominy of a mortal death, by making him reascend before that crisis. It was in the view of the Gnostic, pollution and degradation to the pure and elementary spirit, to mingle with or exercise the remotest influence over the material world.. The creation therefore of this visible world was not made by the great God, who dwelt in distance unapproachable, but by a secondary and hostile deity. God saw every thing that he had made, and behold it was very good. Almost all the creeds of the early churches begin with a confession of Faith in God, the Father Almighty, Maker of Heaven and Earth. With the defense of this fundamental doctrine, Irenæus opens his *refutation* of the Gnostic heresies, saying in the language of Justin Martyr, that he could not have believed Christ himself, if he had announced any other God than the Creator whose work is declared in the first chapter of the Bible. The Church inherited from Judaism the doctrine of the unity of God, the just and holy Creator and upholder of all things, and vindicated it against the polytheism of the pagans, but more especially against the *dualism* of the Gnostics, who supposed matter co-eternal with God and ascribed the creation of our world to an inferior deity or an intermediate Demiurge. The hymns of the Gnostics are said to have exercised much power over the churches of Syria. Their poetry was sung in the churches of Syria, until it was expelled by more orthodox psalmody. We have already spoken of the martyrdoms of Peter and Paul at Rome, of the death of James the Just at Jerusalem by violence in the persecution of Annas, and of the death of St. John at Ephesus; of the fate of the other evangelists and Apostles, little is known with certainty. Legend has been busy in assigning their fields of labor, also the manner of their deaths. It is certain that the disciples of our Lord were scattered abroad, busy with the Master's work, but to what particular country their labors were directed, and where they met their last enemy, death, is not certain. Their good works followed them. Before the reign of Diocletian, A. D. 280, the faith of Christ had been preached in every province and large city of the Roman Empire. The highways, which had been constructed for the use of the legions, opened an easy passage for the Christian missionaries from Damascus to Corinth, and from Italy to the extremity of Spain and Britain. St. Peter, in writing from Chaldea, mentions the presence of Mark; Paul indicates in his letters to Timothy and Titus, their particular charge. Luke we know was the companion of St. Paul in his journeyings, and was busy in writing the Gospel that bears his name, and the Acts of the Apostles. But of Matthew and Bartholomew, and Andrew and the rest, we know nothing of their latter days except from uncertain traditionary legends. It is quite certain that St. Matthew wrote the Gospel that bears his name, *first* in Hebrew. Papias, the contemporary of the Apostle St. John, says positively that Matthew had written the discourses of Jesus Christ in Hebrew, and that each interpreted them as he could. *This* Hebrew was the Syro-Chaldaic dialect, as is proved by many words which he used, and which the Evangelists have translated. St. Paul, addressing the Jews, used the same language, in Acts xxi. 40, and in other places. The Greek version of Matthew appears to have been made in the time of the Apostles, as St. Jerome and St. Augustine both affirm. This subject has been elaborately discussed, and some modern critics have asserted its Greek original, but the general opinion is against them.

CHAPTER V.

EXTENT OF THE CHURCH IN THE SECOND CENTURY.

There is no certain evidence, says Paley, where *some* of the apostles and teachers of the gospel passed their later years, and where and how they closed their mortal career; but from *the work* they accomplished, it is very certain that the original witnesses of the miracles of our Lord passed their lives in labors, dangers and sufferings voluntarily undergone in attestation of the accounts they delivered and solely in consequence of their belief of these accounts ; and that they submitted also from the same motives to *new rules* of *conduct.* A more patient investigator, or one more learned than Paley in the lore of early primitive Christianity, can not be found. As a proof of the earnest work of the apostles and Christian teachers, it is asserted that in A. D. 150, about the middle of the second century, the number of *professed* Christians amounted to *one-tenth* of the subjects of the Roman Empire. Asia was the cradle of Christianity, as it was of civilization. Yet Christianity was a Greek religion for three centuries. Justin Martyr, who lived in the second century, says there is no people, Greek or barbarian, however ignorant of arts and agriculture whether, they live in tents or wander about in covered wagons—among whom prayers and thanksgivings are not said and offered to the Father and Creator of all things, in *the name* of the crucified Jesus.

The apostles themselves had spread the gospel of Christ over Palestine, Syria and Asia Minor. Christianity reached Egypt as early as the apostolic age. Mark the Evangelist laid the foundation of the Church in Alexandria, the metropolis of commerce and of oriental culture. Clement and Origen taught in the schools of Egypt. The Christian religion had its origin among a Syrian people. Jesus spoke an *Aramaic* dialect; it was the popular language of Jerusalem and Galilee, yet nearly all the primal records were written *in Greek*. *Christianity* from the beginning was a Greek religion. The Jews, the first converts to Christ, used the Greek language in their commerce with other countries, and in their intercourse with foreign nations. The most flourishing churches were in Greek cities. The Syriac, or Aramaic, was doubtless spoken by vast numbers of disciples, in Syrian provinces. It spread eastward, beyond the Euphrates, where Greek ceased to be the common tongue. But the Greek language was the language of the Church for more than three centuries. The Grecian Churches of the East, such as Antioch, Alexandria, Ephesus, were held together by common creeds, common usages, common sympathies. The hierarchy were everywhere on the same level. The Bishop of each city in theory had the same power. The *metropolitan* and *patriarchate* were of much later date. Greek Christianity was inquisitive and speculative. Great questions, as the origin of evil, the nature of the deity, the formation of worlds, were agitated among them. The Greeks had many great writers, such as Athanasius, Basil, the Gregories, but they had few worthy successors. Splendid eloquence seemed to expire on the lips of Chrysostom. Tertullian was the first *Latin* writer that commanded the public ear. Africa, not Rome, gave birth to what is called Latin Christianity. Eusebius mentions as a strange fact, that Cyprian, Bishop of Carthage, wrote to the Asiatic Bishops in Latin. None of the Roman Bishops, down to the time of Gregory the Great, were *master minds*. The Church of the *capital* could not but assume somewhat of the dignity of the capital, but Rome had no Origen, no Athanasius, no Cyprian, no Ambrose, no Augustine, no Jerome, no Chrysostom. When our Saviour issued the command, "Go ye into all the world," etc., he spoke to his eleven apostles ; one of the first acts of these apostles was to elect and consecrate another apostle in the place of Judas, giving to him like authority with themselves. Shortly after they appoint other officers, called deacons, with limited powers. Two of these are distinguished for their zeal in preaching—Stephen and Philip. Stephen is regarded as the first Christian martyr. Philip *baptized* many converts in Samaria, but Peter and John came down (Acts viii.) to that city to lay their hands on the converts taught and baptized by Philip. Paul was made an Apostle by the Saviour himself (I. Tim. i. 12); he was baptized by Ananias. Paul was afterwards brought to the apostles by Barnabas, and his miraculous conversion and *ordination* declared unto them. Paul ordained Timothy with his own hands, and with the laying on of the hands of the Presbytery. Paul charges Timothy "to lay hands suddenly on no man," giving him also directions as to the necessary qualifications for Bishops or Elders, and for Deacons. He gives similar advice to Titus. "He hands the torch of truth to Timothy and Titus, which in his *own* grasp had never been dimmed or quenched, nor any faltering amid storms of persecution." Tradition affirms that Timothy was *Bishop* of Ephesus, and Titus of Crete, according to our modern acceptation of the Word. St. John also writes to the *angels* of the seven Churches of Asia these angels are supposed to mean the chief ministers of those Churches. Few points in Christian history have been more contested than the primitive constitution of the Christian Churches; the evidence is chiefly inferential. Milman says the whole of Christianity, when it emerges from the obscurity of the first century, appears uniformly governed by *superiors* in each community called Bishops. But the origin and *extent* of this superiority and the manner in which the Bishop assumed a distinct authority above the Presbyters, is among the *difficult* questions of Church history. "No society," says Guizot, "can exist without a government. But the essence of government resides not in compulsion. The right of compulsion assumed by the Church in the fifth century was contrary to the spirit of the religious society, and to the primitive maxims of the Church. The spirit of compulsion was opposed by Hilary, by Ambrose and by St. Martin. These good men maintained the legitimate liberty of human thought." The Christian Church in its origin was formed round an individual. The apostle or teacher becomes at once the chief religious functionary. Oral instruction was *anterior* to the existence of any book, or any inspired record. The teacher, while he *remained*, would be recognized as the legitimate head of the Christian society. When Paul left Miletus for *the last time*, he sent for "the Elders of the Church from Ephesus," where he had abode three years. Paul gives to the Elders, or *overseers*, of the Church of God the most solemn admonitions. There seems to have been already at Ephesus an organized government. Paul represented the Apostle or Bishop, as the *first order* was called after the days of the apostles. The *second order* in the New Testament are called alternately, Elders, Bishops and Presbyters. The third order are called Deacons. Timothy, as Paul's successor, was Bishop of Ephesus. Two questions have arisen in regard to the Episcopate. Was the Episcopate directly of apostolic origin, as the Roman Catholics and Anglicans, the Moravians, the Swedish Lutherans, and *the Greek Church maintain;* or did it arise, as Presbyterians attest, from the Presidency of the congregational Presbytery? Dean Stanley, the present head of the Westminster, says: "No *existing* Church can find an *exact pattern* of the form of Church government in the earliest times." He says that "it is as sure that nothing like modern Episcopacy existed before the close of the first century, as it is certain that *no* Presbyterianism existed after the beginning of the second century." Timothy, Titus, Silas, Epaphroditus, Mark, and Luke were at first *itinerant* evangelists and legates of the apostles. Afterwards, tradition assigns distinct bishoprics to them. St. John writes to the angels of the seven churches of Asia. We understand these to mean the *superior* minister or bishop of each of those cities, and it indicates the shaping of the church government in the days of St. John. Four of the distinguished fathers say that St. John ordained Polycarp bishop of Smyrna, to whom Irenæus was personally known. The uncontested spread of the episcopate in the second century can not be explained without the sanction of apostolic authority. An uninterrupted line of bishops is traced by ecclesiastical historians to the apostles, without a murmur of remonstrance. No schism, no breach of Christian unity, followed. St. Jerome, quoted by Hooker, assigns the origin of episcopacy to the dissensions of the Church, which required strong exercise of authority, especially in Corinth.

In St. Paul's time three parties seem to have existed: the Pauline, Petrine, and Apolline. Corinth, says Milman, was probably the last Christian community that settled down under the episcopal constitution. In primitive episcopacy there was no sacerdotal idea connected with the word presbyter or priest. They (the early Christians) adopted the word priest both from Judaism and Paganism, without connecting with it any idea of sacrifice, but simply denoting him who was appointed to minister in holy things, to preach the Word, and to dispense the sacraments. They recognized but one priest or mediator between earth and heaven, the man Christ Jesus. As Christianity was a new religion, the Church was obliged to give to *old words* a new meaning. They adopted the word *sacrament*, meaning *oath*, which connects itself with our most holy mysteries. The primitive Episcopal system must by no means be confounded with the later hierarchy. Though the bishops were equal in their dignity and powers as successors of the apostles, they gradually fell into different ranks, according to the political and ecclesiastical importance of the districts in which they resided. Jerusalem, Antioch, Ephesus, Corinth and Rome, were regarded as the mother Churches. In the time of Irenæus and Tertullian they were regarded as the chief bearers of the pure

Church tradition. To the bishop of Antioch fell all Syria as his metropolitan district; to the bishop of Alexandria all Egypt. In these metropolitan divisions we have the germs of the patriarchate of the Greek church. To the bishop of Rome central and lower Italy.

Whence came the precedence of the Church of Rome? The great *political* preëminence of Rome as the capital and mistress of the world doubtless gave potential influence to the See of Rome. St. Paul honored the Romans with his longest and most important epistle. The executive wisdom of the Church of Rome in its management of three questions, that greatly agitated the early Church, redounded much to its credit. These questions were: the proper time for the observance of Easter, heretical baptism, and penitential discipline.

In A. D. 102, Clement was bishop of Rome; he writes a letter to the bishop of Corinth at this time, full of exhortations to love, unity and humility. This epistle was not sent in the name of the bishop, but in the name of the congregation; not in authority, but in love. The authority of the bishop of Rome was that of influence, not power, in the second century. The person most eminent for piety and wisdom was elected to the bishopric by acclamation, which was one of danger as well as distinction. Episcopal government, so long as it remained unleavened by worldly passions and interests, was essentially popular.

The office of a bishop in times of persecution became a post of great danger. Jesus had predicted to his disciples persecution and sorrow. "The time will come when he who killeth you, will think that he doeth God service." It might have been expected, that the Jews would persecute the Christians, as they were in the beginning a secession from their synagogues but that the pagans should become persecutors on account of religion could not be anticipated, when the indifferentism of polytheism is considered. A thousand different forms of religion existed, without molestation, in the great cities of Syria and Egypt, and especially in Rome. The Jews at different times suffered dreadfully from the Romans, on account of their impatience of a foreign government; from rebellions and insurrections, but *not* on account of their religion. They were taught by the law of Moses to treat the stranger with courtesy, and to treat him hospitably. They had been persecutors of their own people, when they had opposed their wicked practices; their kings had persecuted the prophets and other good men, and their hierarchy had now filled up the measure of their iniquity, by crucifying their King and Saviour. Yet they lived in various parts of the world, they had their synagogues in almost every city, but they were undisturbed by the ruling powers. Then why should so innocent a people as the primitive Christians be persecuted — so unspotted in their morals, so gentle in their behaviour? Jesus knew what was in man, and he foresaw the circumstances that would arise. He foretold also a feeling of "shame," that to the present hour, has turned away many a worldly, timid heart from a confession of the "Crucified One." Our Lord knew the jealousy that would arise from the invasive and uncompromising spirit of Christianity. The Jews cared little for proselytes, but the Christian was filled with love for the souls of men, and believed there was no other name given among men by which he could be saved, but the name of Christ. He constantly remembered the command of the great Captain, "Go ye into all the world, and preach the Gospel to every creature," and "Therefore I come not to send *peace* upon earth, but a sword."

We have already spoken of the persecutions of Nero and Domitian. Of the latter it is said that he discovered the *new religion* had entered his own family in the persons of two cousins. Suddenly these harmless kinsmen were arraigned on the charge of *atheism* and *Jewish manners*—they were banished and afterwards put to death.

The third persecution was in the reign of Trajan. With the second century came another *race* of emperors, those that are known in history as the five good emperors. Nerva was the first of these. Adrian, Trajan. and the Antonines were men of larger minds than their predecessors. They reigned not now, as the Cæsars, as monarchs of Rome, but as sovereigns of the *western world*, which had gradually coalesced into one majestic and harmonious system or empire. The rapid progress of the new religion did not escape their notice. These emperors were occupied with the internal as well the external affairs of their empire. The younger Pliny was at this time governor of Bithynia, in Asia Minor, under Trajan. Christianity had advanced with great rapidity in the northern provinces of Asia Minor. It was in Bithynia that paganism was first aroused to the fact that Christianity was undermining her authority. Complaints were brought to the governor that "the temples were deserted and the sacrifices neglected." Then ensued the memorable correspondence between Pliny and Trajan; it is the most valuable record of

Christianity during this period. It presents Paganism, claiming the *alliance* of power, to maintain its decaying influence; Christianity is most imperfectly understood by a wise and polite Pagan, yet still with nothing to offend his moral judgment, "except their contumacy and their repugnance to some of the common usages of society." But this contumacy the Pagans thought must be punished.

CHAPTER VI.

PLINY'S LETTERS TO TRAJAN.

A. D. 98.—Ignatius, Irenæus, Tertullian, Polycarp. Pliny, Roman governor of Bithynia, appeals to Trajan for advice. The answer of Trajan is characterized by moderation. He directs him not to seek for offenders, but when they are brought before his bar, and continue to be contumacious, refusing to *sacrifice*: the emperor intimates that there was an existing law by which the Christians were amenable to the severest penalties, torture and even capital punishment. Pliny had already inflicted *torture* on two females who had been brought before him; these females were probably deaconesses. Pliny writes that after torture he could detect nothing "but a culpable and extravagant superstition. They had a custom," he said, "of meeting together before daylight, and singing a hymn to Christ as God. They were bound together by no unlawful sacrament, but only under mutual obligation not to commit theft, robbery, adultery or fraud. They met again and partook together of food, but that of a perfectly innocent kind." The test of guilt to which the Christians were submitted was *adoration* before the statues of the gods and the emperor, and the *malediction* of Christ. Those who refused were led out to execution. Trajan approves of Pliny's conduct. His rescript established three points: The Christians were not to be sought after; they were not to be proceeded against without a regular accuser and complaint; if accused and found guilty of being Christians, they were to be put to death, unless they retracted and offered sacrifice to the gods. In the public exhibitions, say the historians of those times, the followers of all other religions met as on a common ground. In the theatre or the hippodrome, the worshiper of Mithra or of Isis, mingled with the mass who adhered to the worship of Bacchus or Jupiter. Even the Jews, in some instances, betrayed no aversion to the popular games. But the Christians *stood aloof.* "The sanguinary diversions of the arena," says Milman, "and the licentious voluptuousness of some of the exhibitions were no less offensive, to their humanity and modesty, than those more strictly religious to their piety." They were a peculiar people; they *could not be hid.* In little more than seventy years after the death of Christ, the Christians in the province of Pliny were no longer an obscure sect. It is supposed by some that the acts of persecution ascribed to Trajan were connected with his military movements. A charge of disaffection could easily be brought against the Christians by their enemies. While a persecution against the Christians is raging in the East, the Roman community is in peace and not without influence. Among the most distinguished Christians, who suffered martyrdom in the reign of Trajan, were Simeon, bishop of Jerusalem, and Ignatius, the bishop of Antioch. In the beginning of the second century, the trial of Ignatius is said to have taken place, before Trajan *himself,* when he was preparing for his eastern campaign. The emperor is represented as kindling with anger at the disparagement of those gods on whose protection he *depended* in the impending war. "Is *our* religion," he exclaimed, "to be treated as senseless?" The most trustworthy chronology places the accession of Trajan, A. D. 98, and the martyrdom of Ignatius in A. D. 112. At this time, the emperor is preparing for his Persian war. Ignatius is brought to Rome. While journeying to Rome, to meet his cruel fate, it is said he wrote Epistles to the Churches in Asia. Ignatius was a hearer and convert of St. John, and some say he was made a bishop by St. Peter. The *Acts* of Ignatius are considered as authentic, also *seven* of his letters. He was carried in *chains* to Rome as a public spectacle — his death was terrible — he was thrown to the lions in the amphitheatre. Gibbon says, the martyrs selected for execution by the Roman magistrates were from the two extremes of society; they were either bishops, whose example might strike terror, or from the meanest of the people, who were regarded with careless indifference. Adrian succeeded Trajan.

This emperor, Adrian, withdrew from foreign contests. He wished to bring the empire within narrower and uncontested limits. He traveled over all the countries under Roman dominion; he adorned the cities with public buildings, bridges and acqueducts; inquired into the customs and manners, and into the religion of the distant parts of the world. His personal character showed incessant activity and versatility. His curious and busy temper inquired into every form of religion. At Athens he was in turn the simple philosopher, the restorer of the temple of Jupiter Olympus, and the awe-struck worshiper of the Eleusinian mysteries. It was at Athens that he heard the apologies of Quadratus and of Aristides pleading for the truth and the moral superiority of Christianity. He did not repel their respectful homage. Perhaps these apologies may have influenced his mind in issuing mitigating laws on slavery. It is impossible that the rapid growth of Christianity could have escaped so inquiring a mind as the mind of Adrian. The rescript which he addressed in the early part of his reign to the proconsul of Asia, was dictated by the same policy as Trajan's. Adrian tells the proconsul of Asia Minor, as did Trajan, that he must not listen to the popular cry, that would sometimes break out, "The Christians to the lions," but that the formalities of law must be strictly complied with. The lines that Adrian addressed to his soul when dying* prove that he had some idea of the immortality of the spirit, though a doubtful questioner. The successor of Adrian, Antoninus Pius, maintained the mild policy of his predecessor, either from policy or indifference. Sixty years of almost uninterrupted peace since the beginning of the second century had opened a wide field for the development of Christianity. When Marcus Aurelius, the second Antonine, succeeds to the throne of the empire, A. D. 166, the religion of Christ had spread into every quarter of the Roman dominion. The western provinces, Gaul and Africa, rivalled the East in the *number* if not in the opulence of their Christian congregations. A separate community, seceding from the usages of Pagan life, at least from the public religious ceremonial, had arisen in nearly every city. An intimate *correspondence* connected this new

---

* Animula, vagula, blandula, Hospes, comes que corporis, opuæ nunc a bibis in loca.

The address of Adrian to his soul probably suggested to Pope, our great poet, the address of the dying Christian to his soul: "Vital spark of heavenly flame."

moral republic. Irenæus, the bishop of Lyons, in Gaul, enters into a controversy with the speculative teachers of Antioch, Edessa or Alexandria, while Tertullian, of Carthage, in his rude African Latin, denounces or advocates opinions which spring up in Pontus or Phrygia. Irenæus was the great opponent of the *Gnostics*, and the mediator between the eastern and western Churches. Irenæus of Lyons was the disciple of Polycarp, and has handed down valuable reminiscences of his Apostolic teacher. Irenæus gives the names of the twelve bishops, in succession, who in his day governed the Church at Rome. Irenæus met his death under an edict of Severus in A. D. 202. Marcus Aurelius was a rigid stoic; he sometimes condescended, in pure and elegant Greek, to explain the lofty tenets of the *Porch*, and commend its noble morality to his subjects, while a large portion of the world were *preoccupied* with writings, the writings of the New Testament, which enforced still higher morals. The language of these sacred books were often impregnated with Syrian and foreign barbarisms, yet they commanded the homage and required the diligent study of all the disciples of the new faith. Christians were to be found in the court, in the camp, in the market. They did not decline any of the offices of society, not shunning entirely the forum or yielding interest in the civil administration; they had their mercantile transactions, in common with the rest of that class. "We are no Indian Brahmins or devotees," says Tertullian, "living naked in the woods, or self-banished from civilized life." The Christians admitted *slaves* to an *equality* of religious privileges, yet there was no attempt to disorganize the existing relations of society. There is no proposed interference with the social institution of slavery, in the New Testament. Christianity gives *law* to a master, how a slave should be treated, but leaves the emancipation of the slave to *times* which would be ripe for so admirable and important a change.

Marcus Aurelius assumed the reins of empire A. D. 161. He associated with him the adopted son of Antoninus Pius, Lucius Verus. Marcus claimed as a philosopher to view with calmness and impartiality the actions of his subjects, yet he seemed wholly to misunderstand the character of the Christians. New edicts were promulgated against the Christians, so far departing from the humane regulations of the former emperors, that it was difficult to believe how they could have emanated from an emperor so humane and just to all others. The first year of his association with Verus was one of comparative peace, but calamities began to lower. The public mind was now agitated with gloomy rumors from the frontier|; foreign and civil wars, inundations, earthquakes and pestilence shook the whole Roman people with apprehension. The philosophy of Aurelius could not or did not avail him in a time like this, either to quiet the fears of his subjects, or to quiet superstitious fears that crept into his own heart; he called upon priests from all quarters to celebrate propitiatory rites. An unusual number of sacrifices were offered up for seven days, to purify the infected and horror-stricken city. An extraordinary inundation of the Tiber destroyed many of the granaries of corn on the banks of the river—a famine followed, which pressed heavily on the poor. A German tribe ravaged Belgium; the Parthian war, which commenced disastrously in Syria, now demanded the presence of Verus.

After four years Verus returned bearing the trophies of victory, but bringing with him in his army a pestilence, that spread desolation and death. These numerous troubles were ascribed by the superstitious heathen to the new religion. Precisely at this time, the Christian martyrologies date the commencement of the persecution under Aurelius. In Rome itself, Justin, the apologist of Christianity, ratified with his blood the sincerity of his faith. His death is attributed to the jealousy of Crescens, a cynic, whose audience had been drawn off by the more attractive tenets of the Christian Platonist. Justin was summoned before the prefect, one of the philosophic *teachers* of Aurelius, and commanded to do sacrifice. On his refusal, he was scourged and executed. The emperor was probably absent during this crisis of religious terror; mandates, it is probable, says our historian, were issued to the provinces to imitate the devotion of the capital, and everywhere to appease the offended gods by sacrifice. However this may be, the fact is certain that the persecution raged with violence in the provinces, especially in Asia Minor. The pestilence was not entirely abated when news came of the Marcomanic war. This Marcomanic war, as it was called, was waged by an assemblage of German tribes extending from Gaul to Illyricum. The *presence* of both emperors was needed in this war. It was at this time that Marcus lingered in Rome to offer the sacrifices of which we have spoken. The martyrdom of Polycarp, bishop of Smyrna, occurred about this time, with *many others*, but the fame of Polycarp * has obscured that of other victims. He was the most distinguished Christian of the East; he had heard the

---

* A. D. 167.

Apostle John; he had long presided over the See of Smyrna. This bishop did not ostentatiously expose himself, nor neglect to take measures of security. He retreated from one village to another to elude his pursuers, but was at length betrayed by two slaves, whose confession had been extorted by torture. "The will of God be done," he said. He ordered food to be given to the officers of justice. He requested two hours for prayer. He was placed upon an ass, and on a day of public concourse was conducted to the city. He was met by Herod, the prefect of the city, and his father, Nicetas, who took him with much deference into their own carriage. They vainly endeavored to persuade him to submit to the two tests required—the salutation of the emperor by the title of Lord, and to offer sacrifice. On his refusal, he was thrust from the chariot, and taken to the crowded stadium.

CHAPTER VII.

MARTYRDOM OF POLYCARP.

The merciful proconsul besought him, in respect to his old age, to conceal his name. The Christian spectators imagined that they heard a voice from Heaven, saying, "Polycarp, be firm." He proclaimed aloud that he was *Polycarp*. The trial proceeded: "Swear," they said, "by the genius of Cesar; *retract*, and say, 'Away with the godless.'" The old man, says the narrator, gazed in sorrow at the frantic and raging benches of the spectators, rising above each other, and with his eyes uplifted to heaven said, "Away with the godless." The proconsul, urged him further, "Swear, and I release thee; blaspheme Christ." "Eighty and six years have I served Christ; how can I blaspheme my King and my Saviour?" The proconsul again begged him to swear by the genius of Cæsar. He replied, by requesting *a day* to be appointed on which he might explain the blameless tenets, of Christianity. "Persuade the people to consent," said the compassionate but *overawed* ruler. "We owe respect to authority; to thee I will explain my conduct, but to the populace I will make no explanation." He knew too well the furious passions raging in their minds and how vain it would be to seek to allay them by the rational arguments of Christianity. The proconsul threatened to expose him to the wild beasts, and then he threatened to burn him. "'T is well for me speedily to be released from a life of misery. I fear not the fire that burns for a moment; thou knowest not that which burns forever and ever." His countenance was full of peace and joy, even when the *herald* proclaimed in the midst of the assembly, "Polycarp has professed himself to be a Christian." Then with a shout the people cried, "This is the teacher of all Asia, the overthrower of our gods, he who has turned away so many from sacrifice." The Jews, of whom there were great numbers, joined with the heathen in this assault. They demanded of the president of the games that a lion should be let loose; he excused himself by saying, "The games are over." They declared he should be burned, and immediately both Jews and heathen collected speedily the materials for a funeral pile. He requested not to be nailed; they bound him to the stake. He was unrobed. We will write the prayer he uttered, as it expressed the sentiments of the Christians of that period. "O Lord God Almighty, the Father of the well beloved and ever blessed Son Jesus Christ, by whom we have received the knowledge of Thee; the God of angels, powers and of every creature, and of the whole race of the righteous who live before Thee. I thank Thee that Thou hast thought me worthy of this hour and this day, that I may receive a portion in the number of Thy martyrs, and drink of Christ's cup for the resurrection of eternal life, both of body and soul, in the incorruptibleness of the Holy Spirit; among whom may I be admitted this day as a rich and acceptable sacrifice, as Thou, O true and faithful God, hast prepared and foreshown and accomplished. Wherefore I praise Thee for all Thy mercies; I bless Thee, I glorify Thee, with the eternal and heavenly Jesus Christ, Thy beloved Son, to

Whom with Thee and the Holy Spirit, be glory now and forever."

Polycarp was at least a hundred years old.* His death closed the nameless train of Asiatic martyrs.

Some few years after the martyrdom of this aged bishop, the city of Smryna was visited by an earthquake; a generous sympathy was displayed by the neighboring cities; provisions were poured in from all quarters; homes were offered to the houseless, carriages were furnished to convey the infirm and the children from the scene of ruin. In such humane conduct, may not the progress of Christian benevolence be traced? Many of the sufferers were those whose amphitheatre had been stained with the blood of the aged martyr. They hastened to alleviate the common miseries of both Pagan and Christian, not allowing the thought of divine retribution to interfere with their humane, their Christian work. In circumstances like these, can we not trace an extraordinary revolution in the sentiments of mankind?

In the war with the Marcomanni (of which we have already spoken), in the campaign of the year 174, the army advanced incautiously into a region entirely without water, and in a faint and enfeebled state was exposed, to a formidable attack of the whole barbarian force. Suddenly at an hour of extreme distress, a copious and refreshing rain came down, which supplied their wants, while lightning, and hailstones of an enormous size, drove full upon the adversary, and rendered his army an easy conquest to the Romans. Heathen historians, medals still extant, and the column which bears the name of Antoninus at Rome, concur with

---

* The Christian Legion.

Christian tradition in commemorating the wonderful deliverance of the Roman army, during the war with the German nations. This celebrated event was long current in Christian history as the *legend* of the thundering legion. The Christians attributed the refreshing shower to the prayers they had addressed to the Father, through Christ. The heathen ascribed the victory to Jupiter. Gibbon says, we are assured by monuments of marble and brass, by the imperial medals, and by the Antonine column, that the heathen unanimously attribute their success to the providence of Jupiter and the interposition of Mercury." The skeptical historian concludes his account of this matter with this remark: "Marcus Aurelius despised the Christians as a philosopher, and punished them as a sovereign." That there were many Christians in the army of Marcus in the Marcomanic war seems very probable, from the fact that the conscription was very strict; even gladiators were forced into his army. Whether military service was consistent with Christian principles, was a question that divided the early Christians: some considering it too closely connected with the idolatrous practices of an oath, to the fortunes of Cæsar, and the worship of the standards; but others considered it their duty to give allegiance to their sovereign, and their patriotism and love of country overcame their scruples. This was a time of so great peril to the country, that there were doubtless many Christians in the army—it may be an exaggerated tradition which declares that the Christians formed a whole separate *legion*, in that army. Tradition also says that the Christians believed that the shower was sent in answer to *their* prayers. God was certainly merciful to the whole army. "He maketh the sun to rise upon the evil and upon the good; and sendeth his *rain* upon the *just* and upon the unjust."

The latter part of the reign of Marcus Aurelius was distinguished by another series of martyrdoms. In the year A. D. 177, Ponthius, bishop of Lyons, in his ninetieth year, died in prison from the ill usage he had received. The Christians of Lyons and Vienna appear to have been a colony from Phrygia; they had maintained a close correspondence with their Christian brethren, in the distant communities of Asia Minor. To this district, many years previous, had been banished Archelaus and Herod Antipas; and Pontius Pilate was also banished to this place. It is supposed that a Jewish settlement had been formed around these banished scions of royalty.* It is quite certain that there were many devoted Christians living in the region, round about Lyons and Vienna, and from this point it is probable that Christianity penetrated into Gaul and Britain. The severe persecution that now occurred in this region may have scattered the disciples abroad, as similar calamities had done in the early Christian times. Sanctus, a deacon of Vienna, and Attalus of Pergamus, and Maturus, a new convert, were tortured in the most horrible manner. The amphitheatre was the great public scene of popular barbarity and Christian endurance. Here they were exposed to wild beasts, yet before the ferocity of beasts could dispatch them they were made to sit on heated iron chairs, till their flesh reeked with an offensive odor. One of the most remarkable sufferers, in this memorable martyrdom, was Blandina, a slave. She shared without

---

* Milman.

flinching in the most excruciating tortures with the most distinguished victims. The mistress of Blandina, herself a martyr, trembled lest her humble associate might betray their loved and righteous cause. She was led forth first together with several distinguished men. The only reply that could be extorted from this heroic woman was, "I am a Christian, and no wickedness is practiced among us." The remains of these martyrs were cast into the Rhone, in order to mock and render more improbable their hopes of a resurrection.

With the reign of Marcus Aurelius closed what has been termed the golden days of the Roman empire. But in the weakness and insecurity of the throne lay the strength and safety of Christianity; for little more than a century from the reign of Commodus, the brutal son of Aurelius, to the reign of Diocletian, no systematic policy could be pursued, with regard to the religion or to any of the leading internal interests of the empire. Many of the emperors were involved in foreign wars and had no time for the social changes within the pale of the empire. The persecutions of the Christians which took place during this period seem to have been the result of the personal hostility of the provincial rulers.

CHAPTER VIII.

STORY OF ORIGEN.

During the reign of Commodus the Christians had a friend in Martia, the favorite wife of the Emperor. The Christians had a long, unbroken peace, during the reign of this degraded monarch. Septimius Severus commenced his reign A. D. 194. This emperor wielded the sceptre with great energy, but his early reign was occupied with Eastern wars, and his later years with the affairs of the remote province of Britain. Severus was at one time the protector and at another time the persecutor of Christianity. His son Caracalla had, it is said, a Christian nurse and a Christian preceptor. During his childhood the gentleness of his manners and the sweetness of his temper gave promise of a humane ruler, but, alas, the natural ferocity of his temper ripened under the fatal influence of jealous ambition, which could not endure the rivalry of his brother. Many Christians of distinction enjoyed the avowed favor of the emperor. The persecutions in the reign of Severus in the eastern provinces seem to have resulted from the acts of hostile governors. Alexandria was the chief scene of suffering in this reign. Leonidas, the father of Origen, perished in this persecution. Origen, then a youth of seventeen years, was kept from imprisonment with his father by the prudent care and stratagem of his mother, who concealed all his clothes. The boy wrote to his father, Leonidas, imploring him to be steadfast and not to allow his affection for him and his family to stand in his way of obtaining a martyr's crown. Three hostile parties divided Alexandria at this time: Jews, Christians, and Pagans, the worshipers of Serapis. Severus when in Egypt seemed to be impressed with the mysterious rites of Serapis. The Egyptian priests took advantage of this hour of imperial favor to wreak their vengeance upon the Christians who were making great progress throughout this province of Africa. It is not certainly known whether the Emperor Severus authorized the persecution that was now waged by the Prefect of Alexandria, but he used the most violent measures. The elementary schools of learning by which the Christians trained their pupils were almost deserted in consequence of the persecutions waged against the Christian teachers. Clement and Origen were two of the great teachers of the Alexandrian school. The young Origen labored with unceasing activity in these schools. Origen had some peculiar opinions, but he was very learned and devout. In no part of the Roman Empire had Christianity taken deeper hold than 'in the rich and populous cities of Africa. This country, together with Egypt, was then the granary of the Western World. It is now a thinly peopled desert, made so by Christian feuds, Vandal invasions and Mohammedan barbarism. This was the land of Origen, of Tertullian, of Augustine, of Cyprian. From the ascension of Commodus (son of Marcus Aurelius), to that of Diocletian, A. D. 284, more than twenty emperors flitted like shadows across the tragic theatre of the imperial palace. During the persecution to which we have referred in Africa, Tertullian stood forth as the apologist of

Christianity. African Christianity was not dreamy and speculative, like the religion of the East. It rejected the wild fancies of the Gnostics. It was anti-material and simple and practical in its creed. The address of Tertullian to the Prefect of Africa is no longer the language of mild remonstrance or expostulation, but every sentence breathes defiance and scorn. It hurls contempt upon the gods of paganism. He avows the determination of Christians to expel the idols or *demons* from the respect and adoration of mankind. The language of Tertullian shows the altered *position* of Christianity. Of all the histories of martyrdom none is so unexaggerated in its tone and language and so abounds in touches of nature, and breathes such truth and reality, says our historian, as those of Perpetua and Felicita, two African females. Their deaths are said to have taken place in the first year of Geta the son of Severus and brother of the wicked Caracalla. Perpetua and Felicita were young and delicate women. The father of the former vainly tried to make her recant, in order to save the life of his beloved daughter. The most tender appeals were made by the family of Perpetua, to pervert her from the faith. She belonged to a good family and had a liberal education, and was honorably married. The history of her martyrdom is said to have been written by her own hands. She was cast into prison with an infant in her arms. Perpetua left her child with her family. Felicita, who had been a slave, gave her child to a Christian woman to bring up. The lady and the slave went out hand in hand, to the ampitheatre, to be torn by beasts. A wild cow was let loose upon them. Their heroism and endurance were wonderful. Perpetua seemed to be in a dream, and almost unconscious of her bodily pain. Her last words tenderly admonished her brother to be steadfast in the faith. Five martyrs suffered at this time, three women and two men. After being torn by beasts, they were speedily released from their sufferings, by the merciful sword of the gladiator. Perpetua guiding with her own hand the sword to her throat. This African persecution lasted until the second year of Caracalla, 211-217 A. D.

From the close of the reign of the sons of Severus, except during the reign of Maximin, Christianity enjoyed peace until the reign of Decius. The weak and crumbling edifice of paganism was now shaken to its base, A. D. 218, by the accession of the Syrian Elagabulus. He was the priest of an effeminate superstition. He introduced with much pomp into Rome the worship of the sun, as though he meant to supersede the ancestral deities of the great city. The conical black stone, the idol of Emesa in Syria, was brought to Rome; a magnificent temple was built upon the Palatine hill; hecatombs of oxen and sheep were offered upon numerous altars. The highest dignitaries of the empire, commanders of legions, grave senators, the equestrian order, were required to appear as humble ministers, clad in loose and flowing robes and in linen sandals, among the lascivious dancers and wanton music of oriental drums and cymbals. Nothing was sacred to the voluptuous Syrian. The palladium of the city, that image of Minerva cherished above all the hallowed treasures of the city, was brought forth to be wedded to a Syrian deity worshiped in the East under the name of Astarte. Such insults to the ancient religion, must have disgusted the people, and also deprived them of the veneration they had formerly felt for the majesty of their religion. The pollutions and sensuality of the religion of Elagabulus, together with the rude shocks sustained by the ancient paganism, probably tended to turn the minds of the thinking and moral to embrace a purer faith. The successor of Elagabulus was Alexander Severus, who, though a Syrian, had been educated with some knowledge of Christianity. His mother had held intercourse with the Christians of Syria; she had listened to the lectures of Origen with respect, if not with conviction. Alexander seems to have affected a kind of universalism. In his own palace he enshrined, as it were, the representatives of the different religions which prevailed in the Roman Empire — Orpheus, Abraham, Christ, and Apollonius of Tyana. In Apollonius was centered the modern Theurgy, the magic which commanded the intermediate spirits, between the higher world and the world of man. Abraham rather than Moses was placed at the head of Judaism. Christianity in the person of its founder, even where it did not command *authority* as a religion, had lost the unjust opprobrium under which it so long labored, of animosity to mankind. The followers of Jesus had now lived down the bitter hostility which had prevailed against them. Christian churches began to rise in different parts of the Empire, Christian bishops were admitted at the Court in a recognized official character. To this time at least in Rome, A. D. 222, the religious assemblies of the Christians were held in private; to the wonder of the heathen, their religion *appeared* without temple or altar. The cemeteries of the dead, the sequestered grove, the private chamber, continued their peaceful assemblies.

Their religious usages now became better known. It is said that the Christians at this time published the names of those who had been proposed for ordination, and that Alexander established a similar proceeding with regard to all candidates for civil offices. A piece of ground was also awarded to the Christians by Alexander, upon the principle that it was better to devote it to the worship of God than to any profane use. These circumstances have created a suspicion that Alexander was a believer in Christianity, though he made no public confession. The earliest Christian churches in Rome are assigned by Tillemont to the reign of Alexander Severus. Rooms of small architectural dimensions were doubtless used for worship long before this time, but without observation. The heathen religion had greatly changed at this period from the old beliefs of the Greeks and Romans. They worshiped in the *same* temples and performed many of the same rites, but over all this had risen a kind of speculative Theism, to which the popular worship was subordinate. Celsus, the famous controversialist with Origen, tells him that a philosophical notion of the Deity was perfectly reconcilable with the Deity. This was the commencement of a new Platonism which from this time exercised a supreme authority, to the extinction of the older forms of Grecian philosophy, and grew up into a dangerous antagonist of Christianity. Several of the Fathers of the Church had been students of this new Platonism, before they imbibed the divine Philosophy which cometh from above. This philosophy, however, could exercise no extensive influence; it was merely a *refuge* for the intellectual few. The successor of Alexander was a Thracian savage. The Christian Bishops, like all the other polite and virtuous men, in the court of his predecessor, were exposed to the suspicions and hatred of the brutal and warlike Maximin. The reign of Gordian was short. Philip the Arabian, his successor, has been claimed by some as a Christian, but the splendor with which he celebrated the great religious rites of Rome refutes this idea. It was the thousandth year of Rome from its foundation, and the Roman people demanded extraordinary magnificence. The persecution under Decius for extent and violence was terrible. The Christians were now a recognized body in the State. They were necesarily of the party of the Emperor, whose favor they had enjoyed. Decius hated the adherents of the murdered Philip. The protection of a foreign religion by a foreign Emperor (now that Christianity had begun to erect temple against temple, and the Christian bishop met the pagan pontiff on equal terms around the imperial throne) would be considered among the flagrant departures from the wisdom of Ancient Rome. Decius claimed to be a descendant of the Decii of Republican Rome, though of obscure Pannonian birth. He thought himself called upon to restore the religion as well as the manners of Ancient Rome. He determined to make an effort to purify Rome from the rivalry of Asiatic and modern superstition. The Bishop Fabianus was one of the first victims of his resentment; no successor was elected to the obnoxious office during the brief reign of Decius. Many of the great cities of the Empire followed the example of the capital. In Alexandria, the zeal of the populace outran the fury of the Emperor. Antioch bewailed the loss of her bishop. Carthage was disgraced by the falling away of some even of her clergy—the great test to which the persecuted were liable, was the requirement to sacrifice to their idols. Should any of the Christians be overcome by terror and perform the sacrifice, long years of penitence and humility were required, before they could again be admitted to Christian privileges. Valerian ascended the throne three years after Decius. He revived in his own person the ancient office of censor of public morals. The commencement of the censor's reign, who scrutinized with care the influence of Christianity upon public morals, was favorable to their cause. For a short time, therefore, persecution ceased. The change in Valerian's conduct is attributed to the influence of a man deeply versed in magic. Macrianus is reported to have obtained such mastery over Valerian as to induce him to engage in the most guilty mysteries of magic in tracing the fate of the empire in the entrails of *human* victims. The edict against the Christians in this persecution of Valerian subjected all the bishops who refused to conform to their requirements to the penalty of death, and seized the endowment of their churches. Cyprian, bishop of Carthage, was advanced in life when he embraced the doctrines of Christianity; He passed rapidly through the steps of Christian initiation. On the vacancy of the bishopric of Carthage he was overpowered by the acclamations of the city, which compelled him to assume the distinguished but dangerous office. Cyprian had high notions of Episcopal authority. The inviolable unity of the outward and visible Church appeared to him an integral part of Christianity, and the discipline of the Episcopal order the only means of preserving that unity. The first rumor of persecution designated Cyprian as a victim. Cyprian withdrw from the storm. Inventive cruelty suggested new means of torture.

CHAPTER IX.

Cyprian, in his retreat (A. D. 254), wrote consolatory letters to those not so fortunate as himself. His letters describe the relentless barbarity of their persecutors. During the reign of Decius, Cyprian remained in retirement. He returned to Carthage in the early part of the reign of Valerian. A plague at this time ravaged the Roman world. Its destructive violence thinned the streets of the populous Carthage. Cyprian devoted his energies to the alleviation of human suffering. He exhorted the Christians not to limit their attentions to their own brotherhood, but to extend kindness indiscriminately to their heathen enemies. He determined to remain at Carthage. After a time he was summoned before the proconsul, who told him that the emperor required all those who professed foreign religions to offer sacrifice. Cyprian refused. "Art thou Thasian Cyprian, the bishop of so many impious men?" said the proconsul. "I will not sacrifice," replied Cyprian. He was banished. On the accession of Galerius, he was recalled from exile, but placed in a prison in the city. He was treated with respect and delicacy. A crowd of Christians and heathen assembled at his prison door, to catch glances and hear words from one they loved so well. The proconsul received orders from the *sacred* emperor that the man who had deluded so many must die. Cyprian was taken to a field and beheaded (A. D. 254).

DECIUS.

The proconsul died a few days afterwards (A. D. 249-251). The death of Decius, according to the Pagan account, was worthy of the days of old. He was wounded by the Goths; his son was killed by an arrow. He cried aloud that the life of a single soldier was nothing to the glory of the empire, and soon fell, valiantly fighting. Christian writers say he was betrayed by treachery into a marsh, where he could neither fight nor fly. He perished miserably, leaving his unburied body to the carrion birds and beasts. The captivity of Valerian (A. D. 254) by the Persians took place in 258. It is said that the Persian king used the body of his unhappy captive as a footstool for many years, in order to mount his elephant. He never returned to Rome. Much mystery hung over his death.

Gallienus restored peace to the Church. The edict of Valerian was rescinded. The last transient collision of Christianity with the Government, before its final dreadful conflict with Diocletian, was under Aurelian. The reign of Aurelian (A. D. 271) was much occupied with warlike campaigns. His mother was a priestess of the sun, and the emperor built a temple to his tutelary god at Rome. The sacred ceremony of consulting the sibylline books was directed by him. In their mystic leaves the Roman people *had* believed their destinies were written. The severe emperor now reproaches the Senate for their want of faith in these volumes. He attributes their skepticism to the influence of the Christians. No hostile measures were taken against the Christians in the early part of his reign. Aurelian was summoned as an arbitrator in a Christian controversy.

Paul of Samosata was bishop of Antioch. He brought disgrace on this important See by blending together the elements of Paganism, Judaism and Christianity. His pride and ostentation put to shame the modesty and humble pretensions of former prelates. The zealous vigilance of neighboring bishops soon discovered that his opinions were more nearly allied to Judaism than to the Christian creed. He lived under the protection of Zenobia, queen of Palmyra, who had given him a civil magistracy. He introduced many effeminate ceremonies into his cathedral, which reminded the worshipers of the voluptuous rites of Paganism. He set at defiance the solemn censures and excommunication pronounced by a synod of bishops against him. But when his warlike patroness, Zenobia, was conquered by the armies of Aurelian, the bishops appealed to Aurelian to expel the rebel against their authority, and the partisan of the Palmyrenes. The emperor did not refuse to interfere in this case—so strange to him—but transferred judgment from the bishops of Syria to those of Rome and Italy. By their sentence Paul was degraded from the Episcopate. The sentiments of Aurelian changed towards the Christians near the close of his reign. Sanguinary edicts were issued, but death prevented their general promulgation. Tradition says that a young deacon, St. Lawrence, was put to death in the reign of Valerian. He was roasted on bars of iron. When he was asked to produce the treasures of the church, he assembled together the cripples and aged widows of the church, who were maintained by the *alms* of the charitable. "These are the treasures of the church," said Lawrence. This so enraged his persecutors that they burned him upon a gridiron.

Diocletian ascended the throne of the Cæsars A. D. 284. The necessities of the times now seemed to require more than one person to be invested with sovereign authority. Diocletian, Galerius, Maximian, and Constantius in Britain and Gaul now divided the cares and honors of the Roman world. Among the innovations of Diocletian, none was more closely connected with the interests of Christianity than the virtual degradation of Rome by its ceasing to be the capital of the empire, by the residence of the chief emperor in other cities. Nicomedia, while Diocletian held the reins of power, was the favorite residence. The removal of the seat of government from Rome to Nicomedia made more manifest the magnitude of the danger to existing institutions from the progress of Christianity. Diocletian, A. D. 284: "In Rome, the ancient majesty of the national religion must still have kept down Christianity in comparative obscurity. The Prætor still made way for the pontifical order, and submitted his fasces to the vestal virgin, while the Christian bishop pursued his more humble way." The churches of the Christians could not compare at this time with the stately temples of the heathen, on which the sovereigns of mankind had lavished the treasures of ages. In a letter of Cornelius, bishop of Rome, written during the reign of Decius (A. D. 250), he says: "We have one bishop, forty-six presbyters, fourteen deacons; also readers, acolytes, fifteen hundred widows and poor." The East was more fully peopled with Christians than any part of the Western world, except Africa. The *bishops* of Antioch and Nicomedia, of Carthage and Alexandria, were far more conspicuous and imposing persons than the *prede-*

cessors of the popes, among the consuls and the Senate, and the ministers of the ruling emperor. In Nicomedia, the Christian church stood on an eminence commanding the town, and conspicuous above the palace of the sovereign; whereas, the churches in Rome were in sequestered places, and seemed to avoid the gaze of the heathen inquirer. During the winter of 302-3, the great question of the policy to be adopted towards the Christians was debated, first in a private conference between Diocletian and Galerius. Diocletian, though urged by his vehement partner in the empire, was averse to sanguinary proceedings. He agreed to dismiss the Christians from posts of rank and authority, and expel them from the palace and army. The Christians now formed a considerable part of the army. They were permitted to abstain from idolatrous conformity, but they were sometimes charged with contempt for the auspices. The soothsayer, when disappointed in the appearance of the entrails of the victims, denounced the presence of the profane strangers. Such incidents to a superstitious soldiery* were full of danger and death to the Christians. The palace of Diocletian was divided by conflicting factions. Some of the chief officers of the Emperor's household openly professed Christianity; his wife and daughter were favorably disposed to the same cause. The mother of Galerius was a fanatical Pagan. The oracle of Apollo at Miletus was consulted, and persecution soon began. Diocletian, overcome by the importunity of friends, consented that the church at Nicomedia should be

---

* "Nowhere did the old Roman religion retain so much hold upon the mind as among the sacred eagles."

destroyed, but with no loss of life. Galerius wished all who refused to sacrifice to be burnt alive. At the dawn of day the Prefect of the city appeared at the door of the church. The doors were instantly thrown down; the Pagans beheld with surprise the vacant space, looking in vain for the statue of the Deity. The sacred books were burned and the furniture of the building plundered by the soldiers. The leaders of the Prætorian guard advanced with their tools, and in a few hours the building consecrated by the prayers and penitent tears of the Christians was razed to the ground. The Christians awaited in consternation the promulgation of the fatal edict. It was soon issued. It was a rigorous proscription, short of the punishment of death. It comprehended all orders. The sacred books were to be delivered up by the bishops and proselytes to the imperial officers and publicly burned. The property of the churches was confiscated, whether lands or furniture. Christians of distinction were deprived of their offices. All assemblies for public worship were prohibited—those of the plebeian order were deprived of the right of Roman citizenship. This secured to them the sanctity of their persons from corporal punishment or torture. This dreadful edict was no sooner affixed in the usual place than it was torn down by the hands of a rash, indignant Christian. His life was soon forfeited. He was roasted alive! Suddenly a fire broke out in the palace at Nicomedia, which spread almost to the chamber of the Emperor. No one knew the origin of this conflagration. It was ascribed to the Christians. They retorted by saying that Galerius was the guilty author in order to criminate the Christians and alarm Diocletian into still more violent measures. The consequences were most disastrous to the Christians. The officers of the household and the inmates of the palace were subjected to cruel tortures. Anthimus, the Bishop of Nicomedia, was beheaded. In every part of the world Christianity was assailed by the full force of the civil power. Many were executed, many burned alive, many were bound in prison; some, with stones round their necks, were rowed in boats to the middle of the lake and thrown into the water. From Nicomedia—the center of the persecution—went forth edicts and letters east and west to restore the ancient religion and suppress the hostile faith. The fierce temper of Maximian readily acceded to carry into effect the barbarous edicts. Vague rumors of insurrection in regions densely peopled with Christians gave some countenance to the charge of political ambition brought against the Christians. About this time Diocletian celebrated a triumph at Rome; but weary of the cares of State, soon after his return to Nicomedia he laid aside the robes of Empire. He was seized with a depressing malady, which secluded him for a long time in his palace. It is not known how he was affected, as the secrets of the palace did not reach the popular ear. He retired to Illyria, on the Adriatic. It is said he devoted his attention to horticulture. His colleague, Maximian, followed reluctantly the example of his patron and coadjutor. The abdication of Diocletian left the most implacable enemy of the Christians, Galerius, master of the East. Maxentius, son of Maximian, assumed the purple in the West. He was more remarkable for his licentiousness than for his persecuting spirit. During the persecutions, Constantius alone, of all the Emperors, by a dextrous appearance of submission, had screened the Christians of Gaul and Britain. The persecution had now lasted six or seven years (A. D. 309), but in no part of the world did Christianity betray any signs of vital decay. Constantine, son of Constantius (the first Christian Emperor), had been placed as a hostage in the power of Galerius. Feeling his condition insecure, he determined to escape from his honorable captivity. His father, Constantius, bequeathed him a wise example of humanity and toleration. His mother, Helena, was an active and devout Christian. It is probable that at this time the Christians looked upon Constantine as their protector and the head of the Christian interest.

The most signal and unexpected triumph was over the author of the persecution. Galerius, in the eighteenth year of his reign, was seized with a loathsome malady. An ulcer attacked the lower part of his body that soon proved fatal. "It is singular," says Dean Milman, "that the disease vulgarly called 'eaten of worms' should have been the destiny of Herod Agrippa, of Galerius, and of Philip II. of Spain." From the dying bed of Galerius was issued an edict, which, while it apologized for severities against the Christians, admitted the failure of the measures he had adopted for its suppression. The edict permitted the free exercise of the Christian religion and made an earnest request to Christians to intercede for him in their prayers. The whole Roman world witnessed the confession of the dying Emperor. The edict was issued from Sardica in the name of Galerius, Licinias and Constantine (Edict of Galerius, 311 A. D.) The last persecution of the Christians under Diocletian is regarded as the tenth persecution. The prison doors were now thrown open; the mines rendered up their laborers; long trains of Christian people were seen visiting their ruined churches and former places of devotion. But Maximian, the Cæsar of the East, still continued his harassing oppressions. He restored the Polytheistic ceremonial in all its former magnificence. Armenia, the *first* Christian kingdom, was subjected by him to severe persecution.

CHAPTER X.

The vices of Maximin rendered him hateful to all. In A. D. 312 he insulted Valeria, the widow of Galerius and daughter of Diocletian, with an offer of marriage while *his wife* was still living. Famine and pestilence ensued through all the dominions of Maximin. The ecclesiastical historians of that period claim no exemption from the general calamity, but declare with strong approval that the Christians displayed everywhere the offices of humanity and brotherhood. The sufferers who survived the widespread evils of the time declared that Christianity was stronger than the love of kindred. The Diocletian persecution reached Britain, but did not long continue there, as Constantius was humane in his temper and favorably affected toward the Christians on account of his Christian wife Helena, a British lady.

There is a story told of a British martyr named *Alban*, who was a Roman soldier. A presbyter, flying from his persecutors, took refuge in his house. Alban threw on the dress of the ecclesiastic, and was taken in his stead. When carried to the tribunal, he proclaimed himself a christian, and was beheaded. A church was built upon the spot where he suffered, and was called St. Alban's.

Those who suffered the loss of all except their lives were called confessors.

The victory of Constantine over Maxentius left Constantine master of Rome. He and Licinius reigned over all the European provinces. At the death of

Maximin (A. D. 312) the last hope of Paganism, to maintain itself by the civil government, perished. Eusebius gives a gorgeous description of the reconstruction of a church at Tyre. It was built on the old site of the church where they had at first worshiped Jesus the Son of Mary. The splendor of this second building proves that, even before the accession of Constantine, the Christians possessed sufficient wealth to erect stately temples. We have already alluded to the fact that the biography of the bishops of Rome, their influence and peculiar character, are involved in dimness and obscurity. Gleams of light bring out occasionally the names of Victor, Zephyrinus, Callistus, Stephen, Clement, Cornelius; "but the same providential obscurity that veiled the growing Church threw its modest concealment over the person of the bishop." * But when the emperor of the civilized world adopts Christianity as his religion, the bishop who presides over the Christian clergy becomes at once a prominent functionary. An appeal to the emperor, so long as Rome is an imperial residence, is an appeal to the bishop of Rome.

Melchiades held the See of Rome at the time of Constantiue's conversion, but Sylvester soon succeeded him (A. D. 312–314). Not one of the bishops of Rome down to Leo and Gregory the Great appear among the distinguished writers of Christendom.

The fate of Rome and of Paganism was decided in the battle of Milrian Bridge. Magnentius, the opposing general to Constantine, was utterly routed and slain. It was commonly reported that Constantine, on marching to Rome, had a vision of a cross in the sky, with

---

* Milman.

this inscription: *In hoc signo vince*—by this sign conquer. This vision was followed by a dream, which directed him to cause a standard to be made, to be carried at the head of the army, with the sacred sign and inscription. The shaft of the celebrated standard, called the *Labarum*, was cased with gold. Above the transverse beam was wrought, in a golden crown, the monogram, or the device of two letters which signified the name of Christ. This *Labarum* was *certainly* borne aloft by the officers of Constantine, but this is the only undisputed point connected with this interesting matter. Some, in Constantine's day, really believed that our Lord had condescended to place a token in the firmament, to convince this man of the truth of his religion. Others suppose that his excited mind, *imagined* that he saw a *cross* in the heavens above him. Another theory is that it was an ambitious invention of Constantine, to *impress* the Christian legions of his army, who would, with such a standard, be animated to greater enthusiasm. The object to be obtained, the triumph of Christianity over Paganism, seems not unworthy of a miracle, and nothing is impossible with God; yet the subsequent life of this great man has induced the belief in many minds that the third theory was the true one. Many learned and dispassionate writers, however, accept the second theory. A natural phenomenon, they suppose, was interpreted by the excited vision of the general to be a miraculous sign. "Of all the emperors who had been invested with the purple, either as Augustus or Cæsar, during the persecution of the Christians, *his father only*, the Protector of Christianity, had gone to an honored and peaceful grave!" His mother, Helena, too, was an earnest Christian, though her history has come down to us more in connection with her reverence for sacred *places*, than any enlightenment of Christian doctrine and duty. This, however, is not to be attributed to any defect in her Christian morals, but to the superstitious views of her biographers.

The first public edict of Constantine in favor of Christianity is lost. That issued at Milan, in the joint names of Licinius and Constantine, is the great charter of the liberties of Christianity; but it is an edict of full, unlimited toleration, and no more. The churches that had been destroyed, or property alienated, were to be restored and secured, but the same freedom of worship was allowed to Pagans.

This edict * has the tone of imperial clemency, rather than conviction that Christianity was the *one* true religion.

We have said that his mother was a Christian; some writers suppose that she became a convert after her son† proclaimed himself a Christian. Indeed, on the authority of Eusebius, it is stated that she derived her knowledge of Christianity from her son.

Constantine, though a great general and most consummate statesman, seemed never to comprehend fully the doctrines of Christiaeity, as is proved by his postponement of baptism to the last hour of his life. But his obscure views of Christian truth did not restrain his liberality to the Church. Many of the churches of Rome claim the first Christian emperor as their founder. The most distinguished of these, says Milman, stood on

---

* Edict of Milan.

† This is not probable. The husband of Helena was the *Protector* of Christianity. Christianity had long existed in Britain, *where* her son Constantine was born.

the sites now occupied by the Lateran and St. Peter's. If it could be known at what period in the life of Constantine these churches were built, some *light* might be thrown on the history of his personal religion. As the Lateran was an imperial palace, the grant of a basilica (as the early churches were called) *within* the walls, was a kind of direct recognition, if not of his own personal attendance, at least of his admission of Christianity within the domestic circle. This palace (the Lateran) was afterwards granted to the Christians, the first patrimony of the popes.

Constantine's life and actions have been examined by Pagans and Christians with the most severe scrutiny. Two crimes of the deepest dye are imputed to him — the execution of his eldest son Crispus* and his wife Fausta. Historians are not determined whether the cause of the death of his son was political or domestic jealousy. Some have said that Fausta, the stepmother, stimulated by ambition for her own sons, induced her husband to believe that Crispus, who was popular and beloved for many heroic deeds, was a conspirator against his father and a political rival. It is reported that Constantine discovered too late that his suspicions were groundless, and, filled with rage and remorse, directed that his guilty partner should be sacrificed. Gibbon *doubts* the execution of Fausta ; he says if she was put to death, that the private apartments of the palace must have been the scene of her execution. An imperfect and obscure narrative of the Pagan historian Zosimus is the authority upon which the crimes and death of Fausta are stated. According to this author, "the ancient tragedy of Hippolitus and Phedra was

---
* Crispus' death, A. D. 326.

renewed in the palace of Constantine." Jerome says that several years elapsed between the deaths of Crispus and Fausta.

Both detraction and praise were directed upon every act of this emperor from the beginning of his reign to its close. But so great a change did his statesmanlike acts produce in the Roman empire, that his reign forms an epoch in the history of the world. Christianity with him ascended the throne of the Cæsars, but it was not now the self-denying, pure, spotless religion of earlier times. Wealth flowed in, producing many corruptions.* It was said by one of the pious Fratricelli in the thirteenth century: "After a retrospect of a thousand years, we believe that the gift of a Roman Christian emperor was a *fatal* boon to the Church."

The Christians of apostolic days, and those immediately succeeding them, had received the simple, life-giving doctrines of the New Testament without cavil, or without analytical questionings. They knew how to live and how to die for Christ and His truth. But with the spread of Christianity among Pagan nations, and especially among the *Greeks*, momentous and deep questions began to stir the depths of the heart and intellect by the silent working of the new faith. The nature of the Deity; the state of the soul after death; the origin of evil; the connection of the physical with the moral world—these subjects became topics with the many, and were no longer confined, as they had been, to the intellectual few. The passions of men became warmly enlisted in questions of this character. Man-

---

* It is consoling to reflect that the inner life of Christianity is not known to history; much that was pure, self-sacrificing, and lovely, found no record in the annals of the busy world."

kind within the Christian sphere seemed to retrograde to the stern Jewish spirit, and the Old Testament began ta dominate over the gospel of Christ.

The first civil wars which divided Christianity were those of *Donatism* and the Trinitarian controversy. The Gnostic and Manichean sects were rather *rival religions* than Christian factions. Donatism was a fierce schism in an established community. It began in a disputed appointment to the episcopal dignity at Carthage. The bishop of Carthage was at this time probably more influential than any dignitary in the West. The African churches had suffered greatly during the persecution of Diocletian and the invasion of Magnentius. External troubles, however, did not, as in other places, compress the body of Christians into compact unity, but left behind them a fatal principle of disorganization.

The commanding character of Cyprian and his writings had elevated the episcopal power to a great height.

CHAPTER XI.

THE DONATIST CONTROVERSY.

The origin of the unhappy schism that divided the Church in Africa, though somewhat obscure, has been traced to the following circumstances. It seems to have been more a question of courtesy than of principle. Mensurius, the Bishop of Carthage, dying in 311, the majority of the people and clergy elected Cecilian to the vacant chair. Cecilian was consecrated by the Bishops of Africa proper, the province of which Carthage was the capital. The Bishops in Numidia who had formerly been present at the consecration of the Bishop of Carthage, were greatly offended that they had not been invited and waited for. They called upon Cecilian to appear before them. Cecilian refused. This contumacy so enraged the Numidian Church, that seventy of their Bishops, together with some of the clergy of Carthage, *declared* Cecilian unworthy, and appointed Majorinus, *his* Deacon, Bishop of Carthage. The Church was rent into two factions headed by two Bishops. The Donatists brought this controversy before Constantine in 313. The Emperor referred the matter to Melchiades, Bishop of Rome, with whom were associated nineteen Bishops from Gaul and other countries. They decided against the Donatists. *They* then tried to get a personal decision from Constantine himself. He also gave his voice against them. The Donatists accused the Emperor of an unrighteous decision. The wrath of Constantine was aroused. He ordered the seditious Bishops to be banished. As the Donatist party were numerous and powerful, violent commotions and seditions were aroused in Africa. This controversy lasted with more or less bitterness for a century. The *name*, it is said, was derived from one of the most distinguished of their number who succeeded Majorinus as one of the Bishops of Carthage. Cecilian and the chief minister, Felix, who had taken part in his consecration, were acquitted of the charges brought against them. The great Augustine, first as Presbyter, and afterwards as Bishop of Hippo, in Africa, assailed the Donatists *vigorously* in his writings and speeches; he did much to impair their influence. He roused all Christendom against them. The Donatists were admitted by their enemies to be sound in doctrine and not censurable in their lives. But a party of furious fanatics, composed of the peasantry and rustic populace, espousing the cause of the Donatists, defended them by force of arms, filling the province of Africa with rapine and slaughter. This schism and its effects were happily confined to Africa. Some writers say *it* was not finally extirpated until Mahometanism entered these regions. Constantine the Great did much for his subjects. His wise and vigorous administration had given comparative peace to the Empire. He had relieved the *Christians* from persecution and *all* his people from grievous oppression. He had made two munificent donations to maintain the ceremonial of religion. He had caused the famous Labarum to be made and carried at the head of the army to increase the enthusiasm of the Christian soldier; he had admitted their representatives to his court; he had sought by prudence and wisdom to allay the fierce feuds in Africa. He was present at the great Council of Nice—he called *himself* a Christian, but it is very probable that he was still ignorant of the real character and the profound truths of the religion of Christ.

We have alluded to a trinitarian controversy that disturbed the peace of the church, after the accession of Constantine the Great to the Empire. The first Christians had been content to worship the Deity as revealed in the Gospels and Epistles. They repeated with devout worship the names of the Father, Son and Holy Ghost; they recognized the attributes of God as claimed by our Lord Jesus Christ, and the personality and divinity ascribed by him to the Holy Spirit, but they did not with analytical accuracy define or appropriate peculiar terms to each manifestation of the Godhead. The birth, death and resurrection of Christ, as the Son of God, and the effusion of the Holy Spirit, were truths plainly revealed and received by the *faithful* in all countries where the seed of the Gospel had been sown. Alexandria became about this time the fruitful soil of speculative controversy. Noctus, of Smyrna, dwelt with such exclusive zeal on the unity of the Godhead as to absorb the whole Trinity into one Being. His adversaries called him and his followers Patripassians, as according to the Noctian theory they said, the Father must have suffered on the cross. Sabellianism, however, became more extensively known. Sabellius was an African of Cyrenaica, a Greek province. According to his theory, it was the same Deity who existed under different forms in the Father, the Son and the Holy Ghost. The Sabellians charged those who differed from them with a Tritheistic worship, and the Trinitarians accused the Sabellians of annihilating the separate existence of the Son and the Holy Ghost. But Sabellianism did not divide Christianity into two irreconcilable parties. Alexander, Bishop of Alexandria, surrounded by his Presbyters, expressed his opinions freely with regard to the Trinity. This produced a discussion, when *Arius*, one of the Presbyters present, declared that he agreed with his bishop in all points except in the self-existence of the Son. He admitted the ante-mundane being of the Son and Spirit before all worlds existed, but there was a time, Arius supposed, when the parent Deity dwelt alone. The divine unity, according to this distinguished heresiarch, was broken by an act of God's sovereign will, in creating the Son, the image of the Father—the vicegerent of the Divine power, and the intermediate agent in all the work of creation. These opinions, as it is well known, produced a grievous schism in the church. The indignant Alexander expelled Arius from Alexandria; he retired to Syria, but his opinions had already spread through Egypt and Libya. Two distinguished prelates, both named Eusebius, adopted the opinions of Arius; One of these was the ecclesiastical historian, the other was the Bishop of the important city of Nicomedia. Throughout the East this Arian controversy was propagated with earnest rapidity. The interference of the emperor was again demanded (as in the question of the Donatists), to allay the strife which distracted the Christendom of the *East*. The behavior of Constantine was probably counseled or guided by

---

* It is said, on the authority of Eusebius, that Constantine at the battle of Hadrianople, in A. D. 323, ordered the lives of his enemies to be spared and offered *rewards* for all captives brought in alive.

some ecclesiastic of a humane and conciliatory spirit. The letter sent by Constantine was a model for letters of this character. His letter condemned Alexander for the unnecessary agitation of such deep mysteries, yet unpractical questions, and also censured Arius for not suppressing in respectful *silence* his objections to the doctrines of his Patriarch. It is believed by those who have examined this letter and are intimately cognizant with these times, that the hand of Hosius, Bishop of Cordova, in Spain, is to be traced in this royal and Christian letter. It is by no means, says Milman, an improbable conjecture that Hosius was the Spaniard that administered to Constantine in the hour of mental agony and remorse the balm of Christian penitence. Hosius was sent to Egypt to assuage the fierce disputes that agitated that country from the mouths of the Nile to the Cataracts, on the subject of the unity of God. A general council of the heads of the various Christian communities throughout the Roman Empire was summoned by the imperial mandate to establish on the consenting authority of assembled Christendom, the true doctrine on these disputed points.† In the month of May or June 20th, in the year 325, met the great council of Nice. Not half a century before, the Christian Bishops had been marked as the objects of the most cruel insult and persecution. They had been chosen on account of their eminence in their own communities, as the victims of the stern policy of the government. They had been exiled, set to work in the mines, exposed to every species of humiliation and suffering. Now, they were assembled under the imperial sanction, a religious senate from all parts of the

---

Nicene Creed. Council of Nice.

Empire, at least from the Eastern world: for Italy was represented by only two Presbyters from Rome. Hosius, the good bishop to whom we have already alluded, was the representative for Spain, Gaul and *Britain*. The public establishment of post-horses was commanded to afford every facility, gratuitously, for the journey of the assembling clergy. About three hundred bishops were present at this famous council, Presbyters, Deacons, acolytes without number, and a considerable body of the laity. The presence of the Emperor himself gave great weight and dignity to the assembly. There was one Bishop from Persia and one from Scythia. Hosius, it is believed, presided at this Council. The Bishop of Rome, Julius I., was absent from Nicea; he was also absent from Sardica. The Bishop of Rome, by his absence, happily escaped the dangerous *precedent* which might have been raised, by his appearance in any rank inferior to the Presidency. The council sat for rather more than two months. Constantine seems to have been present during the greater part of the time, exhorting the members of the council to unity and harmony. He was splendidly attired, the gold and precious stones upon his raiment were dazzling to behold. He spoke in the Latin language, and his speech was *interpreted* to the Greek bishops. He *conversed* familiarly with the Prelates in the best Greek he could command. The Nicene Creed was the result of the deliberations of this grave assembly. Hosius of Spain was the first who signed it. *Five*, of the three hundred and eighteen bishops present, contested a single expression, *Homoousios*, of one substance with the Father. Two only of the *five* persevered in opposition. Arius was the leader of the opposition. Eusebius of Cæsarea and Eusebius of Nicomedia were known afterwards as Arians. They consented to subscribe, but sent the *creed* to their people with a comment of their own. The Christian community soon regretted their error in requesting the interference of the emperor in their religious questions. The power which exiled the heretic, could restore him to his place and station. Two years of tranquillity passed after the Council, but it was discovered that Arianism had been condemned, not extirpated. In the same year that the Council of Nice sat, occurred the death of Crispus, the eldest son of Constantine, to whom we have already alluded. It is said the tears and prayers of Constantia, his sister, and the earnest protestations of his grandmother were interposed in vain to save his life. Whether his son was sacrificed to political or domestic jealousy, can never be known. The former is the most probable. Fausta, the stepmother, had three sons to occupy the throne of their father when Crispus was removed. The great popularity and ability of the son, perhaps strengthened the plausibility of the alleged conspiracy against his father. When Constantine visited Rome after the death or murder of his son (which took place in a remote district), he received many insults; pasquinades, charging him with cruelty and murder, were affixed to the gates of his palace. This treatment determined him to leave Rome and never revisit it more. On the foundation of Constantinople, "the master of the Roman world," says Gibbon, "aspired to erect an eternal monument of the glories of his reign; he employed in this great work the wealth, the labor and all that remained of the genius of obedient millions. This city was destined to reign in future times the mistress of the East, and to survive the Empire of Constantine. It is *now*, in the nineteenth century, though still in the possession of the Mohammedans, the object of mighty contention between the most powerful Christian nations of Europe.* The rise of Constantinople was favorable to the progress of Christianity. It removed the seat of government from the presence of those awful temples to which ages of glory in the Roman mind had attached much sanctity. It broke the last link which combined the pontifical with the imperial character. Constantinople was not a pagan city. The new capital had no ancient deities whose worship was connected with majestic buildings. The temples of old Byzantium had fallen when Severus in vengeance razed the city to the ground. No expense was spared to raise a city worthy of the seat of empire.

By the command of Constantine, the cities of Greece and Asia were despoiled of their most valuable ornaments. The productions of Phidias and Lysippus and other masters of art were brought to the city of Constantine. These sculptures had now lost all religious significance. How often has history repeated itself in this way, let modern history declare! In many of the cities both in the East and West there were large buildings called Basilicas, or Halls of Justice. These buildings, says Milman, were singularly adapted for the Christian worship. Two of these, the Sessorian and the Lateran in Rome, had been given to the Christians by Constantine as churches for public worship, and many others were afterwards appropriated for the same purpose. By the consecration of the Basilicas to

---

* Written during the late war of the Russians and Turks.

Christian worship, and the gradual erecting of splendid churches in many of the cities of the East, Christianity began to assume an outward dignity commensurate with its *secret* moral influence. The pious activity of Helena, the mother of Constantine, was chiefly employed in Palestine. Splendid churches arose over the place of our Lord's birth at Bethlehem, and over the place of his burial, near the *supposed* Calvary, and over the place of ascension, on the Mount of Olives. The church called at first the Church of the Resurrection, afterwards that of the Holy Sepulchre, was very magnificent. The erection of these churches was praiseworthy, grateful to Christian hearts in all ages; but alas, superstitious ignorance began to search for the wood of the *true* cross, and for the nails that were used in the crucifixion.* Jerusalem had been trodden down by the Gentiles several times between the death of Christ and the accession of Constantine, yet names cling to remarkable places with great tenacity. It is possible, therefore, that the churches in Jerusalem do cover really the sacred spots so much venerated by Christians.

Eusebius, bishop of Nicomedia, seems to have succeeded to Hosius in the influence exercised by that great prelate over the mind of Constantine.† He accompanied the emperor in his visits to Jerusalem. Eusebius was an Arian. The Arian party gradually grew into favor. Constantia, the sister of Constantine, implored her brother to reconsider the sentence of banishment pronounced against Arius. An imperial mandate was issued to receive Arius and his followers within the pale of the Christian communion. Mean-

---
* Jerusalem, 24th chapter. † Not in excellence and wisdom.

while Athanasius, who had borne a distinguished part at the Council of Nice, and who had been, at thirty years of age, placed over the see of Alexandria, determined to resist the command of the emperor in relation to Arius. Athanasius was the head of the Trinitarian party, and refused to yield to the wishes of the emperor. Many frivolous charges were brought against Athanasius by his enemies, but they were easily disproved. At length he was charged with stopping the supplies of corn from the port of Alexandria, upon which Constantinople depended. Constantine listened with apparent credulity, and thinking it dangerous to leave the power of starving the capital in the hands of one who might become hostile to the government, the guiltless and firm Athanasius was banished to the remote city of Treves, A. D. 336. Arius was recalled to Constantinople. Alexander was the bishop of this city; he refused to admit Arius to the orthodox communion. The Arians threatened to force their way into the church. As he, Arius, was being carried into a church he was suddenly seized with the pains of death. Alexander at the moment was prostrate at the foot of the altar, determined to resist the approach of Arius. The Catholics, as the *Trinitarians* were now called, considered the death of Arius as a judgment of God. We know not the effect of this event upon the mind of Constantine, but it did not change his mind with regard to Athanasius. He continued to regard him "as proud, intractable and turbulent." It was not till his death-bed that he consented to reinstate the bishop of Alexandria. Baptism was administered to Constantine in his last illness.

The general legislation of Constantine bears evidence to an undercurrent of religious opinion and feeling, independent of the edicts which concerned the Christian community. The rescript for the religious observance of the Sunday, which enjoined the suspension of all public business and private labor, seems to have been enjoined upon the whole Roman people. In *one instance* there is direct authority that a certain humane measure was adopted by the advice of an influential Christian. It is this: During the period of anarchy and misery that preceded the reign of Constantine, the sale of infants as slaves, and their exposure, infanticide, too, had become fearfully common. Funds were now assigned for the food and clothing of children whose parents were unable to support them, and as this measure could not prevent the sale of children, parents were declared incapable of reclaiming them unless they paid the price of their own enfranchisement. These humane edicts were issued by the advice of Lactantius, a Christian philosopher, to whom had been entrusted the education of the eldest son of Constantine.

Gladiatorial exhibitions were never permitted in the *new* capital. The master of a slave was now deprived of the arbitrary power of life and death. In the distribution of the royal domains care was taken not to separate husbands and wives, parents and children, brothers and sisters. It can not be doubted that the stricter moral tone of Constantine's legislation emanated from Christianity. All the laws passed by Constantine with the purpose of purifying the social state, in regard to divorce and unlawful marriages, were afterwards embodied in the Theodosian Code, together with the ten commandments (the moral law), and the Apostles'

Creed. During the reign of Constantine Christianity was extended to Ethiopia, now called Nubia and Abyssinia. The Ethiopians attained a degree of civilization, and Arabian commerce was kept up with the other side of the Red Sea. Inscriptions recently discovered in Nubia prove that Greek letters made considerable progress among this barbarous people. These conversions somewhat indemnified Christianity for the losses sustained in Persia by the restoration of the ancient faith in that country, A. D. 250.

In the reading of church history it must be borne in mind that when the Christian Episcopate passes *calmly* down through a succession of beneficent and pious prelates, little is said of them by the annalist, either of church or State. The quiet but earnest Christian who lessens the mass of human misery by his daily charities, and who encourages the faint and weary by his strong faith and love, is beloved and honored by his generation; but he may furnish no *materials* to the chronicler to hand down to posterity. But in times of excitement, in a contested election like that of Liberius in 352, successor to Julius I, and still worse in the case of Damasus and Ursicius, when the partisans of each of these men sought to elect their favorite; unschooled in experience, they little thought how much they would sully the purity of their priestly robes by their vain contentions. The *records* of these matters, made by heathen pens, often exaggerated the fierceness of the contestants. The great Jerome, however, was at Rome when the contest about Damasus occurred. He becomes the historian, and bitterly laments the circumcumstances. Self-seeking is a destructive foe to the love and peace so constantly enjoined by the Master they professed to serve.*

Athanasius was an exile in Belgium at the death of Constantine. Constantius, though an Arian, consented to his return. He entered Alexandria at the head of a triumphal procession, A. D. 340. The bishops of his party resumed their sees. The Arian party in Syria continued to wage a war against him.

---

* The *cross* is the beautiful symbol of self-denial, but alas, self-seeking is often suspected in the nineteenth century, as well as it was in the fourth century. It is more covert now.

CHAPTER XII.

Athanasius stands out as the prominent character of this period in the history, not merely of Christianity, but of the world. Athanasius was born at Alexandria, about A. D. 298. He succeeded to the see of Alexandria when he was 28 years of age. For half a century he was the head of the orthodox party in the Arian controversy. When Gregory, of Cappadocia, took forcible possession of his see, Athanasius fled to Rome for protection : a provincial council held at Rome, and a large council soon afterwards assembled at Sardica, acquitted him fully of all charges brought against him. Constantius continued to persecute him after the death of Constans. He concealed himself at Alexandria for two years and then retired to Egypt and lived among hermits until the death of Constantius. In this retirement he wrote some of his best works. The creed ascribed to him is *spurious*, as is proved from the best authorities. On the accession of Julian he returned to his see, but the Pagans and Arians again uniting, induced Julian to banish him again. He died, however, at last in the possession of the patriarchate of Alexandria, in 373.

Basil, bishop of Cæsarea in Cappadocia, was famous for his skill in debate and eloquence.

Gregory of Nazianzen and Gregory of Nyssa obtained much renown. Their works show that they were worthy to be esteemed.

Among the Syrians, Ephriam made his name immortal by the sanctity of his life, and by numerous writings.

Cyril, bishop of Jerusalem, was born about 315. He succeeded Maximus as bishop about 340. The Arian controversy, together with his dispute with Acacius, bishop of Cæsarea, respecting the *priority* of their episcopal sees, caused him to be twice deposed. Of his works there are twenty-three lectures extant; they are considered as an invaluable treasure, as they contain a complete system of theology, and a circumstantial account of the rites of the Church at so early a time. These lectures were written when he was a Presbyter; he wrote on the Apostles' creed, baptism, confirmation, and the Lord's supper.

Tiberius was bishop of Rome in 352. It appears from the letters of Tiberius, also from the testimony of Jerome, and of Hilary of Poictiers, that this bishop boldly resisted the Arians, and was banished in consequence to Berea, in Thrace; but at the end of two years, he became so eager to return to his bishopric, that he consented to subscribe to the Arian creed set forth by the third council of Sirmium.

When Rome, after the death of Constans, was under the dominion of Constantius, Arianism triumphed for a time. The history of the Church, under Constantius, presents a most stormy period, and of a war among brethren which was carried on without religion or humanity. On the death of Constantius, in 362, the prosperous days of Arianism were ended.

Julian, called the Apostate, succeeded to the empire of the sons of Constantine. Amid much intestine strife within the pale of Christianity, Julian ascended the throne of the Roman empire, A. D. 362. Julian was the nephew of Constantine the Great; at the death of Constantius he was the only surviving descendant of the once numerous family of Constantius Chlorus. Julian seems to have hated his cousin, the emperor, with bitterness, and Constantius, it is said, was jealous of the popularity and rising talents of Julian. Nothwithstanding the alleged alienation that existed between the two cousins, Julian married Helena, the sister of Constantius, and was associated with him in the empire.

Julian was at *Athens* when he was called to share in the toils and glories of the empire. He appeals to the people of Athens to witness his tears of sorrow in separating himself from the schools of the new Platonic philosophy. He had spent six months in the groves of the academy, with the philosophers of the age, who sought to inflame the devotion of their royal pupil. He approached with horror, his historians say, the palace at Milan; though he constantly suspects his cousin of treachery, he gratefully acknowledges the steady friendship of the empress Eusebia. She met him at her husband's court with the tenderness of a sister. "After an obstinate, though secret struggle," says Gibbon, "the opposition of the eunuchs yielded to the ascendency of the empress, and Julian was appointed, with the title of Cæsar, to reign over the countries beyond the Alps."

The provinces of Gaul were overwhelmed with a deluge of barbarians; the Sarmatians (the modern Poles and Russians), no longer respected the barrier of the Danube; the Persian monarch, who was still to be feared, threatened the peace of Asia, both in the east and in the west. The presence of an emperor was required. Constantius now acknowledged his inability to control so great an extent of dominion. Constantius did not consult the senate in the choice of a colleague, but he was anxious to have the approval of the army. Surrounded by the troops whose stations were near Milan, he ascended on this solemn occasion to his lofty tribunal, holding by the hand his cousin Julian, who entered on that day the twenty-fifth year of his age.

Immediately after his investiture, Julian proceeded to Paris, assuming the government of Gaul, and with the command of the forces, intended to drive the German invaders beyond the Rhine. With much skill and energy, he effected this undertaking, and also checked the rapacity of the local governors. His military energy and administrative ability, together with his gracious manners, made him a great favorite with his troops. Reports of Julian's popularity soon reaching Constantius, it excited a jealous hostility.

In 360, Constantius sent a mandate to Julian, to send three of his best legions to the east, to assist in conducting the war in Persia. Disgusted with this requirement, and feeling that it proceeded from the suspicious hostility of Constantius, he determined to accede to the earnest wishes of his attached soldiery. He assumed the purple. The troops, with great unanimity and enthusiasm, proclaimed him emperor.

The domestic connection which might have reconciled the brother and husband, was recently dissolved by the death of the princess Helena.

Julian now prepared to decide the question of his title to *Augustus*, by a civil war. He was marching to attack Constantinople, when he heard of the death of Constantius in Cilicia; this death left him undisputed lord of the empire. His short reign of two years, would find no place in this abridged history, except for his strenuous but fruitless efforts to restore Paganism, and the interesting history of his abortive effort to rebuild the temple of Jerusalem.

A few weeks before Julian determined upon civil war, he had celebrated the Christian feast of Epiphany; up to this time, he had concealed from his most intimate friends his hatred of Christianity and his unbelief of the Christian system. He now publicly renounced the religion in which he had been instructed. He had once been a reader in the Church of Nicomedia, but it is very evident to one who reads his life, that he never sincerely embraced the New Testament. His life was full of dissimulation. He is called an apostate from a faith of which he was never a true disciple. Historians say, "the *unchristian* Christianity of Constantius must bear some part of the guilt of Julian's apostasy." Constantius had sentenced to death Gallus, the brother of Julian, and is also accused of the murder of the father of Julian. Constantius was an Arian,* and a fierce persecutor. On his death-bed he made a bequest of the empire to Julian. It is said that Julian's youth was committed to the instruction and direction of superstitious ecclesiastics, who required of him a course of strict *ceremonial* observances: the midnight vigil, the fast, the long and weary prayer, and visits to the tombs of martyrs, *rather* than an initiation into the principles of the Gospel. He remained a stranger to the originality, the beauty, and the depth of Christian morals, and true Christian sentiment. His teachers seem to have been "blind leaders of the blind." *Julian* himself gives this

---

* We do not believe, or mean to insinuate, that the persecuting spirit of Constantius was the result of his Arian opinions.

account, perhaps exaggerated and prejudiced, of his instructors: For six years, he says, when he lived with his brother Gallus in a fortress of Asia Minor, he was deprived of every kind of useful instruction.

The first care of Julian, on his accession to the throne of the Roman empire, was to restore Paganism and extirpate Christianity. The temples were everywhere to be restored to their former magnificence; where they had been destroyed by the zeal of the Christians, large *fines* were levied on the communities, and became a pretext for the most grinding exactions and in some instances cruel persecutions. It is said that Julian meditated a complete course of religious instruction, in the Platonic philosophy. But he was not content merely with the moral regeneration of Paganism, but attempted to *bring back* the public mind to the sanguinary ritual of sacrifice. "Julian himself *washed off* his Christian baptism by the oriental rite of aspersion by blood." His credulity and superstition in Paganism, seem to have been quite equal to any superstition that his earlier teachers, as *he alleges*, required of *him*. Julian was a more perspicuous writer than any of the philosophers that surrounded him. They seem to to have been degenerate disciples of Plato.

To the Christians, Julian assumed the language of liberal toleration. He abridged many of the privileges of the Christians, and closed their schools. He imitated the benevolence of the Christians so obviously, in connecting hospitals with his Pagan institutions, that he was called the "ape of Christianity."

"While Julian labored with very partial success in attempting to restore the religion of his ancestors, he embraced," says Gibbon, "the extraordinary design of rebuilding the temple of Jerusalem." The vain and ambitious mind of Julian (these are the words of Gibbon), aspired to restore the ancient glory of the temple of Jerusalem. As the Christians were persuaded that a sentence of everlasting destruction had been pronounced against this temple, the imperial sophist would have converted the success of his enterprise, into an argument against the faith of prophecy, and the truth of Revelation. Julian therefore resolved to erect on the eminence of Mount Moriah, a stately temple which should eclipse the splendor of the Church of the Resurrection, on the adjacent Hill of Calvary, built by Constantine under the superintendence of Helena, his mother.

Among the friends of Julian, the first place was assigned to Alypius. This able minister of the emperor obtained the support of the governor of Palestine. The Jews assembled in great numbers to assist in the work of rebuilding on the holy mountain of their fathers, their beautiful house. But the united efforts of Jews and Pagans were unsuccessful. Ammianus, a Pagan, has recorded in the history of his own times the wonderful obstacles which prevented the restoration of the Jewish temple. We quote from Gibbon, who quotes Ammianus: "Whilst Alypius, assisted by the governor, urged the work with great vigor, the execution was suddenly stopped by horrible balls of fire, breaking out near the foundations, which rendered the place inaccessible to the scorched and blasted workmen—the victorious element continuing in this manner, ultimately drove them away—the undertaking was abandoned."

CHAPTER XIII.

> How charming is divine Philosophy!
> Not harsh and crabbed, as dull fools suppose,
> But *musical*, as is Apollo's lute.

"Michaelis," says Guizot, "has given us an ingenious and probable explanation of this remarkable incident,* which the positive testimony of Ammianus Marcellinus, a contemporary and a pagan, will not permit us to *question*. The temple of Jerusalem was a kind of citadel, which had its own walls. The porticos themselves were an excellent fortification. There was a fountain of constantly running water; subterranean excavations under the mountains; reservoirs and cisterns to collect the rainwater."

These excavations and reservoirs must have been large, as they furnished water during the whole siege of Jerusalem to 1,100,000 inhabitants, for whom the fountain of Siloam could not have sufficed. As the siege took place from the month of April to the month of August, they could have had no rainwater. Josephus relates several incidents which show the extent of these excavations. It is probable that the greater part of these excavations were the remains of the time of Solomon, as the people were too poor when they returned from the Captivity, 530 B. C., to undertake such works. Herod the Great, in renovating the temple, made some excavations, but the haste with which the improvements were made "in the days of Herod" preclude the idea

---
*Related in the last chapter.

that they belonged to his period. The temple was destroyed A. D. 70, by Titus; the attempt to rebuild it made by Julian, and the fact related by Ammianus, coincide with the year 363. Between these two epochs an interval had elapsed of nearly 300 years, during which time the excavations, having choked up with ruins, had become full of inflammable air. The workmen employed by Julian, as they were digging, would take torches to explore the excavations; sudden flames repelled those who approached; explosions were heard, and these phenomena were renewed every time that the subterranean passages were penetrated. "It is a fact now popularly known, that when *mines* long closed are opened, one *of two things* takes place. The torches are either extinguished, and the men swoon or die; but if the air is inflammable, a little flame is seen to flicker around the lamp, then *extends* till the conflagration becomes general — an explosion occurs, and all who are in the way are killed."

Whether the designs of God were carried out by the operation of natural causes, or by miracle, it makes no difference in the result. It is certainly beautiful to trace in this incident of the operation of nature, the fulfillment of prophecy. In the words of the Psalmist, we here see, "fire and hail; snow, and vapor; stormy wind fulfilling His word." The temple was not rebuilt; the enemy of the Christians, the apostate Julian, was not allowed to carry out his profane designs. But on the same hill, but *not* on the site, where once stood the glorious temple of the Lord of Hosts, stands a Mahometan mosque, called the Mosque of Omar, built by Omar, the second khalif, in 644.

Julian assumed that he was not a persecutor, but in

various ways he caused the Christians much suffering, by taunts, by contempt, by severe oppression. The monogram of Christ disappeared from the labarum, or standard. Heathen symbols everywhere replaced those of Christianity. As the troops defiled before the emperor on one occasion, each man was ordered to throw a few grains of frankincense upon an altar which stood before him. The Christians were horror-stricken when they discovered that, instead of an act of legitimate respect to the emperor, as they supposed, they had been betrayed into paying homage to idols. Some bitterly lamented the involuntary sacrilege, and indignantly threw down their arms. Some of them surrounded the palace, and avowing that they were Christians, loudly reproached the emperor with his treachery, and cast down the largess they had received. For this breach of discipline they were led out to military execution. They vied with each other for the honors of martyrdom. But the bloody scene was interrupted by a messenger from the emperor, who contented himself with expelling them from the army and sending them into banishment. He refused to call the Christians by the name of their Redeemer, but enjoined the use of the less honorable appellation of Galileans.* He prohibited the Christians from teaching grammar or rhetoric. He directly forbade them to *teach*, and *indirectly* to learn, as they would not frequent the schools of the Pagans.

On Julian's accession to the throne, he had made a decree that the exiles banished during the reign of Constantius should return. The great Athanasius availed himself of this permission, and returned to Alexandria. He once more resumed his place as the patriarch of

---

* Or Nazarenes.

Alexandria. His pastoral labors were not confined to the narrow limits of Egypt.* The state of the Christian world was present to his active and capacious mind; and his age, merit, and reputation enabled him to assume, in a moment of danger, the office of ecclesiastical dictator. By the wisdom of a select synod, to which the name and presence of Athanasius gave the authority of a general council, the bishops who had unwarily deviated into error were admitted to the communion on the condition of subscribing to the Nicene creed, without any formal deprivation of their scholastic opinions.

While Athanasius was thus happily harmonizing the distracted elements of the Church, which had but lately threatened a division of the Greek and Latin churches, the wrath of Julian burst forth with renewed violence against Athanasius. The skill and diligence of the primate of Egypt had greatly tranquillized the churches, before the edicts of Julian were issued. Julian was soon convinced by the earnest solicitation of the people, to stay the hand of persecution, that the majority of the Alexandrians were Christians, and that they were firmly attached to the cause of their oppressed primate. But this knowledge excited him still more, and provoked him to extend to all Egypt, the term of the exile of Athanasius. In writing to the præfect of Egypt, Julian *swore* by the great Serapis, that unless by the calends of December Athanasius had departed from Alexandria, nay, from Egypt, that the government should pay a hundred pounds of gold! He calls Athanasius an abominable wretch, who had been the cause of several Grecian ladies, of the highest rank, receiving Christian

---

* Gibbon.

baptism.* The death of Athanasius was not *commanded*, but the præfect of Egypt understood that it was safer for him to exceed than to neglect the peremptory orders of an irritated master. The bishop prudently retired to the monastaries of the desert, eluded with his usual dexterity the snares of an enemy, and lived to triumph over the ashes of a prince who had declared his wish that the whole venom of the Galilean school were contained in the single person of Athanasius.

"Julian by an artful system," says Gibbon, "proposed to obtain the effects of the Christians, without incurring the reproach of persecution." He abrogated all the exclusive privileges of the clergy; their immunity from taxation, and exemptions from public duties. He would not allow Christians to be præfects, as their law prohibited capital punishments. "But if the deadly spirit of fanaticism perverted the heart of a *virtuous* prince," says Gibbon, "it must be confesssed that the *real* sufferings of the Christians were greatly magnified by human passions and religious enthusiasm. The meekness and resignation of the primitive disciples of the Gospel, was the object of the applause rather than the imitation of their successors." The historian makes an apology for Julian, but not for the *Christians*.

The wealth and power that entered the Church in the time of Constantine and his successors, had a tendency to corrupt the simplicity of the Gospel, and to introduce doctrines, habits and customs that were foreign to the spirit of *the Master*, and the teachings of Him and of His apostles. Still, the Church, in the darkest and most troublous times, was as "a burning and shining light" amid a dark, tempestuous world.

---

* Gibbon.

The Church was an ark of safety and comfort to those who entered it with honest, true and loving hearts. But in the Jewish, as well as in the Christian dispensation, the evil has been mingled with the good. As early as the fourth century, "corruption, fraud and bloodshed had begun to crowd the path that led to the Shepherd's seat." The seed was sown by the Divine Husbandman, and doctrines far surpassing in purity and efficacy any system of theology which the human mind had previously conceived, were widely promulgated. During the continuance of the Apostolic age, Christianity had extended throughout the Roman world and beyond its limits, so that no local power could crush it. Before the death of the last inspired teacher, Christianity had struck its roots deep into the soil of every country between the Euphrates and the Atlantic Ocean.

The true Church is an aggregate of individuals, whose hearts have been quickened from above, and whose dispositions are controlled by the genuine principles of the New Testament. Clouds have darkened the sky in different periods of the history of the Church — the germs of many good seed have died, choked by earthly desires — a cutting wind of controversy about trifles, and about unimportant rites and ceremonies may have destroyed good fruit — yet the Church has much more than *survived*. It has had to contend with many ills — the persecutions of Pagan Rome — the inroads of barbarous hordes, darkening the light of civilization by the dreadful additions brought to *Papal* Rome from Paganism — but the *Word of God* has remained untouched. Christianity uprooted in some places, as in Mahometan countries, has sprung up in other countries. The Lord's promise, that he would always be with his people, seems not to have secured them from some mistakes in doctrine, yet when we review Church history, there is much consolation in the thought, that in the darkest times there has ever been a mystical body — a true Church. It *mitigated* evils which could not be entirely averted — it transmitted to a better age, the elements of natural and religious truth.

The Apostate Julian, soon after the failure of his designs at Jerusalem, set out on an expedition to Persia. He wished to secure by this campaign the Euphratic provinces from a dangerous rival of the Roman power. But death "had marked him for her own." His short reign of two years was brought to an abrupt termination by the arrows of the Persians.

Not only as an emperor, but as a writer, was Julian indefatigable in his efforts to overthrow Christianity. He wrote during the long winter nights of his Persian campaign an elaborate work against the faith of Christ. It has been said that when he received the fatal death-wound, he uttered the bitter sentence, "Thou hast conquered, O Galilean." But his heathen friends give a very different account of his last hours. He comforted his weeping friends, *they* say — expressed his willingness to pay the debt of nature, and his joy that the purer part of his nature was soon to be released from the gross and material body.

Had Julian lived longer, he might have dictated terms of peace and have limited the aggressive designs of Sapor, the Persian Monarch — he might have delayed the fall of the empire, but the fall of Paganism could not have been arrested. "The peaceful stream of *progressive* opinion and religious sentiment, will not *retrograde* or retire at man's bidding. The oppressor holds the body bound, but he knows not what a range the spirit takes."

The short reign of *Jovian*, of a few months, was sufficient to restore the ascendency of Christianity.

CHAPTER XIV.

Valentinian, son of Count Gratian, a distinguished Roman, now succeeded to the empire. He ascended the throne with the fame of having rejected the favor of Julian and the prospect of military distinction for the sake of his religion. He had once provoked the danger of disgrace by the contempt which he expressed for heathenism. At Antioch, where he was obliged by his position to attend the emperor to the table, it is said he struck a Pagan priest who had presumed to purify him with lustral water. Valentinian reigned in the West. He soon appointed his brother Valens, after his elevation, as his associate in the empire. Valens' seat of power was at Constantinople. These brothers allowed perfect freedom to the public ritual of Paganism, but both in the East and West a tremendous persecuting power was waged against magic and unlawful divination. Valens was a fierce Arian and maintained in the East the ascendancy of Arianism. During the life of Athanasius the see of Alexandria remained faithful to the Trinitarian doctrines.

A. D. 364. It was in the year 364 that Valentinian and Valens ascended the two thrones of the empire. The former held the reins of government firmly, but the latter was weak and pusillanimous. Gibbon tells us that Valentinian condemned the exposition of infants, and established in the fourteen quarters of Rome fourteen skillful physicians, with stipends and privileges. He founded useful and liberal institutions for the education of youth and the support of declining science. It was during the reign of Valentinian that there was a fierce conflict at Rome between the followers of Damasus and Ursinus for the seat of the bishop. Damasus prevailed; the schism was extinguished by the exile of Ursinus. Ammianus, a reliable heathen historian, says of this disgraceful contest: "I am not astonished that so valuable a *prize* should inflame the desires of ambitious men; but how much more rationally would these Roman pontiffs consult their true happiness by imitating the exemplary lives of the *provincial bishops*, who recommend their religion by their temperance and sobriety, by their plain apparel and humble demeanor."

Valens is charged with some dreadful crimes against the Trinitarian or Catholic party. But we prefer to relate a memorable interview which occurred between him and the archbishop of Cæsarea, in Cappadocia. The unscrupulous wicked minister of Valens had been sent in advance to persuade the bishop to accept the Arian opinions of the emperor. Basil was inflexible, though the minister, Modestus, threatened him with confiscation and banishment. Basil said to Modestus, "He who possesses nothing can lose nothing; all you can take from me are my clothes and my books, which are my only wealth. As to exile, the earth is the Lord's; everywhere it will be my country, or rather my place of pilgrimage." Modestus was astonished at the intrepidity of Basil. He returned to his master, telling him that neither violence nor menaces could move this man. Valens shrunk from violence. He approached the bishop in a crowd of distinguished worshipers, bearing an oblation. His clergy stood irresolute, doubting whether they ought to receive his offering. Basil advanced and accepted the oblation, but neither supplications nor threats could induce the bishop to receive the sovereign of the Eastern Empire to the communion. In a personal interview, the emperor was so overcome with the eloquence of Basil, as to insist upon the bestowment of a gift for the poor.

Valens listens to the supplications of an immense multitude of Goths, who, alarmed by the inroads of the Huns on the eastern side of the Danube, implore an entrance into the Eastern Empire. They are permitted to cross the Danube, and to take possession of the lands of Thrace. Afterwards incensed by the injustice and cruelty of the ministers of Valens, and knowing their own power, Fritigern, one of the Gothic chiefs, determines to lift the standard of rebellion. Opposing armies of Goths and Romans assemble themselves in the city of Adrianople. The emperor Valens takes the command of his army and is slain by barbarian arrows. A great number of brave officers perished in this battle, which equalled, says Gibbon, in actual loss and far surpassed in fatal consequences the battle of Cannæ. Hordes of barbarians had now made a permanent establishment within the frontiers of the Roman Empire.

A. D. 376. Within the next century Visigoths, Ostrogoths, Huns, Vandals, Heruli, Franks, Saxons, Lombards, migrated from the East and North, settling themselves by colonization or conquest, introducing one or more new races into every country and province in Europe, also settling "like a pitchy cloud of locusts," in the fair and cultivated fields of northern Africa. We have already said that Christianity mitigated evils it could not avert. . In the resettling of Europe and other provinces of the empire, Christianity, says Milman, was the one common bond, the harmonizing principle which subdued to something like unity the adverse and conflicting elements of society. But while it discharged this lofty mission, it could not but undergo itself a great change. It might repress but could not wholly subdue the advance of barbarism. While struggling to counteract barbarism, Christianity itself became barbarized. It lost for a time much of its gentleness and purity, it became splendid and imaginative, and at length warlike and chivalrous. Christianity had in some degree prepared the way for the amalgamation of the Goths with the Roman Empire. During the reign of Gallienus, A. D. 260, in the first inroads of the Goths, when they ravaged quite a large part of the Roman Empire, they carried away numbers of *slaves* from Asia Minor and Cappadocia. There were many Christians among these. The gentle doctrines of Christianity won their way to the hearts of the barbarous warriors. A Gothic bishop with a Greek name was a member of the Council of Nice. The famous Ulphilas, bishop of the Goths in the reign of Valens, was of Cappadocian descent. Thus we see the dispersion of the Christians in the early times, whether as *slaves** or soldiers, contributed to the spread of the doctrines of Christ. The Christian clergy occupied during the resettling of Europe a strange position in the new state of society. The Christian bishop confronted the barbarian sovereign, and though the lands of the clergy themselves were ravaged in the indiscriminate warfare, and were sometimes in-

---

* It must be borne in mind that the Greek and Roman slaves were frequently intelligent and cultivated.

sulted or enslaved, yet before long the minds of the conquerors were subdued by them. The authority claimed and exercised by the clergy at this period in the progress of civilization was of the highest utility. In these warlike times the clergy were almost the exclusive possessors of learning, which commands the reverence of barbarians when not actually engaged in war. The Christian religion rested on a written record; the best minds of the literary ages had been devoted to its elucidation. It became necessary, in the times of invading, devastating armies, that retreats should be sought for the literary, who were anxious to preserve the fruits of knowledge produced in more peaceful and happier times. The cloister or the religious foundation thus became the place of refuge to all that remained of letters or arts. Ulphilas, the most celebrated bishop among the Goths, made a version of the Scriptures in the Mæsic Gothic language. The language of Ulphilas, says Milman, is the link between the East and Europe, between the Sanscrit and the modern Teutonic languages. A large part of *this* version is now extant in the Upsal. It is written in silver letters, on purple parchment.

The whole Gothic nation received the Arian form of Christianity. When Ulphilas and other Gothic prelates visited Constantinople, they found the Arian bishops in chief authority; they were persuaded, it is said, by these men that the difference between Arianism and Trinitarianism consisted in disputes about words. Arianism continued to be the general form of their religious belief until the fall of the Gothic monarchies in Italy and Spain.

"The title, the ensigns, the prerogatives of the sovereign pontiff,* which had been instituted by Numa and assumed by Augustus, were accepted without hesitation by several Christian emperors, who were invested with a more absolute authority over the religion which they deserted, than over that which they professed." We presume those emperors regarded the office as political rather than religious. Gratian, son of Valentinian I., was the first emperor who refused the pontifical robe, A. D. 367. Notwithstanding the steady decadence of Paganism, it was still recognized in many parts of the empire by sacrifices. Many of the Pagan temples, especially in Rome, were undisturbed, though some of them were deserted. The Prefect of Rome in the latter part of the fourth century was a Pagan. Symmachus, a. man of virtue and learning, was the Pagan Prefect of Rome when Valentinian II. succeeded to the sole empire of the West. Symmachus mourned over the aggressive acts of Gratian. This emperor had abrogated the immunities of the Pagan priesthood; he had removed the statue of *victory* from the Senate House which had been restored by Julian. The senate met under the authority of Symmachus, to prepare and present a petition to be offered to the emperor. Symmachus in this oration exercised all his eloquence; he recounts the mighty deeds of Rome in the days of her Republican glory, ascribing to the Pagan rites the potent spell that repelled her enemies. But a counter petition was prepared by Ambrose, the famous bishop of Milan. He asserts the unquestionable obligation of a Christian sovereign to permit no part of the public revenue to be devoted to idolatry. "Man can not serve two masters." Theodosius was at this time em-

---

* Gibbon.

peror of Constantinople. He was justly styled the Great Theodosius; he was at first associated with Gratian; on the death of that monarch he was the protector of Valentinian II., and his restorer to the throne, after the invasion and defeat of Maximus. The accession of Theodosius was hailed with enthusiasm throughout the empire. Theodosius was a Spaniard. In that province Christianity had been established at an early day. Spain through the commanding influence of Hosius, had firmly adhered to the Trinitarian or Athanasian doctrines. Theodosius was by character and education deeply impressed with the truths of Christianity and the Trinitarian doctrines. After the defeat and death of the tyrant of Gaul, Maximus, the Roman world was in the possession of Theodosius. He seated Valentinian on the throne of Milan, and fully restored him to the dominion of all the provinces, from which he had been driven by the arms of Maximus. Before the invasion of Maximus, Justina, a woman of beauty and spirit, the mother of Valentinian II., feeling secure in the government of Italy, insisted that she had a right to claim in the dominions of her son the public exercise of her religion. She had been educated in Arianism, and was zealous in instilling her principles into the mind of her son. She therefore proposed to Ambrose, the bishop of Milan, that he should resign to her control a single church in Milan or in its suburbs. Ambrose would not accede to her request; he thought it would be sacrilege to yield a church where Arian principles would be maintained and taught. The palaces of the earth, he said, indeed belonged to Cæsar; but the churches are the houses of God; and he, within the limits of his *diocese*, as the lawful successor of the apostles, was the only minister of God. He declared with firmness that he would die a martyr rather than yield to the impious sacrilege. Justina prepared to resist, and exert the imperial prerogative of her son, but finally after much trouble and tumult, she was compelled to yield, seeing that the majority coincided with the archbishop, and the laws of the country condemned the Arian heresy. The powers of the earth seemed to interfere in the defense of Ambrose, for now the tyrant of Gaul with an army of barbarians seized the fortresses of the Alps, and rapidly approached the gates of Milan. Justina and the young emperor fled to the court of Theodosius. Justina died shortly after the restoration of her son to the throne by the prowess of Theodosius. After the death of his mother, Valentinian, either from conviction or policy, professed *Trinitarianism.*

Ambrose, of Milan, at this time the presiding mind of the orthodox clergy, united in himself all the episcopal virtues in an eminent degree. The natural disposition of Theodosius, the great captain and emperor,* of whom we have already said so much, was hasty and choleric. "Within *three years,*" says Gibbon, "we must relate the generous *pardon* of the people of Antioch, and the inhuman massacre of the people of

---

*Constantinople, until Theodosius reigned there, had been the *stronghold* of Arianism. It is said this emperor required Demopolus, the archbishop, either to sign the Nicene Creed or to resign his episcopal authority over the great city. He chose to *resign*, and the famous Gregory Nazianzen was installed in his stead. Gregory when he unwillingly accepted the bishopric, was old and unambitious, his manners pure and simple.

Thessalonica. As the recital of the chief incidents connected with these *two cities* illustrates the great power and influence of the bishops of this period, we will attempt to relate them in our next chapter.

CHAPTER XV.

Chrysostom, afterwards so celebrated as the Bishop of Constantinople, presided previously over the churches of Antioch. In consequence of a new taxation laid upon the people of Antioch, whi h they considered exorbitant, a tumultuous insurrection ensued; the people determined to resist the demands of the imperial officers. The mob were roused to fury, and cast down the statues of the emperor and empress; also the statues of their two sons, Arcadius and Honorius. This meeting was soon quelled by the better classes of the citizens, but the populace were seized with alarm at what they had done, and awaited with fear and trembling the sentence of the emperor. The governor of the province had dispatched to the emperor a narration of the whole transaction, and strict inquisition had been made as to the guilt of individuals. Abject terror seemed to take possession of a large number of the community. This commotion at Antioch was previous to the massacre at Thessalonica. Their only hope of pardon rested upon their aged Bishop Flarianus, whom they induced to undertake a journey of eight hundred miles, to intercede for them with the emperor.

Chrysostom, a presbyter, meanwhile remained with the people, to quiet their fears and administer consolation. Twenty-four days after the *sedition*, the masters of the offices declared to the people the terrible sentence of the emperor.

The sentence was that Antioch should be degraded from the rank of a city; the proud metropolis of the East should be subjected to the jurisdiction of Laodicea. The two officers of justice, however, determined to suspend the execution of the terrible edicts against the city until the return of the orator Cæsarius and the Bishop Flarianus.

The resentment of Theodosius subsided. He granted a free and general pardon. The capital of the East was *not* shorn of its ancient dignity and splendor. The bishop left the presence of the emperor, with warm expressions of his respect and gratitude for the intercession he had made. The emperor also thanked the senate of Constantinople for the interest *they* had manifested for their distressed brethren.*

Chrysostom, during this interval of terrible suspense, had ascended the pulpit day after day, and the people in their distress, listening to his eloquence, forgot the forum, the theater, and the circus. The monks, too, from their mountain hermitages, came down to try to impart fortitude and consolation to the despairing people.

There was no repeal nor pardon, however, connected with the more famous *sedition at Thessalonica*. A favorite lieutenant, together with a general and his officers, had been inhumanly murdered. The emperor hastily resolved that the blood of his favorite and that of his brave officers should be expiated in the blood of the *citizens* of Thessalonica. The zeal of the clergy had almost extorted a pardon from the emperor, when the suggestions of his minister Rufinus again inflamed his

---
* Gibbon.

anger. After he had dispatched the messengers of vengeance, he tried too late to recall them.

When Ambrose, Bishop of Milan, heard of the *massacre*, his soul was filled with horror and anguish. When the intelligence of the massacre first reached Ambrose, he kept aloof from the exasperated emperor. He retired to the country, and *wrote* to the sovereign. His letter expressed his own distress and the affliction of his brother bishops, at a deed so inhuman as the massacre at Thessalonica. He and his brethren must not only express their detestation of his guilt, but must also refuse to communicate with a man so stained with blood, not of one, but of thousands. He exhorts him to penitence; he promises the emperor his prayers in his behalf, but tells him the doors of the church must be closed against him.

The emperor of the world was excluded for eight months from the communion of the Church. On Christmas day, when the holy precincts were open to the slave and beggar, the emperor was denied admission. At length Ambrose consented to an interview with the emperor, in the outer porch of the church, the place of public penitents. The interdict was removed on two conditions: that the monarch should issue an edict forbidding the execution of capital punishments for thirty days after conviction, or that the emperor should submit to public penance. Stripped of his imperial ornaments, prostrated on the pavement, watering the ground with his tears, the master of the Roman Empire, the conqueror in so many victories, the legislator of the world, humbled himself before the minister of God and received his absolution.

In this instance, and in many other events of this

age, Christianity appears as the glorious champion of outraged humanity. But in this unlimited sovereignty over the mind, so potent to repress evil, when exercised by the honest and true in the punishment of evil *acts*, there lurked a latent evil. *This* power, in evil counselors and in a darker age, might take cognizance of *opinions*, as well as deeds or overt acts, and would condemn the offender to punishment and death.

In A. D. 385, the first blood wus judicially shed for religious opinions. This was the act of a usurping sovereign, Maximus, and the Spanish bishops Idacius and Ithacius. Priscillian, an eloquent Spaniard, had embraced some Manichean or Gnostic opinions. He and his followers had propagated his opinions in the southern part of Gaul, where they had taken refuge from persecution. This act of persecution was solemnly disclaimed by all the influential dignitaries of the Western Church, by Ambrose, Augustine, and Chrysostom, the Golden-mouthed.

When Ambrose reproached the usurper Maximus with the murder of his sovereign, also with the unjust execution of the Priscillianists, he refused to communicate with the bishops who had any connection in that unchristian and sanguinary transaction. This fatal *precedent* was disowned by the general voice of Christianity. It *required*, says Milman, a long period of ignorance and bigotry so to deaden the moral sense of Christianity as to abandon the spirit of love. Martin of Tours urged his protest in vain against the bloody sentence passed upon the Priscillianists or Gnostics. Martin's life had been an unwearied campaign against idolatry. He had demolished every Pagan edifice within his reach; but persecution for opinion's sake he abhorred. St.

Martin has been a favorite subject for legend. He once met a poor creature at Amiens suffering with cold. Martin had nothing but a cloak. He cut the cloak into two pieces, giving one piece to the poor man. The following night, Jesus appeared to him in a dream, *dressed* in a half cloak. Ambrose of Milan died in A. D. 397. To this devout prelate is ascribed the grand hymn, "*Te Deum Laudamus.*" Tradition says it was first chanted in the cathedral of Milan when Augustine, bishop of Hippo, was baptized.

Of all Christian writers since the apostles, Augustine has maintained the most permanent influence, though some of his opinions were harsh, in view of the certain truth that "God is love." He had comparatively little influence in the Greek Church, but the dominion of Augustine over the opinions of the Western world was eventually over the greater part of Christendom.

The Greek Empire, after the reign of Justinian, greatly contracted its limits. The *Greek Church* seemed for a time to forget her *great writers* on the momentous subjects of religion and morality, for the Church wasted her energies on frivolous and insignificant questions of faith. We have said in the earlier part of this abstract of Church history, that Christianity was a Greek religion for more than three centuries; but from the time of Augustine (A.D. 384), the Latin language became *almost* that of Christianity. The language of Basil and Chrysostom now became foreign or dead to the larger part of the Christian world. Mahometanism at length robbed Christianity of some of her fairest provinces, and narrowed the Greek Church to a smaller circle. In modern days, we see its enlargement in its extension in the Russian Empire.

Of all the Latin writers, Augustine was the most commanding and influential. Abstruse topics, which had been but slightly touched in the apostolic writings, became the prominent points of the Augustinian theology. "Augustinianism has constantly revived, in every period of religious excitement. It formed much of the system of Luther in later days; his doctrines (the doctrines of St. Augustine) were worked up into a rigid and uncompromising system by the severe intellect of Calvin; it was remoulded by Jansenius into the Roman Catholic doctrine. The theology of most of the Protestant sects is but a modified Augustinianism."

St. Augustine was born (A. D. 354) in Tagasta, a city of Numidia (Algiers). His parents were Christians of respectable rank. His mother Monica became quite famous, in consequence of her religious anxiety with regard to her son. While pursuing his studies at Carthage, his ardent mind plunged into the intoxicating enjoyments of the theater, and other sinful gratifications. He was first arrested in his sensual course, it is said, by the remonstrances of Pagan literature; especially from Cicero did he learn the dignity of intellectual attainments. But philosophy would not satisfy the cravings of his spirit. He turned to the religion of his parents, but the inimitable simplicity of the New Testament could not at first satisfy him. He turned aside to the books of the Gnostics, and for several years was deeply imbued with the wild doctrines of Manicheism. His mother, the holy Monica, watched over the irregular development of his powerful mind. His mother's distress at his Manichean errors was consoled by an aged bishop, who had himself been involved in the same opinions: "Be of good cheer; the child of so many tears and prayers can never perish." This answer of the good bishop has infused a ray of comfort into the heart of many a pious mother, all down the ages from the days of the great theologian. How strange, that he who for nine years wandered amid the mazes and reveries of Oriental theology, should have become at length the most logical of theologians!

CHAPTER XVI.

Augustine grew discontented with the Manichean doctrines, which could not satisfy the religious yearnings of his heart. He determined to leave Carthage for Rome, where he would have a more extended sphere as a teacher of rhetoric. The fame of his talents reached Milan. He was born within the magic circle of the great ecclesiastic of Milan. The eloquence of Ambrose induced him to study the writings of the apostles, which until now he had rejected. He thought he saw in the description Paul gives of the dissolute morals of the heathen a fearful picture of his own life. In his religious agony he seemed to hear a voice saying, "Take and read, take and read." He now commenced a strictly religious life; his mother, who followed him to Milan, lived to witness his *baptism* at the hands of Ambrose. He wrote controversial treatises against the Manicheans, Arians and Pelagians, and seemed to have the power to bring down these abtruse subjects to popular comprehension. His great work was called "The City of God." He dedicated thirteen years of his life to this great work. This work was chiefly intended to expel the idea that the decay and fall of Rome was in any regard due to the introduction of Christianity or the alienation of its Pagan deities. The Roman Pagan aristocracy fled to different parts of the world in the hour of peril, many of them to the yet uninvaded, peaceful province of Africa; they ascribed the ruin of their city to the anger of their Pagan deities. "The City of God" is a funeral oration of the old Pagan society, and a gratulatory panegyric on the birth of the new Christian society. Augustine institutes a comparison between the Christian Alaric (barbarian as he was) and the Pagan Radagaisus who left the cities that he entered a pile of ruins, whereas Alaric held Rome six days and did but little mischief. He spared the churches and the lives of unresisting citizens. Our modern historian Gibbon institutes a comparison between Alaric, the Goth, in his treatment of Rome, and that of Charles V., in the sixteenth century, a Roman Catholic prince, who held Rome nine months, when nearly every day was stained by some atrocity of the soldiers.

To return to Augustine's great work. Milman says "The City of God" was undoubtedly the noblest work, both in design and execution, that had yet been contributed to the cause of Christianity. The apologies hitherto written by the Fathers were framed to meet particular emergencies, and were brief and pregnant statements of Christian doctrines. The work of Augustine was a comprehensive survey of the whole religion and philosophy of the school of Christ of antiquity. It has preserved more, on some branches of this subject, than the whole surviving Latin literature. "The City of God" was not merely a *defense*, but a full exposition of Christian doctrine.

The threatened invasion of Florence by Radagaisus, the king of the confederate Germans, is beautifully related by Gibbon. "Radagaisus passed without resistance the Alps, the Po and the Apennines, leaving on one hand the inaccessible palace of Honorius, securely buried among the marshes of Ravenna, and on the other hand the camp of Stilicho, at Paria, who waited to assemble his distant forces before he made battle with Radagaisus." Meanwhile Florence was reduced to the last extremity; their fainting courage was sustained simply by the authority and sympathy of Ambrose, bishop of Milan, who had in a dream the promise of speedy deliverance. On a sudden they beheld from their walls the banners of Stilicho,* who advanced with his united force to the relief of the faithful city, and who soon marked that fatal spot for the grave of the barbarian host. Radagaisus did not go to Rome. While the firmness of the people of Florence checked and delayed the German king in his course, Rome one hundred and eighty miles distant, trembled lest he should approach. Alaric was a Christian and soldier who respected the sanctities of treaties, but Radagaisus was a stranger to the manners, the religion and even the language, of the civilized nations of the South. Stilicho defeated Radagaisus, and deserved a second time the title of Deliverer of Italy. Radagaisus was beheaded, which, says Mr. Gibbon, disgraced the triumph of Rome and Christianity. But when it is remembered, and was certainly believed by the actors in that terrible drama, that he had made a vow to destroy Rome and sacrifice her senators on their altars, it is not surprising that he was punished with death. He had been in the habit of immolating *his* prisoners to his gods—he was taken in arms. At this time Innocent I. was bishop of Rome. When Italy was invaded by Alaric, at the head of the Visigoths, Innocent went to

---

* Stilicho, a great military genius, in the service of Theodosius. He was descended from the Vandals. He was honored with a triumph at Rome for his great services.

Ravenna to solicit the aid of the emperor Honorius. During his absence the city was taken and plundered, A. D. 410. After the departure of the Goths Innocent returned to Rome and exerted himself to relieve the wounds of the scathed metropolis. His zeal and charity endeared him to all classes of the people. This bishop interceded *without avail* in behalf of the famous Chrysostom, bishop of Constantinople, who had been deposed from his see by the wicked Eudocia, empress of Constantinople. Chrysostom, Ambrose and Augustine though younger lived at the same time. Jerome also lived in his cell at Bethlehem about the same time, making his Latin translation of the Bible. Innocent I. though more distinguished perhaps than any of his predecessors in the see of Rome (of whom anything is certainly known) could not compare in mental ability with those of whom we have just spoken. Augustine's personal life contrasts with those of Ambrose and Chrysostom. He had not like Ambrose to interpose between rival emperors, or like Chrysostom to enter into conflict with the vices of a court, and like John the Baptist to reprove a monarch for her sin. He assumed the episcopate in the city of Hippo, in Africa, and was faithful to his first bride, his earliest though humble see. Though Africa had long escaped invasion, it was at length fearfully visited by the Vandals. When the Vandal army gathered around Hippo, one of the few cities which still afforded a refuge for the persecuted, he refused, though more than seventy years old, to abandon his post. In the third month of the siege death gave him deliverance, and he thus escaped the horrors of the capture, the cruelties of the conqueror and the desolation of his church. A. D. 340.

CHAPTER XVII.

MONACHISM. — JEROME.

Jerome was the great advocate of monachism in the West. He began and closed his career as a monk in Palestine. His great work, the translation of the Scriptures into Latin, was performed in Palestine, in a cell at Bethlehem. He engaged in the study of Hebrew as a severe occupation, to withdraw him from impure and worldly thoughts, which his austerities had not entirely subdued. When weary with the difficult task of converting Hebrew into Latin, he would seek solace in the elegant pages of Cicero, or in the musical periods of Plato. But the scrupulous conscience of Jerome would sometimes tremble at the profane admixture of sacred and profane studies. There is little doubt, however, that his love for the great authors of Greece and Rome greatly contributed to the polish of his style in the Latin version of the Scriptures. The purity that distinguished the writers of the Augustan age had greatly degenerated in the time of Tertullian and of Ammianus Marcellinus. The vivid and glowing style of the Vulgate Bible is thought, by scholars, to be the result of an intimate acquaintance with the pages of Tully and Plato.

Jerome was ordained a presbyter, but was never made a bishop. He left to Ambrose, to Chrysostom, and to Augustine the authority of office, and was content with the influence he exercised by personal communication and the effect of his writings. He passed his youth in literary studies at Rome during the episcopate of Damasus. He consulted the libraries of many of the cities of the East. He was received in Cyprus by the bishop Epiphanius. In Syria he plunged into the deepest asceticism.

Jerome was born in Dalmatia, but may be considered as a Roman, as he passed his early years and received his education at Rome. Jerome was deeply imbued, as we have said, with the spirit of monachism; he labored to awaken the tardy West to rival Egypt and Syria in what he considered to be the sublime perfection of Christianity. He influenced, while at Rome, matrons and virgins of patrician families to adopt the monastic life. They attempted to practice in a busy metropolis the rigid observances of the desert.

Christianity in its genius and origin is opposed to monachism, which had little encouragement either from the precepts or practice of its Divine Author. "Go ye into all the world and preach the Gospel to every creature," was His command. Yet the monastic system is not peculiar to Christianity; the Jews had their hermitages and their cenobitic institutions. The Essenes, a sect of the Jews in the days of our Lord, were ascetics.

Anthony is usually regarded as the founder of the monastic life; but it is clear he only imitated and excelled less famous anchorites. He was born of Christian parents, bred up in the faith. At an early age he found himself possessed of considerable wealth. He determined to imitate the example of those Christians who, in primitive times, "had laid their wealth at the apostles' feet." He was a native of Egypt. He retired to the base of a rocky mountain, and took up a solitary abode, but made it a pleasant spot, with vines and shrubs. An ancient monastery in the vicinity of the Red Sea still preserves the name and memory of the saint. He enjoyed the friendship of the great Athanasius, and this Egyptian hermit declined an invitation from the emperor Constantine to visit his court.

Many colonies of monks, after the example of Anthony, settled upon the rocks of Thebais, the deserts of Libya, and in the cities of the Nile. Athanasius, says Gibbon, introduced into Rome the knowledge and practice of the monastic life; and a school of this new philosophy was opened by the disciples of Anthony at the threshold of the Vatican.

"It is impossible to survey monachism," says our author Milman, "in its general influence from the earliest period of its interworking into Christianity, without being perplexed at its opposite effects. *Here*, it is the undoubted parent of the most ferocious bigotry, sometimes of debasing licentiousness — *there*, monastic institutions become the guardians of learning, the authors of civilization, the propagators of an humble and peaceful religion. While much of the gross superstition of the Byzantine Church is to be traced to the dominant spirit of monachism, to the same spirit in the West must be attributed much that was salutary, its constant aggression on barbarism and its connection with Latin literature. If human nature was degraded by the neglect of personal cleanliness and the fanatical self-torture, the callous apathy and occasional sanguinary violence of the Egyptian or Syrian monk, yet it must be recollected that the monastic retreats sent forth men like the Basils and Chrysostoms. Was their devotion to Christianity strengthened by their detachment from mankind? Certainly *not*, we think. The Basils and Chrysostoms were great and good, *in spite* of the monastic system.* These monastic retreats were the best places for education and development that the world then presented. The world, at the time of which we are writing, was a theatre for embattled hosts. Chrysostom and Basil spent much of their time (when they emerged from monasteries), in *great cities*, combating evil. The sermons preached by Chrysostom against the vices of the court of Constantinople, were replete with eloquent invective."

What can be more contrary to the beneficent spirit of Christianity, what more opposed to the attributes of God as revealed to us by our Lord in the New Testament, than *some* features of the monastic system, as revealed in the Byzantine Church and by some of the monks of Egypt? Yet it must be acknowledged that there was a grandeur of soul in *some* of these men and women who rose above worldly cares and anxieties, from a genuine desire of improving the moral condition of their fellow-men, willing to forego all the pleasures of life, as they are termed, that they might impart spiritual hopes to the wretched and barbarous. It must be concluded, that amid the blindness, superstition and ferocity of the monastic life, there were noble characters among them, taught of God, who effected much good.

We see now, in our enlightened days, the obvious evil tendencies of this system. It tends to deaden

---

* It is an irresistible conclusion, that monasteries, in those days when the earth was filled with violence, and was a theatre for embattled hosts, were *the best* places for education and development. They served a good purpose *in a dark age*.

natural affection, it mars the sweet charities of life, it tempts the weak-minded to dissolve the natural ties that our Father and nature have thrown about them, and consort with strangers. Seclusion from mankind is as dangerous to enlightened religion as it is to Christian charity. Yet self-denial is imperative to the Christian, and the limiting and confining our love to those who love us is certainly forbidden by our Great Teacher.

"If ye love your brethren only, what do ye more than others?" Something of the same spirit that induced Anthony and many others to retire from the world and seclude themselves in monasteries, manifests itself in this age by a missionary spirit, that sends them out "into all the world" to teach the ignorant and proclaim to the heathen "the unsearchable riches of Christ." This is a return to the practice of the early Christians in the primitive ages, and in simple obedience to the command of the Master. Both forms of zeal, though seemingly *opposite*, have proceeded from the longings of the immortal soul to reach a higher life. The *missionary* spirit is more consonant to the practice and precepts of our Lord than the conventual system. The *experience* of the world has proved that the assembling of men and women in religious houses, with the fanciful idea of promoting holiness and increasing the knowledge of God, is fallacious, and in some sad instances has tended to fearful superstition and licentiousness. The cloister is *in these days* an unnecessary feature in the religious world. It is as a fungus on trees of righteousness, eating out the heart and healthy substance of true religion.

Good men and women doubtless live within the

walls of a convent; but to immure oneself, and to break asunder the ties that God and nature have imposed, seems to us a sad misinterpretation of the teachings of the New Testament. In times of misrule and war, when armies of barbarians were shaking Europe with a heavy tread, conventual establishments were necessary and served a noble purpose. Then they served as schools for the young, and retreats for the aged. Here learning and religion took refuge from the soldiery and the din of arms. In the monastery, books were transcribed, and valuable archives, both political and religious, were preserved. A great debt is due to the monks of the middle ages for their efforts in preserving valuable records, especially those which related to Christianity. It is true, that, owing to the scarcity of writing materials, many a *palimpsest* or parchment was made valueless by some ignorant monk when he erased the valuable record to transcribe his own musings.

"The abbeys," says Mr. Froude, "that towered in the midst of the English towns, with the houses clustered at their feet, like subjects round some majestic queen, were images of the supremacy which the Church of the middle ages had asserted for itself. The heavenly graces *had* once descended upon the monastic orders, making them ministers of mercy, patterns of celestial life. Then it was that art and genius poured out their treasures to raise fitting tabernacles to the Father of mankind and of His especial servants. The poor outcasts of soeiety gathered around these hallowed walls— the debtor, the felon and the outlaw. These abbeys of the middle ages abode through the storms of war and conquest, like the ark upon the waves of the flood; in the midst of violence remaining inviolate, through the awful reverence that surrounded them. The abbeys at the time they were visited by Henry's ministers, just before their dissolution, were as little like they had been *once*, as a living man in the pride of his growth resembles the loathsome corpse which the *earth* hastens to hide forever."

In the year 1489, Pope Innocent the Eighth, moved by the stories that reached his ears, of the corruption of certain monasteries in England, granted a commission to the Archbishop of Canterbury to investigate this matter. The result of the inquiry contained overwhelming proof of the corruption and defilement of the holy places. The monastery of St. Albans is specially mentioned as having been the theatre of great and abounding iniquity. But the abbot was *not deposed*, but severely reprimanded to amend his doings.

Some say these imputations are false and exaggerated, but the charges to which we have just alluded were brought in the fifteenth century by Morton, Henry VII.'s minister, legate of the Apostolic See, in a letter addressed to the abbot of St. Albans himself. The abbot of St. Albans was a peer of the realm, living but a few miles from London. Queen Mary's agents destroyed the *records* of the visitation of the monasteries in her *father's* time, but there is abundant evidence extant in the official letters of the Cotton library, many of which have been published by the Camden Society.* Bishop Latimer tells us, that when the report of the visitors of the *abbeys* was read in the Commons House, there rose from all sides of the house

---

* Froude.

the cry "*Down* with them." Wolsey, a devoted son of the Church, *first* made public the infamies which disgraced the Roman Catholic monasteries. Their glory had departed, but many modern writers affect to disbelieve the testimony of those great men.

The *general* visitation was made fifty years later than the inquest made by Morton, the minister of Henry VII. It is probable that for several centuries the monasteries had been verging to decay and dissolution, from their hypocrisy and corruption.

Though the dark tints predominate in a true picture drawn of the monasteries in the sixteenth century, yet in the latest era of monasticism in England, there were some *types* yet lingering of an older and better age. There was certainly much heroism shown by some of monks of the Charterhouse, an order of the Carthusians, who chose to die, rather than perjure themselves in the matter of the king's supremacy. Some of these died heroically, as did More and Fisher.

The word monk occurs first in the fourth century. The monks were divided into Cenobites and Eremites, the former class lived in communities, the latter in lonely and desolate places.

Self-denial is certainly a Christian requirement, but the monastic system, as such, fulfilled its destiny more than three hundred years ago.* It is a system *divorced* from healthy life, too often a thing of creed and ceremony, which leaves the lower nature unaffected and unsubdued, and the heart untouched by true love to God and our neighbor. Institutions under the care of the church, whether Roman Catholic or Protestant,

---

* Froude.

whose design is to train persons into useful knowledge, that they may be able to *serve* in this world of ours in any capacity to which they may be called by the providence of God, must ever be necessary "until time shall be no longer."

But while monastic establishments are no longer needed in a land of light and liberty, there is one branch of this system that must commend itself in its *main features* to every Christian heart. We mean the institution of the Sisters of Mercy. These are the missionaries to the desolate garret, seeking the poor, the sick and the friendless. They are found in the obscure retreats of our crowded cities, bearing the message of the Gospel to the dying. Let deaconesses or sisters of mercy be raised up by Christians of every name to carry forward works of benevolence and mercy. *Phebe* was a servant of the Church in apostolic days. She was the messenger of St. Paul on one occasion from Cenchrea, a port of Corinth, to the Romans.

Before we leave the subject of monasticism, we must mention Benedict* of Nursia, as he was called. This famous founder of the Benedictine Order was born in 480. His sister Scolastica, who seems to have been as great an enthusiast as himself, dwelt near him. Their influence in self-denial and energy were manifested by the spread of Benedictine monasteries throughout Italy, from Calabria to the Po. Totila, a Gothic monarch, was reproved by him and induced to lead a better life. St. Maur introduced Benedictine monasteries into France. The name of St. Maur is dear to letters. With Augus-

---

* The Benedictines preserved and copied many volumes of the ancient literature.

tine, the missionary to the Saxons, the Benedictine rule passed into England. The fairest spots in England were chosen for the monasteries. Abbeys rose and fell like other institutions. The rural districts, which in early Christian times were given up to Paganism, were gradually drawn into these communities by the establishment of hermitages and monasteries in their neighborhood. The very name "Pagan" is derived from the fact that the villages* of Italy so long resisted the teaching of Christianity.

We have already alluded to the violent fanaticism of the Eastern monks. The monks of the Western Church were usually very different. They spent their time, as do our modern missionaries, in useful labors.

---

* "Pagus," a village.

CHAPTER XVIII.

A. D. 402.—The fifth century commences with Innocent I. Rome seemed deserted by both her emperors; one reigned in Ravenna, the other in Constantinople. The aristocracy of the sacred city had been scattered by Alaric. In the fifth century the bishops of Rome were respected by the barbarians. In this century the Roman See in dignity and in the regular succession of its prelates, stood alone and unapproachable. Some of the sees of the East had been contaminated by Arian prelates. The fierce rivalries of Alexandria and Constantinople had induced the contending partisans to appeal to Rome.

The great Ambrose * was dead. Chrysostom, though still living, was the victim of persecution. Rome had steadily held the doctrines of Athanasius without wavering. Valentinian II. made a law in 381 that the councils differing in Trinitarian and Arian doctrines should appeal to Rome. There was at this time no commanding mind in the West that could obscure the rising fame of Innocent I. Upon the mind of this bishop now seemed to dawn the ecclesiastical supremacy of Rome. Theophilus, bishop of Alexandria, was a bold, bad man, and a virulent persecutor of the eloquent Chrysostom. Innocent I. took the part of the bishop of Constantinople. This was the popular side. The East, however, resented the interference. The Roman

---

* Once the influential bishop of Milan.

Pontiffs, from the time of Innocent I., began to found their supremacy in their supposed succession of St. Peter; but the world at large looked up to Rome chiefly on account of the civil supremacy of the city. There was a prestige in her former majesty and renown that could not be forgotten. The Pope was head of Christendom, because he was the bishop of the first city in the world. While the bishops of Rome and other cities of the West were strengthening their power over the hearts and minds of men, and not troubling themselves with metaphysical subtleties of doctrine, the bishops of the great Eastern sees were engaged in ignoble strife. Nestorius, Bishop of Constantinople, contended that Christ was the God-man, and repudiated the term,* "Mother of God," that was at this time frequently applied to Mary the Mother of Christ.

Cyril, Bishop of Alexandria, became the fierce persecutor of Nestorius. Who would not, says an eloquent writer, prefer to meet his Redeemer in judgment with the doctrinal errors of Nestorius (if they were errors) rather than with the barbarities of Cyril. Much blame has rested upon the memory of Cyril with regard to Hypatia, who was murdered in the streets of Alexandria by fanatical monks. It is alleged that his great influence might have been used to control the mob that destroyed this accomplished Greek woman. The excitement produced in the Eastern Church by the discussion of abstruse metaphysical questions present some painful chapters in the history of the Greek Church. The Arian controvery was finally settled by Theodosius about the year 380.

---

* We, like Nestorius, are repelled by the term "Mother of God." Mary is nowhere in the New Testament called the Mother of God.

The heresy of Macedonius, Bishop of Constantinople, who taught that the Holy Spirit is a divine energy, and not a person distinct from the Father and the Son, was condemned by the Council of Constantinople in 381.

"Two other controversies after this time produced much excitement. One was headed by Nestorius, to whom we have already alluded. Nestorius maintained there are two *persons* in Christ—the divine and the human. This error was condemned by the Council of Ephesus, A. D. 431. The other controversy was headed by Eutyches, a monk of Constantinople, who taught that there is but one *nature* in Christ—that of the Word, who became incarnate. This opinion was condemned in the Council of Chalcedon, A. D. 451. The doctrine of the Universal Church was *then* defined to be that in Jesus Christ there is but *one person*, yet two natures no way confounded. The decisions of these *four* councils have been received by the whole of Christendom, East and West, as the true exposition of the *faith*."

The Pelagian question agitated the *West* during the last years of Innocent's Pontificate. Pelagius was a Briton. Christianity had been planted in Britain very early. Pelagius went to Rome in 409, and was the founder of a religious system. The peculiar tenet of Pelagius was his denial of original sin. Some obscurity clings to his system. Though an earnest Christian, he seemed to reject the doctrine of "justification by faith." He claimed that infants inherit eternal life, though not baptized. The disciples of St. Augustine opposed him. Pelagius formed no sect, but his system, though condemned, retained its advocates.

The *Church of to-day** doubtless contains many members who hold his peculiar opinions without knowing that they pertain to any system of theology. The African churches repudiated with one voice the reasonings of Pelagius. They adopted entirely, as far as they could understand them, the doctrinal views of St. Augustine, the great Bishop of Hippo. The most distinguished advocate of semi-Pelagian views was Cassianus. He went to Constantinople and became a favorite pupil of Chrysostom, whose writings were adverse to the predestinarian system of Augustine. Semi-Pelagianism aspired to hold the balance between Pelagius and Augustine. It repudiated the heresy of the denial of original sin. It asserted divine grace. The semi-Pelagians, though censured in several councils, formed no separate or hostile communities. Pelagius, it is said, was once arraigned for false doctrine at Lydda, in Palestine, before fourteen prelates. His accusers spoke Latin, while the bishops spoke Greek. Pelagius spoke both languages. It is said the Fathers were imposed on by the plausible dialectics of Pelagius. The confusion of tongues made it difficult for the council to understand with clearness, or to detect heresy in his subtle definitions. He was solemnly acquitted at this council. As a Western monk, however, he was amenable to the tribunal of Rome. His theological opponents lost no time in appealing to the Bishop of Rome. Pelagius, also, wrote a letter explaining fully his views, but before the letter reached Rome Innocent I. was dead! Fosimus, his successor, was a Greek, and was disposed

---

* Leaders of thought to-day reëcho the doctrine of Pelagius in denying orignal sin.

to treat the Pelegian heresy as a matter of little importance.

The whole theology of Chrysostom, of whom we have already spoken, was a practical appeal to the free will of man. The depravity against which he inveighs is a personal spontaneous surrender to evil practices and influences, to be broken off by a vigorous effort of religious faith, to be controlled by self-imposed religious discipline. So far as is consistent with prayer and earnest seeking, man is the master of his own destiny. The two great masters of theology—Augustine and Chrysostom—had grappled deeply with the great mysteries of the New Testament, the sovereignty of God, and the free agency of man." *

> "O, Thou in heaven and earth, the only peace
> Found out for mankind, under wrath!
> Be thou in Adam's room; the Head of all, though Adam's son.
> Thy merit imputed shall absolve all who renounce
> Their *own deeds*, and from Thee receive new life."

God's sovereign grace was the favorite theme of the African Bishop, and the free will of man the inspiring subject of Chrysostom. The predestinarian doctrines of Augustine seemed not to be congenial to the Greek mind. Augustine, after the death of Ambrose, was the great authority in theology. His great work, "The City of God," was written to silence the remonstrances and wipe out the aspersions of Paganism.

Innocent I. was Pope † when Alaric entered Rome. Leo I. was Pope when Genseric sacked Rome. By the middle of the fifth century the grand work of the spiritual monarchy of Rome had been laid by Innocent

---

* Milton. † Or Chief Bishop of Rome.

I. and Leo I. Leo I. died before the conquest of Odoacer, A. D. 476.

The immediate successors of Leo were subordinate to the barbarian kings of Rome. As a proof of the subordinate condition of the bishops of Rome during the adminstration of the Gothic kings, we are told that Theodoric * determined to send John I., who was then Pope, on an embassy to Constantinople. Justin was then Emperor. He had forbidden to the Arians the use and possession of the churches. Theodoric desired the Pope to remonstrate with the Emperor as to his illiberal course. John was very unwilling to undertake the mission, but there was no appeal from the will of the Gothic king. John was required to present to the Eastern Court a written protest in words like these: "To pretend to a dominion over the conscience is to usurp the prerogative of God; in the nature of things, the power of sovereigns ought to be confined to political government. The most dangerous heresy is the belief that a sovereign may separate from a part of his subjects because their creed differs from his own." Yet this king of noble sentiments, who had acted consistently with his "golden words" until the latter part of his reign, suffered himself to be misled by some unprincipled members of his household. These officers of his palace created suspicion in the breast of the monarch against two of the most virtuous and distinguished men of Rome—Boethius and Symmachus. Gibbon depicts with a master's hand the virtues and great learning of these men. He says Boethius was

---

* Theodoric became king of Rome 490. He was an Ostrogoth.

the last of the Romans whom Cato or Tully would have acknowledged as their countryman.

We, however, have introduced this episode to show how submissive the Popes of Rome were compelled to be during the sway of the Gothic king, Theodoric. It is not known certainly how the Pope performed his mission. But on his return from the Greek capital he is thrown into prison, where he died. It is thought that Theodoric suspected the great men* whom he so cruelly executed, of a correspondence with the East, inviting an invasion. An invasion *was* made shortly after the death of Theodoric. This king was an Arian, but he had treated the Trinitarians, or Catholics, as they were now called, with much generosity and consideration. His latest days were greatly troubled with remorse on account of the execution of Boethius and Symmachus.

Leo I.† was the Pope of Rome but a short time previous to the subjugation of Rome by Odoacer and Theodoric. The *sermons* of Leo are the first of a Roman Bishop that have come down to us. The Bishops of Rome before his time were inferior men. Leo dwells on the worship of Christ, not on the Virgin and the saints. The four Popes that preceded Gregory I. were inglorious and feeble. When the sixth century grew to a close, Italy, from being a Gothic kingdom, became a province of the Greek Empire. Theodoric had been killed in a battle against the Vandals.

Rome was now the *second* city of the civilized world. The Lombards had entered Northern Italy,

---

* Boethius and Symmachus.
† Leo I. was Pope 440. Odoacer conquered Rome 476.

invited, it is said, by Narses, the late exarch of Ravenna, who was stimulated by jealousy of the Byzantine Emperor. The Lombards were a fierce heathen people when they entered Italy.

Genseric, the Vandal king, after remaining a year or two in Spain, passed over into Africa, ravaging and desolating the beautiful and populous country. The dioceses of the great Augustine and of Cyprian, of Carthage, were made desolate. The good offices of the Bishop of Carthage must not be forgotten, in trying to ameliorate the condition of the Roman captives carried off by Genseric, the gold of the churches was freely taken to buy their redemption from the cruel conqueror. The narrow tract of the African court filled with monuments of Roman art and magnificence was overwhelmed by the invasion of the Vandals, and soon seven fruitful provinces from Tangier to Tripoli became as a desert.

Genseric, an Arian Christian, nominally united with the Donatists, a powerful schismatical sect, who had long troubled the churches of Africa with their discontents and divisions to effect the ruin of the country. The Donatists were themselves involved in ruin. Religious discord was perhaps almost as fatal to the churches of Northern Africa as the ravages of the Vandals. The Saracens soon followed, and Mahometanism put out the light of Christianity. The *candlestick** was removed from its place, because of sectarian dissensions and persecutions. The Roman world was girt by enemies on every side. The entrance of the heathen Lombards, also the tyranny of the Exarchs of

---

* Revelation of John ii. 5.

Ravenna, caused the Italians to regret the milder sway of the Gothic monarchs.

John, the Bishop of Constantinople, presuming on the civil supremacy of his city,* claimed to be Universal Bishop. Gregory I., Bishop of Rome, reproves the presumptuous John in strong language: "Is this a time to assume so arrogant a title, when we are beset by enemies on every side. Our priests should bewail in dust and ashes the sin and misery of this unhappy time, instead of adopting profane appellations to gratify their pride."

Am I defending my own cause? Is your presumption an injury to Rome? I am pleading for the cause of God, the cause of the whole church. Gregory then declares that he is a prelate of a see where there are many heretics. Let every Christian heart reject the blasphemous name of Universal Bishop. It was once applied, he continues, to the see of Rome by the Council of Chalcedon, in honor of St. Peter, but the more humble pontiffs rejected the title as injurious to the rest of the priesthood. Gregory brands the arrogance of the Bishop of Constantinople as a sign of the coming of Antichrist. He compares this movement to that of Satan, who aspired to be highest in the hierarchy of angels. No one in the church has yet dared to usurp the name of Universal Bishop. It is sacrilege. Gregory I. wrote these words with great sincerity, but a few years after the death of this good Pope the infamous Emperor Phocas pronounced the Bishop of Rome Universal Bishop. The Greek Emperor Phocas gave this title to the prelate at Rome, because he hated

---

* Rome was at this time subject to the Greek Empire.

the patriarch of his own city. This hatred, it is said, arose from the kindness and protection afforded by the Patriarch to the family of *Maurice*, the predecessor of Phocas.

In the interval between Gregory I. and Gregory II. there were twenty-four Bishops or Popes of Rome. Gregory I. was justly called the Great, because of his wise administration of religious affairs at a very trying time. He it was who sent Augustine as a missionary to the Saxons, when he became Bishop of Rome. The old story, with regard to the beautiful fair Saxon boys with flaxen hair, whom Gregory saw in a slave market at Rome, has often been told, but never more strikingly related than *recently* by Dean Stanley.* "Gregory was deeply impressed by the appearance of these heathen children. He resolved to *go* as a missionary to the Saxons, or at once to send one. He was too much needed at Rome *to go*. He, therefore, sent Augustin,† with forty monks, from ‚a convent on the old Celian Hill."

The British Christians had made little effort to Christianize their cruel and savage Saxon conquerors. Augustin was anxious to meet the British clergy. He doubtless intended to usurp authority over the British churches of Wales. The British Bishops and Presbyters met and conferred with Augustin and his monks; but as they differed somewhat in their Liturgy, and in other customs, especially in the time of the proper observance of the Easter festival, the British

---

* "Notes on Canterbury," Stanley.

† Augustin, missionary to the Saxons in England, was very different from the great Augustine of the fourth century.

Christians for a long time refused to obey the Roman rule.

Gregory, in his letters from Rome, gave Augustin wise counsel, urging him to conciliate the Britons, and allow them to use their own liturgy. Gregory I. was wise and conciliatory. He arranged a book of *services*. He did his utmost to train the Romans in self-discipline and to soften the Teutons. He arranged the chants that are still called by his name, though both the chants and the services were probably derived from earlier models. There are letters extant* from Gregory to Augustin, advising him how to deal with other Christian communities, especially with the *old* British churches. When you meet, he said, with anything really good in these churches, you must adopt it. "Things are not to be loved for the sake of places, but *places* for the sake of things." Augustin, however, seems to have been *haughty* in his intercourse with the Britons, and little disposed to regard their prejudices. It is said that when Augustin first met some of the British bishops and clergy in council, under *an oak tree*, the monk Augustin behaved with haughty severity.

The parents of Gregory I. were noble Romans. His grandfather had been Bishop of Rome. When Maurice was Emperor of Constantinople, Gregory was sent to this great city of the East as Nuncio of the See of Rome.

Justin the Younger, in 574, had appointed Gregory Prefect of Rome. He acceded to the Papacy soon after his return from Constantinople. He was distinguished

---
* Dean Stanley.

not only for his religious zeal and charity, but for his learning, his knowledge of philosophy of civil law and the canons of the church. His ample fortune was devoted to works of piety. He built six monasteries in Sicily. In these distracted times monasteries were necessary as houses of refuge from barbarous foes, and as places of *instruction* for the young and ignorant.

The heathen king of Kent, who received Augustin, had a Christian wife, Bertha. She had a chaplain and worshiped in a chapel *once* used by the *British* Christians. When the Saxons drove out the British Christians, they heathenized the places of Christian worship. After the success of Augustin, *they* were *again* converted into places of Christian worship. The baptism of Ethelbert, husband of Bertha, took place A. D. 597.

CHAPTER XIX.

Rome, says Gibbon, at the close of the sixth century was at the point of her lowest depression. By the removal of the seat of the empire, and the loss of many provinces, the sources of public and private wealth were exhausted. The Romans, too, suffered anxiety at this time from the threatening Lombards in North Italy, and from the despotism of the Greek empire. They were blessed, however, with the wise and paternal pontificate of Gregory I. *Un*like most of his successors, he *frequently* ascended the pulpit, and by his pathetic eloquence *kindled* the congenial passions of his audience. The minds of the people, depressed by *calamity*, were directed to the hopes and fears of the invisible world. Till the last days of his life, he officiated in the imposing service of the Church. These services were made more soothing by grand melodious chants. These melodies softened the fierceness of barbarian hearers, and tended to refine the dark enthusiasm of the vulgar, as well as to strengthen their faith in Jesus, "the man of sorrows."

The sixth century knew little of the baneful effects of priestcraft. Gregory I., great and good as he was, was somewhat credulous and superstitious. Under his teaching the Arians in Italy and Spain were reconciled to the Trinitarian, or Catholic Church. He as an apostolic shepherd watched over the faith of the subordinate pastors.

The success of Augustin* in preaching to the Anglo-Saxons reflected much glory on the work of Gregory. The calamities of these times, and the excellence of Gregory, tended greatly to increase the power of the Roman bishop. Rome was a central point, to which Italy and its surrounding States had long looked as a model.

We must now speak of the mission of Augustin. We learn from Bede, a Saxon historian who lived in the early part of the eighth century, that when Augustin invited the *British* bishops to conform to the Roman rule, they positively refused to yield their own customs, and that they retired in disgust at the pride of the Roman agent.

The enmity between the Britons and Anglo-Saxons seems not to have been diminished by the conversion of the latter nation, because their conversion was not derived from the conquered people. The Saxons received Christianity as it existed in the days of Gregory I. The Britons had received their knowledge of Christ through their connection with the Eastern Church. For the sake of protection, they *afterwards*, after much warfare and trouble, acknowledged the supremacy of the See of Rome. A century of cruel warfare with the heathen Saxons, in which they were compelled to yield all the possessions they held dear, did not improve their tempers, or enlighten the minds of the native Britons. Jerome and Chrysostom both testify to the orthodoxy of the *early* British Christians. The representatives of the British Church took part in

---

* The *monk* sent by Gregory. He must not be confounded with St. Augustine of the fourth century.

the councils of Arles and Sardica. The enlightened Pelagius and Celestine were Britons.

When Gregory I. heard of the opposition of the British bishops to the liturgy of Augustin, he counsels him in these wise words: "Choose from each church those things that are pious and good, and when you have made them, as it were, up in one body, let the minds of the people become accustomed thereto." Augustin was successful in Kent, but he made little progress in the other parts of the island.

We have already said, that after the success of Augustin in Kent, the old British churches were purged from their heathenish character and converted into Christian temples. Laurentius was the successor of Augustin in the cathedral of Canterbury. Ethelbert, the king of Kent, was baptized in A. D. 597. The baptisms of that day were performed by immersion in the little rivers of the neighborhood.

The authentic materials for the mission of Augustin are almost entirely derived from Bede's Ecclesiastical History, written in the early part of the eighth century. Augustin died in 605, Gregory I. in 604.

The chief instruments in the conversion of the Anglo-Saxons were Aidan, Finan and Colman, by whom the kingdom of Mercia and the East Saxons were Christianized.

There were three ecclesiastical parties in England in the closing of the sixth century and in the early part of the seventh century, namely: The old British church, that had existed for centuries *before* Augustin came to England ; the Saxons converted by Irish missionaries; and the Saxons converted by Roman missionaries. The Augustinian party prevailed at last, more by diplomacy than by missionary work. A synod for the discussion of the several views of the three parties was held at *Whitby*, at the convent of the famous abbess Hilda.* On one side of the controversy was Colman, bishop of Lindisfarne, on the other was Wilfrid, bishop of York. Wilfrid had visited Rome, and was inclined to favor the Roman view. Colman urged the descent of their tradition from St. John. To this tradition also, Columba, the ardent missionary and bishop of Iona,† clung with much reverence. Wilfrid maintained with great energy the tradition of St. Peter.

Gradually the Scottish clergy and the monks in England ceased to dispute, and occupied themselves with what they deemed more important matters. Those who objected to the peculiar Roman usages retired to Iona, which was long considered a sacred place, famed for its good works and learning. Colman and his clergy retired to Ireland.

The Britons who had lived secluded in their Welsh mountains, indulging in animosities that even Christianity could not allay, were at length brought into peaceful communication by the monasteries of Ireland first with Northumbria, and then with the rest of England. There was a constant flow of missionaries across the British Channel, who possessed much of the knowledge which *still remained* in Europe. The early bishops of Canterbury were foreigners, also other southern sees; but the Anglo-Saxons were soon ambitious of a native clergy. It is said a native

---

* In Hilda's monastery lived Cædmon, the poet, who rehearsed in Saxon verse the whole sacred history as recorded in the Bible.

† A little island in the Hebrides, famous for learned institutions and religion.

clergy grew up in Britain more rapidly than in any other of the Teutonic kingdoms.

Wilfrid of York blended with the rigor of a monk a love of magnificence. His visits to Gaul and Italy made him desire to introduce better church-buildings than Saxon architecture could produce. Houses of rude timber, thatched with reeds, were soon replaced by churches of stone with windows of glass. Wilfrid's present to a church at Ripon, was a copy of the four gospels, written in letters of gold on a purple ground.

Romanism, it must be recollected, had not assumed its modern form in the time of Gregory I., or in the time of Bede. The supremacy of the Pope was not established; the universal dominion of any Pope or bishop was denied and strongly condemned by Gregory himself. Nor was transubstantiation yet accepted, and many other dogmas, now received by the Romanist, were then unknown.

The Anglo-Saxons after they received Christianity made great progress in literature. Bede translated the New Testament (or a part of it), into his own tongue. Bede, by an amanuensis, translated the last chapters of St. John's gospel a few moments before he expired. Adhelm and Cædmon were famous for their Saxon verses. Cædmon engaged the attention of his unlettered congregation by singing to them the essential doctrines of Christianity. It is thought by some that Cædmon's poem on the Creation, or the "Origin of Evil," suggested to Milton Paradise Lost.

We must now revert to a still earlier time, and speak of the most famous missionary of them all. The *early* conversion of Ireland to Christianity is attributed to the zealous preaching of St. Patrick. Much obscurity envelopes the *time* and the *place* of his birth. He was taken to Ireland as a *captive*, say most writers on this subject, about the middle of the fifth century, more than a century before Augustin went to England. He escaped from captivity and went to Brittany, in France (probably his native country; thousands of Britons had passed over to this province in France, during the long war between the Britons and Anglo Saxons, in their contention for Britain or England). The birth-place of Patrick is uncertain, but his zeal for the truth of God and his love for the souls of men is undoubted. He returned to Ireland so soon as he was prepared for teaching, and devoted his *life* to the work of an evangelist. His success as a preacher was wonderful; he had probably several assistants, as Ireland early became an abode of piety and learning. It has been already said that Irish and Scottish missionaries had preceded Augustin in the work of teaching Christianity to some of the Anglo Saxon kingdoms. Columba is said to have founded the monastery of Iona, and to Aidan, monk from Ireland, is attributed the bishopric and monastery of Lindisfarne. Cuthbert, the apostle of the Lowlands of Scotland, traveled over moor and mountain sides to teach the peasants of Scotland and Northumbria. Bede, in *his* day, calls Ireland "the isle of saints." But Ireland was destined to suffer like England from Danish invasions, and for a longer time. The Danes seized the government of Ireland and ruled it with severity for a long time. When the native kings of Ireland were restored they did not exercise the wisdom of Alfred or Athelstan.

But little is known of the history of Ireland, either in Church or State, from the time that *Bede* wrote *his* history until the twelfth century. Bede died about 755. "I spent my whole life in the monastery of Jarrow, in Northumbria," says this learned man. "My pleasure lay in learning, teaching and writing." It is said that Bede learned *Greek* from the school that the Greek Bishop Theodore founded at Canterbury. A late historian,* says that this good and great man was the founder of medieval history, and the *first English* historian. A few weeks before his death he resolved to finish his version of St. John's Gospel in English. As he approached his end he called his scholars around him and bade them *write*. "There is *still* a chapter wanting," said his scribe. "Write it quickly," said the dying man. "It is now finished." Supported in his scholars' arms, his face turned to the spot where he was wont to pray, he passed away chanting "Glory to God." Before the time of Bede and Alcuin, both Saxons, some of the priests knew little more than the Creed and the Lord's Prayer. Hence the importance of the English or Saxon translation of the Gospel of St. John. His ecclesiastical history was written in Latin. He left many works on different subjects to attest his great industry. His death took place about a century and a half after the landing of Augustin.

It is wonderful that so much was accomplished in the propagation of Christianity during this time, when we think how the Roman world was torn by disastrous wars. During the reign of Justinian, the Greek emperor, Rome changed her masters five times. During this period the famous Belisarius made and unmade kingdoms not for himself but for his master Justinian. The calamities of these times tended to increase the

---
* Mr. Green.

power of the bishop of Rome. Rome now began to assert that her episcopate had been founded by St. Peter, a thing hard to disprove in times of ignorance. Nicolas I., in 868, appealed to certain papers called *Decretals*, to strengthen his assumption of Peter's supremacy.

Until the time of Nicolas I. the only documents regarded as genuine was the collection of Dionysius, beginning with Siricius, in the fourth century, together with the documents by authentic councils, given by Isidore. Suddenly the Pope, Nicolas, appeals to a new code. It was *then* discovered that fifty-nine spurious decrees had been added to the old authentic documents. It was pretended that these decrees were made by the twenty oldest popes, from Clement to Melchiades. The pretended donation of Constantine is mentioned in these false decretals. The evident design of these spurious papers and letters was to aggrandize the see of Rome, and to bring all other sees in subjection to it. While the power of Rome was thus sought to be increased, the Patriarchates of Alexandria, of Antioch and of Jerusalem (the mother Church) were cast down and discouraged by the influx of the Mahometans in Northern Africa, Egypt and Syria. The religion of the Moslem threatened almost to quench the light of Christianity in these countries. This extensive manual* of sacerdotal literature, unknown in the earlier ages of the church, claimed for Roman bishops the guardianship and legislation of the Christian Church throughout the world. Those scholars who have thoroughly examined those Decretals say that they were not written at Rome. They were evi-

---
* The Decretals.

dently written, say they, after the council of Paris, in 829. Metz is the place designated where they were written. The archives of Rome show no vestiges of any such writing. This fraud was perpetrated in the ninth century.

It was in this century that Charlemagne made the bishop of Rome *a king*. The bishop of Rome afterwards asserted that the states of the Church given to the Papacy by Pepin and Charlemagne were but a restitution of lands given by Constantine. This gift, claimed in the Decretals as Constantine's, is acknowledged by Roman Catholics to be a forgery. The lands given to the Church by Charlemagne had been wrested from the Lombards. The famous iron crown was bestowed upon a duke of Turin (successor to the Lombard king) as a reward for his *efforts* in reclaiming Lombardy from Arianism. The superstitious of this age alleged that this crown was made out of the nails of the true cross. Though at this time the masses of the people were superstitious and ignorant, it is said that the Lombards, "called the *long-bearded* monsters of the North," had acquired, as exhibited in their laws, the best fruits of civilization. The system of laws framed by the Lombard king, Rotharis, is esteemed the best of the barbarian codes. The kingdom of Lombardy in Italy was more peaceful and prosperous than any other which had been formed from the fragments of the Roman Empire. It was in the reign of Justinian, and it was the chief glory of that reign that the emperor employed the ablest lawyers of his time in compiling the Code, the Pandects and the Institutes. The Institutes contained the elementary principles of law, the Code was a revised edition of all the enactments from the time of Adrian, emperor of Rome. The Pandects were a digest of the precedents and decision of the wisest judges which had been accumulating for a thousand years. To extend the advantages of the new system, schools of law were founded in Rome, Constantinople and Beirut.

In speaking of the events of the sixth century,* both in church and state, we have wandered from Italy to Britain or England and then to Constantinople. It was during the reign of Justinian that the magnificent church of St. Sophia was built (now a mosque), and in this reign the culture of silk was introduced into Greece by two Persian monks. But perhaps the most remarkable feature of Justinian's reign was the trampling of mighty hosts. Narses and Belisarius led armies against the expiring armies of the Goths and against the Vandals, assisted by the Huns and the Turks. Learned men have had much disputation as to the origin of the barbarian hordes. All of them came from Asia at different periods. The Goths were on the Vistula, and the Vandals on the Oder in the days of the Antonines. Though these two people were very diferent in some respects, yet they belonged to the great division of the Suevi. The Vandal race, once so celebrated in the annals of mankind, have so perished from the face of the earth that no language remains to testify to their German, Sclavonic or independent origin. *One* province, Andalusia, in Spain bears witness to their abode in that country for a time. The Goths were incorporated with the Spanish and French under many tribal names. The Lombards impressed their name upon northern Italy,

---
* The sixth, seventh and eighth centuries.

the Huns in Hungary, and the Angles and Burgundians in England and France. Their descendents in the northern countries of Europe are all comprehended by the name of Teutons; as the original inhabitants of Western Europe were known by the name of Celts.

Early in the eighth century Boniface, a native of Devonshire, England, became missionary to some of the German States. The language of Boniface closely resembled the German dialects. He would, therefore, be more readily understood by them than missionaries from Italy.

In 715 Boniface left his native country and attempted in vain to disseminate the doctrines of Christ in Friesland. He was afterwards very successful in Thuringia and other German provinces. He was made bishop by Gregory II. He was assisted by Charles Martel, Mayor of the Palace (he who drove back the Mahometans from Tours), who appointed for him pious and learned associates. With these he had great success. It is evident from traditions that have come down to us that Boniface did not possess the meekness of Columba, who labored before him in Alsace. He had imbibed some of the sacerdotal spirit, which was sometimes conspicuous afterward in those who sought honors from the Court of Rome. He was called the Apostle of Germany, but he was widely different, says Mosheim, from the pattern the genuine apostles have left us.

"The honor and majesty of the Roman Pontiff, whose minister he was, seemed equally his care; nay, more so than the glory of Christ and his religion. He marched into Thuringia at the head of an army and used compulsion or artifice, as it suited him. If Boniface used unjustifiable measures in attempting to bring the heathen into the Church of God, most grievously did he answer for his fault. In 755, when he went back to Friesland with many associates, he was murdered by them, together with fifty of the clergy, who accompanied him. Some years before this time he had received from the Pope Zacharias the Archbishopric of Metz and the Primary of Belgium as a reward for his vast labors. Charlemagne, in 772, attempted the Christianizing of the Saxons. He first sent bishops and monks to instruct them. Charlemagne was as much actuated, perhaps, by political motives as by regard for their religious interest. The Saxons were troublesome neighbors, and often interfered with the rights of the subjects of the great Emperor of the West. The missionaries of peace and love had small success. *War* was tried upon these rebels for two successive years. Alcuin,* a learned Saxon of Charlemagne's Court, gives his views as to the failure of these missions. Had the easy yoke of Christ, with its light burden, been presented to the Saxons with as much earnestness as the payment of tithes and legal satisfaction for small faults, the Saxons would not have rejected the Sacrament of Baptism.

Monarchs were more influenced by a desire for extent of empire than from a desire to improve the moral condition of the people. Charlemagne was a wise statesman. He knew that Christians would make better subjects than the heathen, and that civilization would come with Christianity.

---

* Let the Christian teachers learn from the Master they profess to serve and from *his* apostles. Let them be *preachers*, not plunderers.— ALCUIN.

The general features of the conversion of the Northern races were somewhat different from the Christianizing of the civilized world of Greece and Rome. The gospel, when first preached, spread from soul to soul, and was addressed to earnest inquiring minds, who grasped its truths to direct them in life and sustain them in death; but Christianity had little political significance or importance until the age of Constantine.

"When the missionaries went to the northern countries of Europe, they usually addressed themselves to the barbarous chiefs, kings or warriors. These laid the subject before the free assemblies of the people. There were no powerful pagan hierarchies to dispossess, as in civilized countries; no proud temples to destroy, as at Ephesus or in Athens. Sometimes the people agreed by thousands to follow the example of their chief, and receive the new religion in receiving baptism. When opposing factions arose, preferring the Norse mythology of their ancestors, their disputes would lead to bloodshed. Very little did many of them understand of the nature or power of godliness. The consciences of few of them, perhaps, were stirred with the question, "What must we do to be saved?" Christianity was sometimes extended by a Christian royal marriage with a pagan king.

The Queen would require the free exercise of her religion, with a chapel and clergy to administer the ordinances of her religion. The histories of Clotilda, Bertha, and Ethelberga will recur to the mind in this connection. But one of the most efficient modes was the establishment of monasteries, gradually gathering colonies of people around them. These religious houses in early times were not, as they became afterwards, stately homes of learned leisure, whose *ruins* are still among the architectural glories of the land. No, they were simple dwellings, built by the monks. They felled the trees, erected the mill, plowed the ground. An industrious, civilized community, on the borders of a heathen land. The monasteries to which we allude numbered their inmates by hundreds, and in process of time by thousands. A few of these were the teachers and governors. The Irish monastery at Bangor numbered 4,000, and the Fulda in Germany, at the death of its founder, number as many. Some of the most celebrated missionaries often applied to the bishops of the great cities for a sanction, but many went forward without any other authorization than their love for the souls of men. The oratory often grew into a church, and the cell into a religious house. They taught the heathen by voice and by a self-denying life. In transactions like these all parties were acting honestly for Christ. The Teutonic nations were brought under Christian influence about three centuries before the Sclavonic nations, were brought into the fold of Christ.

CHAPTER XX.

ICONOCLASM.

In 570 the Roman Empire was broken up. The great city of Rome, the "Niobe of nations," submitted to Gothic sway for about the space of fifty years. The feeble Augustulus, the last of the Emperors of Italy, yielded to the superior powers of Odoacer. He, as *King**** of Italy, reigned for seventeen years, and was not unworthy of his high station. He had been instructed in the doctrines of Arian Christianity, but he seems to have revered monastic and episcopal characters, and to have exercised toleration in religion. He was succeeded by Theodoric, the great king of the Ostrogoths, who vanguished Odoacer in battle, and it is supposed he had him assassinated. Gibbon describes Theodoric as a great hero and statesman. His latter days were full of remorse, because of the violent deaths of Boethius and Symmachus, two of the most illustrious of the citizens of Rome. Theodoric reigned thirty-three years.

Italy then became subject to the Exarchs of Ravenna, who were appointed by Justinian, Emperor of Constantinople. Rome, the former "mistress of the world," was now governed as a province. The Greek Empire, though despoiled of some valuable provinces, still possessed great wealth. Her Emperors

---

* He refused to be called Emperor or to wear the Purple.

lived in state and splendor, their palaces were lined with porphyry hung with purple, and filled with gold and silver. Narses and Belisarius commanded her armies. But suddenly, in the early part of the eighth century, Rome burst the bonds that connected her with Constantinople, both politically and ecclesiastically. The immediate cause of this disruption was called Iconoclasm.

In A. D. 726 Leo, the Greek Emperor, commanded all images of saints to be removed from the churches. The image of Christ was alone excepted. Iconoclasm separates Latin from Greek Christianity!

The expressive symbol and the suggestive picture of the fourth century, which were intended to instruct the unlearned, and had been introduced into the churches, simply to explain passages in the lives and deaths of Christ and his apostles, had become in the later centuries a snare to delude the souls of the weak minded. The Emperor Leo was opposed in this measure by Gregory II., Bishop of Rome. A dangerous conflict ensued in Constantinople, and insurrections in Italy. It is probable that the minds of the Eastern Emperors, and especially the bishops and clergy, were aroused to consider the subject of images and their dangerous tendencies from surrounding Mahometanism and Judaism. But for the *monks*, images would forever have disappeared from the East.

"Iconoclasm proscribed idolatry, but it could not kindle or awaken a purer faith. There was in this iconoclastic strife no appeal to principles, as in the Reformation, to justification by faith and to the individual sense of responsibility."* It must be remem-

---
* Milman.

bered, however, that the history of this *movement* comes to us from enemies. Latin historians have cast much obloquy on the names of the two Greek Emperors, Leo the Isaurian and Constantine Copronymus. Hatred of images could become a fanaticism, but it could not become a religion. Some said that in the Greek Empire the State overshadowed the Church, that the Patriarch was a puppet in the hands of the Emperor. This may have been sometimes the case, depending on the character of the Emperor or priest, but much more frequently the bishops and clergy inflamed the zeal of the monarch.

If the secular arm had not interfered the war against Iconoclasm would have been more short-lived and more effectual. Leo, the first Emperor who opposed images, was doubtless honest and right in his opposition. He had been fighting against Mahometans, and *their taunts* of idolatry rankled in his breast. The *restoration* of images was twice effected by women—by Irene, the widow of Leo, and afterwards by Theodora, the widow of Theophilus. The conflict lasted between the East and the West for about 120 years. The Greek Church then declared that no carved, sculptured work, or molten images should be allowed in their churches. This position it holds to-day. They consented that some pictures might be permitted in the churches, as they were not images, but representations. Those images to which the Greeks objected did doubtless minister to superstition. Men prostrated themselves before them, and burned incense before them. They insisted that they simply honored them, but did not adore them.

It was argued that the Jews, to whom the second

commandment was given, had in *their* temple the image of the Cherubim, shadowing the mercy-seat. Since the Incarnation they further argued that all was changed. "God was manifest in the flesh." The Church of Rome was unrelenting in her opposition to the Iconoclasts. The wisest words on this subject, says Milman, are embodied in the books called the *Caroline* books, in honor of Charlemagne. They are said to have been written by Alcuin, the Saxon who resided at the Court of Charles the Great.

In these books, there is distinct condemnation of all religious homage to images,— a vigorous refutation of all arguments that could justify such honor or homage. At the same time the image-breakers are reproved for not distinguishing between these sacred representations and the false idols of the heathen. Man is not all soul; he may, therefore, use sensuous helps, such as the paintings of the Savior and his apostles. It was declared that no one should kneel to any image, picture or statue. These decrees were published fully and specifically in the famous Caroline Books. Yet Charlemagne was not an Iconoclast. He wished some pictures to be retained in the churches as ornaments and reminders of the pious men who had performed pious deeds.

It was at a council in Frankfort, in 797, when Charlemagne presided, and at which a large number of the clergy of different grades were present, that the declarations made in the Caroline Books were proclaimed to the assembly. The learned Alcuin was present. This was a noble protest against the abuse of images, but it can not be determined how much good was effected by them.

Pepin, the father of Charles the Great, had, with the sanction of Pope Zacharias, dispossessed the last of the Merovingian kings of his throne and crown. Some years afterwards, when Desederius, King of the Lombards, invaded the patrimony of St. Peter—*i. e.*, the lands given by Pepin to the Pope, who sanctioned his usurpation, Hadrian I., who was then pontiff, had recourse to Charles the Great, the son of Pepin.

In the year 774 Charlemagne crossed the Alps with a large army. He overturned the kingdom of the Lombards, which had held dominion in Northern Italy for two centuries. He increased the donations that Pepin had made, giving to Hadrian cities and provinces not included in the grant of Pepin. In this manner was the Bishop of Rome made a *temporary king.** Our Lord's solemn prohibition, with regard to worldly titles and honors, was no longer remembered. "It shall not be so among you."

During the seventh and eighth centuries many barbarous nations had entered the Christian Church. When they assumed the name of Christians, they transferred the high prerogatives of their ancient priests to the bishops and ministers of the new religion. Hence originated, says Mosheim, the monstrous authority of the priesthood in the European churches. Their dependence on their former priests and their rev-

---

* "The Holy See was invoked for the *first time* by Pepin as an *international* power. The Pope assumed to depose Childeric, and gave to the royal office of his successor a sanctity hitherto unknown. He gave to Pepin the Hebrew rite of anointing and the Roman diadem. Before this time a Frankish election consisted in raising the chief on a shield amid the clash of arms. Pepin twice rescued the Pope and Rome from the Lombards.

erence for them, had doubtless its influence upon their views of the priestly office, but had the Christian prelates done their duty, the result would have been very different. During this period immense wealth and riches were conferred upon the church. "An idea somehow became prevalent at this time that punishment for sin may be bought off or cancelled by gifts to the churches, to the temples and to the ministers of God."

This was the principal source of these treasures which, from this century (the eighth) onward flowed in upon the clergy, churches and monasteries. Those persons whose duty it was to teach their flocks humility and indifference to worldly things, now became sovereign Lords, Dukes, Counts, and some of them placed themselves at the head of armies. This aggrandizement commenced with their head, the Roman Pontiff. Charlemagne made splendid offerings on the altar of St. Peter.

Charles coming to Rome in the year 800, the Pontiff Leo III. persuaded the Roman people, who were *supposed* to be free, and to have the right of choosing an Emperor, to proclaim him* Emperor of the West. The Pope put the crown on the head of the Monarch while he was kneeling at the altar. He affected surprise. Leo III. was one of the most munificent and splendid of the bishops of Rome. His wealth was great in consequence of the gifts of the Emperor. Buildings in Rome were lined with marble and mosaic. There were priestly robes of silk and embroidery, set with precious stones. Vessels of gold and columns of silver were seen. Leo III. also ob-

---
* Charlemagne.

tained money from heavy exactions levied upon the people. While he was enriching the churches and palaces of Rome, his own life was endangered by a popular insurrection.

Paschal, the successor of Leo III., was accused of being accessory to a great crime committed against two distinguished men. Paschal refused to give up the murderers. He was called before thirty bishops to answer for the imputed crime. He took a great oath, declaring his innocence. In a few days after he was called before a higher tribunal. He died! His death excited a fierce contention in cisalpine and transalpine regions.

The patricians and nobles of Rome call upon Lothair, the grandson of Charlemagne, to settle the difficulty. Lothair issued his mandates, but they were of little avail. He went to Rome in person, and finding that many of the estates of the Roman nobles had been confiscated in consequence of the indolence and avarice of the Popes, he used his power as Emperor of the West, and compelled a restitution of the property to the rightful owners.

In 824, Claudius, of Turin, lived. He was a bishop of blameless life, and his scriptural doctrines were a return to primitive Christianity, or in anticipation of the reformation of later times. The apostolic office, Claudius taught, ceased with St. Peter. The power of the keys, he believed, passed *equally* to the whole *Episcopal* order. Some of the successors of Claudius' opinions lay concealed in the valleys of the Alps, to appear again under the name of Waldenses. He removed from all the churches of his diocese the images that adorned them. He was unrebuked, though he lived in the heart of Italy. Monastic discipline was almost prostrate in this century. Most of the Western monks still followed the order of St. Benedict, but there was little discipline or *vitality* among them, until other orders arose. Supreme power over the whole sacred order was, both in the East and West, vested in the emperors and kings. This power in the East was undeniable, but in the West the flatterers of the popes have labored to conceal the fact.

Hadrian I., in a council at Rome, conferred on Charlemagne and his successors the right of appointing the Roman pontiffs. Charles and his son Louis *declined* the exercise of this power, but they reserved to themselves the power of accepting and confirming the election made by the Roman clergy and people. The emperors of the Franks, by their judges called Legates, inquired into the lives of the clergy.

There were not many famous writers in the eighth century, either in the East or West. Bede and Alcuin belong to the early part of this century. The former died in 755. Charlemagne was a great promoter of learning. He employed amanuenses, who composed and compiled a great deal under his dictation. The four Caroline Books against image-worship were drawn up under his direction and in accordance with his views.

Eginhard wrote the biography of Charlemagne. Several of the popes of this century left epistles. The fundamental doctrines of the Christian faith were yet preserved, both by the Greek and Latin writers. This is certain from the writings of Damaxenus and others of this age. But to the pure seed of the word were *added* many tares. The efficacy of the merits of the Savior were acknowledged, and yet it was maintained that man could appease God by gifts and offerings, and undergoing voluntary punishment.

We have spoken of the riches and treasures of the Roman Church, yet during the controversy about image, worship, the Greeks deprived them (the Romans) of some valuable possessions in Calabria, and Sicily, and Apulia, and exempted the bishops of these districts from the dominion of the Roman Pontiffs, together with the provinces of Illyricum, and placed them under the control of the Bishop or Patriarch of Constantinople. The power of the Pontiff *at this time* was confined within narrow limits. He could not decide by his sole authority, but was obliged to call a council. With the contests respecting images sprung up another controversy respecting the procession of the Holy Spirit. The Latins contended that the Spirit proceeded from the Father and the Son. The Greeks that the Holy Spirit proceeded only from the Father. The Greeks charged the Latins with changing the creed of the church.

It has been alleged that Hosius, Bishop of Cordova, in Spain, added the word *filioque* (from the Son), about the time of the adoption of the Nicene Creed by the Council at Nice.

As an evidence of the increase of superstition in the eighth century, it is related of Gregory III. that he required severe penances of all those who should, through negligence, injure or destroy the Eucharist.

It has been asked by theologians, Was it providence, or permission, or patience, that the dominion called the Papacy grew up in the church? This is a perplexing question. The Papacy was certainly *permitted* for a few centuries to exercise much power. Perhaps, in dark ages, in the time of tyrannical misrule, a great central power in the church averted much evil. Several of the popes did exert themselves to prevent the *wicked divorces* of kings, and took part with the oppressed when civil law was powerless.

CHAPTER XXI.

Gregory I., in 570, as we have already said, had advised Augustine and other missionaries to consult prudence in the arrangement of liturgies, and to permit the Christians of Britain (for instance) to use their own ancient form, if it did not sacrifice the essentials of religion.

But in the time of Gregory VII., 1073, strict conformity was required in the liturgies. The Spaniards were for a long time obdurate, preferring their Gothic liturgy to the Roman form.

There were doubtless some in every country of Europe who received the precious seed of the gospel into honest hearts in this century as in the succeeding centuries; but the prevailing tone of the *visible* church in these middle ages seemed greatly to consist in founding, enriching and embellishing churches and chapels, and in hunting up and venerating the relics of holy men, and in making pilgrimages to the holy places, especially Palestine. Ignorance of the word of God was very general, both in the East and in the West. The true religion of Jesus Christ, if we except the doctrines contained in the Creed, was but little understood or felt at this time. Charlemagne's reverence for the sacred volume was very great. He made many efforts to excite the clergy to a more diligent investigation of the sacred books. He employed Alcuin in revising the Latin translations; indeed, he himself spent a portion of the last years of his life in correcting the errors that had crept in. It has been said that he procured a translation of the sacred books into German; but others attribute this translation to his son Lewis the Pious. Knowing that few of the clergy were competent to explain well the gospels and epistles, as *lessons* used in public worship were called, he directed Diaconus and Alcuin, two of the learned and pious men of his court, to collect from the Fathers *homilies* or discourses on these lessons, that the ignorant teachers might recite them to the people.* The lives of eminent saints, by his direction, were collected into a volume, so that the people might have among them the *dead* examples worthy of imitation, while they had so few among the living.

So long as Charlemagne lived, which was until the year 814, missions were established among the Huns, the Saxons, and others. His son Lewis had the same zeal in propagating Christianity, but he was greatly his inferior in other respects. Two preachers of Christianity were sent under his patronage, in 828, to Jutland and to Sweden. Ansgarius, one of these two missionaries, was very zealous and successful. Returning to Germany in 831, he was made, by the influence of Lewis, Archbishop of Hamburg, a new see, to which Bremen was added. There were more labors and perils in this high position than pecuniary profit. Ansgarius continued to visit the Danes, Cimbrians, and Swedes after his advancement, though sometimes at the peril of his life.

Christian captives, who had been carried by the Normans in their plundering expeditions into Sweden

---

* A chapter in the Old Testament and a chapter in the New Testament are still called first and second lessons.

and other countries, had given these people a favorable idea of Christianity. About the middle of the ninth century two Greek monks — Methodius and Cyril — were sent from Constantinople by the Empress Theodora to the Mesians and Bulgarians, and aftewards to the Bohemians and Moravians. The Teutonic nations had been gradually yielding to the influences of Christianity for three centuries before the Sclavonic nations. The Bulgarians, Moravians, Bohemians, and Poles, inhabited both sides of the Danube.

When Theodora II, in the ninth century, was Empress of the Greek Empire, Bogoris, a prince of Bulgaria, was taken as a captive to Constantinople. He embraced Christianity. When Bulgaria adopted the religion of Christ, Nicholas, Pope of Rome, claimed the country and its *converts*, because it was within the limits of the Western Empire, the Patriarch Photius claimed that Bulgaria belonged to the Greek Church, because Greek Christians had introduced Christianity among them. The Greek monks—Methodius and Cyril—translated the Gospels and the Acts into their own tongue. The Pope Adrian, hearing of their work among the Moravians and Bulgarians, summoned them to Rome. The Pope, after some hesitancy, approved the translation of the Greek bishops.

When Moravia was invaded by the pagan *Magyars*, it was united to Bohemia, and ceased to be an independent kingdom. Bohemia and Poland both received the knowledge of Christ from Moravia. The great achievement of the Byzantine Church was the conversion of Russia.

Ruric, the leader of Scandinavian bands, had established a capital called Novgorod as early as 809. In

955 the Russian Empress Olga visited Constantinople. She then made a profession of Christianity in baptism. The Emperor Constantine Porphyrogenitus was her sponsor. Some years after a Russian Prince, the grandson of Olga, married a sister of the Emperor Basil. The condition required was, that this Prince should accept Christianity. The grandeur of the service in St. Sophia greatly impressed the Russians. It was, however, many years before Christianity gained much ascendency over the old Sclavonic religion. Innocent III, imitating the spirit of Mahomet rather than the master he professed to serve, directed a *crusade* at the sword's point against the heathen of the Northeast of Europe. It was this Pope who permitted and stimulated the fanatical¡De Montfort in a crusade against the Albigenses in the South of France.

We have anticipated the march of events in speaking of the Albigenses in the last chapter. The Albigenses were said to be the remnant of a sect who had sprung up in the seventh century in the Eastern church. They were at first called Paulicians, from the great importance they attached to the writings of St. Paul. Yet this can scarcely be the true origin of the name, inasmuch as they were Gnostics in doctrine and more or less imbued with Manicheism. They protested strongly against the ceremonial character of the ruling church. They rejected baptism by water, but believed in spiritual baptism. The Albigenses, or some of them at least, agreed with the ancient Gnostics in holding to the Persian dualism, and in the opinion that the God of the Old Testament was an evil being. Upon the doctrine of the Trinity there was substantial unity

---

* The Albigenses.

of faith. It is quite certain that their doctrines were not well understood by their enemies, or if understood, they were greatly maligned. Some of them were mystics and ascetics. We find them in 970 in great numbers in Bulgaria. They extended their doctrines by successive migrations in Southern and Western Europe. They became very celebrated in the countries of Provence and Languedoc, in Southern France. Among them were men of learning, rank and substance, with great zeal for their faith.

Raymond, Count of Toulouse, almost an independent sovereign, of the most prosperous and civilized country in Europe refused to persecute his non-Catholic subjects. Pope Innocent III. then proclaimed a crusade against Raymond VI. The war raged from 1208 to 1229. Everywhere fertile fields were laid waste, town and villages depopulated. The Albigenses had among them many enterprising, zealous preachers, who traveled over their land exciting their people to steadfastness. Four councils were called by the Roman See —in 1165, 1176, 1178 and 1179, which successively denounced them as heretics. The war continued through the short reign of Louis VIII.; was ended during the minority of Louis IX. This war *commenced* by Philip Augustus; was, so far as that king was concerned, more a political than a religious movement. The estates of Toulouse were chiefly annexed to the crown, and in this way France gained the control of Mediterranean ports. The most active crusader against the Albigenses was De Montfort, the father of that De Montfort, earl of Leicester, who led the English barons in their opposition to Henry III.

The separation of France and England was made

complete by a law of Louis IX., forbidding any vassal of his to hold estates under another crown. A. D. 1244.

We have spoken of the decline of monasticism in the previous centuries, but now, in the midst of Albigensianism, arose two famous orders. These were the Dominicans and the Franciscans. Dominic was born in 1170, in Old Castile. He could not close his eyes to the contempt in which the clergy had fallen. It is said of him that when he met three legates of Innocent III. returning after a *defeat* by the Albigenses in Languedoc, that he uttered to them a bold rebuke. "It is not by pomp or display that you can impress these people, the heretics; win proselytes by zealous preaching, apostolic humility and seeming holiness." Since the time of the crusades preaching had been greatly neglected by the regular clergy. Now the Friar preachers arose under Dominic and St. Francis. Preaching had been the great forte among the heresiarchs. The *new orders* saw the necessity that these great orators should be answered, whether among the Albigenses or among "the poor men of Lyons," or the disciples of Arnold of Brescia. Dominic sought earnest men from every land and of every tongue, and overspread the land with active, devoted men, whose function was popular instruction.

St. Francis, of Assisi, was full of mystic devotion. He renounced riches both for himself and for his order. All the priests of his order must live upon alms. They must be begging Friars!

It seemed to be the ambition of the Dominicans to make the world one vast *cloister*—not to immure themselves in convents, not to *flee* from the world, as some of the early monks had done, but to subjugate the world. Dominic exercised in Spain the peculiar religious character, which afterwards culminated in Loyola, the founder of the Jesuits, in the sixteenth century. When Dominic and his Friar preachers commenced work at Rome, they were at first received with cold suspicion. But in 1220, seven years after he left Languedoc, he had become Master General of his Order Whenever a Dominican ascended the pulpit a large number of disciples and votaries crowded the churches. Monasteries of their order, for men and women, were established in all the principal places. But, alas, during the dreadful persecution of the heretics in Southern France, the voice of Saint Dominic, lifted in love or pity, was not heard. Throughout the crusade Dominic was not mentioned by either historian or poet. Whether he ever expreased horror or approbation at the cruelties of Simon De Monfort does not appear. His title of founder of the Inquisition,* says Milman, belongs not to history, but to legend. He was born in Old Castile in 1170, of wealthy parentage.

St. Francis was an Italian. He was in early youth gay and full of revelry, but some adverse circumstance led him to view this world through a different medium. His future bride was poverty. He founded the order of Mendicant Friars. The strange, fervent piety of Francis kindled the zeal of many. Innocent III. received St. Francis after some deliberation, saying that the poor men of *the church* must outdo and outwork the "poor man of Lyons." How wise was the policy of Innocent III.

Thus we see that all down the ages new forms of monasticism arose, vitalizing the church in imparting

---

* Dominic's title.

energy and zeal to the people. There was evil mingled with the good, but it was *life*. These orders for a time, the Dominicans and Franciscans, cast into obscurity the Benedictines, the Clugnians and the Cistercians. "The cradle of the first great organization of this kind, A. D. 528, had benefited the world by their care and preservation of the treasures of ancient literature, and by their compilation of great historical works."

The Order of the Carthusians was instituted in 1048. The Monastery of Citeaux became the founder of 3600 convents of the Cistercian Order. The Carmelites founded in Palestine, migrated to Europe in 1238, assuming the rule and name of St. Augustine.*

The Crusades gave rise to several military orders of monks. The Knights of St. John originated in Jerusalem, and derived their name from a hospital in the sacred city, dedicated to John the Baptist. They extended relief to the sick and needy of Jerusalem. They afterwards became military characters, and were divided into three classess: Knights of noble birth, whose business it was to *fight* for religion, priests who conducted the religious services of the order, and *serving* brethren, soldiers of ignoble birth. After the loss of Palestine, the Knights of St. John passed into the island of Cyprus; afterwards they occupied for a long time the Island of Rhodes, until expelled by the Turks. *Malta* then became their possession, obtained by them from Charles V. In 1798 these Knights of Malta betrayed to the French fleet this island, who were then carrying Bonaparte to Egypt. The English then block-

---

* Thalheimer's Medieval History.

aded the island for two years; they took it and still hold it.

The Templars, as an order, derived their name from their residence near the site of Solomon's Temple. They were required, too, to defend the temples of relgion or religious houses, to defend the highways, and protect pilgrims journeying to Palestine. They began at Jerusalem in A. D. 1128.* By their valor and fame they gained vast wealth, which afterwards excited jealousy and cupidity in some of the monarchs of Europe. This order was suppressed by the Pope. They were accused of heresies and crimes. De Molai, the Grand Master, was burned at the stake. He died protesting his innocence.

The third military order were called Teutonic Knights. Frederick Barbarossa raised them to an order of knights. When they returned from Palestine they became missionaries to the Prussians. They introduced Christianity into Prussia. When Dominic and Francis became the institutors of the Mendicant orders, they protested against the wealth and luxury of the monks. About this time Peter Waldo, a rich man of Lyons, sold his possessions, devoting his money to pious uses. His disciples were called the "Poor Men of Lyons." It was to these persons that Innocent III. alluded when he received St. Francis. When Waldo applied to the church for countenance, he was refused. St. Francis remained steadfast to his vows of poverty, but many of his followers wished to be divorced from them. Bonaventura, fifty years after the death of

---

*The Templars. This order was incorporated by Honorius II., under the direction of St. Bernard in 1128. It was suppressed by Clement V. under the influence of the wicked Philip the Fair, 1312.

Francis, said that a begging Friar was dreaded like a robber.

The Institution of Chivalry arose between the time of Charlemagne and the Crusades. This was a strange growth for those rude times. It produced flowers of courtesy, truth and honor, and developed many brave and gallant deeds. This institution, so far as it extended, must have ameliorated the evils of the time. Like every human device, it was not always competent to grapple with fierce passion when interest clashed with fidelity to their vows, their knighthood sometimes trailed in the dust. Chivalry had great sway in France. Mr. Green, the English historian, speaks of Chivalry in France "as a picturesque mimicry of high sentiment, before which all depth and reality disappeared, to give place to a narrow caste spirit and a brutal indifference to human suffering. The word, as it survives among us at this day, is certainly associated with beautiful, manly qualities. We can not but think that this historian's picture is unfair, though there was sometimes affectation and exaggeration mingled with their actions. In the fourteenth century English and French knights united to quell an insurrection, known as La Jaquerie, which threatened to destroy the castles, and which involved the lives and safety of several noble ladies. It is true that war and tyranny had reduced these poor insurgents to a deplorable state, but chivalry was not to blame for that. All classes were not *directly* benefited by it. The time had not come, except in the New Testament, when the rights of the poor and lowly were fully recognized; but chivalry was an advance in the right direction. It was generally the protector of the weak and defenseless. The humanities of chivalry were sanctioned by legal and ecclesiastical power.

The Council of Clermont, 1085, which authorized the first crusade, required that every nobleman's son, at the age of twelve years, should take an oath * before the bishop of his diocese to defend the oppressed, that women of noble birth should have his special care; that traveling must be made secure, and that the evils of tyranny be destroyed. The connection between the church and chivalry was very close. The Tournament ultimately was opposed by the church, because they objected to the expense, and sometimes lives were lost. But these brilliant festivals must have imparted much zest and coloring to the otherwise monotonous lives of the nobility of the middle ages. Gibbon acknowledges the benefits of this institution to refine the temper of barbarians, and its power to infuse some principles of justice and humanity were strongly felt and observed. "Impartial taste," says he, "must prefer a Gothic Tournament to the Olympic games of classic antiquity." Romances of a highly moral and heroic kind appeared in these times, full of incredible adventures, yet the knights were patterns, not of courage merely, but of the higher virtues. They were no less distinguished for modesty, delicacy and dignity of manners.

---

* The *requirements* of a knight when he was instituted seemed to cover the sum of human duty. The union of these English and French knights in the cause of humanity prove that there was among them an esprit de corps.

CHAPTER XXII.

DUNSTAN.

We will now speak of a famous monk of the tenth century. Dunstan was the most remarkable man of his time. "He was the first in a line of ecclesiastical statesmen," says Mr. Green, "who counted among them Lanfranc and Wolsey, and ended in Laud." He was abbot of Glastonbury, bishop of London, and afterwards archbishop of Canterbury. He managed with a master's hand some of the rude kings of Saxon-England. He was energetic and arbitrary. He was a student of books, of music and painting. He built a cell against the walls of Glastonbury cathedral; here he passed much of his time, the people thought in fasting and prayer.

Many legendary stories are told of him. He engraved and illuminated books with the most exquisite designs. He wrought curious patterns in gold and silver, and fashioned utensils of silver for the use of the altar. He so won the love and confidence of Athelstan, by his wisdom in state affairs, by his music and other accomplishments, that it stirred the *jealousy* of the courtiers. These accused Dunstan of magical arts, and so strong was the testimony against him in this superstitious age, that he was banished from the court of his king. He was soon recalled.

One act of cruelty is ascribed to him. When Edwin wished to marry his cousin Elgira, Dunstan, who regarded it as an uncanonized marriage, sent an emissary when she was traveling to brand her face with red-hot iron. This is doubtless a fiction invented by his enemies.

Dunstan introduced the Benedictines into England. He imposed a *penance* of seven years on Edgar, the Saxon king, for his licentiousness. On the accession of the wicked Ethelred, finding that his discipline was unheeded, he retired to Canterbury, and died full of mortification.

Otho III, in 963, the emperor of Germany, sought to raise the character of the Roman bishops. The papacy for sixty years previous had been degraded through the influence of two Roman women of rank and wealth, but unprincipled in morals. They had so controlled Roman affairs as to dispose of the papal crown. The efforts of the young emperor, however, to elevate the papacy were not successful. He died in the dawn of manhood. Two antipopes disputed the title of Gregory VI., bringing the papacy by their unrighteous dealing to the lowest point of degradation. Henry III. then inheriting the empire of Otho, deposed the favorites of the two women to whom we have alluded, and appointed Clement II. A succession of several German popes revived the credit of the Roman See.

During the long minority of the son of Henry III. Hildebrand, a Tuscan monk, produced by his great efforts a strong reaction against the imperial power. He had influenced the election of five popes before he himself was raised to the papal chair, A. D. 1073. He strove for a *celibate* clergy. He sought to fasten opprobrious names on the wives of the married clergy.

He deposed every bishop who had received his *investiture* from lay hands. This matter of investiture was settled in 1122. Lay hands no longer gave the ring and crosier, but the priestly hand touched the scepter in token of homage for the temporalities received.

Hildebrand obtained a *decree* against the married clergy. The Lombard priests quoted the teachings of Ambrose, and the *example* of some of the successors of Ambrose to justify themselves.

One of the flagrant abuses of this time, was the purchase of offices in the church; this crime was called "simony." It was pretended that the Lateran council had desired to avoid this sin when they forbade clergymen to receive benefices from laymen or own allegiance to them.

When Gregory VII. became Pope, Henry IV. being emperor of Germany, there was a bitter struggle between these potentates, that ended only with the life of the pope in exile. It is said that this pope declared to Henry before his election, that when he took the papal chair he would certainly call him to account for the scandals and disorders of which he was known to be guilty. Henry, however, consented to the election of Hildebrand. The Pope commenced his attack on what he deemed the gigantic abuses of the church — "simony" and the marriage of the clergy.

Gregory VII., says Mosheim, was the most daring of all the pontiffs that ever filled the chair of St. Peter. He was greatly excited by the complaints of the Asiatic Christians, in regard to the cruelties of the Mahometans. In the commencement of his pontificate he wished to engage *personally* in a Holy War, and more than fifty thousand men were prepared to march under him. But he was kept too busy at home; it was reserved for others to engage personally in the Crusades, not for him, and of whom we shall speak hereafter.

Hildebrand was a Cluniancier, a monk of the monastery of Clugny. He was a Tuscan. He soon became archdeacon of Rome, and from the time of Leo IX. had governed the pontiffs, as we have before hinted, until his own accession. His great aim and desire was to make the papacy omnipotent; this is proved not only by his acts, but also by his writings. He left certain writings called *dictates*, which embody the most arrogant propositions; he was the vicegerent of Christ, and was not accountable to any mortal. Nearly the whole form of the Latin church was changed by this pontiff; the most valuable rights of councils, of bishops, of religious societies, were subverted and transferred over to the Roman pontiff. His vaulting ambition, so far as he was personally concerned, "overleaped itself." He wished to reduce all kingdoms into fiefs of St Peter; and to subject all causes of kings and princes to the decision of an assembly of bishops who should meet annually at Rome. He was considered a man of extraordinary abilities—intrepid, sagacious and full of resources—but proud, pertinacious, intractable. He had a powerful foe to contend with in Henry IV., the emperor of Germany, and the vigilance of England and France thwarted his ambitious designs.

Much has been said of the humiliation of Henry at Canossa. Gregory VII. was solemnly deposed by the diet at Worms; Henry IV. by the council at Rome. A sentence of excommunication absolved all the subjects of Henry from their allegiance, and declared it a crime to render him any service. The papal authority, more respected in Germany than in *Italy*, encouraged Rudolph of Swabia, with other nobles and bishops, to make a fierce war upon Henry. A diet was called to Augsburg, where the Pope was to preside, and to judge between Henry and his foes. If his excommunication was not then removed, a new sovereign was to be chosen. The emperor in mid-winter traversed some of the wildest passes of the Alps to meet this emergency. It is said he stood bare-foot and fasting for three days at the gate of the castle at Canossa before he obtained a mitigation of the sentence that had been passed upon him; he was required to promise that he would submit his imperial title to the decision of a diet at any place or time his holiness should indicate. The Germans were indignant that their sovereign should have been thus humiliated. As for Henry, he no sooner left the papal presence, than he resumed the war with fresh fury and gained in his next engagement a decisive victory over Rudolph of Swabia. The contest lasted a long time, with alternate victories and defeats. Henry was excommunicated a second time; the Pope sent a crown to Rudolph, who was supported by Swabia and Saxony — also by the wealth of the Countess Matilda, who was the devoted friend of Gregory and who made the church the heir of her vast estate. Ultimately, Rudolph died of a wound received in battle. Henry, in revenge, supported by many German and Italian bishops, in a convention in the Tyrol, created the archbishop of Ravenna supreme pontiff, under the name of Clement III. He was consecrated at Rome, 1080. Henry made several campaigns against the forces of Matilda, who were fighting for Gregory.

Twice Henry besieged Rome in 1084; he became master of a great part of the city.

The Pope Hildebrand meanwhile was shut up in the castle of St. Angelo. He was delivered from his prison by Robert, duke of Calabria and Apulia, and by him taken to Salerno; and *here* it was in the year following that this man, who aspired to rule the world, terminated his days, in the year 1085. His last words were said to be: "I have loved justice, and hated iniquity, therefore I die in exile." In his great desire to have a celibate clergy, he denounced those who lived in virtuous wedlock with their wives, not distinguishing, as he should have done, between honorable men and those who lived in concubinage.

Some of the clergy were at this time very corrupt—there was much outward devotion, but it was not unfrequently divorced from true piety and virtue. The important truth that religion cannot *live*, unless it is based on morality, seems not to have been fully recognized in this age. The Roman head notably took the right side in several instances, in behalf of public morals; as in maintaining the sanctity of the marriage tie, when kings and laymen wished to annul their marriage vows, "but there is a balance sheet on the other side." Unrighteous wars were maintained by some of the popes, and sons were encouraged to rebel against their fathers. The court of Rome in the case of Charles of Anjou did a great wrong in pretending to give what was not hers, and it was attended by terrible results. The blood shed at "the Sicilian vespers cried from the ground against the *foreign* participators."

Western Christendom never fully recognized the Pope as an umpire; there were many dissentients and dissensions in the different kingdoms. "There never was," says Trench in his Medieval History, "a golden age in the Church, nor ever will be, until Christ her Lord shall come."

The *election* * of pope was transferred to the *cardinals* by Nicholas II. under the influence of Hildebrand. This was one of the wisest acts of his policy. Statesmen can consolidate the power of a church, as politicians can increase the power of a state. Leo I., Gregory I., Nicholas I., Gregory VII., Alexander III. and Innocent III. were reckoned as great statesmen.

The exile and death of Gregory VII. were followed by trying times. Clement III., appointed by Henry IV., ruled at Rome, and Henry continued the war with the princes. The friends of Hildebrand had appointed Victor III. to the papacy, but he soon died, having never reigned at Rome.

In 1095, Urban II. having acceded to the papacy, the council of Clermont determined upon the *first crusade* against the Mahometans in Palestine.

But before we enter upon the crusades, we will speak of two remarkable men who lived in England in the eleventh century. One of the first acts of William I. after the conquest † of England, was to send for Lanfranc from Normandy, to aid him in the *reform* of the Church, as he termed it. Lanfranc was raised to the see of Canterbury. His elevation was followed by the removal of most of the English prelates and the appointment of Norman ecclesiastics in their places. The new archbishop did much, says a contemporary, to restore discipline, "as in choosing bishops he consid-

---

* A. D. 1080. † Norman Conquest, A. D. 1066.

ered not so much men's riches or power as their holiness and wisdom." It must, however, have been a grievous thing to the Saxons to see their native clergy displaced for Norman ecclesiastics. Lanfranc opened a famous Benedictine school, to which Berengarius was attracted. He afterwards became celebrated as a controversialist on the subject of the Eucharist. Lanfranc was esteemed as a man of learning and munificence. He improved the monastic system, and built hospitals, churches and cathedrals.

Lanfranc's successor to the see of Canterbury was Anselm. He was so learned and industrious in interpreting the doctrines of the greatest of the Latin fathers, that he has been called the Augustine of the middle ages.* The life of Anselm has been written not only by the brethren of his own order, but by Protestant writers and historians of philosophy.

Anselm was so bold in reproving the rapacity of William Rufus, that he was banished for a time. At the accession of Henry I. he was recalled, and was clothed with much power, both in church and state. Henry wished to marry a Saxon princess, the niece of Edgar Atheling. This lady was detained in a convent by her aunt, the abbess, who maintained that her neice had assumed the *veil*. The princess escaped from the convent and appearing before Anselm at Canterbury, "told her tale in words of passionate earnestness." She had been *veiled* in her childhood, asserted Matilda,

---

* When Anselm was asked by the Norman bishops if he considered *Alfege*, who was killed by the Danes at Greenwich, could be called a martyr, because he died not on behalf of the faith of Christ, he said, "Yes, he was a martyr, because he died for *justice* (to prevent the levying of an unjust tax); justice is the essence of Christ, even though His name is not mentioned.

merely to protect her from rude soldiery. Anselm declared her free from conventual bonds, and when he placed the crown on her head as England's queen, uniting her in marriage to Henry, the joyful shouts of the English multitude drowned the murmurs of either churchman or Norman baron.

Anselm, it is said, possessed much zeal, charity and faith, and differed much in his spirit from his successor, Thomas a Becket.

St. Bernard of Clairvaux was the most influential man of his time. He did not, as Anselm, grapple with the deep questions of philosophy, but with the *practical* issues of his day. St. Bernard was a great organizer. When there were two popes in Europe, Bernard, the abbot of Clairvaux in 1130, was the governing head of Europe. He was the master-spirit that organized the second crusade; his eloquence was irresistible. One hundred and sixty monasteries derived their rules from him. Among his disciples were many bishops and one pontiff, Eugenius III. He left many *writings*. All Christians sing the beautiful hymn attributed to St. Bernard. We will transcribe four verses:—

> " Jesus, the very thought of Thee
> With sweetness fills the breast;
> But sweeter far Thy face to see,
> And in Thy *presence* rest.
>
> No voice can sing, no heart can frame,
> Nor can the memory find,
> A sweeter sound than Jesus' name,
> The Saviour of mankind.
>
> Oh Hope of every contrite heart,
> Oh Joy of all the meek ;

> To those who *fall*, how kind Thou art!
> How good to those who *seek*.
>
> But what to those who *find?*
> Ah *this!* Nor tongue nor pen can show:
> The love of Jesus, what it is
> None but his loved ones *know*.

St. Bernard was called "The Watchdog of the Church." He with energy forbade the persecution of the Jews. There was a schism in the sacred college after the death of Hildebrand. Peter of Leon, the *son* of a Jew, but a cardinal of ability, sought the papacy. He possessed much wealth. Several of the cardinals hostile to Peter called a secret conclave and nominated Innocent II. At the head of this conclave was St. Bernard. Peter for a while by his wealth and ability seemed to overshadow the claims of Innocent. Peter took the name of Anacletus. The Jew's son reigned a short time in Rome. Bernard visited the sovereigns of Europe, and by his earnest appeals secured their assent in setting aside the claims of Anacletus in the secular courts. When he visited the German emperor, he was accompanied by Innocent. Holding the bridle of the horse upon which Innocent rode, the emperor led the candidate for the papacy through the streets of Liége. But *more honored* was the Cistercian monk of Clairvaux than either pope or emperor. He visited the convent of the Carmelites, of which *Heloise* was abbess. Through his influence, it is said, *Abelard* declined to assert his opinions at the council of Sens, in 1140.

St. Bernard was well acquainted with the Scriptures, but quotes chiefly from the Vulgate,* and shows little

---

* "Vulgate," is the translation of the Scriptures in Latin.

acquaintance of the Greek or Hebrew text. It is to be regretted that his sermons in the common tongue have not survived, as he awakened so mighty a revival by his preaching. He once, it is said, healed a feud in an opposing army of the knights and people of Metz on opposite banks of the Moselle. At first they were disposed to despise the eloquent entreaties of the ghost-like old man, but ultimately they united in singing the Gloria in Excelsis, and departed in peace. *He* died at the age of sixty-three, A. D. 1153.

CHAPTER XXIII.

THE CRUSADES.

Palestine was among the earliest conquests of the Saracens.* The Caliph, Omar, took Jerusalem in A. D. 637. The Mahometans *occupied* the Holy City, but the Christians for a long time after its conquest still retained the Holy Sepulchre and the Church of the Resurrection. Pilgrims from all the countries in Europe went thither and were undisturbed. Harounal Raschid, Caliph of Bagdad, and the hero of many Arabian tales, sent the keys of Jerusalem to his great contemporary Charlemagne. These keys were intended as a symbol of safety and security to the Christian visitors of that city. When, however, the Seljukian Turks in the eleventh century took Palestine from the Saracens, they inflicted upon the Christian residents many atrocities, and treated the pilgrims visiting the Holy City with much indignity. The Egyptian Caliphs also sometimes refused protection. These grievances were soon made known to all Christendom. Michael VII., the Byzantine emperor, fearing that the Turks would take Constantinople, sent to Gregory to entreat assistance. Another embassy was sent a few years afterward by Alexis Comnenus to Urban II. Peter the Hermit, an obscure man of Picardy, precipitated the movement. He had gone as a pilgrim to Jerusalem; he had witnessed the wrongs perpetrated upon Chris-

---

* The Arab followers of Mahomet were called Saracens.

tians. His soul was filled with enthusiasm. By his *preaching* he kindled into flame the smouldering fires in the bosoms of the men of the West. In 1096 vast armies left Europe for the East under different leaders. Peter led an army of poor people, many of whom perished miserably. Few of them reached Palestine. A division of this army under Walter * the Penniless, was destroyed in Bulgaria. Peter conducted a large number across the Bosphorus who were destroyed by the Turks. Those cruel barbarians made a pyramid of their bones.

No *king* accompanied the first crusade, but a number of feudal princes. Among these princes was Robert, duke of Normandy, the eldest son of William the Conqueror; Godfrey Bouillon, Raymond, count of Toulouse, Bohemond, of Tarento, Tancred and others. The *first rank*, both in war and council, is due to Godfrey. "Happy," says Gibbon, "would it have been for the crusaders if they had yielded to the sway of that accomplished hero, a worthy representative of Charlemagne, from whom he was descended in the female line. His father was of the noblest race of the counts of Boulogne. Brabant, a province of Lorraine, was the inheritance from his mother. In the service of Henry IV. he had borne the great standard of the empire, he had pierced with his lance Rudolph, the rebel king, and was the *first* to ascend the walls of Rome: he had borne arms against the Pope! His sorrow for that act

---

* Walter was reputed to be a good captain. His followers perished in consequence of the crimes they themselves committed. So little did they comprehend the nature of the mission they had undertaken. Few of them knew anything of the teachings of the Prince of of Peace.

now confirmed, perhaps, a resolution he had made to visit the Holy Sepulchre, not as a pilgrim, but as a deliverer.

Godfrey was accompanied by his brothers Eustace and Baldwin. Godfrey lived on the Rhine and knew the languages spoken on both sides of the river. He was among *heroic men* the hero and the victor of the first crusade, the one who deserved to wear the crown for his good and great qualities.

"*Two* causes, the one moral and the other social, impelled Europe to the crusades. The moral cause was the constant struggle Christianity had had to maintain with Islamism. This struggle began at the close of the seventh century. It succeeded in confining the religion of Mahomet to the south of Spain. The *social* cause was the aspiration of the people for a wider sphere. A vast and unexplored world was laid open to the view of European intelligence by the *consequences* of the crusades. The Crusaders were brought into contact with two states of civilization. The polished Greeks on the one hand (though enervated by luxury), and the Mussulman on the other. Mongol ambassadors, we are told, were sent to Christian kings, to persuade them to enter into alliance for the common interest of the Mongols and Christians.

One of the most conspicuous nobles that assumed the cross in the first crusade was Hugh, count of Vermandois, brother of the king of France. Robert of Normandy attained no distinction, on account of his indolent, easy temper. Stephen, count of Blois, was one of the richest men of his time; he was eloquent and

---

* Guizot.

literary, and was chosen by the chiefs as their president. The legate of the Pope was Adhemar, from southern France. From the same region came Raymond of Toulouse. These two, the prelate and the veteran warrior, assumed the command of large bodies of men. Raymond had fought the Saracens of Spain, he wished now to devote his declining years to the service of the Holy Sepulchre. Bohemond, the son of Robert Guiscard, was already famous for a victory over the Greek emperor. Several Norman princes, together with his cousin, Tancred, accompanied Bohemond. This general is described by historians as unscrupulous and designing, a cool and crafty politician; while Tancred's love of glory and his disdain of wrong and perfidy rendered him the mirror of European chivalry. Both history and poetry describe him as a true knight. He is a favorite of Tasso in his great Epic. It is said that *he*, Tancred, sought diligently to mitigate the sufferings of the defeated at the siege of Jerusalem, when the fanatical crusaders were sating their vengeance in the blood of the Mahometans. It is probable that the romantic interest that surrounds the name of Tancred is chiefly due to Tasso, who in his great poem, "Gerusalemne liberata," makes Tancred the lover of Clorinda, the heroine of the poem. Both poetry and painting have sometimes assumed the garb and authority of history.

Godfrey, of Bouillon, commenced his march from the banks of the Moselle; he conducted his people with admirable prudence and order by the same route that proved so disastrous to the rabble that *preceded* him. When he reached Hungary he demanded from the king an explanation of the circumstances that provoked their destruction. The king exposed the crimes that raised the vengeance of the Hungarians.

Walter was represented as a good captain, but utterly unable to control the host that followed him. He perished in Asia Minor in a conflict with the Turks.

Peter the Hermit reached Palestine in safety, and witnessed the victory that Bouillon and the other leaders achieved. "The grateful multitudes, instructed by the Patriarch of Jerusalem* (who had just arrived in the camp from an exile (in Cyprus), prostrated themselves before the poor *solitary* of Amiens, as a revered and chosen servant of God. How great must have been his joy and gratitude at that moment? His name is never mentioned afterwards." † His success is a striking proof of the power of simple earnestness.

When the crusaders entered the Byzantine provinces their able leader continued to maintain strict discipline. *Alexius, the emperor* of Constantinople, assisted his efforts by supplying the wants of the army in its passage through the desolate forests of Bulgaria, until the first division of the European chivalry had entered into the fertile fields of Thrace. It is possible that the host of Godfrey would have perished, without his aid, in passing amid lands imperfectly cultivated and among barbarous natives. We must look with suspicion upon the reports of some Latin chroniclers, who acknowledge a kind reception at first, but afterwards accuse the emperor of perfidy and hostility. It is probable that the confidence he reposed in the noble designs of Godfrey did not extend to all the

---

* Peter.   † "His work was done."

leaders. Bohemond had been his enemy, and he may have suspected him of a design to subjugate the Eastern world to the spiritual *dominion* of the Latin church, *under the plea* of delivering the Holy Sepulchre from the hands of the Turks. By the decay of the power of the Seljukian Turks,* he had been delivered from the *fear* that his predecessors had felt of the ruin of his empire. The splendor of Constantinople excited great astonishment and perhaps envy in the breasts of the Latins. Hugh, of Vermandois, the two *Roberts* and the Count of Chartres had passed through France and Italy for the purpose of embarkation.

The Pope had given to the brother of the king of France the standard of St. Peter. This Count of France sent a haughty message to the emperor, to *prepare* to receive the standard-bearer of the Pope, and the brother of the king. This message was resented as an insult by the Emperor of Constantinople. The crusaders retaliated. Eventually, the *Count* of Vermandois was taken prisoner, and instead of the magnificent reception he had claimed and contemplated, he entered Durazzo as a suppliant. His brother crusaders now joined their forces with his and compelled or induced Alexius, by severe retaliation, to submit to their wishes. After several collisions of arms and some degrading compliances (as some thought), the crusading levies at length effected a junction on the plains of Asia Minor. The Provençal forces were the last to arise. Tancred had crossed the Bosphorus in disguise, in advance of Bohemond's forces, not wishing to acknowledge himself, as his cousin Bohemond had done, the vassal of a foreign prince.

---

* The Greek emperor.

The Christian hosts now directed their steps to Nice, the former capital of Bithynia, at this time the capital of a Turkish kingdom founded in 1074 by the Seljukian Turks. The Christians captured this city, it is said, by the timely aid and assistance of Alexius. The morning after the defeat of the Turks, the crusading leaders were mortified and infuriated to see the *imperial* banner of Alexius floating over the ramparts of Nice. It will be remembered that in this city *Nice* was the *first council* of the church, held in A. D. 325. The murmurs of the crusading chiefs were soon stifled by honor or interest. In a few days they set out for Antioch. This superb old city, the capital of the Greek Seleucidæ, was *now* in the latter part of the eleventh century, governed by a Turkish Emir. This city had a special historical interest, in the eyes of Christians of every age; to this city, it was said, many Christians had fled after the persecution of Stephen; *here* Paul and Barnabas had preached, and *here*, says the evangelist Luke, "the *disciples* were first called Christians." When the Crusaders reached this famous city there were many (called) Christians yet in Antioch.

Bohemond soon discovering that the Christians were full of discontent, availed himself of the favor of a prominent citizen, who possessed the confidence of the Turkish Emir, to betray the city to them (the Crusaders), but reserving to himself the sovereignty of that great city. But, lo, while the Crusaders were expecting an easy victory, the lieutenant of the Persian king appeared before Antioch with a mighty host; this mighty army had previously been directed against Edessa, the capital that Baldwin had made his own, but hearing that Antioch was likely to fall into the hands of the Christians the Persian general rushed impetuously to Antioch. The *deliverance* of the Crusaders from this mighty host has been ascribed, in a superstitious age, to *miracle*.

The losses of the Christian army had been great before they reached Antioch. The count of Toulouse and the duke of Lorraine were carried in litters. Raymond was ill with disease, Godfrey had been wounded in a contest with a bear. Tancred and Baldwin had been detached sometime before from the main army, with their squadrons of five and seven hundred knights. Honor and fame was the reward of Tancred, but the city of Edessa was the portion of Baldwin, his more selfish rival.

The Christians at Antioch now suddenly find themselves surrounded by the army of Kerbogen, the lieutenant of the king of Persia. The Crusaders were besieged within the city. Among their chiefs there were at least three heroes who were without fear or reproach. Godfrey was sustained by pious hope. Bohemond by ambition; Tancred declared that so long as he had forty knights he would never relinquish a holy enterprise. For twenty-five days the Christian army seemed on the verge of destruction. In this extremity, the choice of servitude or death, they gathered up the *relics* of their strength, sallied from the city, and in *one day* dispersed the host of Turks and Arabians, which consisted, as the uncertain chroniclers of that day report, of hundreds of thousands.

We have alluded to *miracle*. While in great distress at Antioch, a priest of Marseilles pretended that St. Andrew had appeared to him, and disclosed the exact spot where the *sacred lance* lay that had pierced the side of our Lord. This lance was found and put into the hands of one who led the procession of priests on the day that they sallied forth, singing the martial psalm, "Let the Lord arise, and let his enemies be scattered." The enthusiastic shouts were loud and long when the sacred lance was brandished. "Its potent energy was assisted by a rumor or a stratagem of miraculous complexion." Three knights were said to stand on the hill beyond them, dressed in resplendent garments with arms in their hands. Adhemar, the Pope's legate, pointed them out to the people, proclaiming them to be the martyrs St. George, St. Maurice and St. Theodore.* "The tumult of battle," says Gibbon, "gave no time for scrutiny; the welcome apparition kindled into a flame the superstitious enthusiasm of the army." Milman thinks the true cause of the remarkable victory was a terrible feud in Kerbogen's army. Was not this the providence of God? After a delay of several months the *goal* for which they had dared and suffered so much was attained; the reduced army reached Jerusalem. Their victorious banners were planted on the heights of Jerusalem in 1099. Here a new kingdom was established. Godfrey was proclaimed king. It is said he refused the title of king or the crown † from motives of modesty, saying that *he* would not wear a crown of gold where his Master had worn a crown of thorns. He reigned as king, however, and permitted the soldiers who loved him and

---

* This incident at the battle of Antioch *recalls* the old Roman story of the battle of Regillus, when the *leaders* pretended that Castor and Pollux might be seen at the head of their forces. A temple commemorative of this victory was dedicated to them at Rome.

† He refused to be crowned.

wished to remain with him to continue in the city they had helped to conquer, but the discontented and restless returned to Europe. Godfrey died in a year after his conquest, leaving his throne to his brother Baldwin, and his *name* to Christendom,
"One of the few, the immortal names
That were not born to die."

CHAPTER XXIV.

THE CRUSADES—CONTINUED.

Louis VII. of France and Conrad III., emperor of Germany, led the second crusade. They were incited to this by Bernard, abbot of Clairvaux. The new kingdom of Jerusalem was still in the possession of Christians when this second crusade was projected, but Edessa had fallen into the hands of the infidels, and Antioch was threatened. Many of the Christian princes of the first crusade had returned home, and the courage of the Christians in Palestine began to waver. They now begged for new armies of crusaders.

Louis and Conrad collected large armies, and led them to Palestine in 1147. They reached Jerusalem, but did not effect any important results. They returned to Europe in 1149. The second crusade was a failure! A want of harmony among the chiefs of this enterprise rendered futile the great preparations they had made.

In thirty-eight years from the time of their retreat, the famous Saladin, a Saracen, had become viceroy of Egypt and Syria. He had assailed the Christians at the battle of Tiberias, 1187, captured Guy, king of Jerusalem, and in *the same year* captured Jerusalem. For almost a century the Christians had held it as their own. Great was the grief and consternation in Europe when the "Fall of Jerusalem" reached them. The king of the two Sicilies and the kings of England and France at once concentrated plans for a third crusade.

The aged emperor Frederick Barbarossa summoned a diet at Metz, in which he himself and his son, with eighty-eight spiritual and temporal lords, assumed the cross. The emperor crossed the Hellespont, not choosing to go to Constantinople. In Asia Minor he had a battle with the Turks, in which he conquered their capital city, Iconium, after experiencing heavy losses. Shortly after he was *drowned* when bathing in a river of Cilicia. Some writers say, it was the river Cydnus, which had so nearly proved fatal to Alexander the Great. This is the river, too, upon which the Egyptian queen Cleopatra sailed, with great pomp and luxury, to meet Anthony. When the master-spirit, Barbarossa, was taken away, little was done by his army, the remains of which finally reached Acre.

Meanwhile, Richard I.* and Philip Augustus had arrived at Acre. This city surrendered to them 1191. The crusaders, in violation of their word, butchered five thousand Turks, who had been left in their hands as hostages.

During these wars for the possession of the Holy Land arose the three celebrated orders to which we have alluded in another place; the Knights of St. John, the Templars, and the Teutonic Knights, who combined the charities of the Hespitallers with the chivalric vow of the Templars. These last bound themselves to the relief of the sick and the defense of the holy places.

The king of France returned to Europe shortly after the siege of Acre, leaving a part of his army under the conduct of the duke of Burgundy.

---

* King of England—Cœur de Lion.

After Philip's departure, Richard Cœur de Lion prosecuted the war with vigor; he not only vanquished the great Saladin in several battles, but took the cities Jaffa* and Cæsarea in Palestine. When almost in sight of Jerusalem, it is said the French and Italians refused to accompany him, and he was compelled to desist from the undertaking. He made, therefore, a truce with Saladin for three years, three months and three days.

At the close of the first crusade a large portion of Palestine was in the hands of the Christians; at one time only four cities were in the hands of the Turks. But their possessions soon escaped from their grasp, after the third crusade.

Richard at the siege of Acre had offended the duke of Austria, whose revenge was implacable, and caused Richard a long and weary captivity. He regained his liberty by a heavy ransom collected by his mother, Eleanor, and paid to the emperor of Germany.

The fourth crusade was commenced in 1200. Innocent III. was the great mover, and it was chiefly French in its character and composition. They went to Venice in 1202, expecting to be transported in Venetian ships to the Bosphorus. As the people of Venice required a larger sum than they could pay, they agreed to aid the Venetians, in lieu of money, to assist them in taking a town in Dalmatia that had revolted. This they accomplished in defiance of a papal *prohibition*, and without the sanction of their chief, Montserrat. They then went to Constantinople and agreed with

---

* In this city Jaffa, a Christian school is now (1882) taught by some devoted Episcopal missionaries from the *valley* of Virginia, in the United States.

Alexis, the son of the deposed emperor Isaac Angelus, to restore his father to the throne. These princes being restored, soon died in an insurrection of the people. The crusaders, pretending at first to be the champions of the dead princes, waged successful war, took the city, and established a Latin empire at Constantinople which lasted about fifty-seven years. The territory conquered was divided beween the Venetians and their Western associates. In taking the city much that was antique, rare and beautiful was destroyed; sculptures preserved from ancient Greece were destroyed by the rude barbarians. The Venetians, more discerning of beauty, saved the fine bronze horses of Lysippus to adorn a church in Venice.*

Michael Paleologus in 1261 expelled the sixth Venetian usurper and recovered the throne of the Greek empire.

Though Jerusalem had fallen, the Christians still claimed a right to the shadowy crown of Jerusalem. The king of France designated John of Brienne to be the husband of Mary, the daughter of Isabella and Conrad of Montserrat. No nobleman in Palestine was judged so worthy *as he* to share this nominal but perilous honor. John was accompanied from Europe by three hundred knights, the whole contribution at the time, to recover the Holy Sepulchre. This new king of Jerusalem appealed for aid. Innocent III. made a stirring appeal to all western Christendom. Egypt was now the stronghold of the Moslem power.

---

* Over the portals of St. Mark's Cathedral, in Venice, stand the bronze horses of Lysippus, brought from the hippodrome of Constantinople. Lysippus was a sculptor in the time of Alexander the Great, B. C. 330.

The fifth crusade was undertaken by the united forces of Italians and Germans. The commander-in-chief was Andrew, king of Hungary. Honorius III. had now succeeded to Innocent III., 1216. Andrew after one campaign returned to Hungary. The other generals captured the strong city of Damietta in Egypt, A. D. 1220. Their successes were of brief duration, for the next year a Saracen fleet destroyed that of the Christians and cut off their supplies. They lost Damietta.

A new army of crusaders was now enrolled by the legate and missionaries of the pontiff; this army was increased by the idea that their *commander* would be the great Frederick II. This monarch had promised the pope that he would command the army in his own person. Frederick had married Jolanda, the daughter of Brienne, king of Jerusalem, which was an additional reason why he should keep his crusading vow. But under various pretexts he delayed going to Palestine until 1228. Frederick being then excommunicated, he set out with a small retinue to join the forces that were anxiously awaiting his arrival in Palestine. Instead of carrying on the war, he soon terminated it. *

Yet he did much; he made a treaty with the sultan, by which the Christians were to be allowed freely to visit Jerusalem; and Bethlehem, Nazareth and other places were made over to them. He made a truce of ten years with the sultan; the principal condition was that he should be regarded as the king of Jerusalem. When he visited the church of the Holy Sepulchre, it is said

---

*Gibbon says, "Frederick II. despised the phantoms of superstition, and the kingdoms of Asia. He wished to establish the Italian monarchy from Sicily to the Alps."

he took the crown from the altar and put it upon his own head. We suppose the priests would not crown him, as he had been excommunicated.

The fifth crusade was brought to a happy termination, yet the pope's* anger still raged against the emperor. He attempted to inflict many injuries upon him during his absence. The emperor returned to Germany in 1229.

The quarrels of the crusaders in Palestine led to the loss of the good that Frederick had obtained for them. A sixth crusade was proclaimed. The sultan of Egypt determined to be beforehand with his enemies. He entered Palestine, and drove the Christians from Jerusalem. The nobility of England and France determined to go yet again to the relief of Palestine. Theobald, count of Campania and king of Navarre, with other French and German princes, went in 1239; Richard of Cornwall, the brother of Henry III. of England, in 1240. The English were well received by the Christians, whose affairs they reëstablished. Jerusalem and the greater part of Palestine were surrendered by the sultan of Egypt; the walls of Jerusalem were rebuilt and the churches reconsecrated.

The objects of this expedition having been gained by negotiation, some writers do not reckon it in the number of crusades. It is usually, however, called the sixth crusade.

A seventh crusade was proclaimed in 1245. Jerusalem was again in the hands of the Egyptians. This crusade, it is said, grew out of a great Mongol movement that terrified the world in the thirteenth century.

---

* Gregory IX.

Christians and Mussulmans now leagued together against the common enemy. Acre had now become the refuge of the Christians, and was the only important place left of all their former possessions in Palestine.

Louis IX., St. Louis of France, was the leader of the seventh crusade. A large army assembled at Cyprus. The English joined it there under the command of Edward,* prince of Wales, afterwards Edward I. of England. After much delay they went to Egypt. Louis had some success at first, having captured Damietta, a strong city of Egypt, but disasters dire soon followed. The heroic king was taken prisoner, and after spending four years in Palestine, an immense sum of money was paid for his ransom, and he returned to France with a few followers in 1254. Great, indeed, was the cost of blood and treasure paid for the temporary victories and uncertain tenure by which they held the holy places.

Louis renewed the war in 1269, as he supposed he had not yet satisfied his solemn vow to God. He died at Tunis, in 1270, of a pestilence which swept off the greater part of his forces.

In 1291, by the capture of *Ptolemais* by the Mohammedans, the empire of the Latins in the East became extinct.

The loss of Palestine was attributed far more to the disunion of the Christians than to the valor of the enemy. There was much profligacy among those who called themselves Christ's soldiers, and there was much ignorance and obstinacy among the papal legates, who

---

* Edward was two years in Palestine. His feats of valor, according to Gibbon, were as great as those of his uncle, Richard I.

often thwarted the well-planned measures of the heroic and the true.

With Gregory X. the crusades ended, one hundred and seventy-seven years from the time the first had been preached. The king of Jerusalem, the patriarch, and the great master of the Hospital escaped to Cyprus. Many thousands at the last storming of Acre were slain with the sword; some perished on the scaffold. The churches and fortifications of the Latin cities were demolished. *Silence* reigned upon the coast which had so long resounded " with *the world's debate.*"

CHAPTER XXV.

END OF THE CRUSADES.—LOUIS IX.

The crusades *began* at the close of the eleventh century and lasted through the twelfth and thirteenth. Until the war for the recovery of Jerusalem, Europe had never been moved by a common sentiment, nor acted in a common cause.

"The principal effect of the crusades," says Guizot, "was their tendency to the emancipation of the mind and a decided progress towards liberal ideas. With Gregory expired the crusades! For nearly two centuries these wars had connected as a principle of union the countries of Western Asia with Europe. This tie was broken. No longer could the Pope *claim* a title to exact a tribute from a vassal world. The high tides of the Papacy began to ebb in 1303. The last convulsive effort for the world's dominion was made by Boniface VIII. It ended in the *captivity* of Avignon.

For seventy years Rome was deprived of the presence of her chief bishop. Avignon was their place of exile. After the death of Gregory X. three successive Popes passed away in three years — Innocent V., Hadrian V., and John XXII. The last was killed by the falling of a roof of a noble chamber, which had been erected specially for him. We have spoken of two crusading expeditions of the good Louis IX., of France. There was an interval of twenty years between the two visits of Louis to the East. He spent this time in improving the condition of the Gallican State and church. Louis, assisted by the lawyers of France, issued an edict called the Pragmatic Sanction. This edict limited the power of the clergy, in denying to the *Court of Rome* the power of ecclesiastical taxation ; also limiting their interference in the election of the clergy. This Pragmatic Sanction became a charter of independence to the Gallican Church. Among the dearest objects of St. Louis was the reformation of the clergy. The high religiousness of this king, together with the unsettled state of the Papal hierarchy, enabled him to promulgate this charter of liberty without disturbance.

Henry II. of England had labored in the twelfth century to achieve a similar result, but he had to contend with a most formidable opponent in Thomas à Becket, Archbishop of Canterbury. Henry's solicitude was not on account of the corrupt lives of the clergy, but his anxiety was directed to the curtailment of their power. In the Council of Clarendon, A. D. 1164, articles were drawn up by the king and ratified in a full assembly of the great lords, barons, and prelates, wherein the prerogatives of the bishops and clergy were circumscribed within narrower limits, and the regal power in respect to the clergy more accurately defined. By these articles the clergy were made amenable to the laws of the land, if they were guilty of crime, and as liable to punishment as laymen.

There were many other points discussed at this council, all tending to show that the king, and not the priest, should govern the *State* in England. Becket refused to submit to these regulations, pretending that they were injurious to the divine rights of the church at large, and of the Roman Pontiffs. Becket, as Chancellor of England, had administered his high office with great ability, living, however, in great luxury and ostentation. When he was afterwards made Archbishop of Canterbury, he renounced the vain pomp of the world, and living as an ascetic he induced the people to believe that he was possessed of great sanctity and holiness. He refused to sign the constitution of Clarendon. He fled to Avignon, to Alexander III., who was an exile there.

Becket returned to England, but was still inflexible in his opposition to the salutary laws enacted at Clarendon. This contest of Becket was a struggle for power. Henry II. had kingly qualities. He was chivalrous and brave, but *passionate*, lustful, and sometimes cruel. But through all this trouble between the king and Becket the Archbishop utters no warning voice against the vices of Henry and his infractions of the moral law, but complains loudly of the king's disobedience to the hierarchy. The tragical death of Becket is well known. Henry was annoyed with the dogmatism of this prelate and his interference with the affairs of the State. In hasty passion he cried out, "Will no one rid me of this turbulent man?" Some servile courtiers heard his rash words. Hoping for reward, they secretly set out for Canterbury. These ruffians slew the prelate at the foot of the altar. Becket had fled thither, hoping that the sanctity of the place would protect him. But these degraded ones were dead to any such influence. The king was overcome with remorse when he heard of the deed. He went to Canterbury and submitted to a scourging on *his body*, as a penance for the *sin* of *his soul*. He could not have given to *man* an evidence of more bitter repentance. Was it acceptable to God? *It is said* the wretched assassins fled in abject fear to the Pope, and obtained absolution on *condition of perpetual exile.* Who can forgive sins but God alone? "The blood of Jesus Christ cleanseth from all sin." Christ, the High Priest, has given authority to his ministers to *declare* forgiveness of sins to all who, by repentance and faith, turn to him. A declaration of absolution on the conditions of true faith and penitence may give, and has given, comfort to souls distressed on account of sin.

But in a wilderness, in every place and nation without priest or altar or audible voice, the offering of a contrite heart will be accepted and absolved. This *absolution* rests upon the word of God, that can not be broken. Nevertheless, Christ did appoint special ministers of his word to administer consolation to his disciples when he had ascended to his father. Becket was murdered in the year 1170. He was enrolled, as we have said, among the martyrs and glorified saints.

NOTE ON BECKET'S TOMB AT CANTERBURY.—The shrine of Becket was for three centuries a centre of reverence and adoration, not only to the English, but to all the countries of Europe. It was in the twelfth century that the relics of the dead bodies of those esteemed to be saints were held in the highest reverence. Multitudes of people and the proudest monarchs journeyed to Canterbury with votive offerings of gold and jewels. In 1370 the spirit of Sudbury, Bishop of London, was stirred within him when he saw blind devotees journeying to the shrine of Becket. He remonstrated with the people on the "mischievous superstition," but some of them hurled imprecations against him. In 1513, at the dawn of the reformation, Erasmus and Colet visited this famous shrine. The treasures amassed on this altar were enormous. They were filled with disgust and contempt at the idolatry they witnessed. In 1538 this jeweled shrine, this hold of superstition was destroyed by the order of Cranmer. It is said that Mary Tudor, during her reign of five years, wore upon her breast the most precious gem taken from this famous shrine.

Numerous pilgrimages were made to Canterbury, the place of his burial. Monarchs from France and Germany, at different periods, prostrated themselves on the pavement that covered the bones of St. Thomas à Becket. There is a vulgar superstition among kings as among other men. The honest voice of Wickliffe denounced this mummery with much effect. So gorgeous were the decorations of art, so resplendent the jeweled memorials that past centuries had gathered round this tomb, that some lovers of the beautiful in art, even Dean Stanley in his "Notes on Canterbury," seemed almost inclined to drop a tear on the now vacant places. In his own eloquent words he says, "It is true that reverence for the dead ought never to stand in the way of *the living*, that when any *evil* is avoided, or any good attained by destroying old recollections, no historical or antiquarian tenderness can be pleaded for their preservation. No great institution perishes without cause."

Alexander III., the same Pope to whom Becket had fled for refuge, deprived bishops and councils of the right of *designating* who should be worshiped as saints. He determined that canonization should be decided solely by the Pontiff. Alexander III. also claimed the right of creating kings. This power had been claimed by the Popes since the time of Hildebrand, but Alexander was the first Pope that actually *used* this power. At this time the election of Popes by cardinals assumed the forms they still retain. In the same century that Becket lived in England, Arnold, of Brescia lived in Italy. He was a pupil of the famous Abelard. Arnold was a man of learning and pure morals. Arnold attempted, in the middle of the twelfth century, a civil and ecclesiastical revolution in Italy. He saw th evils that arose from the vast riches of the clergy. He thought that the interests of the Church required that they should be deprived of many prerogatives. He was persecuted by St. Bernard, who probably misunderstood him regarding him as a dangerous man. Adrian IV. so feared the spread of his doctrines that he sent him, into exile. The people sustained him. Fredcrick I. delivered him up to the pope. He was executed, his body was burned, and his ashes cast into the sea lest the people should venerate his corpse. But of all the leaders and sects that arose in this century, none obtained so great reputation for probity and innocence as the Waldenses. Peter Waldo did not aim to inculcate new articles of faith, but he strove to restore the Church to its primitive form, to purify the morals of the clergy, and to restore the apostolic simplicity which they had learned from the words of Christ. The Waldensian Church was governed by bishops, presbyters, and deacons, for they supposed these orders were instituted by Christ or his apostles. They taught, as our modern Protestants do, that in the time of Constantime the Great, the Church began to degenerate from her original sanctity. They denied the *supremacy* of the bishop of Rome. Their doctrines seem to have been almost identical with the teachings of Claude, bishop of Turin, who lived in the ninth century, and of many others all down the ages, whose names are not conspicuous in the calendars of earth, but whose registry is in heaven.

In the fourth council of the Lateran, A. D. 1215, Innocent III. published three decrees which contained enactments not only to increase the power of the pontiffs, but attempted to widen the religious system by adding new doctrines, or as they are called, articles of faith. Previous to this time there had been various opinions as to the manner in which the body and blood of our Lord are present in the Eucharist. No public decision had as yet * *defined* what must be held and taught on this point. Innocent pronounced at this fourth council of the Lateran that *view* to be the true one, which is now universal in the Roman Church. He consecrated also the hitherto unknown term of transubstantiation. He required it to be held as an article of faith that *all* are bound to confess to a priest. Confession of sin was held to be a duty; but until now every one was at liberty to confess mentally to God alone, or orally to a priest.

The reception of both these dogmas was enforced simply upon the injunction of Innocent III. In 1260 a strange fanatical sect arose, called Flagellants. These deluded people ran about the cities and town with whips in their hands lacerating their almost naked bodies, that by this voluntary punishment they might obtain pardon for their sins. These extreme views had doubtless arisen from the teachings they had received from the monks of the mendicant orders. Their turbulence and extravagance soon produced disgust, and both emperors and pontiffs issued decrees to stop this religious or superstitious frenzy.

A strange controversy filled all the schools of Europe for many centuries. The respective disputants were called Nominalists and Realists. There was also a third called Conceptualists, an intermediate doctrine between the two. So very metaphysical were these

---

* Thirteenth century.

points of controversy that we shall merely hint at the existence of the controversy and some of its consequences, without attempting definition.

Some maintained that *general ideas* are *things* that have real existence. These supported their opinions by Plato and Boethius, and were called Realists. Nominalists, on the contrary, asserted that *general ideas* are nothing more than *words* or *names*. These quoted the authority of Aristotle. Its origin, says Mosheim, some trace back to the controversy with Berengarius on the Lord's Supper, because the opinions of the Nominalists might be used *very* conveniently in defending the doctrine of Berengarius respecting that sacrament. The germ of this scholastic controversy is doubtless to be found in the opposition of Plato and Aristotle concerning the nature of ideas. The eloquent Abelard * was a Nominalist.

Albert Magnus and his disciple, the famous Thomas Aquinas, were Realists. Roscellinus, in the eleventh century, in applying his Nominalist doctrines to theology, was accused of *tritheism*, since by denying the validity of abstract ideas he could respresent the Trinity as only a nominal and unreal unity. He was condemned by the synod of Soissons in 1092, and obliged to retract his assertions. Nominalism from this time fell under the suspicion of the church. Anselm, Archbishop of Canterbury, was its chief opponent. "John, of Salisbury, wrote that there had been more time consumed in the discussion of these metaphysical points than

---

* Abelard has been accused of heresy in doctrine. He was probably a *heretic* in *morals*.

† Nominalists claimed that there was no such thing as an *abstract* animal or tree in general, but individual objects.

the Cæsars had employed in the conquest of the world; that the riches of Crœsus had been exhausted upon it, and that the contending parties, having spent their whole lives upon this point, could not determine it to their satisfaction, nor could they find in the labyrinths of science, where they so long groped, that it was worth the pains they had taken."

So shadowy, so intangible and unsubstantial was this question of dialectics! Yet in this long quest these learned, ingenious intellects doubtless found many grains of golden truth, amid the depths of dross they attempted to sound.

The era of schoolmen and mystics was a remarkable era in medieval times. Bonaventura, a Franciscan of Lyons, in France, was a remarkable man. He, like Aquinas, was a celebrated lecturer. The thirteenth century boasted of many men of inquisitive minds, acute understanding, and uncommon penetration in regard to abstruse and difficult subjects, though they assented to various things that have since been proved incorrect. The great mistake some of these learned doctors made was an attempt to examine religious subjects by the powers of reason and human sagacity, rather than by the Scriptures. Some pious men warned the theologians of Paris to avoid the subtleties of philosophy, and to teach the doctrines of Christ by his *word.*

CHAPTER XXVI.

"Sir, didst not thou sow good seed, in thy field? Whence then hath it tares? And he said, An enemy hath done this" (Matt. xiii. 27).

It is not remarkable that after transubstantiation began to be received by the Church (though with many dissentients *), that the consecrated bread of the Eucharist should receive divine honors. Splendid caskets containing this bread, or *the host*, as it was called, were carried from house to house.

This superstition reached its zenith, when the festival of the body of Christ was instituted. A *nun* of Liége declared that she had been instructed that an annual festival should be kept in honor of the Holy Supper, or rather of the body of Christ. Few persons believed in her vision. Yet such was the superstition of the time, and *the power* of the hierarchy, that Robert, a bishop of Liége, affecting to believe in this *vision*, ordered this *new* festal day in 1246. But it was not generally observed until Urban IV., in 1264, *imposed* the festival of Corpus Christi on the whole church. Clement V., in 1311, confirmed the edict of Urban at the council of Vienna.

We suppose the observance of this festival of Corpus Christi has done no special harm, but we are simply attempting to relate *how* many superstitious ceremonies crept into the Church without any authority

---

* Scotus strongly opposed this doctrine in the ninth century, and the famous Beranger of Tours in the eleventh century.

from the Chart,* by which they professed to be guided, and without the tradition or example of the primitive Church.

Boniface VIII. added the year of Jubilee to the ceremonies of the Church in the fourteenth century. This pontiff declared to all Christendom that all who should visit the temples of Peter and Paul at Rome, at the close of each centennial year,† should have plenary forgiveness of their sins. When *his* successors found that it brought much *gain* to the Church of Rome, they shortened the period, first to half a century, then to thirty-three years, and lastly to twenty-five years, continuing, as we believe, to the present time.

A humiliating succession of false *doctrines* had now been brought in the Church — Mariolatry; the invocation of saints; the great value of virginity; the working of miracles by relics; the satisfaction of sins by gifts to the clergy; transubstantiation; the virtue of pilgrimages; the forbidding of the Bible to the laity.

In speaking of the false tenets that had been adopted by the Church, or at least by many of its teachers, during the dark ages, an ingenious writer ‡ supposes that it was due to a deterioration of *race*. "The old Roman element," he says, "had been eliminated through the republican and imperial wars, and also through the slave system. The half-breeds, of which the Peninsula was full, degenerated more and more. Blood degeneration implies *thought* degeneration. The early bishops of Rome were men of Roman blood and Roman heroism, but the later pontiffs, whose

---

* The New Testament. † A centennial year was approaching.
‡ Mr. Draper.

lives were so infamous, and thoughts so base, were engendered of half-breeds. Ideas and dogmas, that would not have been tolerated in the old Roman race, found acceptance in the festering mass of the new Italian population."

This is indeed a subtle question ; the physiological state, has, as he suggests, doubtless some connection with the ethnical element, but when it is remembered, that the old Roman race previous to Christianity embraced the most absurd superstitions, we must look to a more obvious cause for this adulteration of doctrine. The false views of religion that crept into the Church were mainly due to the ignorance of the people of the written word of God, and also to the great power and wealth that were lodged in the hands of fallible men. Some of these men, aspiring to be "Lords over God's heritage," brought evil of every kind into the Church that Christ and His apostles had established. With many attendant evils, however, there was Christian truth at the foundation that could not pass away, giving rise to many blessings, in spite of the degradation and wickedness of man. The civil law had been greatly improved by Christianity. The idea of personal moral accountibility was more precise than formerly. The sentiment of charity was exemplified not only in individual acts, but in permanent establishments for the relief of affliction, and the spread of knowledge and truth as they held it. Some of the ecclesiastics who had risen from the humblest ranks, true to their democratic instincts, were inflexible. supporters of right against might.

Rome, from her central seat, aspired to be all-seeing and take in a hemisphere at a glance. Her influence touched the king in his palace and the beggar at the monastery gate. Every one received their names at her altar; her bells chimed at the marriage or tolled at the funeral. Her prayers claimed a power to give repose to the souls of the dead. Thus did a chain of sweet influences bind the sons and daughters of the Church.

Christian funerals were *sometimes* celebrated with magnificence as early as the fourth century. Jerome speaks of the funeral of Fabiola as comparing in splendor with the triumphs of Roman generals. This Roman lady had spent a large fortune in alms-giving, and had founded the *first* hospital at Rome.

As regards the sacred and consoling services of the Church at the baptism, the bridal, or the tomb, these things are as true of Protestant Christianity as they ever were or are of Roman Christianity. But we must say of the Church of the Dark Ages (as it is called), that while it was often oppressive and exacting to the rich and powerful, to the poor and penitent it was usually "as the shadow of a great rock in a weary land."

In the thirteenth and fourteenth centuries the pontiffs had fierce conflicts with heretics, as the Romish Church called those who questioned their authority, or who rejected their dogmas — dogmas or opinions not taught in Scripture, but imposed on their consciences by the arbritrary power of *some* of the popes.

The Albigenses, the Waldenses and other sectaries, had spread themselves over the valleys among the Alps, Southern France, Germany and portions of Spain, threatening danger to the Roman domination. These people were remarkable for their spirited preaching. Preaching among the regular clergy had become almost obsolete until the rise of the Dominican and

Franciscan clergy, who, seeing the success of the Albigenses, became zealous preachers from country to country.

The monks had kept through very troubled times of social life the best pattern of religious devotion; they had executed wonders in illuminating and preserving manuscripts; but there came a time,* especially in England, when their rules fell into neglect and disuse. In the time of Wyckliffe the mendicant monks had become objects of ridicule and scorn.

Eyery reader of Church history must feel, as he comes down the ages, that, despite the corruption of the clergy and the ignorance of the laity, there were some loving and true hearts that burned with a desire to open the Scriptures, and to enlighten the people as to the true teaching of the Word of God. As in the days of Elijah the prophet there were seven thousand who had never bowed the knee to Baal, though the prophet blindly supposed he was the *only* true worshiper in the land of Israel, *so* in Christian Europe, in the fourteenth century, there were many who turned their faces heavenward, and who sought the lips of the Priest that kept knowledge.

The power at Rome did sometimes repress an injustice, but in calling so many cases to Rome for decision, she deprived in this way the national churches and States of their rights of self-government. The monasteries sometimes desired exemption from the bishops of their dioceses, and were willing *to pay* the papal court to decide for them according to their wishes. The papacy became the seat during the four-

---

* In the fourteenth century.

teenth and fifteenth centuries of enormous *simony*, from the decision of causes, from indulgences, and from selling the offices of the Church. The papacy sunk into a slough so deep, that she could not *of herself abate them*—some futile efforts were made. The riches of the papal court were to *many* as the breath of life. Some of the popes saw and felt the need of reform, but during the *few years* they sat in the papal chair, they were unable to cope with the tremendous issues.

The scholar and the mystic were united in some of the great characters of this period. Eckart, a Dominican, was a leader among the mystics. As scholasticism declined, mysticism increased. Thomas à Kempis, whose writings are well known in modern days, was a famous mystic. In 1324 the terrible disease black death stalked abroad, in seven years sweeping away two-thirds of the population. There was something in mysticism that seemed adapted to such awful periods. There was, too, at this time a great *conflict* between Church and Empire.

But religion, as we have already said, found a sanctuary in some devout hearts. In the darkest periods, our Lord has had a Church upon earth, an *invisible* within the visible. There were many *names*, doubtless, written in the Lamb's Book of Life that were not registered or canonized upon earth. The great head of the church, though not so *manifestly*, was carrying forward then, as now, a work of grace and power in the hearts of his people.

The first teacher who shook with lasting effect the power of the hierarchy, was John Wycliffe, of Lutterworth, England, in 1348. The Teutonic constitution of England, as we have said in another place, had not only restrained the Norman power of the crown, but the Latin despotism of the papacy. In the days of Becket, the clergy had striven to escape trial for crimes in the civil courts, but in the time of Wycliffe, a century and a half later, the hand of the civil law did not scruple to arrest an ecclesiastic accused of crime. In the reign of the feeble Edward II., Clement V. commanded the persecution and ruin of the Templars. With some opposition the mandate was ultimately obeyed. The papal power exercised in England varied with the ability of the monarch; this was manifested in the reign of the cowardly King John, who became a vassal to the pope, A. D. 1215.

John Wycliffe was born in Yorkshire in 1324, just before the accession of Edward III. to the throne of England. England was at this period a land of schools; Oxford and Cambridge were in high repute—they were then thronged with thousands, instead of the *hundreds* who now enter their classic halls. Wycliffe became a student at Oxford. These instutions of learning were open to the humble; this was an element of strength to the Church in the fourteenth century, as it is a source of strength to the Romanists in the nineteenth century. The most humble were brought through their colleges of learning, to take rank with the highest in the realm. Arms, and the Church, were then the only two *professions*. The lawyers and physicians of this day were ecclesiastics. .

John Wycliffe was admitted to Queen's College, Oxford. This college had just been founded by Philippa, the noble wife of Edward III. In the latter part of the thirteenth century Roger Bacon had been a lecturer at Oxford. Bacon was esteemed the father of

English science. His researches opened the way for many modern discoveries, especially the use of gunpowder, which he is said first to have made.

NOTE.—From the days of Cædmon in the seventh century, portions of Scripture had been translated into the vulgar tongue, but they were fragmentary and had fallen out of use. Wycliffe determined to translate the *whole Bible*, and send it through the land. Like the apostles, he put the ministry of the Word, not *the Sacraments, in front*. In the Eucharist, the reformers of Wycliffe's day saw *unchanged* the bread and wine, but they believed Christ's body and blood were truly present.

CHAPTER XXVII.

WYCLIFFE CONTINUED—HUSS.

Wycliffe, shortly after he entered Oxford, removed to Merton, the older, wealthier and more famous of the Oxford foundations. Statesmen and prelates, kings and queens had founded six colleges at Oxford for poor scholars. The university held the supreme authority. There were also some halls where some scholars dwelt and studied under the ordinary academic discipline. There must have been a renaissance or revival of learning in England as well as in Italy in the early part of the fourteenth century. Some great teachers had preceded Wycliffe at Merton, such as William of Ockham, whose teachings shattered the foundations of Papal supremacy; also the learned Bradwardine, who adopted the predestinarian doctrines of Augustin.

Wycliffe's promotion to offices of high trust prove the extent and depth of his studies. His varied erudition, says Milman, is probably due to his studies at Oxford; but his mastery over the vernacular English, the high supremacy which he vindicated for the Scriptures, which, by great toil, he promulgated in the vulgar tongue, these were his own, to be learned *in no school*. These were to be attained by none of the ordinary courses of study. As Chaucer, his contemporary, was the father of English poetry, so was Wycliffe the father of English prose.

When Wyccliffe was first summoned to appear at

St. Paul's, before the Archbishop of Canterbury, he was accompanied by the Duke of Lancaster, John of Gaunt, as he was usually called, the son of Edward III. Nothing is known of the specific charges made against Wycliffe at this examination. About this time the king's ministers were anxious to procure a sum of money which was in the hands of the Pope's bankers. They applied to the University of Oxford for legal sanction to obtain this money. Wycliffe was employed by these ministers to give his opinion as to the *right* of possession. Wycliffe declared boldly that the necessities of the nation have the *first claim* to all moneys raised within the realm. Wycliffe quoted the venerated name of St. Bernard as *authority*. Meanwhile information of the opinions of Wycliffe and his bold advocacy of them reached the Papal Court at *Avignon*. Gregory XI. dispatched three bulls to Canterbury. The Pope demanded that *his* opinions should be examined, and if erroneous, that he should be imprisoned or cited to appear before him (the Pope) at Avignon. His mandates were coldly received. The opinions at first that were censured as wrong, entirely related to the ecclesiastical power. His creed was not as yet charged with heresy.

A second trial came. He is not now attended by the nobles, but by the common people. They forced their way into the chapel, and by violent menaces and gestures, alarmed the prelates. In the midst of this tumult a nobleman entered, and in the name of the Princess of Wales, now at the head of the administration, forbade further proceedings.

Wycliffe drew up replies to some of the charges relating to political disputes between the ecclesiastics and the State. He boldly declared that church property was not *inalienable* if not applied to a proper use. It may be forfeited, and under certain circumstances the temporal power can enforce the forfeiture. He taught that the spiritual power of excommunication and absolution depend for their validity on strict conformity to the law of God. Wycliffe declares himself a sincere churchman, and by no means denies the jurisdiction of the Church. His opinions have been formed from Holy Scripture,* and he is ready to defend them to the death.

The death of Gregory XI. stops for a time the prosecution of Wycliffe. A schism follows in the Papacy. Wycliffe became more and more the antagonist of the hierarchy. The lower clergy reverenced him. Oxford did not repudiate him. He organizes an order, who travel through the land, preaching sometimes in the churches and sometimes in the highways and market-places. These itinerant teachers supplanted the mendicant orders in popularity, who had now fallen from their high estate. The gross corruption of the begging friars in the days of Wcycliffe drew him into a controversy with them. In their early history these Friars had been estimable and devout. They had sunk at this time into the worst repute. The itinerants sent out by Wycliffe, with the English Bible in their hands, presented the foundation truths of the New Testament with such power, that the depths of the soul were stirred and thrilled. Many of these hearers had had only the symbolic teaching of the ritual. Others were without any instruction.

---

* And the teachings of holy doctors.

But under the preaching of Wycliffe and his followers "the dry bones of unbelief and ignorance" were breathed upon by the Spirit of God, as in the days of the prophets. He sent *out* the portions of the English version to the people as he finished them. It was the bitter complaint of one of Wycliffe's adversaries that laymen and women who could read were better acquainted with the Scriptures than some of the lettered clergy.

As Wycliffe advanced in his studies he began to question not only the power of the Pope, but some of the doctrines of the Church. He now rejects unequivocally the materialism of transubstantiation. The Eucharist, he declares, is Christ's body and blood, spiritually, sacramentally; but the bread and wine are not changed. They co-exist in the mind of the believer. Wycliffe was summoned *to appear at Grey Friars* before Courtenay. The meek and moderate Sudbury, the predecessor of Courtenay, had been murdered by a mob. This synod was called together to examine for the third time into the doctrines of the great preacher. This assembly cunningly tried to prove Wycliffe an enemy to temporal as well as ecclesiastical authority. Unfortunately about the time of this trial there was some insurrection and disturbances, which had not any connection with the teaching of Wycliffe's disciples. These troubles evidently arose from excessive taxation.

The famous seditions of Wat Tyler, Jack Straw

NOTE.—The Council at Constance condemned the books of Wycliffe to be burned. His bones were dug up after his honored remains had laid under the choir at Lutterworth forty-eight years. His ashes were thrown into the nearest river.—GEIKE.

and others occurred about this time. The wars of Edward III., and the minority of Richard II., caused much pecuniary pressure and financial disturbance. The wily enemies of Wycliffe tried to connect the new doctrines with the disturbed state of the country, which was obviously the result of odious and unwise taxation. Twenty-four *articles* of Wycliffe were arraigned; ten were condemned. Among these was the denial of transubstantiation. An act was passed by the lords and promulgated by the king, that all the preachers of Wycliffe, as his disciples were called, should be imprisoned, that they might answer in the bishop's court. This was the first statute of heresy ever passed in the realm of England. It is well known that the opinions of all reformers are liable to exaggeration. The grand courage of Wycliffe enabled him to sustain the odium, strengthened as he was by the sublime desire of enlightening and converting the souls of his fellow-men Oxford continued to be the centre of his influence. Scholars crowded around the university pulpit, while the Carmelites, who also preached at Oxford were compelled to declaim to empty churches. Wycliffe, when summoned to appear for the last time, declined to appear. No special notice was taken of his contumacy. He may have been suffering from sickness. He cast back upon the council of the Grey Friars the calumnious aspersions with which they had assaulted him. *Wycliffe, at his home in Lutterworth, and in the villages around it, was a bold preacher in the vernacular or vulgar tongue, understood by the people; but at Oxford, before the convocation, his

---

* Milman's Christianity.

speech was full of acuteness and subtility and logical versatility; the most experienced master in the university.

The Augustinian monks publicly promulgated his condemnation on the subject of the Eucharist. He was unyielding on this point. When he received his *censure* he was sitting in the professor's chair. With calm pertinacity he said, "On this point all have erred but * Berengarius."

Wycliffe retired unmolested to Lutterworth. There was as yet no statute in England for the *burning* of heretics. No officer in England would have obeyed the mandate of the church without legal warrant. Wycliffe died in 1384. The austere life of Wycliffe has defied calumny. He was exemplary in his whole conduct.†

Chaucer's sympathy with Wycliffe is expressed in his praise of the poor parson, who followed Christ's love and his apostles, before he taught it to his flock. His industry was wonderful. The number of his tracts almost baffles calculation. His translation of the Scriptures, *in parts*, was a prodigious achievement. His ideal was the restoration of the pure, moral and religious supremacy in religion—refusing to separate the weighty matters of the law from the anise and cumin.

In Wycliffe's translation of the Scriptures is laid

---

* Berengarius lived in the eleventh century. He appeared before Hildebrand to be examined on his views. He was not condemned by Gregory VII. In his controversies with *Lanfranc* he certainly denied transubstantiation; but it is difficult to arrive at his precise views, as he used ambiguous phrases.

† Thalheimer.

the foundation of Protestantism; but he built no edifice, nor created any new sect, but (like the English reformers in the sixteenth centuy) he brushed away many of the webs of superstition wherein had been hatched dangerous and false doctrines. He sought to wipe out from the minds of his disciples many of the tenets that had made a lodgment in the church in dark, medieval times, such as pardons, pilgrimages, indulgences, absolutions, excommunications.

"Teutonic Christianity," says Milman, "waited more than two centuries for a *finished creed*, such as the thirty-nine articles of the Church of England, or the Augsburg Confession. His doctrines (Wycliffe's), drawn from the fountain of truth, sank into the hearts of multitudes. They spread into Bohemia and kindled fires of martyrdom. Wycliffe's personal influence had affected the most distinguished personages of the land. John of Gaunt, and the widow of the Black Prince, and especially Anne, of Bohemia, the wife of Richard II., were his disciples and friends. This Bohemian princess was called the good Queen Anne, and seems to have been truly religious. She had the gospels in Bohemian, English and Latin. It was through the attendants of the Queen that an intimate religious connection grew up between Bohemia and England. Wycliffe was the morning star of the reformation for Bohemia as well as England.

Many knights of property became disciples of Wycliffe. Sir John Oldcastle, Lord Cobham, was their head. His whole soul was devoted to religion. His enemies accuse him of treasonable designs against the government. Henry IV., in order to strengthen his usurped power, became subservient to the hierarchy.

The king and parliament now, for the first time in England, enacted a statute for the burning of heretics. About thirty years after the death of Wycliffe Lord Cobham was put to death, on the double charge of treason and heresy. He published a confession of his belief, calm, guarded and conciliatory; but his enemies were determined to crush him. Insurrections of the lower classes of the people who loved Richard II. gave color to the false charge of Cobham's enemies. "To you as my king," addressing Henry IV., "I owe under God my obedience; but to the Pope of Rome, I owe neither suit or service." He said to the Primate and other bishops, "Many have been my sins. I have broken in times past God's commandments; but for these transgressions you have never rebuked me; but for neglecting your *traditions* and your laws I and others are thus cruelly treated." When told to confess his sins, he knelt with deep devotion on the stone pavement, saying: "I *shrive* me to thee, Almighty God, through the Lord Jesus, who alone can give me forgiveness." He addressed the multitudes who surrounded his funeral pile, begging them to obey the Scriptures, and reject all evil in their lives. His last words were ascriptions of praise, but they became inaudible from the crackling thorns.

The persecution of this noble man was probably attributable more to his political than to his religious faith. He was opposed to the Lancastrians.* Some wild schemes may have been formed by some of the Lollards, as the disciples of Wycliffe were called, but Cobham was probably ignorant and innocent of any

---

* Henry IV. was a Lancastrian.

treasonable designs. The fears of the government were evidently much aroused. It was reported that the disaffected in the realm desired to make Cobham regent of the realm. It is still a question for what cause these fears were grounded.

Before Henry V. came to the throne, two or three humble men were burned for their heretical opinions. The prince rode around the pile, prepared for the martyrs, begging them to recant. He was in great distress to see the holocaust, but had not the *courage* to forbid the sacrifice. When he became king he enterd into close alliance with the most powerful of the church that he might get subsidies to carry on war with France.

CHAPTER XXVIII.

In the beginning of the fifteenth century (1400), the Latin Church had two pontiffs, Boniface IX., resident at Rome, and Benedict XIII., at Avignon. On the death of Boniface, the cardinals of his party elected (1404) Innocent VII.; he soon died. His place was filled by Gregory XII.

Both of these popes promised, under oath, that they would resign the pontificate whenever the interests of the Church seemed to require it; but they violated their promise. Benedict, when beseiged by the king of France at Avignon, fled to Catalonia. A council of nine cardinals met at Pisa, in order to put an end to the protracted schism in the papacy. This council declared both Benedict and Gregory unworthy of their position; they then excommunicated them, and appointed a new pope, who assumed the name of Alexander V.; he died in 1410. John XXIII. was appointed in his place by sixteen cardinals. This man proved to be destitute of moral principle and piety.

Sigismund, emperor of Germany, the king of France and other princes of Europe, seeing the vast evils incident to the distracted condition both in Church and State, resolved upon a general council. This council met at Constance. Sigismund, with many princes of Germany, was present. The principal object of this great council was to extinguish the discord among the pontiffs. This point was accomplished. John XXIII. was removed, on account of criminal offenses. Gregory

XII. resigned, and Benedict in 1417 was deprived of his office by a solemn decree of this council. He continued to claim his apostolical rights until his death, but he was disregarded.

Martin V. became sole pontiff in 1417, by the unanimous suffrages of the cardinals. Sigismund, the emperor of Germany, stood higher than any successor of Charlemagne since the days of the Othos, the Fredericks, or Rudolph of Hapsburg.

The crowned heads, together with the contestants for the Tiara, did not create in that famous assembly at Constance so much excitement and interest as did the presence of *John Huss*. He was escorted by three nobles of his country, with a great troop of other followers. Huss had a special safe-conduct from Sigismund for his safe arrival and departure from Constance. He was a pale, thin man, in mean attire. One of the professed objects of this council was the *reformation* of the Church, not only in its head but in its members. This *wise* council deemed that one mode of purgation from the many vices and corruptions that stained the purity of the Church, would be to extirpate heretical doctrines. John Huss was summoned to appear at this dignified council as a heresiarch.

The opinions of Wycliffe had been received in the Sclavonic country of Bohemia with eager zeal; scholars from Bohemia had sat at the feet of the bold professor of theology at Oxford. Prague, the capital of Bohemia, had received and disseminated Wycliffe's writings. The kings of this country, even before the time of the English reformer, had not discouraged their preachers in inveighing against the vices of the Roman court and the many abuses that had become so rife in the Church at this period. The schism in the papacy, the residence of the popes at Avignon, controlled as most of them were by the kings of France, had shaken the awe of the hierarchy to its very base. The popes that had been set aside by the Pisan council still claimed power; John was dispised for his immoralities.

John Huss was a preacher in the University chapel at Prague and the confessor of Queen Sophia. He was learned and eloquent; he was a man of severe morals, but gentle, friendly and accessible to all. He had come to Constance to be *judged*, far removed from his home, but surrounded by friends who appreciated his great worth. It is said that John Huss examined with great deliberation the works of Wycliffe, but his doctrine worked by slow degrees into his mind. His preaching at first was not doctrinal, but directed chiefly against the vices of the time. The clergy at first admired his eloquence, but when he began to point out the abuses of the Church, condemning the luxury and immorality that prevailed, the clergy became his persecutors.

Huss was protected by the court, but, alas! the friendship of the king of Bohemia, with the nobles, availed him little at the council of Constance. Though half of Bohemia espoused his doctrines, he was burned at the stake in a strange city.

Gerson, chancellor of the University of Paris, was at the council of Constance. He tried hard to reform the abuses of the Church. He reasoned powerfully against the infallibility of the pope. "Who has made," he inquires, "the pope a saint? Not the Holy Ghost, for high station can not bring the influence of the Holy Ghost, *but the grace of God.*" Under the influence of Gerson, the council declared their decisions *above the pope.*

The Nominalists and Realists were furious in their controversies about this time. Mosheim supposes that Huss, a Realist, was a martyr to the violence of the Nominalists, who were most numerous at the council of Constance. Milman says, he was a martyr to the hierarchy. He held all the great truths of Christianity; also some tenets that were afterwards rejected by English and German Reformers.

Jerome of Prague, his devoted disciple, also suffered death. Huss had implored Jerome not to come to the council, fearing that his fortitude might yield. Jerome, though not as bold as his master, was devout and sincere, and *at the last* was unflinching, as the faggots blazed around him.

The Bohemian reformers were very strenuous with regard to the denial of the cup to the laity. They insisted upon their right to receive it, as our Lord had first administered it. Both symbols were equally precious to them.

The death of Robert Hallam, bishop of Salisbury, England, in 1416, was a great blow to the liberal party. At the council of Constance he had been the right arm of the emperor, and was the most influential man who had opposed *death* as the penalty of heresy. The proud, luxurious hierarchy knew that *truth* and sound argument were on the side of John Huss. This celebrated man was perhaps too dogmatical in his dialectics. The council of Constance threatened to shake the papal supremacy, but in the election of Martin V. the papacy was strengthened for a short time, as Martin was a man of dignity and ability.

In the next century Italy became a battle-ground for the world, and the Italian wars *seemed* to quench in every part the spirit of religion. Then the popes sunk to the same level they had occupied when Boniface VIII. and others like him had disgraced the tiara. Alexander VI. has been called the *Nero* of the pontiffs. His name was Roderick Borgia. This shameless man had four illegitimate children, Cæsar Borgia being one of them—so famous for his vices. Lucretia Borgia was his daughter. Alexander VI. died in 1503. He died of poison which had been prepared for others.*

While this wicked man ruled at *Rome*, the noble preacher *Savonarola* declaimed at Florence with all the zeal and eloquence of a Christian orator against the sin and corruption of the time. As in the time of the prophets of old, he was one of the seven thousand who had not bowed the knee to Baal. Savonarola summoned the princes of Europe to convene a council and depose the wicked pope. Alexander replied in excommunicating the good and great Florentine. Savonarola denounced, too, the family of the Medici, who, though lovers of art and magnificence, had robbed the city of Florence of her *political* rights, while they adorned her with the statues of men who had loved religion and liberty.

---

* NOTE ON THE DEATH OF ALEXANDER VI.—"This pope was doomed to perish by his own wicked devices. It is said, that in his appointment of his forty-three cardinals, the majority gained their dignity by paying to the pope enormous sums of gold. When these cardinals had again become rich, through their employments in the Church, they were *poisoned*, that the papal coffers might again be filled by the confiscation of their estates. A similar fate was reserved for the cardinal of Caneto, who was invited with Cæsar Borgia to the Belvedere, a favorite retreat of the pope near the Vatican. A servant was instructed to serve the guest with poisoned wine. By mistake the bottles were interchanged and the *pope* partook of the fatal drug."—THALHEIMER.

This remarkable man, Savonarola, attacked vice and infidelity with great freedom in the pulpit; he probed the corrupt ulcers of the Church and of the State with an unsparing hand. Though a devout Catholic, he denied the infallibility of the pope, and was filled with horror at the baseness of Alexander VI. When Savonarola was commanded by this unscrupulous pope to come to Rome, and to quit preaching, he deemed it his duty to disregard these mandates.

Savonarola was a child of Italy; he was warm and passionate. This temperament led him to think that he saw visions, and that his dreams sometimes were revelations from God. He was holy and spiritual, and possessed a marvellous gift of oratory which he used to elevate and purify his fellow-men.

Savonarola's influence in the cities of Italy, especially in Florence, was for a long time very great. His crafty enemies, encouraged by the pope, seized him by force, put him to the rack to extort confessions, and finally burned his body, throwing his ashes into the sea.

Savonarola denounced the immoral amusements of the Florentines; their *lascivious dances*, and their demoralizing *theatrical representations*. This opposition to their guilty pleasures called down cruel violence upon the devoted head of Savonarola. A biographer of Dante has said, in speaking of the persecutions and exile of the great Florentine patriot and poet, that all who have striven to elevate their race, have been forced to wear "a crown of thorns." This seems to have been especially true for many centuries in the history of Italy; but now, in her national unity, for which patriots so long sighed in vain, there seems to be *a ground of hope* for more enlightened liberty and purer religion. We must, however, retrace our steps.

Though the council of Constance asserted the right of a council to impose restrictions on the papacy, it remained a barren, abstract proposition. This right of councils to reform the Church and restrict the papal power, was asserted again at the council of Basle. It was futile.

CHAPTER XXIX.

ROME — RIENZI — BOHEMIA.

Martin V.* after his election to the papacy at the Council of Constance, feared for a time to return to Rome. The state of the Eternal City was deplorable. An inundation of the Tiber had added to the wretchedness of the people, growing out of anarchy and confusion. A new power had now arisen in Italy. The captains of the free companies, as these lawless military men were called, had possessed themselves of a great part of the papal dominions. Ludovico Sforza was sent against them, but he was defeated. One of these captains, Braccio Montone, received overtures from Pope Martin, and he agreed to cede to him several cities.

Rome, during the time that her bishops or popes lived at Avignon, in France, was the theatre of the wildest excesses and revolutions. For the space of seventy years the popes lived at Avignon, subject to the predominant influence of France, especially during the reign of Philip the Fair. The rival houses of Colonna and Ursini had brought much misery upon all classes of the people in Rome. During this time the famous *Cola de Rienzi* rose to great power. He was first roused to action by the murder of a beloved brother in a broil growing out of the feuds of the

---

* This pope became the *sole* pontiff in 1417 by the suffrages of all the cardinals.

nobles. His course for a time was as brilliant as a meteor, or as a burning comet athwart the sky of Rome.

Rienzi appeared about the middle of the fourteenth century. He lived at the same time in Italy when the sober, earnest, practical mind of Wycliffe in England, was engaged in translating the Scriptures, and in resolving high questions connected with our eternal state.

Rienzi was the cotemporary of Petrarch. Petrarch was, in the days of Rienzi's prosperity, his friend and correspondent. He hoped that this brilliant man would bring back the golden days of Roman law and liberty. Alas! it was a vision that was soon dispelled. There was no solid foundation in the virtue and intelligence of her people, upon which a permanent and pure structure could rest. But it was gorgeous and brilliant while it lasted.

The parents of Rienzi afforded him a liberal education. His enthusiastic mind perused with great diligence the manuscripts and marbles of antiquity. He studied history and eloquence in the pages of Cicero, Livy, Cæsar, Seneca. He fondly hoped to be a restorer of Roman liberty. "Like Crescentius and Arnold of Brescia," says Madame de Stael, "Rienzi has taken memories for hopes."

We now quote from Gibbon: "Never, perhaps, has the energy and effect of a single mind been more remarkably felt than in the sudden reformation of Rome by the tribune Rienzi. A den of robbers was converted to the discipline of a camp or convent. He was patient to hear, swift to redress, inexorable to punish; his tribunal was always accessible to the poor, and to the stranger; nor could birth or dignity, or the immunities of the Church, protect the offender or his accomplices. The privileged houses, the private sanctuaries in Rome on which no officer of justice would presume to trespass, were abolished; and Rienzi applied the timber and iron of their barricades to the fortifications of the capitol."

. When an embassy was sent to the Papal court at Avignon, Rienzi was selected as one of the thirteen deputies of the Commons to recommend their cause by his spirit and eloquence. He had the honor of haranguing Clement VI., and the satisfaction of conversing with Petrarch, a congenial mind. He was then poor, but the employment of an apostolic notary gave him five florins of gold; this daily stipend enabled him to appear more respectably, for it is said, when he entered Avignon he had but a single garment. His persuasive eloquence commended him to all.

Rienzi attributed, in a great degree, the *evils* that preyed upon the vitals of Rome, to the absence of the chief shepherd. His oratory was constantly used to persuade the pope to leave the banks of the Rhone and return to Rome. The religion of Rienzi was deeply tinctured with the superstition of the times; but he applied, without fear of sacrilege, the revenues of the apostolic chamber, to widows and orphans, and to indigent convents. After unparalleled success, in restoring order and law in Rome, he became the chief actor in the most extravagant theatrical pageants — and he who had conferred so many blessings on his city became the victim of personal vanity, and of reckless extravagance in living. He grieved and disgusted his warmest admirers by his presumption, and yet more by the jealousy and hatred of the nobles. He abdicated his high place, retiring from Rome and spending seven years in exile. It must have been to him a grievous banishment. Again he was recalled. His reception was brilliant; but, after an administration of *four months*, he was killed in a tumult. In his last contest with the mob, feelings of reverence and compassion still struggled in his favor, but the dagger of a bold assassin was plunged in his breast; he fell senseless with the first stroke.

Had this gifted man been true to himself, his career would be beautiful to contemplate. It is said that he disfigured his handsome countenance in his later days by intemperate drinking — he did not remain master of himself. His failings and virtues have often been contrasted, and in periods of anarchy and servitude the name of Rienzi has been a watchword; and he has been claimed as the deliverer of his country and "the last of the Roman tribunes." The most exalted *virtue*, alas! can not always turn aside the dagger or the pistol of a fanatical assassin in times of revolution.

We must now return to the acts of the Council of Constance. Bohemia seemed to rise with one impulse of grief and indignation when *she* heard of the martyrdom of Huss, followed by that of Jerome of Prague. Her king, Wenzel denounced the treachery of Sigismund the emperor, and the barbarous injustice of the Council of Constance. As the Council closed, the Hussite War commenced. It lasted during the whole pontificate of Martin V. This pope seems to have been so busy with the regulation of affairs at Rome, as to give no heed to the misery of Bohemia. Rome rose from her ruins under his diligent administration as from a master's hand. It became populous and prosperous, and was again the capital of the Christian world. "Safe in Rome, Martin heard at a distance the roll of Ziska's chariots, the shrieks of cities stormed, the wail of armies mowed down by the scythe." This Bohemian war was still raging when the Pope Martin closed his earthly career, and opened a way for Eugenius IV.

While King Wenzel lived, the Hussite War was restrained in its fierceness, but at his death, Sigismund was the next heir to the throne. To receive this traitor as their king was more than Bohemia would bear — the torch of sedition had first been kindled in consequence of the betrayal by Sigismund of the safe-conduct of Huss. A wronged people now called the wonderful military talents of Procopius and Ziska to their aid. The emperor tried to awe the people into obedience. No war was ever more remorselessly cruel than this war — Sigismund burned without scruple all heretics who fell into his hands. The reprisals of the Bohemians were terrible, the voice of religion was no longer heard; it was political and national indignation lashed to fury by injustice and cruelty.

This dreadful strife commenced in an honest difference of religious opinions, together with a desire to repress or lessen the power of the hierarchy. The pope's legate now published a bull for a crusade against Bohemia. The famous Ziska had become almost irresistible; he had produced a panic among the Germans, and revenged upon them the unspeakable barbarities practiced on his countrymen. When, in the third year of the war, Sigismund entered Moravia at the head of Hungarian forces they, too, fled from the war chariots of Ziska.

The Council of Basle, 1433, attempted to put an end to this war in Bohemia. Envoys from that country appeared at Basle. But little was accomplished, until Eneas Sylvius went into Bohemia; he was sent by the council, and he managed matters with some success. The four articles that the Bohemians specially desired were granted: The Eucharist must be given to the clergy and laity in both kinds; the clergy must not possess temporal power; the Word of God should be free to all; public crimes must be punished.

We have merely alluded to the residence of the popes at Avignon. Five popes, from Clement V. to Gregory XI., made their residence on the Rhone at Avignon, from the years 1308 to 1376. This period of seventy years the Italians called the Babylonian captivity. The residence of the pontiffs at Avignon tended greatly to weaken the authority of the Romish see. Gregory XI. in the year 1376 transferred his residence from Avignon to Rome.

This residence at Avignon must not be confounded with the great *schism* of the West, which lasted fifty years, and took place shortly after the death of Gregory XI. The cardinals hastened to elect a successor to Gregory, fearing that a Frenchman might be elected. The Roman people demanded that an Italian should be placed at the head of the Church. The cardinals, terrified by the Roman clamor, elected hastily a pontiff under the name of Urban VI. This pontiff soon alienated the minds of the cardinals by his coarse and haughty conduct. The cardinals withdrew to the kingdom of Naples, and there appointed another head, who took the name of Clement VII. Urban lived at Rome, while Clement removed to Avignon. From 1378 to 1418 one of the rival popes lived at Avignon.

In this way the *unity* of the Latin Church was destroyed for a time, as existing under one head. This disunion continued for fifty years, and is called the great schism of the West. France, Spain, Scotland, Sicily, Cyprus, espoused the cause of Clement; while England, with other countries, thought Urban was the true pope.

This schism, as we have already said, was healed at the Council of Constance; it was there determined that a pontiff is subject to a council of the whole Church. Eugenius IV. succeeded Martin V.

A council at Basle was held soon after his accession. The two objects of this assembly were, first, an union between the Greeks and Latins, and secondly, a reformation of the Church, *both in its head and members*. Though all the serious minded of the Church had grieved over the general corruption, both in doctrine and practice, nothing was done towards its reformation. Eugenius the pontiff fearing that the reformers in the council (of Basle) would do some earnest work, threatened to dissolve it.

The Greek emperor, John Paleologus, came to this council, together with the patriarch and the principal bishops of Constantinople, hoping to form an union with the Latin Church. The Greeks were now reduced to great extremities with the Turks, and anxiously sought to be reconciled to the pope, hoping in this way to gain succor and sympathy from the Latins. Bessarion, a learned man among the Greeks, exerted his influence to induce the other Greeks to consent to acknowledge that the Holy Spirit did proceed from the Son, and that departed souls undergo purgation by fire before they can have a vision of God. Some of the Greeks yielded, and a peace was extorted, but it was not permanent. Bessarion was made a cardinal, in consequence of his concessions.

Eugenius IV. by his conduct at the council disaffected the fathers at Basle, and they threatened to deprive him of the pontificate. They, in 1439, elected a new pontiff, who lived in retirement on Lake Leman. He assumed the name of Felix V. This schism was of short duration, as Eugenius died in 1447. Felix two years after resigned his supremacy.

By the efforts of the kings and princes of Europe, especially of the king of France, tranquillity was once more restored to the Church. Nicholas V. was now made pope, a man of learning and moderation, and a preat patron of literature. His election to the popedom took place before the abdication of Felix. Nicholas was assisted in literary work by means of the Greeks who came from Constantinople. Nicholas died on the 24th of March, 1455, principally from grief at the capture of Constantinople by the Turks.

Calixtus III., *his successor*, was chiefly remarkable in urging Christian princes to fight against the Turks.

Eneas Sylvius Peccolemini, bishop of Sienna, was made pope in 1458. He took the name of Pius II. He was a man renowned for his writings and other achievements. Posterity would have accounted him a much greater man, if he had not been guilty of the inconsistency of defending the rights of *councils* against the pontiffs when he was Eneas Sylvius, and, after he was made pope, *denying* that a council is superior to a pontiff. In 1461 he obtained from Louis XI., king of France, the abrogation of the *Pragmatic Sanction*, which had been passed by the good Louis IX. in behalf of liberty.

CHAPTER XXX.

In the early part of the fifteenth century Christianity suffered much from the inroads of the Turks and Tartars, until the final overthrow of the Greek Empire in 1455 by the taking of Constantinople. In Asiatic Tartary, among the Mongols and adjacent nations, the ground which had been so long occupied by the religion of Christ had become the seat of gross superstition. Mosheim says that as late as the beginning of the fifteenth century the Nestorian patriarch sent certain men to Cathay and China to preside as bishops in the churches existing in those countries and their remote provinces. Nestorian Christian light still glimmered amid surrounding darkness. Nestorianism is still found, in the nineteenth century, in Armenia, and will doubtless increase and shine when brought more in contact with the enlightening influences of the present age.

To return, one part of Constantinople was taken by storm, the other part surrendered on terms of capitulation. The outward form of the Christian Church was left untouched until the time of Selim I. He deprived them of their temples and interfered with their worship and Christian usages. The grand church of St. Sophia was converted into a Mahometan mosque. The tyranny of the Turks almost silenced for a time the Grecian and Oriental muses. But the loss of the East was the gain of the West. Many scholars found a home in Italy, which greatly contributed to the Renaissance, in stirring up the minds of Dante, Petrarch, and others, and in recovering from the dust of ages Greek and Latin books of the Augustan age.

Two schools of philosophy — Aristotelian and Platonic — contended with each other which of the two should have the preëminence. This controversy was probably of little advantage to the school of Christ. It was not in Italy that the wave of the Reformation was lifted, notwithstanding the noble struggles of Savonarola to purify the current of ecclesiastical affairs. The Scholastics, who were the disciples of the loved and learned Thomas Aquinas, Duns Scotus, and others, had long been losing ground, because their disquisitions and essays were loaded with dialectics and with terms unmeaning to the people, instead of demonstrating the plain declarations of the sacred volume. As the Scholastics declined in popularity, the *Mystics* gained strength. There were many differences of opinion among the Mystics. One characteristic seems to have been to ascribe little efficacy to the external rites of religion. Religion, the Mystic said, consisted chiefly in the contemplation of God ; and at the same time they attempted to reason about the Trinity and of the soul of man with a subtlety that the capacity of that age could not comprehend. Among the Mystics there were excellent men ; Thomas á Kempis is a shining example of these. The author of the treatise on the Imitation of Christ was born in the diocese of Cologne. He assumed the habit of a monk in 1406. He lived to the age of ninety-two.

We doubt not that among the Fratricelli there were some true Christians. These people were Franciscan monks, who insisted upon observing strictly the rules of their order. They were sometimes found in opposition to the pontiffs, and were persecuted as heretics. One of these, Celestine V., was made Pope, but he soon resigned the papal chair.

John Wesselius was a contemporary of Savonarola, but of another clime and country. When Martin Luther read the works of Wesselius, he said: "Had I *previously* read these books, it might have been said that Luther derived all his views from Wesselius, so perfectly accordant are they in spirit. This increases my joy and confidence in the correctness of my own opinions, since with such uniform agreement, nearly in the same words, though at a different period, and in another country, he harmonizes with me throughout."

Thus, we see, all *down* the ages, amid darkness that could be felt and shadows that obscured the sacred page, there were witnesses for Christ that lived, suffered and died for Him. Though the wise and good saw the necessity of diminishing ceremonies and festal days, some in the fifteenth century desired to add to them. Sixtus IV. ordered the festival of the Transfiguration of Christ. He also promised remission of sins to all who would keep, from year to year, the memorial of the immaculate conception of the Blessed Virgin.

Of all the religious fraternities that were prominent in the fifteenth century, none was more distinguished than "the Brethren or Clerks of the Common Life," under the rule of St. Augustine. In these schools were trained nearly all the restorers of polite learning in Germany and in Holland.

Erasmus of Rotterdam was trained in one of these schools — he who was so celebrated as a teacher of Greek in Oxford, England.

While the Turks were darkening counsel and exercising dreadful tyrannies on the eastern side of Europe, a people of the same *religion*, but of a different race, lived harmoniously in the southwest of Europe — we mean the Spanish Arabs. They were called Saracens as the followers of Mahomet, but in Spain they were called Moors (afterwards Moriscoes). This people came into Spain in the beginning of the eighth century, while all the states of Europe were in a condition of unrest or disintegration. It was nearly three centuries before the Norman conquest (1066). It was long before Rome acquired temporal power.

The Latin and Greek Churches were, at that time, in the midst of the iconoclastic controversy. The Lombards had entered Italy. The Danes and the Normans were intruding on the courts of England and France.

It was the grandfather of Charlemagne, Charles Martel, who, by his great victory at Tours, France, drove back the first Moslem army that threatened to overrun Christian Europe. It was about one hundred years after the death of Mahomet that a *dynasty* allied to or descended from Mahomet, called the Abassides, took up their residence in Andalusia, the most fertile and beautiful portion of Spain. They gained this country by overcoming in battle Roderic, the last of the Goths. Here they lived for nearly eight centuries.

After the memorable defeat at Tours, the energies of the Spanish Arabs were no longer expended in the career of conquest. They became the most literary people in Europe. After the conquest, such of the Christians as chose were permitted to remain in the conquered territory. They were permitted to worship in their own way.*

The Spanish caliphs supported a large military force. The flower of these forces was a body-guard of twelve thousand men, *one-third* of whom were Christians. They made Cordova the capital of their empire. A glowing picture has been drawn by historians of the great progress made by the Saracenic Moors, in knowledge and in all the elegant arts of life.

A period of brilliant illumination with the Saracens corresponds with the deepest barbarism in Europe. Some notion may be formed of the taste and magnificence of this era, from the *remains* of the far-famed mosque of Cordova. Most of its ancient glories have *departed*, but its thousand columns of variegated marble still remain.

The French Pope Sylvester II. is said to have drawn much of his knowledge † from the schools of the Spanish Arabs. The beautiful frescoes still to be seen on the walls of the Alhambra (the palace so beautifully described by Irving) are corroborative of the wonderful excellence of the Saracenic Moors in art. Their fondness for luxury and letters was derived, it is said, from their intercourse and correspondence with Bagdad and other cities of the East, after their conquest of Granada.

The Koran does not contain, says Prescott, a single precept in favor of the cultivation of science. The climate and soil of Spain were eminently propitious to growth and progress.

---

* Prescott.

† It has often been said that the Saracens derived their early learning from Christians in the East.

Algebra and the higher mathematics were taught in the Saracenic schools of Spain, and in this way were diffused over Europe. Manuscripts of cotton paper as early as 1009 have been found in the Escurial, and in 1106 manuscripts of linen paper. The application of gunpowder to military science was learned through the same channel.* They introduced into Europe a variety of salutary elixirs, but their medical prescriptions were regulated by the aspect of the stars. Their physics was debased by magic, their chemistry degenerated into alchemy, their astronomy into astrology. They were the subjects of a despotic government, and the disciples of fatalism. Man appeared to them in the contrasted aspects of master and slave. There was no such precept in Mahomet's Bible as "Do unto others as you would have them do to you." But their sway over their *subjects*, whether Moslem or Christian, was mild and considerate.

* Prescott.

CHAPTER XXXI.

THE INQUISITION.

For centuries after the great Saracenic invasion, *Spain* consisted of small *independent* states, often at war with each other. This is, doubtless, the reason why the Moors were so long permitted an undisturbed residence in the fairest parts of Spain. About the middle of the ninth century the Spaniards had reached the Douro and the Ebro. In the eleventh century, under the banner of the Cid,* the Spaniards extended their line of conquest to the Tagus. The poem of the Cid, written a century afterwards, is supposed to have engendered, or aroused, a patriotic desire to reconquer their country from the Moslem. By the middle of the thirteenth century the dominion of the Moors was restricted to the province of Granada. This little kingdom resisted for a long time the united forces of the Spanish monarchies.

Ferdinand and Isabella began to reign over the kingdoms of Arragon, Castile and Leon in 1474. Historians have cast a beautiful halo over the name and character of Isabella, both as a woman and as a queen. *We* think of her as the sympathizing, intelligent patroness who befriended Columbus, who found for us a home in this new world. Yet it was in her reign that one of the greatest abuses of power that ever disgraced

---
* The Cid was a famous champion of Christianity in the eleventh century. He has been a great favorite of poets and historians.

humanity, received the royal sanction. We mean the *Inquisition;* and it is to introduce this monster of iniquity that we have made this digression into Spanish history.

We do not understand that the tribunal of confession, or the confessional, is necessarily a device to cheat unwary souls; but, the reader of Church history must discover that, in times of ignorance, and in the hands of fanatical, designing men, the *confessional* may become a terrible engine of tyranny. This truth is fully exemplified in the life of Isabella. Her earliest confessor was a wicked fanatic, whose name, Torquemada, became afterwards so famous in his active work in the Inquisition.

The Jews for centuries had been very numerous in Spain; they had frequently occupied positions of high trust in the government. They were at this time very rich; and, in order to evade legislative enactments, which were very severe upon them, some thousands professed conversion to Christianity. The situation of these new converts, after they had intermarried in noble Christian families, suddenly became very insecure. The Dominicans, who were very watchful for heresy, discovered their indifference to Christian rites; they sounded the alarm, and insisted that "the Holy Office of the Inquisition" should be introduced into Castile. It had existed for a time in southern France, an inquisitorial office being established there for the punishment of the Albigenses.

When the cruel scheme was mentioned to Ferdinand, he listened with complacency; but it was not an easy matter to vanquish the repugnance of Isabella to a scheme so contrary to her natural benevolence and magnanimity. This scheme promised an ample source of revenue in the confiscations it involved. We may readily believe in the *sincere* opposition the queen made to the introduction of the Inquisition, when we remember the controversies she afterwards had with the able Ximenes in regard to his interference with the religion of the Moors. The objections of the queen of Castile at length yielded to the arguments of wicked advocates when she called to mind the injunctions of Torquemada with regard to her duty of extirpating heresy. She probably never knew the horrible details that were connected with its practical use. The abuses of it were greater after her death.*

Llorente, the historian of the Inquisition, computes that during the administration of Torquemada in eighteen years, there were upwards of ten thousand burnt, together with six thousand who were condemned and burnt in effigy — ninety-seven thousand *reconciled* by various penances.

The persecutions under Torquemada were confined almost wholly to the Jews. "The fires of the Inquisition," says Prescott, "which were lighted for the Jews, were destined eventually to consume their oppressors. They were still more *deeply avenged in the moral influence* of this tribunal, which, eating like a canker into the heart of the monarchy, at the very time *it* exhibited such goodly promise, left it, at length, a bare and sapless trunk."

Sixtus IV. at one time rebuked the intemperate zeal of the inquisitors, but afterwards we find him seeking to quiet the *scruples* of the queen respecting the

---

* It is quite certain that Isabella was ignorant of the cruel details. Witness her tenderness and humanity to the Indians.

appropriation of the confiscated property; he also exhorts the monarchs of Castile and Arragon to proceed with the work of purification.

In the same year that this iniquitous court commenced its operations, a *plague* desolated Seville which swept off fifteen thousand of the inhabitants.

"Let me not fall into the hands of man," says David, when a choice of evils was presented to him. The history of the Inquisition proves that *fanaticism*, armed with power, is the most dreadful evil that can befall a nation. *The odium excited by Tórquemada's cruelty was so great, that he thrice sent an agent to Rome to defend his cause before the infamous pontiff Alexander VI. The sufferings entailed upon those accused of heresy by the Inquisition were terrible.† Many of the accessories of this Satanic ceremony were not used or practiced until after the demise of Isabella. It is the *tendency* of all evil institutions to grow worse, until the wrath of man, under the mighty power of God, rises in majesty and blots them out forever.

The influence that first kindled the fires of the Spanish Inquisition, was the mean impulse of greed, or covetousness. The extortion of money from the rich Jews, was the first thought; but hypocrisy called to her aid fanaticism, a bird of evil omen with fierce talons and hungry beak — how unlike the symbol of holy influences, the gentle dove.

---

* Prescott.

† The sentence pronounced by the Inquisitors, just before the execution by burning, was called Auto-da-fè. Except the last act of burning, the proudest grandees of the land sometimes witnessed the dismal tragedy.

We can comprehend how the heathen, in the age of Nero, could fancy that they might be doing God service in their persecution of the primitive Christians, supposing, in their deep ignorance, that blood was propitiatory; but how one bearing the name of Christ can be a persecutor, presents a problem in human history very difficult to solve. The truth of history declares, however, that the murderous engine called the Inquisition existed nearly three centuries in Christian Spain; a country that had been free, but in the reigns of Ferdinand, Charles V., and especially under Philip II., the government became a grinding despotism. The Inquisition was not entirely suppressed until 1808.

This *Holy Office* was chiefly in the hands of Dominicans; but it is not true, as has been sometimes imputed to him, that St. Dominic was the founder. His character, if there is truth in history, or symmetry in the qualities of the heart and mind, falsifies this idea.

It is somewhat refreshing to know that even in this age (we mean the latter part of the fifteenth, and in the sixteenth century), there were some consistent and beautiful characters. Among these we can not reckon Isabella's prime minister, Ximenes, because he did not possess charity, which the apostle declares is greater than faith and hope.

Ximenes was intellectually great; he was a great statesman, and severely punished every offense against his state; as a churchman he identified himself with the interests of his religion, and punished delinquents with severity. He freely forgave, it is said, every *personal* injury; *this* is admirable. He built up no family; he dispensed his large revenues on great public objects and upon the poor. His condition in early life was lowly ; he was not ashamed of it. He was not destitute of *sensibility*, as is evident from kind acts to his early humble friends.' He was irreproachable in his morals. This proves his strength of character, and his fear of God, as he lived in a very corrupt time.

When he entered on the duties of his office as archbishop of Toledo, he devoted his energies to schemes of reform ; in this his royal mistress was also much interested. The clergy had widely departed from the rule of St. Augustine, by which they were bound. Nothwithstanding much opposition, he effected thorough outward reform. The monasteries, too, were in great need of review and renovation. A great clamor was raised against him, but Ximenes was steadfast and inexorable in his proceedings to work a reform. The general of the Franciscans came from Rome to Spain to compel him to desist in his inquisitorial proceedings, but, sustained by the queen, he persevered under all opposition. The Spanish clergy had been noted for their dissolute way of life, and the beneficial changes wrought by the example, discipline and teaching of Ximenes and the queen, are the subject of great praise with their contemporaries.

The moral energy and brilliant talents of Ximenes, stimulated as they were by patriotism and religion, entitle him to be considered the leading man in the momentous reign of Ferdinand and Isabella. He was the centre of influence and action, from the high positions of trust he occupied. Several remarkable men belong to this age, some, perhaps, better and nobler than he ; but their position did not permit them to wield *at the time* so great an influence. The great and good Columbus, as *all* know, belongs to this era. The venerable and benevolent Las Casas was also a contemporary. Las Casas devoted his energies to the improvement of the condition of the Indians in the newly discovered islands, who were most cruelly treated by those Spaniards who were intent on enriching themselves. This good man, Las Casas, refused a rich bishopric in Cuzco and afterwards accepted, in Mexico, the bishopric of Chiapa, that he might convert and instruct the heathen. His was a soul of love and gentleness.

But to return to Ximenes and the policy he pursued in Granada. This country had been admirably governed for eight years after its conquest. Fernando de Talavera, a mild and moderate man, had been made bishop of the see of Granada. The conversion of the Moors to Christianity was his great anxiety. He regarded them with tenderness and charity, and with a very different spirit from most of his brethren.* Though late in life, he determined to learn Arabic, that he might commune with the Arabs in their own language. He caused vocabularies, grammars and catechisms to be compiled; also some selections from the Gospels. He unsealed the sacred oracles which had been shut out from their sight — he opened to them the only true source of Christian knowledge, "the ministration of the Word." His wise, benevolent measures and exemplary manners gave him great authority among the Moors. His progress was necessarily slow, but it would have been *effective*, had it not been for the interference of zealots, without knowledge, who thought more active measures ought to be pursued.

Ximenes in 1499 communicated with Talavera upon this subject, and requested leave to participate with

---

* Prescott.

him in this labor of love. The sovereigns, understanding the disposition of Ximenes, enjoined upon *him* and other prelates to observe the temperate and wise policy hitherto pursued, and to *beware* of giving the Moors any cause of discontent.

Ximenes was not of the temper to *follow* the pacific Christian practice of Talavera.

Ximenes summoned a conference of leading men, and expounded with all the eloquence and learning at his command the true foundations of the Christian faith, and the errors of Mahometanism. He enforced his arguments by rich and costly presents, consisting chiefly of elegant dresses, of which the Moors were very fond. Whether arguments, or gifts, availed most, is not known; but many of these learned men soon expressed their willingness to be baptized. They were followed by illiterate disciples, so that, in one day, four thousand are said to have offered themselves for baptism. Ximenes, unable to baptize them individually, adopted the expedient of baptizing them by *aspersion*— he scattered the holy water from a mop or hyssop, and threw it upon the heads of the multitude.

Some opposers soon rose up against the work of Ximenes; they declared he was violating the treaty made at the conquest. This opposition seemed to stimulate the arbitrary Ximenes, who began to use some violent measures. This led to an insurrection, and the sovereigns to their dismay perceived that the zeal of the propagandist Ximenes would lead to a fearful war. Meanwhile, Ximenes had caused all the Arabic manuscripts he could procure to be heaped together in one of the great squares of the city of Granada, and burned! The largest part were copies of the Koran, or books of Moslem theology — but they were beautifully executed, sumptuously bound and decorated; for in these things the Spanish Arabs exceeded every people in Europe. He reserved for his University of Alcala, of which he was the founder, three hundred volumes relating to medical science. When Ximenes was afterwards attacked by an enraged populace in his own palace, he was as intrepid in facing danger as he had been remorseless in burning the Arabian libraries. Talavera by his personal influence quieted them for a time

Many of the people from this time migrated to Barbary, and the remainder of the population abjured Mahometanism and consented to receive baptism.

The whole blame of the disturbances at Granada were rightly imputed to Ximenes; but afterwards, when they saw how many *converts* were made, they declared the triumphs of Ximenes were *great*.

CHAPTER XXXII.

In the two foregoing chapters we have written somewhat of the history of Spain, both in Church and State. We have seen, not only in Spain, but in all the countries of Europe, the great need of reform. Licentiousness stalked abroad, not only in the persons of the inferior clergy, but in those who claimed to be at the head of spiritual affairs.

A truly interesting era had now arrived. Printing had been introduced in all the countries of Europe. Much of the indifference and immorality among the clergy and people was doubtless due to the ignorance of the New Testament. Not only were the manuscripts of the gospels and epistles rare and expensive, but they were written in languages not generally understood by the people. Wycliffe, as we have said, one hundred and fifty years before this time had sent abroad the Word of God, written in a vulgar tongue, and a few other reformers had made efforts of enlightenment in other countries; but at the dawn of the sixteenth century most of these translations had died out. But about this time a great revival of learning took place, commencing in Italy; this revival *extended* to Holland, Germany, France and England. Many things marvellous and strange had been revealed — a new continent had been discovered; the Pacific Ocean had been seen by Balboa, from the hills of Panama; the dusky savages of the Indies, together with other unexpected wonders, led to credulity in the people which induced them to receive as truths monstrous fables, recited by designing adventurers. The world was awakened from the sleep of ages.

Nicholas V. aspired to make Italy the domicile and Rome the capital of letters and art. His death was hastened by thè taking of Constantinople. In 1458 Eneas Sylvius Piccolimini became Pius II. He was a man of consummate ability. Pius II. was the only pope who risked his life in a crusade against the Turks. Nicholas V. built the Vatican. Julius II. and Leo X. did but accomplish, says Milman, that which had *dawned* upon the mind of Nicholas V. We mean the Cathedral of the Apostle of St. Peter. In Nicholas V. *closed* one great age of the papacy.

The revival of learning in Italy seemed to do little for true religion in closely uniting the moral and holy with the ritual. But in England and Germany the results were different. The principal chairs of the universities had been long held by men unfit for these places; some of these were filled by mendicant monks, others by men who pretended to teach the philosophy of Aristotle. There were a few of them who taught with ability and earnestness the doctrines of the Bible. The little piety that remained at this time, seemed to be with the Mystics. This people tried to demonstrate the vanity of external worship without holiness of heart and life. When Luther arose in the University of Paris to dispute with her learned sons, out of the Scriptures, there was not one competent to discuss with him.

Under the popes Nicholas V. and Pius II. Italy became the great school of Christendom. Multitudes resorted thither to learn the ancient languages, and buy the manuscripts of the classics. Nicholas V. did not forsee that this great patronage of learning would be a foremost cause of *the ruin of medieval* religion. The *dominion* of Latin Christianity was drawing to a close.

Erasmus in 1498 met at Oxford, in England, some learned men who had studied in Italy. Of Dean Colet he says, "when I hear him it seems that I am listening to Plato himself." At Oxford Erasmus prepared himself to publish the New Testament in Greek, which was of inestimable value in the work of the Reformation. This work appeared at Basle, in 1516. The "Colloquies" of Erasmus ridiculed and condemned the superstitions of the day—the indulgences; the lying miracles; the idolatry of images and saints which prevailed.

Though Erasmus did so much good work for the Reformation — causing the pure stream of Christian truth to flow over the land by the translation of the New Testament, yet it has been said he was half-hearted in the *love* of Christian truth. Yet Erasmus said, "I wish that all men and all *women* might read the gospels and epistles of St. Paul. I *long* for the day when the husbandman * shall sing parts of them to himself as he follows the plow, and the weaver shall hum them to the shuttle, and the traveller shall while away the reveries of his journey, with their stories." Erasmus did not relish the *heat* of controversy, but he diffused so much light over the path of the inquiring Christian, that we do not think his hearty love of

---

* We think such sentiments show love and heartiness for the Word of God and for the souls of men. Is not this religion?

Christian truth, as understood by the great reformers of the sixteenth century, should be questioned.

The disciples of the "new learning" on the eve of the Reformation were called "Humanists." Sir Thomas Moore was one of these. At first tolerant in his opinions, and seeing clearly the necessity of Church reformation, yet, when he read the attacks of Luther on the Church, he was greatly excited; this man, so much admired in the flower of his days by all parties, became a persecutor. He was made Lord Chancellor after Wolsey's fall, and this was a signal for the fires of Smithfield to be lighted.

Wolsey, with all his faults, was not a persecutor. "I hear no widows' sighs, nor see any orphans' tears, says Thomas Fuller, "caused by him." Wolsey was a many-sided man; he loved pageantry, place and preferment; and in these things no man was ever more largely gratified. Honors followed one another in rapid succession. He was dean of Lincoln, archbishop of York, cardinal, priest; then Lord Chancellor of England. Having been in early life chaplain to Henry VII., he became counselor and companion to his son, Henry VIII. Wolsey is charged with the great crime of permitting young Henry to play the profligate without restraint, so that he might hold the reigns of government unchecked. Henry VIII. had a strong will, but singularly subject to whom he loved, and in whom he had confidence. "The best eulogy on Wolsey's character," says Lingard, "is to be found in the contrast between the conduct of Henry *before* and *after* Wolsey's fall."

Wolsey had more *ambition* than *faith*. His life was not regulated by the Word of God; his *morals* were not pure. In this respect he *unfavorably* compares with Ximenes; and in his self-seeking, he reminds us of Richelieu.

One crime of this age, and for long ages before, was the custom of permitting one man to hold many offices at a time. Some of the clergy of the fourteenth century held as many as twenty benefices. By this shameful system the popes rewarded their officials and enriched themselves.

This custom lasted in a *modified* form for a long time *after* the Reformation. Simony prevailed in Wolsey's time to a very great degree; and no one availed himself more of this bribery than Wolsey. He knew that reform was needed in every department of the ecclesiastical state, but he seemed not to know how much he himself needed reformation, until he was despoiled of his earthly dignities, and was about to die. Shakespeare has given him a magnificent place on the canvas of history. His words, we will quote a few of them, will help us to form a true conception of his character:

> " He was a man of an unbounded stomach, ever ranking
> Himself with princes; one, that by suggestion,
> Tied all the kingdom; simony was fair play;
> His own opinion was his law: i' the presence
> He would say untruths: and be ever double,
> Both in his words and meaning—
> Of his own body he was ill, and gave
> The clergy ill example.
>   This Cardinal, though from
> An humble stock, was fashioned to much honor
> From his cradle. He was a scholar; a ripe and good one;
> Exceeding wise, fair spoken and persuading:
> Lofty and sour to them that loved him not;
> But to those men that sought him, sweet as summer.

And though he were unsatisfied in getting,
Which was a *sin*, yet in *bestowing*—
He was most princely: ever witness for him
Those twins of learning Ipswich and Oxford!
One of which fell with him, unwilling to outlive the good
    that did it;
The other though unfinished, yet so famous,
So excellent in art, and still so *rising*,
That Christendom shall ever speak his virtue.
His overthrow heaped happiness upon him;
For then, and not till then, he felt himself,
And found the blessedness of being little:
And, to add greater honors to his age,
Than man could give him, he died *fearing God*.

Archbishop Warham, of Canterbury, was a great and good man. He saw the necessity of reform, but shrank from the steps necessary to accomplish it, and from any thought of secession from the existing state of things. Erasmus speaks of him as a favorer of the new learning, and of his kindness and generosity to himself. Warham resigned the office of Lord Chancellor in 1515. Wolsey succeeded him.

Dean Colet was one of the most fearless and independent men of his time. In 1511 he preached before the Convocation of Canterbury. He denounced the sin of his brethren; both priests and bishops, he said, were too much engaged with secular concerns; this brought dishonor on the priesthood and confounded it with the laity; reformation, he cried, must begin with the bishops. This sermon of Colet's, says *Mr. Geike*, in his work on the Reformation, was the first trumpet blast of coming events.

Colet endowed St. Paul's school for the free education of children in the *new learning;* he had also dared to translate into English the Lord's Prayer, with comments. He condemned images, auricular confession, and purgatory. He was saved from prosecution by the regard of Warham and the friendship of Erasmus. The young king, too, was an admirer of Colet.

"*At the accession of Henry VIII. the English language was spoken only in England. The people of Wales spoke Welsh, and the people of Cornwall spoke Cornish. *Spain* was then the greatest European power, and France was nearly her equal. The Holy Roman Empire was the first State in rank, and when united with the Spanish crown under Charles V., it made the Pope apparently the Dictator of Europe."

Prussia was then a desert; Holland under the feet of Spain.

How grand and impressive is the change that three centuries have made! England's laws and language compass the world. The great military kingdoms of Prussia and Russia require the other civilized peoples of the earth "to stand to their arms." The Pope is restricted to his own ecclesiastical domain. Italy, so long the battle-ground, of the nations, is ruled by a lawful monarch in the City of the Cæsars, and has her own legislative councils. Some portions of heathen India, China and Africa are reaching out their hands to God.

We must now return to the sixteenth century. Romanists have said much, and all right-minded people have condemned Henry's divorce from Katharine, his virtuous wife of twenty years; but it was a union that should never have been sanctioned. Henry's conscientious scruples on this subject was a *pretense*, but the

---

* Geike.

iniquity was not all on his side. His marriage with his brother's widow had been forced upon him by the politic monarchs of Spain. They urged the pope Julius II. to grant a bull authorizing a marriage which they believed to be contrary to the Word of God. The pope at first refused his consent, but the powerful influence of Spain induced him to yield. Henry had submitted the matter to the two leading men of his council, Fox, bishop of Manchester, and archbishop Warham. The former took it into consideration, but the latter rejected the proposals at once as abhorrent to religion and directly opposed to the *letter* of the Old Testament. These doubts and scruples as to the lawfulness of his first marriage must have been remembered by him, when he was searching for a pretext to dissolve the union of which he had become tired, and when unbridled passion suggested a marriage with another — with Anne Boleyn, the mother of Elizabeth.

Some historians tell us that Ferdinand would not consent to the marriage of Arthur with his daughter until all other pretenders to the throne of England were removed. To remove every barrier, Edward, earl of Warwick, was beheaded.

The Lady Katherine said, when she knew of the trouble that awaited her, "that she had not offended, but it was a *judgment* of God, for that her former marriage was made in blood."

"The king Henry VII.," says Lord Bacon, "did bring a kind of malediction on this marriage."

Henry VIII. had just reached his eighteenth year when he ascended the throne. No accession ever excited higher expectations among a people than that of Henry VIII. He was distinguished for personal beauty and for vigor and skill in arms. He was the friend of the new learning; the admirer and protector of Colet and Erasmus. His early years were spent amid tournaments and revelry.

He had some experience in war; he joined a league of the Italian States to drive out of Italy Charles VIII., king of France. He succeeded in this effort, but it was a fruitless campaign to England. In this war Ferdinand secured Navarre, for the possession of which he had made the war, and then treacherously deserted his son-in-law, leaving him to fight alone. Ferdinand promised the king of England to ratify a marriage between his grandson Charles and Mary, Henry's sister. Soon after, however, Henry learned, to his disgust, that Charles had been promised to a young daughter of the French king.

Henry's heart seemed now to be turning against everything Spanish. The alliance with Spain was broken off, and Mary, a girl of sixteen, was married to Louis XII. of France, a broken-down man of fifty-three. She early became a widow, and afterwards married the duke of Suffolk, and was the mother of the famous Lady Jane Grey and Catharine Grey.

Never had pope a more faithful supporter than the king of England at this time. He wrote a book against the so-called heresies of Luther, which so gratified the pope that he styled Henry "the Defender of the Faith."

Through all the changes of his terrible career, the king's court was the *home* of letters. Even as a boy his son, Edward VI., was a fair scholar in both the classical languages. His daughter Mary wrote good Latin letters. Elizabeth, who spoke French and Italian as fluently as English, began every day with an hour's reading in the Greek *Testament*, together with the tragedies of Sophocles or the orations of Demosthenes.* Henry's ministers, much as they differed on many subjects, all agreed in the protection and encouragement of the culture around them.

Julius II., who had passed much of his life in camps, died in 1512. Some of his cardinals, relying on the help of Louis, king of France, summoned a council at Pisa to curb the madness of Julius, and to deliberate on measures for a general reformation of the gross corruptions of the Church. Julius called a counter-council at his Lateran palace in 1512 to annul the acts of the council of Pisa. During its session, or shortly thereafter, this pope was called to a higher tribunal.

He was succeeded by Leo X., who gave a great impulse to the cultivation of letters and the patronage of art. Julius II. had commenced St. Peter's Church at Rome; Leo now devoted his energies to the prosecution of this work. With such a coadjutor as Michael Angelo, this crowning work of architecture made elegant progress. But money was an important factor in this splendid enterprise.

This want gave rise to the embassy of Tetzel through Germany to make sale of Indulgences. How this shameful traffic opened the eyes of Luther, and enabled him to probe deeply into the ulcerous condition of ecclesiastical affairs, is known to all readers of history.

---

* Green's History of the English People.

The sale of Indulgences was not a new thing. In what are called the Jubilee years, this lucrative invention had been much used. In 1300, all who came to Rome and spent there fifteen days, were promised the forgiveness of their sins. This brought so much money into Rome, that Jubilees were repeated every twenty-fifth year.

Julius II. had offered this easy way of remission of sin to all who contributed to St. Peter's. "It was given out that the infinite merits of Christ, and the excess of the good works of the saints, beyond those needed for their own salvation, formed a treasury from which the Church might *draw* for the benefit of any one on special conditions." Our Lord declared that after we have done *all*, we are unprofitable servants; but the church at Rome in the sixteenth century taught another *gospel*.

Tetzel and his assistants roused the public indignation by their shameful immorality as well as by their absurd teachings. On the 31st of October Martin Luther, who was soon to become the great Reformer of the World, then a University professor, nailed to the door of the Church of All Saints, at Wittemberg, a *challenge* of the whole system of Indulgences.

When Luther was first sent to Rome, in 1510, by his monastery, his soul was full of reverence * for the

---

" Blessed Rome! he cried, as he entered the gate. Alas! the Rome of reality was far from blessed. The *name* of religion was there. The thinnest veil was spread over the utter disbelief with which God and Christ were at heart regarded. There was, *culture*. It was the Rome of Raphael and Michael Angelo; but to the poor German monk who had come there to find relief for his suffering soul, what was culture?"—FROUDE.

city of which St. Paul had spoken. He thought of the martyrs of the early Church. On arriving, he fell on his knees, raised his hands to heaven and exclaimed, "Hail, holy Rome!" But alas! he soon perceived that he was in a city of unbelievers. Christianity seemed forgotten in the centre of the Christian world.

In the year 1517 Martin Luther, a monk of Saxony, of the town of Eisleben, and belonging to the order of Augustinian Eremites, which was one of the four mendicant orders, opposed himself alone to the whole Romish power. He was a professor of theology in the University of Wittemberg, which Frederic the Wise, elector of Saxony, had established a few years before. Leo X. was now at the head of the Church. Maximilian I. of Austria governed the German empire, to which Charles V. was soon after elected. Frederic ruled over Saxony. Henry VIII. was king of England. Francis I. was king of France. All these crowned heads were men of unusual ability; it was a time, as we have already said, of great enthusiasm in learning and literature.

Luther was born in 1483, at Eisleben. His father was a miner of Mansfield. His celebrated son attended the schools of Magdeburg and Eisenach; he studied scholastic philosophy and jurisprudence at Erfurt, and read also the ancient Latin authors. While at Erfurt he was much impressed by the sudden death of an intimate friend killed by lightning.

CHAPTER XXXIII.

MELANCHTHON—ZUINGLIUS—LUTHER.

Luther was stunned by the electric bolt that killed his friend, and now awakened to a deeper sense of the preciousness of the soul and his duty to his fellowmen. He resolved to devote himself to a religious life. With this view, which was not in accordance with his father's wishes, he joined the rigid order of Augustinian Eremites. His vicar general seeing his ability, sent him to Wittemberg to teach philosophy and theology. He soon discovered the defects of the scholastic system, and began to reject human authorities in matters of religion. He was doctor of divinity in 1512, and then applied himself assiduously to Hebrew and Greek. John von Stanpitz was his vicar general. He wrote his own language with greater purity, elegance and force than any German author of that age. His translation of the Bible first appeared in 1534. His faults were the faults of a warm, earnest, nature, and the effects of the education and of the times in which he lived. It is well known that he answered his opposers with too much acrimony, and sometimes with personal abuse. His own soul was deeply penetrated with the truths he embraced. He had witnessed the working of "the mystery of iniquity" at Rome. He knew the fatal influence of falsehood, and this seemed to deprive his impetuous, sincere mind of the patience and meekness that so greatly adorn it. In many instances he believed that he was contending with hypocrites or half-hearted Christians. He was, however, the *sun* of the Reformation, and his defects were *spots* that could not hide or obscure the warmth and brilliancy of his light.

We are told by some writers that in the early part of his career in the convent, his remorse for sin was so great that one of his brother monks pointed out to him a cardinal doctrine of the creed, the forgiveness of sins; also read with him in the Scriptures of justification by faith, which was to him ever afterwards the central doctrine of his creed.

Staupitz was probably the monk that enlightened Luther when he was in his great spiritual trouble. It is known that he approved of Luther's theses against the papal indulgences, and that he demanded at Augsburg that Luther should not be condemned unheard. It is comforting to know that, notwithstanding the corruption and infidelity of this age, there was still "a little flock" that held the truth and practiced it. Had it not been for the great celebrity of Luther, we should probably have never heard of the humble faith of the monks of the Augustinian monastery at Erfurt.

In Luther's controversy with Tetzel, he was applauded by the best part of Germany; but there were many sycophants who cried out against him. Leo X. at first seemed to disregard Luther's arguments and opposition, but being informed by the emperor that Germany was much agitated upon this question, he summoned Luther to appear at Rome and take his trial. Frederic of Saxony interposed, and requested that Luther's cause should be heard in Germany. The pontiff yielded and ordered Luther to appear before his legate, Cardinal Cajetan, at Augsburg, and *there* to defend his doctrines and conduct. Cajetan was a Dominican. The Dominican order and the Augustinian seem to have been inimical to each other. A more unfit person than Cajetan could not have been selected. The cardinal required Luther to revoke the errors in his theses—namely, that there was not any treasury of the merits of the saints at Rome from which the pope could dispense indulgences, and that without faith no forgiveness of sin could be obtained from God. Luther held fast to his opinions. The cardinal, though a learned man, was no biblical scholar, and could not produce any proofs in refutation of Luther's doctrine. When Cajetan threatened him with ecclesiastical censures, Luther appealed from the pontiff ill-informed to the same better informed.

The Romish court perceived its mistake in the appointment of Cajetan, and appointed another legate to confer with Luther. This legate persuaded Luther to write to the pope, in which he promised that he would be silent if his enemies remained so.

This was the period, however, of many literary combats. Eckius, a famous papal theologian of this time, disputed with Cardostadt * on the subject of *free will*, but the disputants accomplished nothing. Luther then engaged with Eckius in a contest respecting the supremacy and authority of the Roman pontiff (a question far more easy to settle), but the literary combatants referred the decision to the universities of Paris and Erfurt. Eckius was forever after the enemy of Luther. But among the witnesses of this dispute was

---

* A friend of Luther.

one who became the second reformer, next to Luther, in Germany. This person was Melanchthon. He had studied at Heidelberg, and afterwards became Professor of Greek at Wittemberg. He taught and wrote and debated in furtherance of the same objects with Luther, but with more mildness and gentleness than he. Melanchthon composed the Augsburg Confession, and the apology for it. He was an active but gentle reformer.

While these controversies were agitating Germany, and shaking the very throne of the pontiff at Rome, a very bold, erudite reformer appeared at Zurich, in Switzerland. Ulrich Zwingle was a canon and priest. Zwingle, it is said, commenced to preach before Luther contended with the pope. He perhaps discovered the corruptions of the church somewhat earlier. He had contended in his courts with an emissary of like kind with Tetzel. Both began gradually without any concert, to cast off from the church "the wood, hay and stubble" that had gathered over the divine and hoary edifice in the flight of ages. Luther had a wider field of action than Zuinglius (as he is sometimes called). The latter moved only in the narrow circle of a single canton in Switzerland. Zwingle was a ripe classical scholar. He studied diligently, too, the eminent fathers of the Church, as Ambrose, Augustine, and Chrysostom, and pressed upon his students the study of Hebrew, but inculcated with force that the Bible was the only *standard* of religious truth. Luther and his followers had long and severe contests with Zwingle and the reformed,* respecting the corporeal

---

* The disciples of Zuinglius.

presence of Christ in the Eucharist. This difference of opinion caused much alienation and prejudice between the two bodies during the whole of the fifteenth century.

The Lutherans believing in what Luther called *consubstantiation;* he believed in the presence of Christ in the *elements*, but not in their change or *transubstantiation*. The Zuinglians regarded the Eucharistic sacrifice or offering simply as a memorial.

In 1524, the Council of Zurich reformed the public worship according to the advice of Zwingle. He continued to guide his flock until October, 1531, when an army from the popish cantons marched against Zwingle. Zwingle, according to the usage of his country, bore the *standard* that attempted to repel them. The enemy were victorious; Zwingle was slain, and his body cut to pieces and burned to ashes.

Overcome, it is said, by the importunity of the Dominicans, Leo X. issued the first *bull* against Luther on the 15th of June, 1520. As soon as Luther heard of this first sentence of the pontiff against him, he appealed to the supreme tribunal of the future council. Believing that his appeal would be disregarded at Rome, he determined to proclaim his secession from the Romish community by a public act. He caused, on the 10th of December, 1520, a fire to be kindled without the walls of his city, and in the presence of a vast multitude, he committed to the flames the bull issued against him, together with a copy of the pontifical canon law. In this way he publicly signified that he would no longer be a subject of the Roman pontiff. Luther withdrew, however, only from the Romish Church which looks upon the pontiff as infallible; not from the church *universal,* the sentence of which, pronounced in a legitimate and free council, he did not refuse to obey.

Many Roman Catholics, who were attached to the liberties of Germany, looked upon this bold act of Luther without offense.* In diffusing the principles of the Reformation through Germany, Luther had the aid of other excellent men in various parts of Europe, and especially was he assisted by the doctors of Wittemberg and the great learning of Melanchthon. Meanwhile, in 1519, Maximilian I. died, and his grandson, Charles V., King of Spain, was elected his successor. Leo X. reminded the new emperor of Germany that he had assumed the place of advocate and defender of the Church, and called upon him to inflict punishment upon Martin Luther, a rebellious member of the Church.

Frederick IX. counseled Charles to proceed with great caution. Charles felt under greater obligations to Frederic than to any other German Prince. In order, therefore, to gratify this friend, and also the pontiff, he determined to summon Luther to appear before the diet, which would assemble at Worms, before the passing of any decree against him.

Luther appeared at Worms, protected by a safe-conduct from the Emperor, and boldly pleaded his cause before the diet. Some of his friends regarded it † as a perilous undertaking. When his friend Spalatin warned him of his danger, he replied "he would go *thither* if there were as many devils there as there were tiles upon the houses." He was conducted in his monkish dress

---

* Mosheim. † His journey to Worms.

by Von Pappenheim, the marshal of the empire, to the assembled diet. He was asked two questions—namely, whether he was the author of the books laid upon the table before him, and whether he would recall any of the opinions contained in them. To the first question he answed yes. To answer the second question, he waited until the next day. He answered by making distinctions.

Some of his writings, he said, related to a Christian's faith and life; others were directed against the Papacy, and others against private individuals who defended the Romish tyranny. He could not renounce the first, because even his enemies agreed they contained much good matter; nor could he renounce the second, because that would be lending support to papal tyranny; as to the third, he acknowledged he had often been too vehement. The official said to him, *You* must have erred, because you have contradicted the Pope and council. He answered, The Pope and the council have often contradicted themselves. He closed with this declaration:* "Here I stand. I can say no more. God help me. Amen." Neither promises or menaces could move him. When called upon to renounce his opinions, and to become reconciled to the Pope, he said he could never yield, unless convinced of error by proofs from Holy Scripture and sound reason. He obtained leave from the emperor to return home unmolested, but Prince Frederic, fearing mischief should befall him, caused him to be intercepted near Eisenach by

---

* "There on the raised dais stood the sovereign of half the world. On either side were the ministers of state, archbishops, the princes of the empire, gathered together to judge the son of a poor miner, who had made the world ring with his name."

persons in disguise, and conducted to the castle of Wartburg; in that castle, which he called his Patmos, he lay ten months, beguiling the time with writing and study.

The emperor and Luther never met again. The emperor, many years after the debate at Worms, and after the death of Luther, went to Wittemberg, at the head of his army. He desired to be conducted to Luther's tomb. When some one suggested that the body should be taken up and burned at the stake in the market place, Charles nobly replied: "I war not with the dead." His body lay in the grave, but there was scarcely any part of Europe where the light of the religious reformation by Luther did not shed its radiance. While Luther remained in the castle of Wartburg (ten months) the monasteries were broken up. The old ecclesiastical institutions of Germany were crumbling.

The Elector of Saxony, the Landgrave of Hesse, and other princes declared for the reformation. The Protestants had a majority in the diet and controlled the force of the empire. During Luther's retirement at Wartburg he translated the Bible. A diet at Spire in 1526 resulted most favorably to the reformers. Ferdinand, the brother of the Emperor Charles, presided at this diet. The emperor, by his envoys, required that all contentions about religion should cease, but said that the edict at Worms against Luther should be confirmed. Many of the princes declared that a general council ought to be assembled to take cognizance of this edict. The emperor was at this time so perplexed with his French, Spanish, and Italian affairs, that he could not give, during several years, much attention to the affairs of Germany or to the subject of religion.

Clement VII., fearing the power of the emperor in Italy, entered into an alliance with Francis I. and the Venetians against the emperor. This so inflamed the resentment of Charles, that he made war upon the Pope in Italy, captured the city of Rome in 1527, by his General Charles, of Bourbon, and shut up the pontiff in the castle of St. Angelo. The Lutherans improved this opportunity to extend their cause. It was about this time that the Elector of Saxony caused a visitation of the churches throughout his dominions. Luther was the clerical writer for Saxony, and Melanchthon for Misnia. They were to examine into the condition of the parishes, schools, monasteries and cathedrals, with power to make any changes that were necessary to their well-being. Luther, impressed with the ignorance of both clergy and laity, busied himself, after his return home, in writing catechisms for their use.

How blessed is the work of those who strive to elevate the moral and intellectual condition of their fellow-creatures. This tranquillity was interrupted by the second diet of Spire, in 1529. The emperor was anxious to make a compromise with the Pontiff, Clement VII. The decree which had been passed three years before, that every prince should regulate religious matters in his own territories as he saw fit, was now *revoked*, and all changes declared unlawful until the decision of the council should determine what was best to be done. The reformers understood perfectly that a legitimate and free council could not be obtained from the pontiff. They, therefore, at this second diet at Spire remonstrated and protested against the revocation of the decree that each prince should have the liberty to regulate affairs in his own district. The Landgrave of Hesse, the Elector of Saxony, and other patrons of the reformation *protested* and appealed to the Emperor and a future council. Hence originated the name of *Protestants* borne from this time onward by all who left the communion of the Roman pontiff. As no good *formula* of the doctrines professed by the followers of Luther now existed, Luther was requested by John, elector of Saxony, to prepare a brief summary of his doctrines.

Luther had drawn up, in 1529, seventeen articles which had been agreed to in the convention of Schwabach. He exhibited these to the Elector at Torgau, hence they were called the articles of Torgau. From these articles as the basis of the Lutheran formula, Philip Melanchthon was requested by the Protestant German princes (holding consultation with Luther all the time), to draw up that confession of faith which is known as the *Augsburg Confession.* The greatest hindrance to a cordial union between the Saxon and Helvetic, or Swiss, reformers was their disagreement in regard to the Lord's Supper.

Philip, Landgrave of Hesse, appointed a conference between Luther and Zwingle and other learned doctors, to be held at Marburg in 1529. They debated four days together. They agreed satisfactorily together as regarded the divinity of the Saviour, the efficacy of the divine word, original sin, etc. ; but they could not reconcile their differences with regard to the Last Supper.

How much wiser now seem to us, on this subject, the reformers of the Church of England? They did not attempt, in this great mystery, to analyze so much as the German reformers. They adopted the words of our Lord and the scriptural teachings concerning it, leaving the sense or interpretation of the words to each individual conscience. It plainly teaches, however, that the bread and wine are not changed, but consecrated to a holy purpose.

As early as 1523 there were multitudes in France opposed to the principles and laws of the Romish Church. Margaret, Queen of Navarre, sister of Francis I., was pleased with the principles of the reformed religion. She took under her protection pious and learned men, who formed religious societies in different places. Le Fevre and Roussel betook themselves to Navarre, where they did not openly break with the Romish Church, but they taught the doctrines of the reformers. But cruel persecutions soon arose. Margaret was forbidden to encourage any innovations. At a convention held in Smalcald, in 1537, another summary of the religious faith of the German reformers was drawn up. This writing of Luther is called the articles of Smalcald. They were drawn up in the German language. These articles cover twenty-eight pages. The first part contained four articles, in which the Protestants professed to agree entirely with the Papists. These four were the Trinity, the Incarnation, Passion and Ascension of Christ.

On other points of doctrine there was great difference between the Papists and Lutherans. When the Protestants signed the articles of Smalcald, "Melanchthon annexed a reservation to his signature, purporting that he could admit of a Pope provided he would allow the gospel to be preached in its purity, and would give up his pretensions to a divine right to rule, and would found his claims wholly on expediency and human compact." This is annexed to the articles. A young scholar from Oxford, England, heard of Luther's doings at Wittemberg. He soon directed his course to the sacred city of the reformation. Students of all nations were flocking to Wittemberg. Tyndale was the young Oxford student to whom we have alluded. Luther advised him to translate there the gospels and epistles. The press which Tyndale established at Antwerp, where he was joined by a few students from Cambridge, who was soon busy with his versions of the Scriptures, and with reprints of the tracts of Wycliffe and Luther.

Some one has said that without the Greek Testament of Erasmus the reformation would have been impossible. It is certainly true that Tyndale's English Bibles and Testaments were of inestimable value to the people of England. These volumes of Tyndale were smuggled over to England and circulated among the poorer and trading classes through the agency of an association of "Christian Brethren." They found their way to the universities, where the intellectual impulse given by the new learning was quickening religious speculation. The rapid diffusion of Tyndale's works roused Wolsey at length to action.

At Oxford the brethren were seized and put in prison. In London a large number of Testaments were burned. But in spite of the panic of the Protestants, who fled in crowds over the sea, but little severity was exercised until after Wolsey's fall, when forbearance was thrown aside.

CHAPTER XXXIV.

It has often been said by the frivolous, who are incapable of tracing effects to causes, that Henry VIII. was the author of the Reformation of the Church of England. The great predisposing cause of the Reformation in England, as in other countries, was the corruption of the Church, both in its docrines and in its practice.* Many honest, true men within her fold had felt the need of purification, and the great necessity of a return to the primitive source of spiritual life, in the oracles of God. Henry VIII. was not one of these. He was perfectly satisfied with the papacy and all its claims, until it contradicted his will. He was "a Defender of the Faith" as it then existed. All Germany and Switzerland were aflame at this time with the teachings of Luther and Zuinglius. Oxford scholars had gone to Wittemberg, they had seen Luther, they had set up printing-presses in Antwerp and in other places, they had returned to England, laden with their versions of the Scriptures, especially with the Gospels and Epistles. Through the agency of associations, the

---

* The deliverance of the Church of England from the power of the papacy was effected partly by convocation and parliament. The papacy, in its greed of gold, drained the kingdom annually of large sums of money. Convocation petitioned the king that this drain should be stopped. The extracts from this petition are still extant, says Blunt, in the British Museum. A book put forth in 1537, called "The Institution of a Christian Man," did good work for the Reformation. Forty-six of the leading men in England had published it. It explained the creed, sacraments, Ten Commandments, etc.

work of these zealous, God-fearing men was spread over the country. They found their way to the universities. Cambridge had already won a name for heresy; the intellectual impetus given by the new learning was quickening religious thought both here * and at Oxford. Henry cared nothing for religion, as his wicked acts most plainly prove; but he was fond of learning, fond of theology. He was a pedant, and loved to discuss doctrinal points. He was surrounded by learned men, with reforming views. Latimer (afterwards burned at the stake) was the court preacher, and Cranmer, his private counselor, singularly intent upon the instruction of the people, was watching every opportunity that he might obtain from his tyrannical monarch the privilege of translating portions of the church service into the English tongue. A great literary reform was in progress. Some who were not thirsting to drink at "the fountain of living waters" were yet anxious for *intellectual* advancement.

More, Colet and Erasmus were styled the three Oxford reformers. Colet was a doctrinal reformer, as well as a literary one. He was taken off by death before the time came that tried men's souls, and sometimes burned their bodies. There were many men also of low estate and position, who dearly loved to read any books that taught them the precious practical truths of the Bible.

Henry VIII. was, as we have said, fond of learning. He was a sagacious prince, and comprehended somewhat of the signs of the times. His sympathy with learning therefore disposed him to listen to the solicita-

---

* At Cambridge.

tions of Cranmer, in his great desire to convert into English the service of the Church.

But he lived and died a Romanist, as the existence of the *six Articles* proved. In his rage against the pope for refusing to grant him a divorce, he had cast off his allegiance to him, affecting to believe what the early Church did *in truth* believe, that the bishop of Rome should claim no priority over the bishops of other metropolitan cities, and to restrict himself to ecclesiastical affairs.

We see in the history of this world how our Almighty Father educes good from evil : it was wicked passion that induced Henry VIII. to dissolve the bond that connected papal Rome with his kingdom ; yet the friends of reform hailed it with joy, knowing that the illegal and unrighteous authority that had so long interfered with their desire to purify and renovate the Church, was ended.

In the year 1525, an association was enrolled in London called the "Christian Brothers."* It was composed chiefly of poor men, tradesmen and artisans. There were a few of *the clergy* with them. These men employed agents to go up and down the country, carrying Testaments and tracts with them. The records of the bishops' courts in the early part of this century were filled with accounts of prosecution for heresy. The persecuted were men and women who rose up against the *masses*, the pilgrimages and the *indulgences*. These things had become intolerable. They had

---

* We read of "Christian Brothers" as early as the thirteenth century. Tauler and Groote were distinguished preachers of the "Brothers of Common Life." Thomas á Kempis united with some of these in his day, and was of like spirit.

learned enough of the truth in Wycliffe's Testaments to know that these things were false.

When Wolsey had founded the great college at Oxford (now called Christ Church), desiring to make his magnificent institution as perfect as art could make it, he had not only sought Professors in Rome, and from other cities in Italy, but he had introduced several students from Cambridge represented to be of unusual promise. These students were deeply imbued with the enthusiasm of Tyndale. The names of some of these were Clark, Frith, Sumner, Taverner and Garret. The last mentioned was a secret member of the London society. He sought all such young men as were given to Hebrew, Greek and Latin. He also introduced into Oxford treasures of *forbidden* books imported by the "Christian Brothers." It is said that Wolsey knew that the *taint* of heresy rested upon some of these men, but thinking they were unsubstantiated rumors, allowed them not to weigh against ability and character. These men were in the habit of reading the New Testament in their rooms, especially studying St. Paul's epistles. They had a gradually increasing circle of interested hearers from the undergraduates of the University.

After these students of the Word of God had conferred together about six months, within the limits of the university, suspicion rested upon them. Several of these were imprisoned. Garret was fiercely pursued from place to place; but falling into the hands of Wolsey, he refused to deliver him up. Clark died of the treatment he received in prison. His last words are recorded. He desired the communion, but was refused, *lest* the holy thing should be profaned by the touch of a heretic. When told he could not be permitted to have it, he* said: "*Crede est manducâsti*," "Faith is the communion." Some of these students recanted, but afterwards repented of their weakness, and suffered heroically at the stake. Of such men as these were Bilney and Bainham. Bilney had escaped through Wolsey's hands in 1527, but in 1529 he was again cited before the bishop of London. Three times he refused to recant. He was offered another chance, and he fell. After spending two years in misery he began to preach in the fields. He exposed the licentiousness of some of the priests, and this formed the ground of his last arrest. He still believed in the mass and in the power of the keys, but he was found heterodox on the papacy and the mediation of the saints. He was sent to the stake by the bishop of Norwich.

The crime of the offenders varied. Sometimes it was a denial of the corporal presence, more frequently a denunciation of the habits of some of the clergy. It is said that Bilney once chose Latimer for his confessor, that he might confer with him, and that Latimer said that Bilney poured a flood of light on his soul, and called him the instrument whereby God called him to knowledge.

Sir Thomas More was successor to Wolsey, and under him the fires of Smithfield burned more frequently. "With Wolsey heresy was an error, with More it was a crime." Of these first martyrs of the reign of Henry VIII., Mr. Froude says: "These were the first Paladins of the Reformation, the knights who slew the dragons and the enchanters, and who made

---

* Froude.

the earth habitable for flesh and blood." They were rarely men of much ability, but of clear sense and honest hearts. Tyndale was a remarkable man, and so Clark and Smith promised to become, but they were cut off. William Tyndale lived to see the Bible, for whose translation into English he had so faithfully labored in exile, carried into his own country with the will of *the king*, solemnly recognized (no longer a hidden possession) as the Word of God. Tyndale was in Flanders at this time. He was denounced to the regent by an English fanatic, who had enticed him to leave the city where he would have been secure. He died the martyr's death amid smoke and flame.*

Every monastery, every parish church had in these superstitious days something to attract the interest of the people. The people brought offerings to the shrines where it was supposed the relics were of the greatest power. The clergy, to secure the offerings, had invented the relics and invented the stories of the wonders.

The greatest *exposure* of these things took place at the visitation of the religious houses. There were images of the Virgin and crucifixes or roods, the virtues of which many had begun to doubt. There was a famous crucifix in Boxley in Kent, which was said to smile or frown as its worshipers were generous or close-handed. About the time of the imprisonment of Bainham and others, four young men in the vicinage of Boxley determined to experiment on the virtues of this rood or crucifix. They carried it on their shoulders for some distance, and, feeling no resistance from

---

* Froude.

the idol, they fastened some tapers to it, and the image was soon reduced to a heap of ashes. For this night's work, three of these young men swung in chains (one having made his escape) on the scene of their exploit.

As yet but two men of the highest *position* in power and ability were on the side of Protestantism. But we have seen the upturnings among the people and the tendencies of many in the universities. Three editions of Tyndale's translation in English were sold before 1530. The king now gave his sanction to the work. Cromwell gave a license to Miles Coverdale to go abroad, and, with Tyndale's help, to collect and edit the scattered portions; and in 1536 there appeared in London the first *complete* edition of the English Bible. It was dedicated to Henry VIII. Cranmer and Cromwell were represented on a portion of the frontispiece as presenting the Bible to kneeling priests and laymen.

"I came not to send peace on earth, but a sword," was fully demonstrated in many of the scenes and acts of the Reformation. In all great revolutions, whether political or religious, it seems the destiny of nations to be baptized in blood. The state of England in 1434 seemed very critical. There was evidently much disaffection and discontent among the people.

Anne Boleyn had interceded for others, but the time soon came when Queen Anne herself had to die by the axe of the headsman. She was condemned to die on a false charge. She left one child, the famous Queen Elizabeth. Anne Boleyn wrote from the Tower a letter, which is still preserved in the British Museum, in which, with simple earnestness, she declares her innocence. She had tried to influence the king to favor the cause of the Reformation by forming a union with

the Protestants of Germany. The Protestants of Germany, including Luther, were generally hostile to Henry. But Cromwell, who was at this time the great and energetic leader of the affairs of England, seeing that conspiracies were rife in England, and that the throne was in danger from the *ambition* of some parties and from the fanaticism of others, determined, if possible, to form a Protestant League. Parliament in 1534 adopted a variety of measures, under Cromwell's lead, to widen the separation between Rome and England. Convocation declared that the pope had no more authority in England than any other bishop. An *act* of supremacy was passed, making Henry "head of the Church." Oh, dreadful act! Could not the independence of England have been secured in some other way! This term was applied to him simply to stop the *encroachments* of spiritual powers, within and without the realm. It was a symbol of the independence *
of England; but it has been fearfully misunderstood.

A distinction should be carefully drawn between the *nomination* of a king and the *ordination* by the clergy. As early as 1537, the reforming clergy instructed the people *not* to confound the *presentation* of a monarch with the *religious authority* conferred by the bishops and clergy. The *presentation* was simply a *nomination* to a living by a patron; the other was the holy rite of ordi-

---

* The Annates or First-fruits were at this time transferred to the crown (1532). They were afterwards restored to the Church by Queen Anne, and destined to the support of the poorer livings. A late writer on "The Property of the Church of England" says: "The property of that Church is not the property of the state. The Church of England, instead of being maintained by the state, *contributes* annually out of its own funds, for the welfare of the nation, between fifty and fifty-five millions of dollars."

nation conferred by an *authorized* clergy. Henry VIII. abused the *supremacy* given him by the convocation in putting to death some noble men who refused to acknowledge his *headship* in Church affairs. The election or nomination of the bishops by the chapters of the cathedrals had long been *formal*, and their appointment since the time of the Edwards had been practically made by the papacy, *on the nomination of the crown*. The privilege of *election* was still left to the chapters of the cathedral churches, but they were compelled to receive the candidate chosen by the king. This *strange* thing has lasted until the present time, but its *character* is wholly changed. The nomination of bishops ever since the accession of the Georges has passed from the king in person to the minister who represents the will of the people. Practically, therefore, an English prelate, among all the prelates of the world, is now raised to the episcopate by the same popular vote which raised Ambrose to the episcopal chair at Milan.

But the policy of Cromwell in Henry VIII.'s time reduced for a time the English bishops to mere dependents on the crown. Cromwell, as Vicar-General, aspired to make his monarch the center of all power, spiritual as well as temporal. Cromwell did not follow the beautiful counsel given him by Wolsey, which the great dramatist puts in his mouth. On the contrary, his cruel policy brought to the scaffold or block several noble men.

The accomplished Sir Thomas More and Fisher, bishop of Rochester, were executed because they refused to take the oath of supremacy. The Charter House monks of the Carthusian order were brought to trial for this cause. The Prior of the Charter House was executed, and many others connected with this establishment suffered imprisonment, exile and other evils. The members of the Charter House were said to be monks of pure morals and simple faith. Their fate seemed to be universally mourned.*

The same historian from whom we have already quoted says that Cromwell had a long and bitter debate to meet in the suppression of the monasteries; although the House of Commons had cried "Down with them!" when overwhelming proofs of the general corruption of the religious houses were laid before them, yet there was much wrath and hate seething in the minds of a large number of the people. Especially did they hate the measure when they saw that the money derived from the spoliation was not *all* devoted to educational purposes, but a large portion, it is alleged, was used for enriching the king, his minister Cromwell, and that minister's satellites.

"Before Cromwell's *rise* and *after* his fall from power the reign of Henry VIII. witnessed no more than the common bloodshed of the time." Cranmer, who was now Archbishop of Canterbury, never soiled his hands with any portion of the spoils of the monasteries.

Cromwell seems, from his great talents, energy and decision, to be a favorite with historians. But he set a human life at "a pin's fee." The only good we know of him was his faithful service to Cardinal Wolsey. But he did not "fling away ambition," but he hugged it to his soul. He was a pupil of Machiavel, and, like that great politician, his only aim seemed to be to make his state or country the most powerful nation of the

---

* Green.

earth, whatever costly sacrifices must be made to achieve it. His great desire to connect his monarch and country with the Protestant powers of Germany was the cause of his fall. The blow of the headsman's axe was the guerdon of his splendid services he at last received. He had caused so much blood to flow that little regret was felt at his death. Cranmer interceded strongly in his behalf, but to no avail.

In the year 1536, Henry, with the sanction of the convocation, prescribed that the Scriptures and the ancient creeds be made the standards of faith; the doctrine of justification by faith is stated; four of the sacraments are passed over, and purgatory is left doubtful. But transubstantiation, auricular confession, the worship of images and saints, were still retained. In the year 1539, however, the king and the opposers of the Reformation procured a statute to be passed in both houses of parliament, making it *penal* to speak or write against any of the six following articles, namely: 1. That there remained in the sacrament of the altar after consecration no substance of bread and wine, but under these forms the natural body and blood were present. 2. That communion in both kinds was not necessary. 3. That priests might not marry by the law of God. 4. That vows of chastity ought to be observed. 5. That masses should be continued, the use of private masses. 6. That auricular confession was expedient and necessary, and ought to be retained in the Church.

This six-article law was called the bloody statute, because it was enforced during the residue of Henry's reign, and brought many to the stake or to prison. It caused the Reformation to recede during the last eight years of Henry's reign. It was enforced until 1547.

Cromwell was executed in 1540. His fall has usually been attributed to his connection with the German marriage. He, like Wolsey, is thought to have forfeited his high position on account of a woman. Cromwell daily became more identified with the Protestants, and this must have disaffected the king, as we have seen from the "six-article act" that he became more stringent in his Romish views in the latter part of his life. Cromwell, too, had failed in the Anglo-German League. Henry was left alone politically at the very time that Charles V. and Francis I. were drawing together. The Lutherans were deluded by the emperor.

Have we maintained the position with which we set out in this chapter, that Henry VIII. was not the author of the Reformation of the Church in England? It is conceded that, through the Providence of God, opportunities were afforded in this reign for an increase of knowledge. Light from the Lutheran Reformation dawned upon England. The Bible and other books were translated. It matters not whether England's king broke the fetters that bound him to the papacy, through passion or through righteous conviction — he could break down a barrier, but he could not create or build up.

CHAPTER XXXV.

Much sarcasm has been leveled at the assumption of Henry's title, "Head of the Church."* On the accession of Elizabeth, it was deemed prudent to retire from the designation.† When the Act of Supremacy was passed, in order to guard against misconception, an explanatory document was drawn up. "The king's grace," says this paper, "has no new authority given hereby in being recognized as supreme head of the Church of England, for in that recognition is included only that he have such power as to a king appertaineth by the law of God, and not that he should take any spiritual power from ministers that is given them by the gospel. So that the words "Head of the Church" serve rather to declare to the world that the king hath power to suppress all powers, as well of the bishop of Rome as any other within *this* realm, whereby his subjects might be grieved, and to correct and remove any disquiet among the people, rather than he should pretend thereby to take away from the successors of the apostles that which was given to them by God."

In the session of this former Parliament in the twenty-fifth year of this reign, when the exactions done to the king's subjects by a power *from without* were put away, then the promise was made that nothing should

---

* Mr. Froude. † While retaining the authority.

be interpreted upon that statute that the king's grace, his nobles or subjects intended to vary from the congregation of Christ's Church, in anything in the articles of the Catholic Church, or anything declared by the word of God necessary for salvation.

"It is not *meet* lightly to think that the selfsame persons, continuing the selfsame Parliment, would, in the next year following, make an act whereby his majesty, his nobles and his subjects should so vary. And no man may *with conscience* judge that they did so."

There is no authority of Scripture that will prove that any *one* of the apostles should be head of the *Universal* Church of Christendom.

The suppression of the monasteries, as we have already hinted, produced much discontent and disorder. All the gold, silver and other property pertaining to these religious houses had been confiscated. The abbots were pensioned, and part of the revenues were expended in founding schools and colleges, and six new bishoprics; but a very large portion of the church property, the people believed, had been grasped by the courtiers and favorites of the king.

In the northern counties an army of 40,000 people undertook what they called a "pilgrimage of grace." Many towns and castles fell into their hands. A Parliament of the north met at Pomfret and demanded reunion with Rome, the restoration of Princess Mary to her rights as heiress to the crown and the fall of Cromwell. To that great statesman (Comwell) they attributed all the evils of the time. This rebellion was put down with the most summary vengeance. Four abbots were hung, and several feudal chiefs were executed. At the first outbreak the king yielded to several of their demands, and a compromise was made, but a second insurrection was put down, as we have said, with terrible violence. Much odium rested on the head of Cromwell on account of these executions, and it doubtless contributed to his overthrow, though this "pilgrimage of grace" occurred in 1536 and his execution in 1540.

Towards the close of Henry's reign the conservatives gained the ascendancy. The Protestants were persecuted. Anne Askew was racked and burned because she refused to believe in the real presence. Latimer was arrested, and an attempt was made against the life of Katharine Parr, the Protestant wife of the king. She saved her life by a little well-timed flattery of the king, who was fond of conversing with his wife on the controverted points of religion. Her enemies narrowly escaped the fate they had prepared for her. Gardiner, bishop of Winchester, was her enemy. Henry, it is said, in his last speech to Parliament, 1545, spoke as favorably of toleration as a statesman of that age could be expected to do.

Several distinguished nobles suffered upon the scaffold during this reign, but to the masses of the people it was not so tyrannical as many previous reigns. More than once Henry was compelled to yield to the popular will. A very distinguished man of this reign was Reginald Pole. He was a cousin to Henry, and wrote a book filled with arguments, which he sent to the king, protesting against the divorce and his separation from Rome.

Paul III., the successor of Clement VII., made Pole a cardinal, but he lived away from England, which was the home of his childhood and youth, until the reign of Mary Tudor. Philip Melanchthon wrote a noble protest to the king against the "Bloody Statute." He insists that Henry should repeal the barbarous decree, but the appeal was unavailing. The Protestants of Germany had been greatly grieved by what is called "the Peasants' War."

There arose in the year 1525 a multitude of seditious, delirious fanatics, who declared war against the laws and magistrates, and spread rapine and slaughter through the land. Thomas Munzer, a fanatical Anabaptist, was one of the chief incendiaries and leaders in this peasants' war. The storm subsided after the battle of Mulhausen, A. D. 1525, in which Munzer was taken and suffered capital punishment. The enemies of the Lutherans pretended to ascribe *this sedition* to the spread of the new doctrines.

The great Luther died in 1546. He had witnessed the extension of the religious doctrines he had so labored to propagate, not only throughout Germany, but also in Denmark, and Sweden. In these two last mentioned counties the Episcopate was retained; the bishops† were reformed with the people, as was the case in England.

To return to Luther. He had married, much to the surprise of his friends, in 1526, Catharine von Bora. The marriage was a happy one. He had three sons. From 1521 to 1530 Luther's pious labors were devoted to the translation of the Bible, hymns and choral services in the vernacular tongue. Luther wrote some famous hymns. Luther has been called the Elijah of the reformation. In unrolling the scroll of his-

---

* Melanchthon in 1560.   † At least *some* of them.

tory we see impressed upon it great peculiar characters, who seem to have been created for trying emergencies. Luther was one of these. He had to bear the burden of ages of superstition and ignorance, and to open and clear the way, that the world might see the light of truth. He possessed the boldness, the energy and the endurance to accomplish a grand, moral work, even the work of regenerating Christendom. He was the forerunner, the voice (not the echo) crying in the wilderness of sin and death, "Make straight in the desert a highway for our God." Under different circumstances, and different conditions many men after Luther nobly *helped* to accomplish the grand result of a glorious reformation, in giving Christian liberty to man, and in enabling him to burst the shackles of superstition.

Cranmer, the great reformer during the reigns of Henry VIII. and Edward VI., had a most difficult part to act. His path was beset with thorns during the reign of Henry. His province was to calm the irascible temper of the monarch and to sue for privileges to the church that would elevate and instruct the people. He has been called timeserving and compliant, but it is very certain from the fruits of his labor that he served the time manfully and well.

The year 1552 must be remembered as the year in which Cranmer and other divines prepared for the church in Great Britain the priceless gift of the English liturgy. The Creed, the Lord's Prayer and the Ten Commandments had already been given to the people in English. A prayer book, known as the *First Book* of Edward, had been published in 1549; but much remained in this book in the service of popery. It pleased neither party. A commission of six bishops, with Cranmer as primate, was appointed to prepare a new book, the Second Book of Edward VI., 1552.* They used the treasures of the past, that had been bequeathed to them, ancient liturgies, collects and offices which had happily survived. The present was thus connected with the past by golden links of prayer and praise, reaching down through the ages. The Songs of Zion, the Psalms of Moses and David, the noble Ode of Zachariah, the Magnificat of Mary, the Gloria in Excelsis of the Angels, and, more than all, the prayer given to us by our Lord, were as precious jewels set in this book, together with the holy and wise *collects* of the fathers of the early church and the Te Deum of Hilary. For this crowning service the arrangement of the prayer-book, England is indebted to Cranmer and his associates, next in importance to the gift of the English Bible. The people could now intelligently unite in the public worship of God. The prayers were repeated aloud. This drew multitudes to hear the *prayers* in their own native tongue.

The absolution was turned into a prayer! The prayers *for the dead* were *removed*; also, the invocation of the saints. Much credit is due to Cranmer, that he

---

* The prayer-book is the genuine flower and fruit of the Church of England, put forth by her own *inward* life, indorsed and sanctioned by her clergy in convocation and her laity in Parliament assembled. The authority of the bishop of Rome was from the first as exercised in England, an *invasion* of the rights of the British Church. This usurpation, against which the English nation vainly struggled for centuries, became intolerable as its pretenses and abuses grew. The revival of learning and the translation of the Scriptures unveiled to the people more clearly the enormities of the papacy. At length the church and nation threw off forever the usurper.

gave so much beauty and simplicity of expression to his native tongue.* As the translation of the Bible bears the impress of Tyndale, so is the image of Cranmer reflected on the calm surface of the liturgy. Many beautiful portions are translations of the Breviary. Cranmer's translations of these prayers chime like church bells in the ears of the English-speaking nation.

The English liturgy was the one admirable thing produced in the reign of Edward VI. The accession of Edward was in 1547. His father had appointed a council of regency under the Duke of Somerset, the brother of Edward's mother, Jane Seymour. Somerset surrounded Edward with Protestant teachers.

Gardiner, Bishop of Winchester, a strong opponent of the reformation, and himself a fierce persecutor, was thrown into prison by Somerset. Somerset afterwards sought to release Gardiner, but he was overcome in his conscientious scruples by Warwick, his wicked brother, and some ultra-Protestants.

Ridley was not so loving in his spirit, to those who differed from him, as we would hope to see in one so good and true. He was destined to become in the reign of Mary one of "the army of martyrs." Ridley once said to Gardiner, when referring to his

---

* Froude.

† To class the Church of England, says a late writer on "The Continuity of the Church," among the many *sects* produced by the reformation is to act in defiance of history and common sense. Not one link in the chain of her apostolic order was severed. *She* had been, and continued to be, the apostolically founded and divinely commissioned witness and keeper of Holy Writ " to preserve in England and *hand on* to future ages—to all who would seek authority and instruction "—the faith once delivered to the saints.

persecution: "The hand of God is upon me, because I have troubled other men." The spell of the past long held *some* men stern but true in the idea that certain *opinons* deemed false should be punished.

Calvin and Bullinger were not free from this mischievous error, as well as Bonner and Gardiner. A thoughtful writer says that the Roman Catholic *was* intolerant upon principle; persecution was the corollary of his creed. The Protestant *was* a persecutor *in spite of* his creed, led by vindictive temper. The Protestant brings his Bible to the door of every Christian family. He recognizes the ability of the Church in defining Scripture, but denies the infallibility of human testimony. We can not find gold unalloyed in the work of the reformation. In all revolutions there will be some base metal mixed with the pure ore.

While the unscrupulous Dudley was forming a conspiracy against his brother Somerset, while he and others of the laity were devising wicked plots, Lever, Latimer, Ridley and Cranmer held on unflinchingly to their honest convictions. With aching hearts and perplexed intellects they witnessed the prevailing corruption and cruelty. Cranmer kept aloof now from State matters, and was devoutly engaged in arranging the prayer-book. No fibre of political intrigue or conspiracy could be traced to the palace at Lambeth. No plunder of church or crown had touched his hands.

It is to be regretted,* says a late historian, that Cranmer deposed Bonner and Gardiner. There was about was time a vestment controversy. Hooker, Bishop of Gloucester, had some doubts as to the propriety of

---

* Froude.

the square cap, etc. He consulted Martyr and Bucer on this subject. They gave him wise answers. His scruples were finally overcome.

In these pages of our history we have sought to prove that the Church of England did not take its shape and form through the counsel of Henry VIII. On the contrary, that Henry maintained and promulgated the six-article law which embodied the cardinal doctrines of the Romish Church. It is conceded that through the prudent and pious intervention of learned men during this reign, important principles were gained by the friends of reform.

Henry was a sagacious prince, and in this era of reviving literature he was persuaded by Erasmus (who made the translation) and by Cranmer and others to consent to the translation of the Greek Testament into the English tongue; also the Ten Commandments and Lord's Prayer. Henry's Protestantism extended no further than a protest against the infallibility of the Pope, with regard to his divorce and a determination that he should not interfere with the affairs of his kingdom.

The dissolution of the monasteries, of which we have already spoken,* was doubtless an entering wedge to the battering down of many of the corrupt incrustations which had gathered upon the Church during the ignorance and violent misrule of the middle ages. A cry for reform from within the Church had been heard from all the countries of Europe, from the days of Wycliffe, and afterwards from the holy Savonarola, but

---

*Chapters XXXI V–XXXV.

the cry was stifled and discouraged and overcome by obstacles that seemed insurmountable.

But now the time was come. Leaders of thought in Germany, in Switzerland, and in France were earnest and active in the cause of reform. In the last years of Henry's life *reform* had retrograded in England because of the terrors of the "six articles."

In 1547, Edward VI. ascended ihe throne. The parliament in 1547 repealed the laws which sanctioned persecution, but previous to this time Bonner and Gardiner, refusing to obey the injunctions of the court of Edward, had been sent to prison. Injunctions were issued to regulate worship and religious order. They who prepared and revised the English prayer-book were engaged in selecting the treasures of the past. They retained all that was in unison with the word of God. They did not, says Bishop Hall, take the prayer-book out of the *mass*, but they thrust the mass out of the prayer-book. They did not adopt much that was new. They were reformers, not revolutionists.

In 1551 *forty-two* articles of faith were adopted. In 1552 the prayer-book was organized and made nearly as it is now in the Church of England and the Episcopal Church of the United States. By the act of supremacy the right of reforming the Church was in the crown; but, says Mr. Gladstone, when the convocation acknowledged the *headship of the crown* in 1531, Archbishop Warham was primate. Not one of the bishops or prelates who determined the royal supremacy had aught to do with the reformation. Cranmer was not a bishop when this act of supremacy was passed. The leading reformers of Edward's reign (sixteen years after the act of supremacy was passed), were young Edward himself, the Duke of Somerset, the king's uncle, the lord protector, the Archbishops Cranmer and Holgate, Paget, secretary of state, Lisle high admiral, the Bishops Holbeach, Goodrich, Latimer, and Ridley.

Peter Martyr, of Florence, was appointed divinity professor at Oxford, and Martin Bucer was professor at Cambridge. Both these men were liberal enlightened reformers. The king, though a child in years, was remarkably mature in intelligence and virtue. The dependents of Dudley, earl of Northumberland, appropriated to themselves all the public property they could lay their hands upon. The young prince, on the contrary, stimulated the lord mayor and aldermen to establish hospitals and schools.

Parliament had ratified the *first* book of Edward published in 1549, and aftewards the revised book of Edward, published in 1552. As a proof of the intolerance of the times parliament made it a penal offense to use any other liturgy. Some tumults were excited by this measure, but they were soon quieted. Edward VI. seemed to have just notions of government, and was truly a religious prince.

Many learned men had gathered around from every quarter holding Protestant opinions, The leading opponents to reform were the Princess Mary, Wrothesley, the Bishops Tonstal, Gardiner, and Bonner. The first book of Homilies was appointed to be read in the church when the incumbents were not well qualified to preach.

CHAPTER XXXVI.

ACCESSION OF MARY TUDOR.

Edward died in 1553. As soon as Mary, the daughter of Katherine of Arragon, was established upon the throne, she proceeded to release from prison Bonner, Gardiner, Tonstal, and to restore them to their sees. The reforming bishops, Cranmer, Hopper, Latimer and Ridley, Coverdale, Rogers, Holgate, were incarcerated. Eight hundred friends of the Reformation fled from their country and settled upon the Rhine. Among these were bishops, deans, archdeacons, doctors of divinity, together with noblemen, merchants, etc. A compliant parliament repealed the laws that Edward had made, and restored things to the state in which Henry had left them. The Protestant professors, Martyr and Bucer, were expelled.

Mary had had a brief struggle for the throne in a contest with the partisans of the Dudleys and Greys, who had urged Lady Jane Grey, against her will and judgment, to pretend to the throne, which was the rightful inheritance of Mary Tudor.

Lady Jane was a Protestant, distinguished for her learning and accomplishments, and for a lovely, religious character, as all historians testify. Unfortunately, she became the *tool* of the unprincipled Dudley, her father-in-law, who, to serve his own selfish ends, wished to make her Queen. She was the granddaughter of Mary, the youngest sister of Henry VIII. Her father also was descended from Margaret, Henry's eldest sister.

But the people of England had too strong a sense of justice, despite her Catholicism, to ignore the claims of Mary to the throne of England.

It is said that Edward VI. heartily desired that his cousin, Lady Jane, should succeed him, on account of her Protestant opinions, and her excellence of character. Edward had been educated with his cousin, and fully understood the purity of her religious principles; in his languishing state of health, Dudley, now Earl of Northumberland, persuaded the young king to execute a deed, whereby Lady Jane Grey, to the exclusion of his sister's superior legal rights, was made heir to England, and Queen of England. After wearing a crown for ten days, the noble princess resigned the vain pageantry and returned to domestic life.

Mary immediately ascended the throne. She at first concealed her violent bigotry, and assured the people that she would not alter the laws of Edward VI. An entire change, however, quickly followed her accession, both in men and measures. All the popish rites were everywhere restored. The imprisoned bishops were released. A compliant parliament in October, 1553, repealed the reforming laws of King Edward. The married and recusant clergy, some thousands in number, were deprived of their parishes and sees.

Much displeasure was now manifested at the violent measures of the Queen, and especially her proposed marriage with Philip II., king of Spain. An entensive conspiracy was formed by Sir Thomas Wyatt, Sir Peter Carew and the Duke of Suffolk. The strong motive with the latter was the hope of recovering the crown for Lady Jane Grey. This rebellion ended in disaster and defeat. Lady Jane Grey, who had been spared when her father-in-law expiated his guilt on the scaffold, on account of her youth and innocence, was now attainted for treason, together with her youthful husband, Guilford Dudley, and suffered the extreme penalty of the law. It is said that the council, dreading the compassion of the people for one so loved, ordered that she should be beheaded privately, within the verge of the Tower, while her husband was executed on Tower Hill.*

The fires of Smithfield burned fiercely during Mary's short reign of *five years*. Rogers, prebendary of St. Paul's, a man distinguished for piety and learning, was the first martyr. Hooper, Bishop of Gloucester, was condemned at the same time with Rogers; he was sent to his own diocese to be punished, in order to strike more terror into his flock. But his constancy had the opposite effect. He bore testimony to the truths he had proclaimed among them, until the violence of his sufferings denied him utterance. Ferrar, bishop of St. David's, also suffered martyrdom in his own diocese. Ridley, Bishop of London, and Latimer, of Worcester, perished together in the same fire at Oxford. Latimer called to his companion when tied to the stake, "Be of good cheer, my brother! We shall *this* day kindle such a flame in England as I trust, in God, will never be

---

* "The husband was first executed. When *she* heard of the magnanimity and calmness that her husband evinced on the scaffold, she was encouraged to write upon her tablets three sentences — one in Greek, one in Latin and one in English; purporting that, though *human* justice was against her husband's body, divine mercy would be favorable to his soul."—RUSSEL'S MODERN EUROPE.

extinguished." Sanders was committed to the flames at Coventry; he rejected with scorn a pardon offered him if he would recant, crying out, "Welcome cross of Christ! Welcome everlasting life!"

But the man who had been most active in Edward's reign, he who had given shape and form and consistency to the work of reformation, now faltered *for a time* when he was called upon to die. We mean Archbishop Cranmer!

He was now an old man; his body was enfeebled by a long imprisonment; in a moment of infirmity he signed a recantation. When it was known that he had signed this paper, he was required by Mary and her council to come to the church, that he might acknowledge publicly his errors. He came to the church, weary and weak with suffering, but he surprised his audience with a very different declaration from that which the Queen expected. After explaining his sense of what he owed to God and his sovereign, he said, "There is one miscarriage in my life, which above all others, I heartily repent — I mean, the insincere declaration of faith to which I had the weakness to subscribe. I take this opportunity of atoning for my sin by a public declaration. I am willing to seal with my blood those doctrines, which, in an hour of infirmity I denied — *doctrines* which I firmly believe to have been communicated from heaven."

But little time was lost before he was led to the stake. When the fire burned around him, he thrust his right hand into the fierce flame, exclaiming, "This hand has offended." He seemed to find some relief when he had sacrificed this instrument of his crime to divine justice.

The whole number put to death in this reign was about two hundred and eighty-eight. Some died in prison and many, as we have said, fled the country. Cardinal Pole, after a long absence, was recalled to England. He, it is believed, tried to restrain the court of Mary in their ferocious proceedings. Bonner has been charged with the chief agency in these cruel proceedings. Queen Mary died in 1558.

Elizabeth was immediately proclaimed. She determined to restore the reformed religion. She first inhibited preaching until church affairs were more settled. The exiles hastened back to their homes in England. They were somewhat divided in their views as to discipline, rites and ceremonies. The court secured a parliament in 1559, which repealed the persecuting laws of Mary Tudor, and invested the sovereign with power to regulate the discipline and forms of worship. She consulted the clergy as to these measures. The Queen appointed Parker, Grindal, Cox and others to revise the liturgy of King Edward, which had been so carefully revised and compiled by Cranmer Very slight alterations were made; it was ratified by parliament and established by law.

Much prudence had been exercised by Elizabeth during the reign of her sister. When pressed as to her belief in the *real presence*, she replied:

> "Christ was the Word, that spake it,
> He took the bread, and brake it;
> And what that Word did make it,
> Thus I believe, and take it."

About forms of prayer, there has been and ever will be, much thought and discussion in the religious world. When the disciples of our Lord asked from

Him instruction in prayer, He gave them a *form* of prayer; a form forever hallowed in the hearts of His people. The wants of individual human hearts are the same in every age and country, when looking to the Father of our spirits, the source of all hope and help. In the worship of the congregation, however, not only *similarity*, but some degree of uniformity, seems to be necessary. Accordingly, we find from very early times, the existence of liturgies.

The Jews used precomposed forms of prayer. The Greek, in the chorus of the tragedy and in singing pœans to their gods, *united* in lofty religious harmonies. The Psalms were introduced early into the public Christian service. "The Church," says Dean Milman, "succeeded to an inheritance of religious lyrics as unrivalled in the history of poetry as of religion." The Psalms, and *perhaps* the Psalmody that had filled the spacious courts of the temple, may have been adopted by the Christians. The earliest recorded hymns are fragments from the Scripture — those hymns that are now constantly sung in our Episcopal churches, viz., the Doxology, the angelic hymn, Glory be to God on High; the Cherubic Hymn, and the Hymn of Victory, are both taken from Revelation. The Magnificat, and the Nunc Dimittis, are still sung in the Church of England.

In the early Christian churches each nation had its liturgy. In these there was much similarity, but not entire uniformity. When Gregory I. writes to Austin, in the sixth century, on the discipline of the British Church (which had come into contact with the church of his Saxon converts), he tells him not to interfere with the worship of the Britons, but to allow them to use their own liturgy, which had been received from another source.

The liturgy used in the church at Jerusalem can be traced back to the second century. The liturgies of Basil and Chrysostom are revisions of the early church at Jerusalem. These form the basis of the liturgies of the Greek Church in Russia and Greece, and Armenia. The liturgy of Cyril of Alexandria forms the principal part of the worship of the Copts in Egypt and Abyssinia. The Ambrosian liturgy, ascribed to Barnabas, is still used in the churches of Milan. The liturgy used in Spain is very ancient. The Gallican church had a liturgy of its own until the rise of the Carlovingians. The Roman liturgy gradually supplanted the Gallican liturgy, which has been ascribed to Hilary of Poictiers.

The Roman liturgies are traced to the time of Leo I., 440. To Hilary of Poictiers has been ascribed the grand anthem of the Te Deum; but it has usually been styled the Hymn of Ambrose, as tradition says he sang it in the church at Milan, at the baptism of St. Augustine, in the fourth century.

Many liturgies were written in the sixteenth century during the reforming movement; but the most celebrated of these was the liturgy of the Church of England, which was carefully revised from the treasures of the past. Of this we have fully spoken. Calvin, Luther and Zuingliu published liturgies, but no uniformity was arrived at among them. The Swiss and Germans retained their liturgies until the close of the eighteenth century, when a new theology (rationalism), produced a radical change in the spirit and form of Divine worship in those countries. At the present day, however, these churches have returned to their liturgies of the sixteenth century, and now seem to value liturgical worship.

We have spoken of the accession of Elizabeth in 1559, and of the clergy she appointed to revise the liturgy adopted during Edward's reign. It was slightly altered, but all that savored of idolatry, all the notions about purgatory, were rigorously excluded; the precious services of the early church were retained, and the bishops, pri sts and deacons continued in an uninterrupted line, as from the beginning. When the bishops of Mary's reign were called upon to take the oath of supremacy, all refused except one. New bishops were consecrated by the ex-bishops of Edward's reign. The Queen now ordered a visitation of all the churches in her realm and issued injunctions regulating worship and discipline, and the duties of clergymen; also holy days, etc., with penalties against the recusant clergy. Two hundred refused obedience; these lost their livings.

The convocation, in revising the Forty-two Articles of Religion, as they are called, reduced them to thirty-nine, the number in which they *now* exist in the English and American prayer-books. The Puritan argued at this convocation for a still more simple worship, but the book, as prepared by Cranmer, has remained substantially the *same* from that time to the present day.

A NOTE ON ROMAN CATACOMBS. — Inquiries are frequently made in late years about the Catacombs of Rome: What are they? They are galleries dug in the rock, used as places of burial. The Christians, following the examples of the Jews, buried *their dead* in rock-hewn galleries. In times of *persecution*, the early Christians used them as places of worship. They wrote on the graves of their friends consoling words, and painted symbols of their happiness in heaven. From the sixth century to the seventeenth, nothing was known of the Catacombs, as they were deserted at the invasion of the barbarians, and filled with ruins.

"These Catacombs," says Dean Stanley, "are a standing monument of the Oriental and Jewish character even of Western Christianity."

The *primitive Christians* of Rome were an Eastern community, speaking Greek. All the paintings on these Catacombs are cheerful and joyous. There is neither the cross of the fifth century, nor the crucifix of the twelfth. There is the Good Shepherd, the Vine with its branches, also the Lamb at the foot of the Cross. There are many symbols of the Resurrection.

> "I say to thee, do thou repeat
> To the first man thou mayest meet
> In lane, highway or open street,
> That he and I and all men move
> Under a *canopy* of love
> As broad as the blue sky above."
> — TRENCH.

CHAPTER XXXVII.

JOHN KNOX — REFORMATION IN SCOTLAND AND SWITZERLAND.

The affairs of Scotland, civil and ecclesiastical, were in great confusion from the death of James V., in 1542, to the accession of Mary, Queen of Scots, in 1561. As early as 1527, Protestant doctrines had made their way in Scotland. Perhaps some of the writings of Luther, that Latimer, Bilney, and Tyndale had circulated in England, had reached Scotland. It is quite certain that in 1527 Patrick Hamilton was arraigned for heresy and burned at the stake at St. Andrews. Hamilton had visited seminaries of learning on the continent, and was greatly esteemed for his accomplishments. Hamilton was abbot of Ferne, a young nobleman of blameless life. He suffered martyrdom in the twenty-fourth year of his age. From this time Protestantism made *slow* but sure progress in Scotland.

For nineteen years Mary Guise held arbitrary sway over the kingdom. She was the widow of James V. and mother of Mary Queen of Scots, and the sister of the famous Guises of France. With little observation or opposition the reformed doctrines were quietly spreading in Scotland until the martyrdom of George Wishart, a reformed preacher, by Beatoun, Archbishop of St. Andrews. This occurred in 1545, and created the wildest excitement.

Norman Leslie, a young nobleman, assembled an

armed force, surprised and murdered the cardinal in his castle of St. Andrews. Leslie and his adherents held possession of St. Andrews for fourteen months. John Knox was the leading spirit at this time among the preachers, and boldly preached the doctrines of the reformation. The Regent, Mary Guise, assisted by a French squadron, forced the garrison of St. Andrews to submit. Knox was among the prisoners. He was sent out of the country to France. He was on the *galleys* nineteen months. John Knox had been educated in the University of Glasgow. He was a teacher of philosophy and theology at St. Andrews in 1530, devoting himself in his hours of study to the works of Augustine and Jerome, and doubtless contrasted the doctrines of these ancient fathers of the church with the traditional teachings of the court of Rome in the sixteenth century. After his release from the French galleys he became for a short time one of the chaplains at the court of Edward VI.

On the accession of Mary Tudor* he fled from England. He resided in Geneva for two years with Calvin, Beza, and other learned reformers. In 1559 Knox left Geneva for his native country, greatly strengthened and encouraged by his intimate communion with Calvin.

Knox, in his theological views, was an ardent disciple of Calvin, and a bold and fearless preacher. He was a leader in the political affairs of his country, as well as in the ecclesiastical. The tyranny and dissimulation of the unpopular Regent, Mary Guise, together with the violent intolerance of the reforming preachers,

---

* To the throne of England.

produced violent and disgraceful scenes. Iconoclasm was a prominent feature in the Scottish reformation. An insurrection ensued on one occassion, when some of the were priests preparing to celebrate mass. In the mad fury of the people the images of the churches were demolished, pictures torn from the walls, and the houses of some of the Franciscan and Dominican Friars were destroyed.

Civil war raged through the kingdom between the regent, assisted by French troops and the *lords* of the congregation, as the Protestant leaders were called. Elizabeth, Queen of England, sent powerful assistance to the Protestants. The death of the regent, while the city of Edinburgh was invested, led to a truce and to the call of a parliament to settle differences. Parliament, in 1560, established the reformed religion and Roman Catholicism was interdicted. When Mary Queen of Scots, came to her kingdom in 1561, she summoned John Knox to her presence. He discussed with undaunted vigor the questions she proposed to him. She had him arrested in 1563, but all except the dependents of the court acquitted him.

The Presbyterian churches accepted the order of Geneva. The Scots have inflexibly held to the Presbyterian form of government, doctrine, and discipline through many trials. Though we may not fully sympathize in their mode of worship, nor feel satisfied with their ordination (seeing that they exclude what we deem the apostolic mode), yet it must be conceded by every candid mind that the Calvinists of Scotland and Geneva have been able defenders of the cardinal truths of our holy religion, and warm advocates of civil liberty.

In this world of sin they have been active in battering down the strongholds of Satan by well directed engines of the press and pulpit. Mosheim, in tracing the origin and progress of the Lutheran Church, says this church was *called* Lutheran because it would not be ungrateful to the man who first dispersed the clouds that had gathered around gospel truth, teaching his hearers to place no reliance upon their own doings, or upon glorified saints, but to give all their confidence to Christ.

We date the commencement of the Lutheran Church from the time when Leo X. expelled Martin Luther and his adherents from the Roman Church in 1520. It acquired a permanent form in 1530, when the confession of its faith was drawn up and presented to the diet of Augsburg. It was freed from the jurisdiction of the pope in 1552, when Maurice of Saxony made a *pacification* with Charles V. at Passau. Like all Protestant churches, the Lutheran holds that the rule for a correct faith and holy life is to be drawn from the Bible itself. This church has certain books, such as the Augsburg Confession, the Articles of Smalcald, and the Catechisms of Luther. These, like the "Book of Common Prayer," are deemed to be digests of the *sacred* oracles.

The prayer-book of Episcopalians derives much of its *significance* from its being a record of the utterances of distinguished *saints* in the primitive and uncorrupted ages of the church. The internal regulation of the Lutheran Church is intermediate between the Episcopal and Presbyterian forms or systems, except in Sweden and Denmark, where the Episcopal form is retained. The Lutherans have a liturgy. These liturgies have been often amended, as circumstances required or as sovereigns demanded. They commemorate the *great* festivals of the Christian year, as Christmas, Easter, Ascension, Pentecost.

The Reformed Church in Switzerland (called usually the German Reformed) had for her founder and most zealous defender Zwingle or Zuinglius. This church differed but little in the beginning from the Lutherans, except in regard to "the Lord's Supper." The father of the Swiss Church taught that the bread and wine *represent* the body and blood of Christ. The Lord's Supper, said the early followers of Zuinglius, is simply a memorial of Christ.

Several leading men † among the reformers tried to assimulate the doctrine of Zuinglius to the view of Luther, who taught consubstantiation of the spiritual presence of Christ in the Eucharist. One of the illustrations used by the Lutherans to denote this idea was "as *heat* dwells in iron, but it does not change it." John Calvin was of Noyon in France. He obtained the direction of the Church in Geneva in 1541, and had vast influence in the republic. It was his aim to make Geneva the mother of the whole Reformed Church and the focus of light, as Wittemberg had been to the Lutheran community. His chief influence outside of Switzerland was felt in France; its churches looked to him for counsel and received his creed and polity. He had ceaseless industry. Calvin was an intellectual giant. How wonderful and rich were his mental gifts! But, alas! his hard temper, together with the inherited spirit of the times, betrayed him into a fearful crime— the persecution unto death of Michel Servetus for her-

---

NOTE.—The *Mercersburg* professors are said to entertain *now* different views from Zuinglius.

† Especially Martin Bucer.

esy. This dark shadow constantly rises up to intercept his brilliant fame, and to lessen his influence as a great reformer.

Beza, who succeeded to the chair of theology occupied by Calvin, wrote at Calvin's request a defense of the execution of Servetus, in which he pleaded the right of the civil power to punish heresy. Beza afterwards greatly modified his opinions. He was a man of admirable temper. An edict of toleration in France made it safe for Beza to return to his own country. He was very anxious to proclaim the reformed doctrines in Paris. While there some of the retainers of the Duke of Guise attacked a congregation of Huguenots, assembled in a barn for worship. A frightful massacre ensued. Beza hastened to the court to remonstrate. One of the nobles present threw all the blame upon the Huguenots. "I admit, sire," said the reformer, "it is the part of God's church, in whose name I speak, to endure rather than to inflict blows; but may it please you to remember that it is an *anvil* which has worn out many a hammer."

We must not forget while speaking of the many righteous Protestants of this era to mention Borromeo, a Romanist of Milan, who reminded his people of the good deeds of Ambrose, so devoted was he to the duties of his bishopric. Borromeo was the agent in finishing the work of the council of Trent in 1563. He was the most unworldly of men, and as benevolent as he was unworldly.

To return to Calvin. The institution of Calvin continued to flourish long after his death, in 1564. By his writings and his famous academy of learning he induced many eminent persons to emigrate to Geneva.

Calvin introduced at Geneva the Presbyterian form of church government. The disciples of Zuinglius would not accept the views of Calvin on the Lord's Supper, and were also much opposed to his views of predestination. But the reformed religion, as shaped by Calvin, took up a permanent residence not only at Geneva, but it had many adherents in France and Germany.

Frederick III., in 1560, substituted Calvinistic teachers for Lutheran teachers. There were friends of the reformation in France from a very early time. The encouragement that Francis I. gave to learned men induced many persons of genius to reside in France. Some of these were reformers, and they brought with them Protestant writings.

William Brissonet, bishop of Meaux, 1530, felt and deplored the corruptions of the Romish Church. He wished to work a reformation in his diocese without producing a schism. He associated with himself several pure spirits. His efforts were rendered abortive by persecution. He protected for a time Le Fevre, Farrel, and Roussel, who were known to be earnest reformers.

The lovely Margaret Valois, of Navarre, the sister of Francis I., was an earnest promoter of the spread of evangelical religion. Her brother rebuked her for the protection she afforded to Lutherans. She promised not to proceed further, if he would grant certain concessions. Two of these concessions were that the *host* should not be worshiped, and that the *cup* should be given to the laity. This famous woman was the maternal grandmother of Henry IV., of Navarre.

"The reformation in France," says d'Aubigné, "was *self-adopted.*" It put out shoots in the *university* itself, having germinated in Paris. Be this as it may, there is no country where the Huguenots were more fiercely persecuted than in France. Their confession of faith was drawn by the strong hand of Calvin at a general synod in May, 1559.

It was during the reign of Henry II. that the Huguenots gained so much strength that they attempted to become the dominant party. The love of political power was a leading feature in some of the members of the reform party, as well as those of the Romanist party. Antony, king of Navarre, his brother, the Prince of Condé, and many of the nobility were Protestants in their feelings and opinions. They belonged to the Huguenot party, with perhaps little personal piety. But Admiral de Coligny, the greatest general and statesman of them all, combined with the genius of a warrior the fervor of a religious reformer. How grand is the opportunity of doing good in the State, when men like de Coligny preside in its council.*

Catharine de Medicis, the widow of Henry II., has become a synonym for the most monstrous vices. She cared not for religion. Power was the idol she worshiped. She was the ruler behind the throne during the short successive reigns of two of her sons. The Duke of Guise, a Romanist leader, and the Princes of Bourbon, supported by the Huguenots, also contended for the mastery during the feeble administration of Catharine's sons. Some concessions made by the Guises and the Queen to the Huguenots, to serve political ends, stirred up the jealousy of the Romanists.

---

* The world has presented few such models. Washington, in our own land, Guizot in France, and the present Premier in England, Mr. Gladstane, are striking examples.

In order to pacify them war was renewed with the Huguenots. After a bitter contest peace was declared at St. Germain in 1570. The daughter of Catharine, and sister of Charles IX., was given to Henry of Navarre, the great military leader of the Huguenot party. This seeming peace culminated in the massacre of St. Bartholomew, 1572. It was instigated by the queen mother, and occurred on the night of the marriage of her daughter.

CHAPTER XXXVIII.

MASSACRE OF ST. BARTHOLOMEW, 1572.

This horrible massacre was instigated by the queen mother; it filled Protestant Europe with horror. On this night perished Coligny, the benefactor of France, of whom we have already spoken, with many other worthy people. Five thousand persons perished in Paris alone. One mayor only in the numerous cities of France, it is said, had the moral courage to despise the edict of the young king, Charles IX. This boy* died in less than two years of nervous prostration and remorse. Henry III, successor to Charles, was more jealous of the League than of the Huguenots. The Guises, the Duke and the Cardinal, were at the head of the League. This League, it is alleged, had been formed for the extermination of the Protestants, but more probably with the purpose of transferring the crown of France to the head of the Duke of Guise at the death of Henry III, whose health was very feeble. Henry III. procured the assassination of the brothers, the Duke of Guise and the Cardinal, but was himself murdered in a short time, 1589, by Clement, a Dominican fanatic. Henry IV. now acceded to the throne; he reached it by *one* † of the three methods of obtaining it, the success of his sword. He refused to take Paris *by assault*, lest he should sacrifice too many lives. To give *peace* to

---

* He was but nineteen years old.
† By inheritance, by *election*, by the sword.

his distracted country, he declared himself a Roman Catholic, thus forsaking the faith of his fathers. He issued immediately as a reparation "the Edict of Nantes," which gave to the Huguenots the same *rights* as the Romanists. They enjoyed by this edict full religious liberty.

We now *recede* a little to speak of *a body* that did not wholly sympathize with the kings and queens. The parliament of Paris refused to register some of the decrees against the Huguenots made by the wicked Katharine. That parliament also refused to register an edict for the establishment of the Inquisition in France. A discussion in 1559 took place in the parliament condemning former rigors and urging a more merciful policy. Henry II., husband of Katharine de Medicis, interposed and ordered *seven* of the men who recommended mercy to be imprisoned. This cruel monarch, who threatened that he would himself *see* the Huguenots burned, was called a few days after to a higher tribunal. He was wounded in the eye at a tournament, which caused his death.

Henry, duke of Navarre (afterwards Henry IV:), was a heroic, humane man, but *fanaticism* would not suffer him to live. He was murdered in 1610, leaving the Huguenots without a protector. They had *rest*, however, during the administrations of Richelieu and Mazarin. They (the Huguenots) were *faithful* during the minority of Louis XIV., and actually fought against Condé to sustain the throne of Louis. In 1685 this *Grande Monarque revoked* the Edict of Nantes. This revocation made 500,000 of the best citizens of France to flee to other countries and live in exile. Large numbers were sheltered in England. Many came to America. The names of their descendants are still recognized among *our* people.

Among the sects that arose in Germany about this time were the Anabaptists of Westphalia. This sect, *now* so learned and pious, were in their *origin* connected with fanaticism and sedition. Some of the princes of Germany, incensed by the seditious leaders of the Anabaptists, persecuted the whole society. Munzer and his associates in Saxony and in other German provinces proclaimed war in 1525 against all law and civil government, declaring that Christ alone would reign from that time forward. The Anabaptists, by the favor of William I., Prince of Orange, acquired a quiet residence in Belgium. William I., the great vindicator of Batavian liberty, accepted the simple affirmation of these enthusiasts, not requiring from them a citizen's oath. In 1689 messengers from a hundred congregations in England and Wales, met in London, and drew up a confession, very similar to the Westminster and Savoy Conferences.

The troubles of the Baptists seem to have resulted chiefly from their interference with the civil governments. Some of them had very just views of civil and religious liberty, but they brought much odium upon themselves in railing at "the higher powers." It was under very different circumstances that Roger Williams denied the right of the magistrate to impose faith and worship, also the right of the king to take the lands of the Indians without purchase. To obtain the freedom he desired he retired to the shores of Narragansett, R. I., where he founded the city called Providence. Williams and his coadjutors founded the first Baptist church in America. They instituted baptism by immersion, Holliman, a lay *elder*, baptizing Williams and he baptizing the elder. Williams had been a minister of the Church of England, and afterwards an elder among the Puritans at Salem, Massachusetts. Persecution drove him to Rhode Island. Roger Williams was a noble, large-hearted man. Civil and religious liberty are greatly indebted to him. The history of Williams, say his biographers, was for half a century the history of Providence, R. I. He made several trips to England, where he received assistance for his colony. He was made president of the colony in 1654. He enjoyed when in England intimate communion with John Milton. Williams would not persecute the Quakers, but discussed with some of their leaders the importance of the sacraments.

Washings and sprinklings have formed a part of the religious ceremonies of all nations. This rite of initiation arose doubtless from a sense of impurity. When the Jewish ceremonial law was instituted by Moses, with its various *washings* prescribed to priest and people, they were intended to convey to their darkened minds the idea of holiness, and the necessity of purification in approaching God in worship. These people understood the power of Jehovah, but they had little conception of his holiness or love. They were brutalized by the superstitions of Egypt and the evil treatment they had received.

John the Baptist called upon his followers to be baptized. Our Lord received baptism either by immersion or pouring, and he commanded his disciples to teach and baptize all nations. Baptists claim that the immersion of believing adults was the primitive baptism. It is conceded by many who now use sprinkling that immersion was the most usual mode in the early church. It is still exclusively practiced by the Oriental churches and the Greek church, but these immerse their infants. The Western church, some centuries before the Reformation, adopted sprinkling as most convenient, especially in the cold countries of Northern Europe.

An effort was made in the sixteenth century to restore immersion to the church; but except in the case of the Anabaptists the effort was unsuccessful. The Episcopal Church makes it optional with the *subject* whether immersion or sprinkling should be used. Baptists refuse to accept infants as proper subjects of baptism. A large class of Baptists, inasmuch as they consider *baptism* as the door of entrance to their communion, decline to partake of the "sacrament of the Lord's Supper" with other Christian denominations. Open communion, however, has been eloquently advocated by Robert Hall, the great Baptist divine of England. Within the present century the Baptists have advanced rapidly in numbers and influence.* Under the name of Baptists, a great variety of sects are embraced. John Bunyan, who lived in the seventeenth century, and the author of "Pilgrim's Progress," was a Baptist. Baptists all agree in maintaining the congregational form of church government.

The advocates of infant baptism argue somewhat in this manner: "God said to Abraham, every man child among you shall be circumcised." By this command circumcision became the *rite* of the Abrahamic cove-

---

* The disciples of Carey who planted a Baptist mission in India in 1796, have done much to evangelize India; also Mr. and Mrs. Judson, who went thither from the United States.

nant, and is declared by St. Paul to be the sign and seal of that covenant; this sign and seal was administered to infants. If baptism comes in the place of circumcision, the presumption is that Jesus, by the words "make disciples of all nations," baptizing them meant that baptism should be administered to infants. When Jesus said "Suffer little children to come unto me, for of such is the kingdom of heaven," nothing is said of baptism, but there is no prohibition. If by the kingdom of heaven is meant the heavenly society and church of Christ's kingdom, then there is encouragement to parents to bring their children to God in baptism.

We have no account in Scripture of the baptism of Christ's disciples. They were probably baptized by John the Baptist, but there is no record of it. We read of the baptism of households. In such cases the faith of the parent or guardian was accepted. In physical diseases our Lord sometimes accepted the faith of the parent in the healing of the child. When Peter says "Be baptized every one of you . . . . for the *promise* is unto you and your children," he was speaking to Jews who knew that the promise of Abraham was to them and to their children, they would naturally infer that the blessings of the gospel would not be less extensive. Infant baptism was practiced in the early church, and in whatever way administered it devolved upon the children to confirm this dedication when they reached mature years.

Church history asserts that the *baptized* presented themselves to the bishop to receive the laying on of hands. In this *rite* they declared their personal faith in Christ, and made a solemn renunciation of a worldly, sinful life. Confirmation, or laying on of hands, is not regarded by Protestants as a sacrament but as a holy rite.

Our Lord said to Nicodemus, "Except ye be born of water and of the Spirit ye can not enter into the kingdom of God." (St. John, third chapter). Some Christians suppose that this declaration means that no person can be admitted to heaven who has not been baptized with water. St. Paul's language perhaps strengthens this opinion, "He saved us by the washing of regeneration, and the renewing of the Holy Ghost." The Church of Rome considers baptism when administered by a priest with good intention, as applying the merits of Christ to the person baptized. Hence their great anxiety for the early baptism of children, believing this sacrament necessary to salvation. Augustine, the famous bishop and writer of the fourth century, made a distinction between the regeneration produced by the waters of baptism and the *predestinated*. The reception of this sacrament either by an infant or adult would deliver them, *he* taught, from the *wrath* or sin which the children of Adam inherit, but unless they were predestined to salvation they would not *persevere* in that state to which they had been regenerated. Inasmuch as our Lord invites all to come to him and partake of the water of life freely, and as St. Paul too declares that the sacrifice of Christ was a propitiation for the sins of *the whole world*, we can not sympathize in this view of the great theologian Augustine. We believe that all who come to God in sincerity will be accepted. All who are baptized by an authorized minister, whether infant or adult, in the exercise of faith, are brought into covenant with God, into *a state* of salvation. Christ has not established a *nullity* in giving us baptism, if we receive it according to his command by faith and repentance. The blood of Christ is surely available to the *unbaptized* when opportunity is wanting. God is a God of love.

CHAPTER XXXIX.

The Quakers, a sect that arose in England in the early part of the seventeenth century, whose founder was George Fox, refuse to accept either baptism or the Lord's supper as obligatory upon them. They consider these sacraments merely as symbolical actions, the one shadowing forth the inward purification of the soul; the other, the intimate communion which Christians enjoy with Christ. They say our Lord condescended to use these sacraments in accommodation to the weakness of his disciples and followers, but all sacraments became unnecessary after the outpouring of the Holy Ghost, upon the day of Pentecost. They consider it wrong to prepare a sermon, or to *preach*, in the ordinary sense of that word; they must not indeed "neglect the assembling of themselves together," but in their assemblies they must wait for the impulse of the Spirit before they attempt to pray aloud or exhort. They did not acknowledge the necessity of a regular ministry; each man or woman in their meetings, who was *moved*, as they supposed, by the Spirit of God, stood upon the same plane and possessed equal authority.

Notwithstanding their fanatical and fanciful views on many points in religion, they incorporated into their system some sound practical principles, which have challenged the respect of all. They have adopted literally, under all circumstances, the words of our Saviour as to non-resistance. They say that war is wholly at variance with the spirit of the Gospel, which continually breathes peace on earth and good will to all men. The Quaker, therefore, never engages in war, and would never hold in bondage a fellow-creature.

As it regards slavery and war, the principles of the Quaker must ever be accepted, in the abstract, by Christians of every name; but in the question of self-defense, either of individuals or nations, a formidable obstacle is presented to its practical working. But, if the doctrines of the Quakers were carried out, "nation would not lift up the sword against nation, nor would men learn war any more."

George Fox, the founder of the Society of Friends, was educated in the Church of England. From childhood he led a religious life. He was apprenticed to a shoemaker, who also kept sheep; his occupation was chiefly that of a shepherd. Passing much of his time in retirement, and being earnestly engaged for the salvation of his soul, he diligently read the Holy Scriptures, waiting on the Lord to be taught by His Spirit their true meaning.

"This sect had its birth," says Mr. Bancroft (he has given us a beautiful chapter on the rise of Quakerism), "in a period of intense public activity — when the heart of England was swelling with passions, and the public mind turbulent with factious leaders; when a zeal for reform was invading the Church, subverting the *throne*, and repealing the privileges of feudalism; when Presbyterians in every village were quarreling with Independents and Anabaptists, and all with the English Church and with the Roman Catholics."*

---

* History of the United States.

George Fox was set by his employer to watch sheep. He was a shepherd, like David, and Tamerlane, and Sixtus V. The occupation was grateful to his mind; the years thus engaged were passed away in prayer and in reading the Bible, in frequent fasts, and in reveries of contemplative devotion. He commenced preaching at nineteen years of age. One day the thought rose in his mind that a man might be bred at Oxford and Cambridge, and yet be unable to solve the problem of his existence. Again, he reflected that God lives not in temples of brick or stone, but in the hearts of the living. From the parish priest, he turned to the dissenters, but he found them unable to reach his condition. He now determined, within himself, that truth is to be sought for by listening to the voice of God in the soul.

The "inner light" from henceforth must be the guide of the Quaker. The Bible is the religion of Protestants. Had the Quaker a better guide? The Quaker rejoined, that he believed in the unity of truth; there can be no contradiction between right reason and previous revelation, between just tradition and an enlightened conscience. The *letter* is not the spirit; the Bible is not religion, but a *record* of religion. The Scriptures (said one of their leaders) are a declaration of the fountain, and not the fountain itself.

"They are a people," said Oliver Cromwell, "whom I can not win with gifts, honors, offices, or places."

"We agree with other professors of the Christian name," say the most reliable Quaker authorities, "in the belief in one eternal God, the Creator of the universe; and in Jesus Christ His Son, the Messiah, and Mediator of the New Covenant. To Christ alone we give the title of the Word of God; although we highly esteem these sacred writings in subordination to the Spirit. We believe that, in order to put in practice those sacred precepts, some of which are contrary to the unregenerate heart or will of man, every man is endued with a measure of the Spirit, sufficient, if cherished, to enable him to distinguish good from evil; and to correct his evil propensities, which mere reason is insufficient to overcome. We believe, true worship is not confined to time and place; but we think it incumbent on Christians to meet often together, in testimony of their dependence upon God, and for a renewal of their spiritual strength. Nevertheless, we dare not depend for our acceptance with him, on a formal repetition of the words and experiences of others. We dare not encourage any ministry, but that which we believe to spring from the influence of the Holy Spirit. We attempt not to restrain this influence to persons of any condition in life, or to the male sex alone; but, as male and female are one in Christ Jesus, we allow such of the female sex as are endued with qualifications for the ministry, to exercise their gifts for the edifying of the Church."

We have already spoken of their rejection of the sacraments, of their opposition to war and slavery, and their testimony against oaths. One of their most peculiar customs, is the refusal of the men to take off the hat in any presence. It is related of William Penn, the celebrated founder of Pennsylvania, that when his father, Admiral Penn, earnestly solicited his son, then a young man, to doff his hat in respect to the King and Duke of York, he persistently refused. He preferred to break the commandment of God, Honor thy father, rather than depart from the unmeaning custom of his sect. When he was a student at Oxford, England, he not only refused to conform to the worship of the established Church, or to wear the dress prescribed for students, which *he* considered a relic of superstition, but with some of his companions who had embraced his views, assaulted several of the students in public and stripped them of their linen surplices or robes. For this outrage he was expelled.

Quakers in the seventeenth century were frequently imprisoned for refusing to take the prescribed oaths, also their refusal to pay taxes or tithes. Penn, however, was a great favorite of Charles II. and James II. Penn interceded with these monarchs very successfully for his Quaker brethren, and for himself he received large grants of land on the Delaware, in America. He also had powerful friends afterwards at the court of William and Mary, in Locke and Tillotson, and in the Duke of Buckingham.

The wise and Christian government of William Penn* in Pennsylvania, and his kind and honest dealings with the Indians, have entirely overshadowed the fanatacism and inconsistencies of his youth. The name and character of this lover of freedom and of equal rights have come down to the sect whom he loved so much, as a noble inheritance.

Fox, Barclay and Penn were the three great leaders of this peculiar people. It is believed that this sect has somewhat dwindled in numbers in the nineteenth century. Many of their descendants in England have

---

* William Penn, however, freely employed negroes, and died a slave-holder — though his people generally refused to consider them as property.

gone into the Episcopal Church, and have adopted those forms of worship, which, in their early history, seemed to be most obnoxious. The decline in their numbers is most probably to be ascribed to the neglect of the Sacraments, appointed by our Lord Himself. Their excellent principles and moral virtues as a community, must be conceded.

The Independents, a sect who arose in the seventeenth century and became very conspicuous during the time of Cromwell's rule in England, express as follows the leading principle of their system: "Every particular society of visible professors agreeing to walk together in the faith and order of the gospel is a complete church, and has full power within itself to elect and ordain all church officers, to exclude all offenders, and to do all other acts relating to the edification and well-being of the Church." Their *doctrines* were very similar to the Presbyterians, adopting the system of Calvin for their creed.

Robinson, the author of the sect of the Independents, regarded a standing ministry as useless. He was the leading teacher of the Pilgrim Fathers. Cromwell and his Ironsides belonged to this sect. The whole body sets apart with religious solemnity certain persons under the name of pastors, teachers or elders, who derive their title to act in that capacity solely from the nomination of their society, and who, in virtue of that nomination, are the only persons entitled to perform the acts, such as the administration of the sacraments and other offices that may minister to edification. The name of Independent was afterwards changed to the present name they bear—Congregationalist.

The Presbyterians, on the contrary, have a system of church government, by presbyteries or associations, of teaching or ruling elders. This system is established by law in Scotland, as the Episcopal system is established by law in England. Both* claim to have derived the power of ordination from the apostles, the one through the line of bishops by apostolic succession, the other through the presbyters or elders.

When Christianity emerges from the obscurity o the first century, says Milman, it appears uniformly governed by *superiors* in each community, called bishops. Some learned writers, as Mosheim, Neander, and Gibbon, consent to the fact of the government of these superiors or bishops in the early part of the second century; but believing from the *beginning* it was not so, they attempted to account for this total revolution by supposing that each community or church was governed by a college of presbyters, one of whom naturally presided at their meetings, and gradually assumed, and was recognized as possessing, a superior function.

But the almost simultaneous elevation of the bishop in every part of the Christian world (though the bishop was for a long time assisted by his presbyters) appears to me an insuperable objection to this hypothesis.† According to this view (the view of Mosheim) they allowed themselves to be deprived of their co-equal dignity, without resistance and without controversy. The uninterrupted line of bishops is traced by the ecclesiastical historian up to the apostles; but no murmur of remonstrance against this usurpation has transpired. Episcopalians believe that the bishops spoken of in the third chapter of Paul's epistle to Timothy were

---

*The Episcopalian and Presbyterian both claim. † Milman.

identical with the presbyters and elders, but that the Bishops of Ephesus and Crete were office-bearers of the same order as the Bishops in after ages.

The Presbyterians argue that Timothy and Titus were extraordinary office-bearers, suited to the infant state of the Christian Church. The Presbyterians say that their church government has its germ in the Old Testament, inasmuch as the people of Israel, at various periods of their history, had wise and able men set over them who were styled elders, and that this was a distinctive feature of the synagogue system up to the time of the Savior. The model of the ancient community would naturally, as far as circumstances might admit, become that of the new. But in their primary constitution there was an essential point of difference. The Jews were a *civil*, as well as a religious; the Christians, exclusively a religious, community.

In making an epitome of the several Protestant sects who arose in the sixteenth and seventeenth centuries, we must not forget "the little flock" of the Moravians, also called the United Brethren. Christianity was introduced into Moravia and Bohemia by missionaries who came from countries in which the apostle Paul had preached and founded churches. These were provinces doubtless connected with the Greek Church. For several centuries the people of Bohemia and Moravia manifested matters of faith, a close adherence to the doctrines of the New Testament. They held fast to church principles, in opposition sometimes to the injunctions of the bishop at Rome. They insisted that the Bible was the only rule of faith and practice. They claim John Huss as one of their martyrs, who, in 1415, was burned at the stake by the order of the Council of

Constance. We have already spoken fully of his martyrdom, and also of the interchange of religious sentiments that passed freely between England and Bohemia in Wycliffe's time, through the religious efforts of Anne of Bohemia, the wife of Richard II.

Whether indigenous or transplanted, the doctrines of our Lord flourished in Moravia and Bohemia as in a kindly soil. But after the martyrdom of Huss, and after much dreadful persecution and opposition, they seemed to forget for a time, in the war waged against them, that *love* or charity is the essence of Christ's religion.

In 1433, the Council of Basle granted to the Hussites (as the people are called, from whom the Moravians are descended), the famous compacts, thereby granting their essential demands. One party refused to receive these concessions, whereupon the other party, the Calixtines, made war upon them and entirely defeated them. The Calixtines now became the national church of Bohemia. A remnant of the other party,* not liking the *corrupt* practices of the Calixtines, determined to recede from them. Through the instrumentality of their bishop they obtained leave from the Regent of Bohemia to settle on one of his estates, called the Barony of Litiz. Their pastors were Calixtine priests, who held evangelical views, and who had joined their society. This was the beginning of the modern Moravian Church.

In 1461, by the treachery and at the instigation of one of their leaders, a fierce persecution fell upon them. After much deliberation they † determined to separate from the national establishment, and to change their

---
* Taborites.   † The Taborites.

society into an independent church. To do this it was necessary to institute a ministry of their own. Anxious to secure a ministry whose validity was unquestionable, and one that the Calixtines and Roman Catholics must acknowledge, they determined to seek the Episcopal succession from a colony of Waldenses, living on the confines of Bohemia and Austria, who had obtained this succession. The Waldensian bishop consecrated three men who had been sent them by their synod, as their bishops. About the close of the fifteenth century they had more than 200 churches. They had published a Bohemian version of the Bible. In the sixteenth century they sent deputations to Luther. There were some differences of opinion between them and the Lutherans, yet their conferences were friendly. When the Moravian deputation took leave of Luther, the great reformer said, when he bade them Godspeed: "Do you be apostles of the Bohemians as I and my brethren are apostles of the Germans."

In the beginning of the seventeenth century the outward prosperity of the "United Brethren," as they were now called, was fully established. In 1621, Ferdinand II. began a series of persecutions, directed against all the Protestants of Bohemia and Moravia. Protestantism was overthrown in these countries. But more than 50,000 emigrated. The church of the United Brethren seemed to disappear, but a hidden seed was preserved for ninety-four years. This seed was fostered by Comenius, a bishop of the Moravian line. In Moravia many families had cherished in secret the views of their fathers. Just fifty years after the death of Comenius, their bishop, a colony of Moravians established themselves on an estate of a pious nobleman, Count Zinzendorf. They built here a town, called it Herrnhut, introduced the discipline of their fathers, preserved by the writings of their last bishop. They now obtained the episcopate from the Unitas Fratrum (the national church from which they had sepated). In this way the ancient Moravian society was again renewed. Zinzendorf renounced all worldly honors and became a bishop, devoting himself to the service of the Church.

Churches were planted in various parts of the continent in Great Britain and North America. In North America, they were devoted to the missions among the Indians. In 1749 the British Parliament acknowledged the Moravia brethren as an Episcopal Church, and passed an act encouraging them to settle in the North American colonies. They established several mission stations in Southern Greenland. These missions were paid for by the Church of England, but the missionaries were Moravian.

The Moravian brethren have not increased in the United States as other denominations. Two causes have been assigned. First, the entire strength of the Moravian Brethren in this country was concentrated on the foreign mission field. Secondly, their *exclusive* system. No one was permitted to own real estate in their communities unless they were members of their church. This system was changed in a general synod held in 1857, and a way opened for a more general development of the church resources in the home field. A community of goods never existed among them, as has been sometimes stated. In early times, during Indian wars, they combined their efforts for the protection of their people. The Moravian ministry, like that of the Protestant Episcopal Church, has bishops, priests, and deacons. Their ritual also is very similar. They have love feasts in imitation of the apostolical Agapæ. Their ritual also is very similar. They have regular forms for adult and infant baptism, for the Lord's Supper, for marriage and burial, and for confirmation.

CHAPTER XL.

ACCESSION OF ELIZABETH — CONSECRATION OF PARKER.

It were an arduous task in one who has attempted to give the Annals of the Church from the beginning, to tread all the mazes of the Reformed Church of England, from the accession of Elizabeth to the reign of William and Mary. When we look at the distractions and dissensions of the Church during the *Commonwealth*, followed by the immoral reign of Charles II., and that of his more wicked brother, James II., and to go further back and observe the varied and difficult questions that were presented to the clergy and the worldly queen at her accession, we are constrained to say, "What hath God wrought in bringing the Church of England, as we see it to-day, a church of order and beauty, out of the chaotic mass of trouble and gloom that encompassed it in the sixteenth century?"

We will try, during that stormy time, to seize upon some salient points of interest without wearying or disgusting the reader. During the five years of Mary Tudor's reign, much that was perishable had been destroyed. The fires of Smithfield had burned fiercely, but a living flame still glowed in the hearts of those who loved the reforming work of Cranmer, Ridley, Latimer, Hooper, and a cloud of other witnesses, whose bodies had been burned, but the books in which they had preserved the treasures of the best, earliest ages of the Church *remained.* Thousands who had fled to the continent returned when they knew a friend to reform was on the throne. Thirteen bishops had died just before Elizabeth's accession. Not one had conformed but the Bishop of Llandaff. It was a responsible and difficult matter to fill the vacant sees with good, efficient men. A primate must be chosen. Matthew Parker, who had been the chaplain of Anne Boleyn, and much beloved by Elizabeth, was made primate. He was a devout man. He had been Dean of Lincoln in King Edward's time, but seemed unwilling at first to assume the onerous duties of the Episcopate, the responsibilities involved were so great. The Lord Keeper, who was his intimate friend, used his encouraging influence, and perhaps high moral considerations overcame his scruples.

Parker was elected in August, and on the 9th of September an order for his consecration was given under the great seal. Tonstal, Boure and Poole were invited to consecrate him, but they refused to act. Barlow, late Bishop of Bath and Wells; Scory, late Bishop of Chichester; Coverdale, late of Exeter, and Hodgkins, expressed their willingness to consecrate. On December 9th the election of Parker was confirmed, and in the chapel of Lambeth Palace he was duly consecrated according to the ordinal of King Edward's second book, which, having been incorporated with the prayer-book, was now *legalized* by the recent act of uniformity.

"Of this consecration," says Canon Perry, "there remains a minute and detailed account in the register of Lambeth and in the registers of the court of Canterbury; in many documents in the rolls; in contemporary letters; in papers preserved at Zurich, not known in England until 1685, and Parker's own book, printed in 1572. No historical fact, says the same authority, can be supported with evidence more overwhelming.

These details are given because a story called "The Nag's Head Fable," invented forty years after by Romanists, who wished to make it appear that Parker had not received proper consecration, and to disparage the apostolic succession, which is claimed by the bishops of the Church of England. The new archbishop, with the assistance of other bishops, consecrated five other bishops. One of these was Jewel, who wrote the first of a series of works, that became afterwards so famous in English theology. This man had been marked for destruction in Mary's reign, but saved his life by *subscribing* a formula, presented to him by his enemies. Ashamed of his weakness, he left England and took up his abode in Zurich with a distinguished reformer. His great talents as a preacher, soon after his return from his exile, marked him out for preferment. Before his consecration as Bishop of Salisbury he had gained distinction in a controversy with Romanists. This controversy led to his writing in Latin a celebrated work, "The Apology for the Church of England." This work was translated into English by Lady Bacon, the wife of the Lord Keeper, and afterwards into the several languages of Europe.

Jewel was inclined from his tastes and antecedents to the extreme school of the reformers, but he exercised wise moderation in the administration of his diocese. He has received much praise for the discrimination he evinced in his encouragement of Richard Hooker, the author of "Ecclesiastical Polity." He procured Hooker's admission to Corpus Christi College, Oxford, and settled a pension on him.

After Jewel's death this great man was befriended by Dr. Sandys, Archbishop of York. Having neither "family nor fortune," Hooker, in these disjointed times, required friends to introduce him to a career, which he afterwards pursued with so much honor to himself and with such great advantage to others. It is no small Christian virtue for men to use their opportunities in the advancement of the poor and meritorious, as did Jewel and Sandys. Hooker was born of poor parents in 1554, near Exeter. He took orders in 1581. In 1585 he was made master of the temple. Here he became involved in a controversy with Walter Travers. The controversy was carried on in their sermons, so that it was said that in the morning Canterbury spoke, and in the afternoon Geneva.

It is said that Hooker's distaste for disputation drove him from London to a Wiltshire vicarage, which he exchanged at a later time for the parsonage of Bishopsbourne, among the quiet meadows of Kent. Parker, the first Archbishop of Canterbury, under Elizabeth, was buried in Lambeth Church, June 6, 1575. Moderate in his views, but firmly opposed to Romanism and Puritanism, he desired to enforce the laws, not because "he cared for cap, tippet, surplice, wafer, bread, or such," but for the laws established. He was specially valuable to the church as an organizer. He was resolute to restore order in the worship and discipline of the church. The whole machinery of publication had been thrown out of gear by the rapid and radical changes of the last two reigns. A large number of the priests in the North were still Roman Catholic at heart.

The first difficulty with which Parker and the new bishops had to contend was with the queen herself. Elizabeth was unwilling to give up the crucifix and lights in her chapel. The bishops were compelled to minister, much to their annoyance, at the altar thus ornamented.

Jewel writes to Ballinger: "It comes to this, that either the crosses or *roods* must be restored, or our bishoprics relinquished." At length a compromise was effected with the queen. Sandys writes that the queen had agreed that the images should not be restored, but the popish vestments, I mean *the copes*,* are still to remain, which, however, we hope will not last long.

It is probable that the queen was influenced in this matter, says her biographer, not so much by religious as by political considerations. There was a great want, too, of competent ministers to preach the word of God. In order to supply this want, the bishops consented to admit illiterate men to orders. This, however, proved to be an unwise expedient, and we find Parker writing to Grindal, then Bishop of London, not to ordain or admit any to orders who had not some suitable education.

Another formidable difficulty met the bishops in the resolution of the queen to grasp with unblushing rapacity the *revenues of the church*. The archbishop and four other bishops elect, addressed a letter to the queen appealing to her to stop her proceedings. The property, Elizabeth contrasts unfavorably with her sis-

---

* A rich habit covering the person, with a cape or hood.

queen would not consent to relax her grasp of episcopal manors, but she remitted to the bishops half of the *first fruits*, payable to the crown. In regard to church ter Mary. The primate and certain of the bishops, being ecclesiastical commissioners, determined to draw up a paper for the guidance of the clergy, and at the same time to prepare a *short* confession of faith, which all clergy appointed to *livings* might be required to *sign*. The document they now issued was styled "interpretations and further considerations." These considerations related to *suitable* apparel for the bishops and other clergy while engaged in the ministrations of the church. Only one *apparel* should be used in the church, as the *cope* in the administration of the Lord's Supper, and the surplice in all other ministrations. The principal articles of religion drawn up were as follows: The first asserts the doctrine of the Trinity. The second; the *sufficiency of Scripture* and the three creeds, the Apostles' Creed, the Nicene Creed, and the Athanasian Creed.* Third, the power of the Church to change ceremonies and rites. Fourth, the necessities of appointment to the ministry by the "high authorities." Fifth, asserts the supremacy as "expounded and declared" by the injunctions. Sixth, that the Bishop of Rome has *no more* authority than other bishops. Seventh, that the Book of Common Prayer is Catholic, apostolic, and most fit for the advancing of God's glory, and the edifying of God's people. Eighth, that though the old ceremonies be

---

* Efforts have been made at different times in the Church of England to get rid of the last-mentioned creed. It is, however, we believe, a *dead letter*. This creed was not written by Athanasius. The name is spurious.

omitted in baptism, yet that it is validly performed in the Church of England. Ninth, that private masses, and the doctrine that *the mass* is a *propitiatory* sacrifice are to be condemned. Tenth, the holy communion ought to be received in both kinds. Lastly, that images are vain things, and God must be served by works of obedience, faith, and charity.

Archbishop Parker turned his attention to the revision of the Bible. Some of the reformers in their exile at Geneva, had occupied themselves in this holy work. The Genevan Bible, with notes, had appeared about 1560. The "injunctions" ordered, as those of Edward had done, a copy of the "Great Bible" to be set up in all the churches. But the translation of the "Great Bible" was by no means perfect. The Genevan Bible was not fully approved. The archbishop, therefore, determined to have all the authorized versions revised by learned divines. This revision was completed in 1568, and as the majority of the revisers were bishops it was called the Bishops' Bible. The ecclesiastical courts greatly needed reformation. They had become a legalized tyranny. But in Elizabeth's reign the needed reformation was not made.

On the accession of James I., a millenary petition was presented to him, signed by a tenth of all the clergymen in his kingdom, praying that the church courts should be reformed. This petition asked for no change in the organization of the church, but for a thorough reform in the courts. "Why should," says Bacon, "the civil state be purged as *time* breedeth mischief, and the ecclesiastical state continue upon the *dregs* of time and receive no alteration *these many years?*"

When the Queen made a progress, in 1561, in the eastern counties of her kingdom, she was greatly incensed to see the irregularities in the public worship. The queen was disposed to attribute the seeming indifference of the clergy and their carelessness in the administration of the rites of the church to clerical matrimony. In her displeasure she was disposed to issue a proclamation forbidding the marriage of her clergy. Cecil used his influence to prevent so unbecoming a step on the part of the queen. Some of the bishops were indignant and expressed horror at the language of the queen, with regard to God's holy ordinance of matrimony. That there was some disorder in the churches at this time during the hours of public worship, appears from the following statement:

"Some say their prayers in the chancel, some in the body of the church; some attend to the order of the book, others intermeddle psalms in metre; some minister in a surplice, others without a surplice. In some churches the table standeth in the chancel; sometimes persons receive the Lord's Supper kneeling, others standing or sitting. This disorder was distasteful to the queen. The love of order and ceremonial, say the writers of that day, was her strongest religious sentiment.

Queen Elizabeth had, perhaps, but little personal piety, but her love of a gorgeous ceremonial was no proof of the want of it. She was not a persecutor. A late historian, Mr. Green, says she was a persecutor, but she was the first English ruler who felt the charge of persecution to be a *stigma*. Her ministers boldly asserted the right of every religious subject to freedom. It is true that Walsingham, her minister, pursued the

Douay priests. Those Jesuits came to England, the people thought, to sow treason and revolt. Those who were put to death died as traitors, not as religionists.

Thousands of Flemish exiles and French Huguenots found homes in England. Statements of doctrine were distasteful to Elizabeth. She would not ratify the articles until she made a change in them. She kept the homilies a long time under consideration. In her youth she had been strictly subjected to Romanist surveillance, and was assailed afterwards with so many differing creeds that we are not surprised at her impatience in listening to doctrinal disputations. When she was made queen she reverently kissed the Bible, pronouncing that they (the evangelists) should be no longer prisoners. She blamed the bishops for the prevalent disorders in the church, yet she would not permit them to enforce subscription to the articles by statute. She desired to govern the church by her prerogative and by the ecclesiastical commission, and not by statute law.

It was the policy of Leicester and other anti-church counsellors who surrounded her, to stir up the Puritans to resistance, and on the other hand to represent that all the non-conformity in the land was due to the bishops' want of discipline.

Parker had made an effort, in 1565, to reduce the London clergy to conformity. At that time 140 appeared before him at Lambeth, of whom all but thirty promised conformity. In 1566 they were again called to Lambeth. On this occasion sixty-one promised obedience; thirty-seven refused. The recusants were now suspended or *deprived*. The archbishop had now commenced the policy of coercion. He did it with a foreboding that it would not succeed. Among the deprived ministers themselves there was some anxious deliberation. Were they to decline to separate from a church in which the word and sacraments were truly administered, though defiled with superstition? or were they, inasmuch as they could not have the word of God preached, or the sacraments administered without idolatrous gear, to break off from the public churches, and assemble elsewhere to worship God in a manner which would not offend the light of their consciences? There was a division among them. Some of the most able objectors continued in communion with the church; another section broke off entirely from the church and established a discipline and worship of their own.

This was the first formal act of schism in the Church of England. No charge of false doctrine was made. It was simply the *vestments* to which they objected. The name of *Puritan* was first applied to those men who left the church on account of "the idolatrous gear," * as they termed it. Truly it may be said that religion has received, in all ages, the severest wounds in the house of her friends. All who read church history must acknowledge this humiliating truth.

Archbishop Parker was succeeded in the primacy by Edmund Grindal. Grindal had been one of the Marian exiles. In 1549 he had been president of Pembroke Hall, Cambridge, having become distin-

---

* Throughout the earlier years of Elizabeth's reign, the vestments of which there is such frequent mention in "the Zurich letters," were only the cope and surplice. Copes were used chiefly in the cathedral churches.

guished as a preacher. He was appointed, in 1550, a chaplain of Ridley, bishop of London. In 1551 he became the chaplain of Edward VI., but on Mary's accession he fled to Strasburg, where he remained until Mary's death. As soon as he returned to England he was employed, with seven other Protestants, to revise the liturgy, and also to oppose the Roman Catholic prelates in public debate. He succeeded Bonner as Bishop of London, and was afterwards translated to the see of York.

Grindal had shown a becoming spirit in repressing disorders both in the North and at Durham. Grindal was recommended to the queen by Lord Burleigh, who believed that the exercise of his gentle and amiable disposition would be more effectual in quelling disturbance than arbitrary moroseness. A quiet term of office could not be anticipated, as non-conformists and puritanical *conformists* were making attacks upon the Church of England, as it had been settled in the early days of Elizabeth and Archbishop Parker. Grindal says he had many conflicts with himself in accepting the great responsibility. "He did so lest, resisting his vocation, he might, with Jonas, offend God, and occasion a tempest."

"Our affairs, says Grindal, "after the settlement of the ceremonies, were for some time very quiet when some virulent pamphlets came forth in which almost the whole external polity of our church was attacked. The writers of these papers maintain that the archbishops and bishops should be reduced to the ranks; that the ministers of the church ought to be solely elected by the people; that in every city, town and parish a consistory should be established, consisting of the minister and elders of the place, who alone are to decide on all ecclesiastical affairs."

The persons who held these sentiments were the forerunners of the Independents, who increased so greatly during the reigns of the arbitrary James I. and his successor, Charles I., that in the era of the Commonwealth they became the governing party. We have seen that the epithet Puritan was first applied to the frivolous objectors to the vestments worn by the Episcopal clergy. The term Puritan was afterwards applied to all who refused to conform to the Church of the State. Some who did fully conform to the establishment, but who attached more importance to the essentials of religion, humility, justice, mercy, and truth, than to its outward symbols and ceremonies, were often called Puritans by the worldly and evil-minded.

In the summer of the year 1570, Archbishop Grindal made a metropolitan visitation. He soon found that the great want of the church was earnest, efficient preachers. Grindal testifies to the advance that had been made during the primacy of Parker, yet they had been very irregularly distributed. Grindal, noble missionary as he was, determined to use his best efforts to supply the need. Grindal encouraged the frequent meetings of his clergy for mutual improvement. These meetings were called "prophesyings," and there was doubtless an element of usefulness in these exchanges of sentiment, helping the clergy to think definitely, and to express themselves correctly. They were well calculated to increase Christian fellowship. Many of the laity also attended these meetings, but afterwards it was thought best to restrict them to the clergy. The queen became prejudiced against them, either through misrepresentation of those who did not understand them, or perhaps through the evil influence of Leiscester, who was very inimical to the Church. These "prophesyings" commenced about the year 1571. They became very popular. In 1574 the Bishop of Lincoln issued directions to the clergy as to their direction, recommending that not only doctrines were to be discussed, but practical religious duties were to be indicated and commented upon. The new Archbishop of the Canterbury Convocation laid before the synod a body of articles relating to the qualifications of the candidates for the ministry or clerical office. Grindal was anxious in these articles to meet and overcome puritanical objections, so far as it was expedient. When these articles were submitted to the queen she struck off *two* of them—*one* that allowed marriage to be celebrated at any convenient time without regard to Lent; and another which declared that baptism could only fitly be performed by a lawful minister. The queen wished to make them remember that she had the power to strike out that which was offensive to her, though she had withdrawn the title of "Head of the Church."

These canons or articles said that "unlearned ministers" must not be promoted in the Church.* When these "exercises" or prophesyings had extended to Norwich, the headquarters of non-conformity, the queen became impatient; she severely reproved Grindal for licensing so many preachers. She also commanded him at once to put a stop to the "prophesyings." The Archbishop was grieved at this peremptory and imperious mandate. As soon as he deliberated

---

* Canon Perry's History of the Church.

upon this *matter*, that he thought so important, he determined to write to her majesty a letter of remonmonstrance. In this letter he reminds her of the great duty and value of preaching. He tells her that ten of his *suffragans* greatly esteemed the religious exercises in which they had been engaged. He laments the *spoliation* the church had suffered, which had been the cause that every parish could not now have a pastor. Hence the origin of these associations in parishes without pastoral care. "I can not," he says, "with safe conscience, and without the offense of the majesty of God, give my consent to the suppressing of these 'prophesyings.' I choose rather to offend your earthly majesty than the heavenly majesty of God. In God's matters all princes ought to bow their sceptres to the Son of God, and to ask counsel at His mouth what they ought to do.

"Remember, madam, that you are a mortal creature. Must not you also one day appear before the judgment seat of the Crucified, to receive there what ye have done in the body, whether good or evil? And although ye are a mighty prince, yet remember that He which dwelleth in heaven is mightier."

The boldness and independence of this opposition is specially to be admired when it is borne in mind how much *Erastian* principles prevailed at this era, that is, an idea that ecclesiastical authority is subordinate to the civil power. The queen's answer to the *noble* letter of Grindal was to order a meeting of the Star Chamber to propose that the Archbishop should be *deprived*. She was prevailed upon, however, to consent to a milder sentence. The Archbishop was suspended and confined to his own house. Another peremptory epistle was then sent to all the Bishops, warning them to desist from these "prophesyings." Most of the Bishops liked these *meetings*, but they did not evince the boldness of their chief.

*Bishop Cox writes to Burleigh: "I trust that her majesty, when she examines into this matter, if she seeks the glory of God and the edifying of the people; when she sees the ignorance and idleness of a great number of poor blind priests, she may deem it necessary to drive them or encourage them to some travail and exercise of God's holy word, whereby they may be better able to discharge their bounden duty to their flock."

The suspension of the Archbishop did not incapacitate him from the performance of much episcopal duty. He was unable to act as president of the Convocation. His compeers earnestly besought the queen fully to restore him.

In the meeting of the Convocation in 1580, the clergy were directed to look into the subject of excommunication. Much irritation had been produced among the laity by the conduct of *lay judges*, who had caused the penalty of excommunication to be inflicted for very inadequate causes.

A paper was drawn up by Grindal insisting that excommunication should be taken away except for great crimes, then the sentence was to be pronounced by the bishop. His views were not fully carried out at this time on this delicate subject.

In January, 1583, the queen sent to Grindal to prepare his resignation. He professed himself ready to resign, but before his arrangements were made for the

---

*Canon Perry's Book of the Church.

resignation of the see death released him from its cares.

In 1586 we learn that the Bishop of Chester issued directions as to "prophesyings." In his letter he says, "Her majesty's privy council have recommended their use and extension."

CHAPTER XLI.

Whitgift became archbishop of Canterbury on the death of Grindal; he was bishop of Worcester when called on to take the primacy. The withdrawal of Grindal from active work seems to have encouraged the Nonconformists in a bolder expression of their views. Whitgift was full of energy and decision. There were at least three formidable sects of Nonconformists when Whitgift commenced the administration of ecclesiastical affairs.

The Brownists were the most considerable sect. Their leader, Robert Brown, had left the Church of England on account of its "vain ceremonies." Whitgift's first step was to present the test of the "Three Articles" to many of the preachers who pretended to conform, and yet disregarded the Prayer Book — the Queen's supremacy, the Book of Common Prayer, and the Articles of Religion (the Thirty-nine Articles). Whitgift presented no new test, but he presented very frequently the old tests for subscription. He prepared for much opposition, as he knew he would have great trouble in enforcing conformity. Therefore, in 1583, the great seal was affixed to a new ecclesiastical commission, with fuller powers than any before issued. The queen supported Whitgift in this tyrannical procedure, considering that the recusants could only be silenced by this weapon, which they vainly thought might be effective.

Whitgift drew up twenty-four articles for the use of

the ecclesiastical commission, that were so stringent as to bring upon him the displeasure of many of his former friends. He insisted that the critical state of the Church required such proceedings. Lord Burleigh wrote to him on the subject in much displeasure. He tells him that "the Inquisition in Spain *use not so many questions* to entrap their prey." The queen herself was appealed to in favor of the nonconforming ministers. She desired the archbishop to answer the objections made against his proceedings.

Whitgift was constrained, by the opposition he received, to allow conferences to be held at Lambeth between the Church divines and the Puritans, in the presence of Lord Leicester and the other ministers of the court.

We can see very clearly, in the light of the nineteenth century, the weakness and ineffective tyranny of Whitgift's policy; but it was not so apparent in the sixteenth century. Yet Burleigh seemed to understand that "the spirit of gentleness would be more winning than severity." *Some men*, either in political or religious crises, seem incapable of conciliation. Whitgift and Laud, though possessing some qualities that adorn a man, belonged to the class of uncompromising zealots. These men belonged to different schools in theology, yet they were both equally devoted to non-essentials. Whitgift was a Calvinist, and Laud an Arminian.

The parliament of 1593 made a law that those who refused to conform, by non-attendance on the service of God, should be banished or imprisoned within three months. In this way the country was cleared of many of the sectaries, who preferred exile to imprisonment. The greater number of the disaffected emigrated with their ministers to Holland.

We have spoken of conferences at Lambeth. The chief topics at these debates were the reading of the apocrypha, the use of private baptism by laymen, the use of the cross, private communion, the clerical dress. Let us look at these unimportant questions with charity; they were doubtless perplexing to weak but conscientious minds at that time. It is a mortifying concession to make, that Whitgift and others seemed to plead for the "institutions of the Church" on *Erastian* principles. They were called *Erastian* from a learned physician of Switzerland. Erastus thought it the best policy, in view of the claims of the Pope, and the extravagant claims, too, of some of the heads of the Reformed Churches, as a Protestant, to resolve all the powers exercised by Church governors into *the will of the State*.

On three occasions our Lord declares His kingdom upon earth is spiritual, not civil — Matt. xx. 25, 26; Luke xii. 13; John xviii. 36, 37.

The men who conferred at Lambeth believed that their Church in important points was in accordance with the Bible, and with the primitive Church. Yet they said (Erastians) it was within the power of the sovereign to appoint Church government.

It is true that many valuable concessions were gained for the Church by ecclesiastics who gained influence over the sovereign. Cranmer and other good men availed themselves of the circumstances of the disjointed times of Henry VIII. and his successor to gain religious ends. Was this time-serving? If they did acquiesce in questionable measures, it was not for personal emolument; it was that they might gain benefits for the Church they loved so well, that they sought conciliation rather than debate. The claim of a king to be the *head of a Church in the full sense* is more revolting than the claim of Bishop or Pope. "My kingdom is not of this world," said our Lord.

But the men of whom we have been speaking did not bask in the calm sunshine of political favor. They were required to act, to *re*form systems amid storms of political and ecclesiastical strife.

During the reign of Elizabeth there were many controversies on the respective merits of Episcopacy and Presbyterianism. Whitgift, the archbishop, and Cartwright, a university professor, had a famous controversy on this subject. Whitgift did not prove himself to be very learned in theology. Cartwright defended with ability the Presbyterian basis as the most scriptural.

Dr. Bancroft preached, in February, 1589, a sermon that challenged much interest and attention. He asserted that there was no scriptural basis whatever for the Presbyterian mode of ordination, but claimed it for Episcopacy. There was never ancient father, nor church, nor synod, he said, from the apostles' time to the present, that ever dreamed of a Presbyterian basis. Sararia also, a learned divine from Holland, held the same views. In a controversy that he held with Beza he said that the apostles did not appoint anything that they had not received from the Lord; but they *did* appoint bishops (such as were Timothy and Titus) wherever there was need.

This earnest introduction of the question of Church government upon such exclusive grounds *alarmed* the fears of many *churchmen* of this time, lest in adopting such views they should *unchurch* the foreign reformed communities, for whose piety and learning they had great respect. Such feelings greatly modified the opinions of many, in embracing what the Episcopal controversialists called the truth of history. The moderate or Low Church party contented themselves in thinking that Presbyterian ordination was irregular, but they would not presume to say it was invalid.

We will now quote on this vexed subject the opinion of Hooker, the author of "Ecclesiastical Polity." He is the great standard authority of the Church of England. Hooker occupies a middle ground between differing schools of theology. He says bishops have indeed a Divine sanction, but are not indispensably necessary to a Church. Church government, according to him, is a thing which the Church constitutes under a Divine authority. The Church has, in accordance with this Divine power, constituted the regimen of bishops; but the Church might, if it pleased, under certain circumstances, dispense with this order, and arrange otherwise. Whether or not the justifying circumstances had arisen in the case of the foreign churches, Hooker does not say. "We must note," he says, "that he that affirmeth speech to be necessary to all men, doth not necessarily import that all men must speak of necessity one kind of language. Unto the complete form of Church polity much may be necessary that the Scripture teacheth not, and much that it hath taught become unrequisite, sometime because we need not use it, and sometime because we can not. I see that certain reformed churches, the Scottish especially, and the French, have not that which best agreeth with sacred Scripture; I mean the government that is by *bishops*, inasmuch as both these churches have fallen under a different kind of regimen. I had rather lament than excogitate, considering that men often, without any blame of their own, may be driven to want that kind of polity which is best, and to content themselves with that which the irremediable error of former times, or the necessity of the present, hath cast upon them. Bishops, though many avouch with conformity of truth that their authority hath *thus* descended, even from the very apostles themselves, yet the everlasting and absolute *continuance* of it, they can not say that any commandment of the Lord doth enjoin, and, therefore, must acknowledge that the Church hath power by *universal* consent, upon urgent cause, to take it away—if thereunto she be constrained through the proud, the tyrannical and unreformable dealings of her bishops, whose regimen she hath long delighted in, because she hath found it good and requisite to be so governed."

Hooker allows to Episcopacy scriptural sanction, yet does not assert its *divine right*. He leaves it to the conscience to determine, or to the reason of man, whether Church polity is a mutable thing, under the control of circumstances.

The Lutherans in Germany, and the Calvinists of France, Holland, and Scotland, made up their minds that they could do without bishops. There was sad warfare through the center of Europe, and the Spaniards and French persecuted the Protestants, some of them thinking in their blindness that they were doing God service. Queen Elizabeth was a friend in need to all the distressed reformers.

There were *four* branches of the Reformed Church of Christ that kept their bishops: the English and

American Episcopalians, the Swedish Lutherans, and the Moravians.

A proper observance of the Lord's day became now a subject of interest. A book came out on this subject in 1595, which had the effect of giving a peculiar character to the religious and social life of England. The bishops had issued directions about Sunday observance, but they restricted their injunctions to buying and selling on the Lord's day. They forbade all games being carried on during the time of divine service.

As early as 1449 an act was passed in England to prohibit *merchandise* on Sunday. In 1678 all secular work was forbidden, except works of charity and mercy. How precious are the Sabbaths of our lives! Oh, that they could be hallowed to all classes in the community! See in Isa. lvi. 2 and lviii. 13 the promises made to *all* who hallow the sacred day.

The book to which we have alluded was written by a Puritan minister in 1595. Fuller testifies to its remarkable effects: "The fencer laid down his buckler, the archer his bow. May-games and morris-dances grew out of repute."

Although the *proper* observance of the Sabbath, or a seventh part of our time, is a blessed institution to all God's creatures, yet some well-meaning sectaries have carried their views to as absurd an extreme as did the Jews in the days of our Lord. The Sunday had been shamefully desecrated in the age just previous to the Reformation. "The rites of sacrifice and circumcision have vanished away, but the *name and duties* of the Sabbath, enshrined as it is in the moral code, must forever remain."

The doctrines of predestination and election have produced much controversy. Since the day that the question was asked of our Lord, "Are there few that be saved?" the question of election has agitated the Church of God. St. Augustine, in the fourth century, sounded its deep mysteries, but was not quite able to satisfy himself. His theology, as we have said, has influenced the Church in every age. We see it in the Thirty-nine Articles of the Protestant Episcopal Church.

"Work out your own salvation with fear and trembling, for it is God that worketh in us, to will and to do, of his own good pleasure." In this passage of Scripture we see declared, not only the sovereignty of God, but the free agency of man. On the mysterious question of the operation of grace, the English Church was long dominated by the opinions of Calvin and Beza.

During the reign of Mary, the Protestant exiles had received much kindness from the leaders of the Genevan and from the Zurich schools of theology. During a large part of the reign of Elizabeth the English divines were strongly tinctured with Calvinism. Now and then a bold man would declare his belief in free will, as Bishop Cheyney of Gloucester.

Mr. Barrett, in a sermon which he preached at Cambridge, said that *sin* was the true, proper and first cause of reprobation. This assault on Calvinism was distasteful to the most influential doctors at Cambridge. Dr. Whitaker, the Regius Professor of Divinity, brought the matter before the archbishop. Whitgift called to his aid several divines to *settle* the controversy. At Lambeth a paper of articles was drawn up, known as the "Lambeth Articles." There were nine of these articles. We will only quote the first: "God from eternity hath predestinated some to life, some He hath reprobated to death." If these articles prove anything, they prove that man, when he presumes to understand the "secret decrees" of God, plunges into absurdity and blasphemy. Many were shocked at this document, denying, as *they thought*, the attribute of justice to the Most High.

The queen, when she heard of these articles, said that "she misliked them very much, regretting that the prelate had allowed such points to be discussed, as being matter tender and dangerous to weak minds." A protest was soon made against these articles.

Baro, in a Latin sermon at Cambridge, 1596, took the position that God created all men in the likeness of Adam, and consequently to eternal life — as Christ gave Himself a propitiation for all. Baro was cited before the vice-chancellor to answer for heresy. The primate wrote to the chancellor to proceed cautiously. Burleigh reproved the vice-chancellor for his citation of Baro: "Ye sift him with interrogatories, as if he were a thief. If you punish him, it will be for holding the truth." The queen said these *articles* must be suppressed.

Andrews, a bishop of much ability, placed the doctrines of the articles in their true light before Whitgift. Baro was permitted to keep his place.

Calvin was indeed an intellectual giant and a deeply religious man. His "Institutes" prove that he possessed great logical powers. He elaborated a system of theology in all its parts, on the basis of the Divine will as supreme.* That *will*, in Calvin's view, though

---

* Calvin seemed to square and triangulate and systematize the doctrinal mysteries of the Scripture, as a problem in mathematics.

hidden to us, is not arbitrary, but most wise and holy. The human race, corrupted radically in the fall of Adam, has upon it the guilt and impotence of original sin ; its redemption could only be achieved through a propitiation ; of this redemption only *electing* grace can make the soul a participant, and such grace once given is never lost. This election can come only from God, and it includes only a part of the race, the rest being left to perdition. Justification is by faith alone, and this faith is the gift of God.

All Christians embrace a large part of Calvin's creed; but there are *two* points in his faith that ordinary minds can not receive. *One* is that a loving Father, as the Bible represents our God to be, could ever pass by or reprobate *any* of the creatures He has made. "Whosoever *will* may take of the waters of life freely" is the doctrine of our Lord, who gave Himself a propitiation for the sins of the world. The other point in Calvin's theology that we can not receive is, that we can "never depart from grace given." We know that nothing but *our sins* can separate us from God. If we are diligent in our Master's work, "our calling and election" will be sure.

The execution of Servetus, the Socinian physician, was in accordance with the laws of the European states of that time. It was, say his friends, the inherited spirit of the times. His condemnation was an act of the council, after some deliberation, and in accordance with the opinions of other cantons. Calvin, it is said, interceded that he might not be burned, but decapitated. If Calvin had possessed as much *love* as he did *learning*, we believe he would have heartily interceded with the council, to save the life of Servetus.

Religion without love or *charity* is as sounding brass or a tinkling cymbal. Oh, how lamentable is it that some of the lights of the world have almost gone out in darkness on account of the persecution unto death of a fellow-creature, not for crime, but for error in opinion!

At the close of the reign of Queen Elizabeth, a generation had arisen which knew nothing of any religion which differed greatly from the Church of England. The peculiarities of this Church, the ceremonies and vestments which had at an earlier period been exposed to bitter attacks, were now connected with hallowed associations. The time, however, was not very far distant, when kings, by their absolutist principles, and ecclesiastics, in magnifying non-essentials and in the exercise of an uncompromising spirit, brought tribulation and woe upon the Church of God.

In 1603 James I. became king of England. There was some doubt upon the minds of Englishmen as to the religious opinions of James, coming as he did from Scotland, and from under the instruction of the learned but Calvinistic Buchanan. He showed soon his preference for the Church of England, but, we think, his embrace was one of death and dishonor to the Church. There was a conference at Hampton Court which amounted to nothing. This took place in 1604. The Puritans were very unfairly represented, and afterwards scoffed at its proceedings. There were numerous objections made to the ritual — the cross in baptism, the ring in marriage, and the surplice in preaching. Soon after this conference Whitgift died. It is said of Whitgift that he spoke very plainly to the queen with regard to Church spoliation. The rescue of its property from her covetous grasp is ascribed to Whitgift. He was not a time-server, as were some of the bishops during the reign of James.

Bancroft succeeded Whitgift to the primacy. Bancroft, says Southey, had neither the wisdom nor moderation of Parker or Whitgift. He framed canons by which all persons who spoke in derogation of the Church of England were to be excommunicated, and with an *impolicy* as gross as his intolerance, when several Puritans wished to migrate to some of the colonies of America, he, instead of rejoicing that intractable spirits, as some of the Puritans were, were willing to leave the country, obtained a proclamation whereby they were forbidden to leave it without a special license from the king.

He ejected from their benefices all who would not conform to the rules. The Church was weakened under his policy, and at the accession of Abbott it was found that opponents of the Church system had increased in number. Abbott was appointed to the primacy, not on account of any peculiar fitness for his high office, but from favoritism. The appointment of Andrews, a man of marked ability and excellent spirit, was desired by the true friends of the Church, but they were overruled. Abbott, however, seems to have been a good man, though without great qualities. He showed his steady virtue in refusing to grant a divorce to the Earl of Rochester that he might marry the wicked Countess of Essex. For this independence he lost for a time the favor of the king. At the same time he is accused of making the tribunal of the High Commission more terrible than ever from the imposition of heavy fines. Yet his sensibility was so wounded by causing the death accidentally of a man when he was hunting, that his own life was shortened by sorrow. This seems hardly consistent with the disposition ascribed by some historians to him of moroseness and tyranny.* Abbott from his death-bed implored James I. to raise an army to assist his son-in-law, the elector, who was fighting for Protestantism.

James was vain, selfish, and vacillating. He supposed himself capable of settling everything in the Church, because theology had been his favorite study. There was much time-serving in the reign of James. He attempted to defeat justice by brow-beating the judges, but Sir Edward Coke bravely refused to be influenced by him. Sir Francis Bacon is said to have sanctioned torture in this reign.

---

* Abbott was a Calvinist, and was accused of being too lenient to the Puritans.

CHAPTER XLII.

The discovery of the gunpowder plot in 1605 naturally awakened suspicion in the king and his court. Bishop Andrews, the great preacher of the day, was exhorted to write against the Romanists. The spirit of controversy infected many of the great divines of that day. They should have been differently employed. A great crisis was approaching. "If the Marian fires," says Canon Perry, "the French St. Bartholomew, the 50,000 victims of the Low Countries, did not avail to destroy their influence or lessen their power, what hope of usefulness could reasonably be expected from controversy?"

Now for the first time a *sacramental* test was used in the service of persecution. Recusants were required not only to attend the parish church, but to receive the Lord's Supper. One noble work must not be forgotten as belonging peculiarly to the reign of James I. The encouragement that James gave to the translation of the Bible must be heartily recognized. The king was well aware, from his scholastic attainments, of the deficiences of the Bishops' Bible, and as a theologian, he had an antipathy to the Calvinistic perversions of Scripture in the Genevan Bible.* He wrote to Bancroft, who was Bishop of London, that he had selected fifty-four divines for the work. Bancroft informed his brother bishops of the wishes of the king.

---

*Canon Perry. Or rather, the marginal notes.

They were expected to consult all the learned men of their diocese, and ask their suggestions in all passages of difficulty. When the work was begun, in 1607, the fifty-four divines were reduced to forty-seven. How thorough, true, grand and beautiful this translation was, and is, all Protestant English-speaking people have declared with uniform acclaim.

In 1610, three bishops were consecrated for Scotland. An objection was urged by some of the Scotch clergy to consecration by the Archbishop of Canterbery, lest the Scotch Church should be subjected to the English Church. To avoid any subject of jealousy, neither of the archbishops took any part in the consecration. Several years after this time, 1637, when the liturgy was read in the Cathedral of Edinburg, a furious riot ensued. James I. and his advisers understood the temper of the Scotch people far better than the indiscreet ecclesiastics of Charles I. James had positively refused to adopt the stringent policy that was afterwards attempted in the reign of his son. These objections to a harsh policy probably arose in his mind after he had permitted a great crime to be committed, in allowing two unhappy men to be *burned* for their religious opinions. One of these men was brought into the presence of the king, that he might convince him of his Socinian errors. When the man refused to accept his arguments, it is said he spurned him with his foot. The usual excuse has been made for James, that toleration was not understood, and that heresy was believed to be high treason against the Almighty.

These burnings excited, however, such horror among the people, who had become strangers to such cruelties, that the king was obviously ashamed of what he had done. James was an absolutist in politics, and very impatient of contradiction in his religious opinions. Under his rule had taken place an *ominous* union of Patriots and Puritans. Many of these men loved the Church, but unwilling to lose their political rights, they formed an alliance with men who thought with them on political subjects. This was a natural result. James claimed "the divine right of kings," and to their shame be it spoken, there were clergymen in his day who sustained him in this idea. Strange as it may appear to us, there were really good men who believed in "passive obedience."

The claims of James, however, startled many thoughtful Englishmen, who concluded that "if the practice should follow the king's theories, they would not be likely to leave to their successors the freedom they had derived from their ancestors."

We must now, for a short space, retrace our steps. About the time that Luther cast aside the veil that covered the corruptions of Rome, a great man arose in Spain—Ignatius Loyola, the founder of the Jesuits. He saw the corruption of the Romish communion, which he loved, and determined to create an order which would enter into all the ramifications of society, lay hold of the springs of social life, and seize by a skillful policy upon all the schools and colleges. We have already spoken of the introduction of Jesuit priests into England during the reign of Elizabeth, and the summary measures that were adopted to drive them from the country and to prevent the establishment of their schools in England. They were punished as traitors, rather than heretics. The efforts of Loyola had been endorsed by the Pope. He had constructed a wonderful system, a deeply laid scheme to control the destinies of the world.

Before the actors in the busy drama of European politics had specially marked the course of this enterprising astute order, it had sent out emissaries into all the world. Loyola's successors had followed the track of maritime discovery. Their missions were sent out into all the world, to India, South America, China; but above all, they in little more than fifty years had filched from Protestantism many of her provinces. They produced a counter reformation.* The provinces of Southern Germany, Bohemia and Poland were *restored* to the papal see. The Huguenots in France lost in numbers and in power. Many left the country at the revocation of the edict of Nantes. Great efforts were made to seduce Sweden, but in this they utterly failed. There were doubtless assisting causes besides the energetic efforts of the disciples of Loyola. Protestantism had wasted its strength in theological controversies, in bitter disputes, between the churches which followed Luther and the churches which followed Calvin. The German princes who espoused the cause of the reformation used it and prostituted it to their political ends and aims. The papacy meanwhile rallied the Catholic world to revise the Council of Trent. At this council (impelled, it is probable, by the knowledge of the superior morality of the Protestants), they deliberated seriously on the *morals* of their clergy. They passed decrees on this subject which challenged general approbation.

The Council of Trent, which was summoned, it was

---

* We have alluded to this counter reformation in our sketch of Moravianism.

alleged, to explain and reform the doctrine and discipline of the Church, produced new *enormities*, inasmuch as they placed among the doctrines necessary to be believed, and guarded by anathemas, the doctrine of the seven sacraments, the necessity of auricular confession, the canonical authority of the Apocryphal books, etc.

No pope was personally present at this Council, but it was governed by his legates. This Council seemed more anxious to serve the interests of the papal dominion than the general interests of the Christian Church.

Some provinces of the Romish church receive the decrees of the Council of Trent entire, without exceptions or conditions, as Portugal, Italy, portions of Germany.* That part of the Council which related to the *doctrines* of religion was admitted as a rule of faith among the French. But that part which relates to discipline and ecclesiastical law has been constantly rejected by France, as it was deemed hostile to the rights of the French Church. The Vulgate, the old Latin version, was declared authentic.

Both sacred and secular learning were held in greater esteem, after the time of Luther, by Romish Christians, than ever before, especially by the Jesuits. The written word of God, and the *unwritten*, *i. e.*, the traditions of the Church, are *the two* sources of Christian knowledge.

At the death of Elizabeth, the Protestants saw their losses. The dream of a reformation of the Universal Church was at an end. When awakened from this dream many of the Protestants of England became

---

* Mosheim.

excited and restless. Any *ceremony*, however beautiful and innocent, if it was *retained* or used by the Roman Catholics, became distasteful to them. We have already said that James claimed the divine right of kings. His aggressive tone on the rights of freemen soon evolved an *alarmingly* aggressive tone in the House of Commons towards the monarchy and the Church. Three-fourths of the Parliament that met in 1604 were in sympathy Puritan, *not* Presbyterian. James had been frightened by the Presbyterians in his youth, and he now chose to confound them.*

The name was of little consequence. All the great and good, with few exceptions, were opposed to the extravagant claims of James and the high-churchism that threatened the Church.

In our inquiry as to the causes that seemed to arrest Protestantism in its onward march, near the close of the sixteenth century, we must not forget certain individuals who, though within the fold of the Church of Rome, labored with a true Christian spirit to extend the knowledge of Christ. Among the Jesuits who took the lead in the work of missions was Francis Xavier, commonly called the Apostle of the Indies. He was a contemporary of Loyola. Both teacher and disciple were very different in their spirit and teaching from many of the Jesuits who came after them, those "who compassed sea and land to make proselytes," yet taught their benighted hearers but little of the gospel of our Lord.

In 1549 Xavier went to Japan and laid the foundation of a numerous body of Christians, which flourished for many years in the empire. Xavier

---

* Green's History of Englad.

composed some delightful hymns that Protestants now sing in their churches with much zeal.

Ricci, a learned Jesuit, went to China, 1582, and by practicing many ingenious devices attracted the attention of the Chinese. After twenty years' labor he gained access to the Emperor, and soon gained a numerous body of converts.

St. Theresa, in Spain, was preëminent in seeking to effect a reform amid the Carmelite nuns. She was a true disciple of Christ. She tried to convince her sisters that no seclusion from the world, no discipline of mind, was sufficient without useful labor. By suitable employment the mind was best preserved from unprofitable, sinful and wandering thoughts. She desired to inspire them with what she calls the prayer of love, where the soul forgets itself, and listens only to the voice of the Heavenly Master.

The institutions of St. Francis de Sales were established in the same spirit as those of Theresa. He founded the order of Visitation. This order was intended to protect delicate females from direct penances and from austere communities. His order is said to have exercised a beneficent influence in France. About this time the Ursuline Nuns went to France and placed themselves over the schools of young girls. Vincent de St. Paul appeared also in France as the missionary of the people. He founded the order of the Sisters of Mercy.

THE JANSENISTS.

The society of the Jesuits, however, departed more and more from the principles of their founder. They constantly acted upon the dangerous principle that "the end sanctifies the means." Some of them said, "To take a false oath is in itself a deadly sin; but he who swears outwardly, without inwardly intending to do so, is not bound by his oath. He does not mean, he only jests." It had been a principle that he who took the Jesuits' vow should abandon temporal possessions; but they now so managed property that they received all the benefits by transferring property to the respective colleges with which they were connected. When the Jesuits became corrupt, an opposition to their false doctrines arose in Jansenism, so called from their teacher, Jansen. This man, with his friend, Du Verger, studied at the University of Lourain, Holland,[*] where the true doctrines of the gospel had never been entirely forsaken, the learned theologians say. His associate, Du Verger, labored in the Abbey of St. Cyran to do the same work that Jansenius did at the university. They endeavored to revive true doctrine as taught by Augustin. Jansenius boldly attacked the Jesuits in their doctrines. He taught the necessity of grace, "the baptism of the Spirit," to aid the *will* which is in bondage to earthly desires.

Du Verger devoted himself in the midst of Paris to the study of the Scriptures and the early Christian Fathers. Many distinguished persons attached themselves to his tenets, such as Arnauld, an intimate friend of Richelieu, and of Anne of Austria. Angelique Arnauld, with her nuns of Port Royal, became Jansenists and were renowned for good works. Port Royal authors became very celebrated. Blaise Pascal was one of these. Jansenius died before his book was printed. St. Cyran, his coadjutor, was thrown into

---

[*] There is still Jansenism in Holland.

prison by Richelieu, who had an antipathy to such effective doctrines as were preached by the Jansenists.

St. Cyran tried to do good to the souls of men while in prison. Like Paul and Silas, he preached to his jailers. He was released after the death of Richelieu, 1643. The Jansenists bore a close analogy to those Protestants who have retained episcopacy or government by bishops. The Jansenists, however, never left the fold of Rome, though at times fiercely persecuted. They were devoted to the writings of Augustin, Jerome and Chrysostom. They believed they possessed a pure tradition to the time of St. Bernard.

The hermitage of Port Royal became very celebrated as the *nucleus* of the holy doctrines of the Jansenists. They translated the Scriptures into their own native tongue; also the writings of the Fathers and the Latin prayer-books. This community of men, the Port Royal authors, endowed with the highest intellect, and actuated by the most noble aims, exercised an extensive influence on the literature of France for many years. "The literary splendors of the age of Louis XIV. may safely be attributed to the Jansenist authors of Port Royal."*

During the pontificate of Innocent X. Jansenist divines were heard preaching from the pulpits of Rome. Their *essential* doctrines, consisting of five propositions, were examined and passed upon by a court of Rome. Innocent X. cared not for the investigation of doctrine, but he was forced to issue a bull condemning the five propositions. The Jansenists were remarkable for holiness of life and great devotion to good works. Some of them were called Mystics or Quietists.

---

* Draper.

About the same time, 1668, lived Madame Guyon, a distinguished Quietist. She propagated her religious views by books and tracts. She was befriended by the great Fenelon, Archbishop of Cambray.

Bossuet, Bishop of Meaux, wrote a book, controverting, as he supposed, the doctrines of Madame Guyon. He applied to the good Fenelon to endorse his book against the heresies of Guyon. Fenelon objected, saying that he considered the errors of the book consisted rather in fervid expressions than in heretical doctrines. Fenelon published a book in 1697, declaring that he adopted some of her opinions, especially the mystical precept that we ought to love God purely, without the expectation of any reward. This produced a controversy with Bossuet, who sent Fenelon's book to the Pope. It was indeed a defense of Quietism.

Innocent XII., after a long silence, passed a mild censure upon the book, but censuring still more the *enemies* of Fenelon, who had written so violently against it. It is said Fenelon withdrew his book, and accepted the condemnation of the Pope. Previous to his controversy with Bossuet, Fenelon had stood high in the royal favor and with Madame de Maintenon. He had first been appointed missionary to the Protestants, in the vicinity of Paris, after the revocation of the edict of Nantes. In receiving this appointment, he preferred to the king one petition—that there should be *no violence* permitted in his diocese. He, by his mild measures and great eloquence, is said to have been very successful in winning many Protestants to Catholicism, or at least to the doctrines he taught, which were full of Christian love. For some years Fenelon was the preceptor of the grandsons of Louis, the Dukes of Burgundy, Anjou and Berry. He wrote admirable books for their instruction. One of these was, "Telemaque," in which the author significantly points out the duties of a monarch to his subjects. The book was anonymous, but so soon as the king discovered that Fenelon was the author of the book, the good archbishop was restricted to the diocese of Cambray, and not permitted to appear again at court. He devoted himself to good works, and it is supposed, retained to the last his Mystic or Quietist opinions, though for the sake of the peace of the Church he withdrew his book.

Madame Guyon, after enduring some persecutions, died in obscurity in 1702. She had been always charitable to the poor, and devoted her whole time to religion.

Port Royal, the celebrated retreat for penitents, and learned men, and noble women, was *destroyed* in 1709. It had exercised much influence over the religieuses of France for nearly a century. Louis XIV., at the instigation of the Jesuits, ordered the edifice to be entirely demolished, and the nuns, who still lived there, were transferred to Paris. The institution at Port Royal would have been destroyed long before, had not the powers of the papacy been restrained by the political and clashing interests of France and Austria, and even Spain sometimes attempted to restrict papal interference.

In 1660 the papacy seemed to be shorn of some of its power. Louis XIV., though superstitiously devoted to Romanism, historians say, avenged himself upon the court of Rome by trying to lessen her power, because the Popes Innocent X. and Alexander VII. and Clement IX. and Clement X. were on the side of Spain. Louis XIV. also encountered opposition from Innocent XI. in his spoliations.

Certain bishops of Jansenist opinions had been subjected to oppression because they resisted the will of the king with regard to the revenues of some bishoprics. On this account they appealed to Pope Innocent XI., who seems to have been a good man. He adopted their cause, and warned Louis to abstain from using the immunities of the church.

It had been the maxim of the French court that the papal power should be restricted by the French clergy, and the clergy to be kept within proper limits by the Pope. The king, in 1682, assembled a Convocation, his clergy sustaining him, in which he stated propositions declaring the independence of the secular power, and the king was declared free from the spiritual power. The Pope now determined to refuse ordination or institution to all who were members of the Convocation assembled by Louis XIV. At this very time the king of France pretended to prove his orthodoxy by a relentless persecution of the Huguenots. It is said that this Pope Clement XIV. disapproved of the king's cruelty to the Huguenots. In 1773 he (Clement) expelled the Jesuits, extirpating their offices, houses and institutions. This order has been repeatedly suppressed by kings, from a jealousy of the power and influence wielded by this body.

The effect of Jansenism in France, like Puritanism in England, seems to have awakened religious thought, and to have stimulated intellectual inquiry. The Jansenists were more speculative and mystical in their religion than the Puritans or Protestants of England. They cared little for politics or earthly power. They were submissive to authority, finding happiness in the monastic institutions. The *Old Catholics* of the present time seem to be Jansenists.

The Protestants of Sweden, Germany and England had a powerful leader to defend their rights when Gustavus Adolphus arose to fight their battles. The king of Sweden arrested, by his victories over the Catholic powers, the papal inroads that had been made since the close of the sixteenth century.

By the peace of Westphalia the great conflict between Catholic and Protestant powers was brought *to an end*. But a bitter struggle of a different kind awaited the Church of England; "the foes were those of her own household." The *people* of England were a mighty bulwark against either civil or religious tyranny, real or imaginary. The condition of the Church at the death of James I. seemed prosperous, but its condition was critical, its security was only seeming. A fatal—*no, not fatal*, but—a fearful crisis was at hand. The world, says Southey, did not contain men of stronger talents, sounder learning, and more exemplary lives, than the clergy of the Church of England at that time. Their works have stood, and will continue to stand, the test of time.

These men were to be tried in the furnace. Many and various were the circumstances that led to violent measures. The times must have been terribly out of joint when it was deemed necessary that the three foremost men in the realm—the pillars of Church and State—should bare their necks to the headman's ax. No moral stain could be imputed to any of these men. Their trangressions were political! Strafford, Laud and Charles I. The first was considered by his former compeers in the House of Commons as an apostate in political principle. He was tempted by the honors offered by the king, and threw off the cloak of patriotism worn for a time. He died for political offenses. The purity and decorum of the life of Charles reflected no discredit upon his religion. But his views of government were false. He seemed not to comprehend that a king could not with impunity break the laws of his country. Laud, the Archbishop of Canterbury, was as intolerant in the Church, as Charles was exorbitant in the State, in his claims of kingly authority. These men ultimately fell under the power of a body of men— Cromwell and his Ironsides—whose will for the time was resistless, and who knew no mercy until the blood of the victims flowed from the scaffold. This terrible drama was enacted before the eyes of the English people, and was *permitted*, we may humbly suppose, that the world might learn that a heavy penalty will follow in the train of *disregarded* human rights, both civil and religious.

Laud was brought to the block at eighty-two years of age. He died with the most devout prayers upon his lips. Laud had done many unwise things, and acted in a very arbitrary way when he tried to compel the Scots to receive episcopacy against their will. He attempted to increase the ritualistic ceremonies of the Church of England, when he ought to have seen that the prejudices of the Puritans (who still attended the Episcopal churches) were increasing more and more. They suspected Laud of Romanism. These suspicions were not *just*, as was proved by the fact that a cardinal's hat was offered him and he positively refused this much-coveted honor.

Laud sinned with many of his time in trying to bind the consciences of men. He seemed incapable of conciliation. The arbitrary measures of Laud caused emigration to America.

George Herbert said:

> "Religon stands tiptoe in our land,
> Ready to pass to the American strand."

Laud injured the church he loved so well by his taste for show and ceremony. In his time a painted window was regarded as a relic of idolatry, and kneeling at the chancel to receive the "sacred symbols," which we now do so innocently, was regarded as very sinful, as intimating that the bending of the knee meant worship.

Laud grievously answered for his faults. Few characters have excited more controversy. He was a benefactor to learning. He purchased rare books and manuscripts. He encouraged the learned labors of Ussher, of Jeremy Taylor, Hall and Sanderson; but his own vision was too much restricted to one range of subjects. It is said that his opposition to Calvinism was one cause of his unpopularity. Laud perished in 1644; Charles in 1648. Some of Charles's best soldiers clung to him, such as Lord Falkland — not that they approved his political views, but because they loved the Episcopal Church of England, and plainly saw that it was the object of the Revolutionists not only to overturn the throne, but subvert the altars. About the time of Laud's death, the liturgy, a blood-boughtt reasure, was suppressed. In Edward's time, iconoclasm had dashed into pieces its stained glass. In Elizabeth's time, the communion table was moved into the middle of the chapel. Archbishop Abbott tried to check all attempts at a higher ceremonial. But Laud studiously tried to replace the stained window and the broken crucifix.

CHAPTER XLIII.

In 1643, the English Parliament selected one hundred and twenty of the ablest divines of England, with thirty lay assessors, whom they commanded to meet at Westminster to *settle* the worship, government and doctrines of the Church. This famous Westminster Assembly continued to meet and discuss such subjects as the Parliament submitted for several years in succession. They were men of different religious views — Presbyterians, Erastians, Independents, and some *moderate* Episcopalians. A deputation was sent, soon after the assembling of this body, from Scotland, requesting the Westminster Assembly to sign the "League and Covenant," thereby agreeing to establish one uniform religion in the three kingdoms. The Parliament assented reluctantly to the proposition of the Scottish Church, in order that they might have their assistance in their political designs. They drew up a Directory for Public Worship, also a Directory for the Ordination of Ministers and for Discipline and Government, in 1645. Ruling elders were chosen in 1646, and the erection of Presbyteries, Synods and a General Assembly, for a *trial* of the system.

The Scotch Church objected to an appeal from the highest ecclesiastical judicatory to the Parliament. The English Presbyterians sided with the Scotch. The king was at this time in the hands of the Scots. The English Presbyterians determined to enforce Presbyterianism *jure divino* on all England, and to allow no toleration for dissenters.

From 1644 to 1647, the Independents greatly increased in number. They uniformly pleaded for the toleration of all sects who held the fundamental doctrines of Christianity.*

The intolerant measures of the Presbyterians alienated the Independents and the army, and finally led to the *subversion* of the Presbyterian establishment set up in England.

Not one of the leading Puritans, says Mr. Green, of the Long Parliament was a Presbyterian. Pym and Hampden were disposed to Episcopacy, but the adoption of the Presbyterian system was forced upon the Puritan patriots by political considerations.

The demand of the House of Commons for scriptural proofs of the divine authority of Presbyterianism produced warm debates in the Westminster Assembly. The Independents and Erastians at length withdrew and protested. The Presbyterians, fifty-three in number, now left alone, voted almost unanimously that "Christ has appointed a Church government, distinct from the civil magistrate." No opinion can be more correct than this; but what government did he appoint? This still remains a question in many minds.

In 1847, provincial synods met in London, and continued to meet until the end of Cromwell's reign.

The king, though a prisoner, and moved by the entreaties of his queen, refused steadily to yield his assent to the new ecclesiastical constitution of England. At the same time, he tried to detach the Scotch from the English by promising them Presbyterianism in Scotland and Episcopacy in England. But

---

* Murdock's Mosheim.

they rejected his offers, hoping still to bless England as well as Scotland with Presbyterianism.

The country now swarmed with sectarians. Mr. Baxter mentions the chief separatists as Independents, Anabaptists, and Antinomians. The Antinomians were very rigid Calvinists. Some of these fanatics seemed to consider themselves free from the moral law, arguing that if they were the elect of Christ, and that Christ in their stead had obeyed the law and suffered its penalty, nothing more could be required of those who were satisfied of their election. Doctrines like these could only be maintained by madmen and hypocrites, with the New Testament in their hands.

The king also tried to gain over the Independents, promising them free toleration; but his concessions failed to benefit him.

The Assembly's short Catechism was presented to parliament in 1647, and the larger Catechism in 1648. The army *demanded* of the Parliament free toleration for all Protestant dissenters. The Presbyterians vigorously opposed this, and endeavored to disband the army. The army now took the king from the hands of the Parliament and became peremptory in their demands.

In May, 1648, the Scots invaded England, in order to rescue the king. The Parliament likewise commenced a negotiation with the king for his restoration, upon the basis of a single religion, with no toleration for any other. The king insisted upon Episcopacy, the Parliament on Presbyterianism.

The army drove back the Scotch army, seized again the king's person, purged the House of Commons of many of its members, remodeled the government, impeached the king, Charles Stuart, and beheaded him. A short time previous to the death of the king, Parliament had enacted a *ferocious* law in its sectarian zeal. The death-penalty was fixed upon all who should deny the doctrine of the Trinity, the divinity of Christ, the inspiration of the Scriptures, or the resurrection of the body; while persons believing that man by nature hath free will to turn to God, or denying the lawfulness of Church Government by Presbytery, were to be punished with imprisonment. This statute was *never* enforced, but it suggested extraordinary means of resistance.

Charles perished January, 1649. The House of Lords and the monarchy were abolished a few days after his death. The solemn League and Covenant was laid aside, and nothing but an engagement or oath of allegiance to government was required of any man to qualify him civilly for any *living* in the country. Hence many Episcopal divines now returned and became parish ministers.

In 1653, the Parliament that had sat for thirteen years, and for *four* years without a king or House of Lords, was ordered to disperse.

Cromwell the Protector tried to make men of all religions feel easy under his government, yet all Papists and Episcopalians were excluded from full toleration. Cromwell, however, forbade all the clergy from meddling with politics. The Presbyterians, in 1659, seeing no prospect of restoring the League and Covenant under the Cromwellian Protectorate, formed a coalition with the Royalists to put Charles II. upon the throne. The remains of the Long Parliament were restored. Charles II. came back in 1660, amid bonfires and rejoicing. No stipulations had been made as to the national religion. Episcopacy was soon restored. Some hundreds of the Presbyterian ministers were displaced to make way for the old Episcopal incumbents.

In 1662, an act of *uniformity* was passed which made it criminal to dissent from the Established or Episcopal Church. A number of Presbyterian ministers conformed, but about 2,000, most of them Presbyterians, lost their places. A far wider change had been made during the civil war, when 7,000 Episcopal clergy had been ejected from their parishes, to suffer the extreme of poverty. But, says a late historian, the Episcopal clergy were ejected as much on political as on religious grounds. The fidelity of those men to their Church and *king* did not lessen their sufferings. We see, during those times, Prideaux, Bishop of Exeter, was forced to sell all his household stuff that he might procure food for his family, and we see Chillingworth, a lover of toleration, taken prisoner by Sir William Waller and treated with great indignity.*

In the new Parliament of 1661, the new members were yet better Churchmen than they were Royalists. A common suffering had thrown the gentry and the English clergy together, and the squires were now zealous for the Church.

Some attempts at *conciliation* were made in the Convention that met soon after the restoration of Charles II., so that the bulk of the Puritan party could remain in the Church of Cranmer and Latimer. No compromise with the Independents was possible. Archbishop Ussher and Sir Matthew Hale were both anxious that some concessions should be made to the Puritans. Many moderate Presbyterians seemed disposed to

---

* Green."

accept terms. They (Ussher and Hale) proposed some amendments in the Liturgy, omitting, as the Puritans called them, "superstitious practices," also proposing to give Episcopacy the synodical government of the ancient Church. Hyde, Earl of Clarendon, however, objected, and the compromise was never made. The ejected Episcopal clergy entered into their livings (many of them had died), the bishops returned to their sees, the Convention Parliament was dissolved, and every hope of compromise was removed. Had the concessions been made that were so earnestly wished for by some of the greatest and best of both parties, it is believed that Howe and Baxter, and many others, would have been reconciled to the Church of England. At the dissolution of this Convention 2,000 Presbyterian divines, as we have already said, some of them distinguished for learning and piety, gave up their livings.

Jeremy Taylor and Chillingworth were now dead, but in their successors were found the pious, good sense of Burnet, the enlightened wisdom of Tillotson, and the logical philosophy of Bishop Butler. A class of divines came to the front *at the Restoration*, who were neither High Church nor Puritans. We mean Jeremy Taylor, Stillingfleet, Hales, Chillingworth, Sherlock, Burnet, Butler. These were enlightened, devout men, but they *abhorred* persecution. Some of these men, though devoted to their Church, as it then existed, desired to include dissenters. They opposed dogma, and insisted that the Apostles' Creed seemed to them the one term of Christian union that the Church had a right to impose. Chillingworth, in his meetings, said, "Take away this persecution, this burning and damning of men, because they refuse to subscribe to the *words* of men as the words of God." Call no man Master but Christ. Hale based his love and loyalty to the Church of England on the fact that it was the most tolerant church in Christendom. Jeremy Taylor pleaded for the Anabaptist and the Romanist. For all religions he would plead freedom, except those that would destroy government or teach ill life.

These men were called in their day Latitudinarians, because they simplified belief, and required only essential doctrines as taught in the New Testament.

A halo encircles the names of those clergymen of whom we have just spoken, who refused to persecute for opinions' sake, and whose only motive was a respect for the rights of man and a love for humanity.

The Quakers, in the reign of Charles II., excited alarm by their extravagance of manner, their refusal to take oaths, and other peculiarities. Many of them were put in prison. When Charles II. published the "Declaration of Indulgence," in 1672, thousands of Quakers were set free. The famous John Bunyan, the author of Pilgrim's Progress, came out of Bedford jail at this time. Roman Catholics at this time practiced their religion only in private houses. Charles made this "Declaration," not that he cared for religious liberty, but that he might serve his own political aims. Charles, however, had not a persecuting spirit. Charles II., if he had any religious faith, was a Roman Catholic. Our readers will remember Macaulay's graphic description of the last scene in his death-chamber—when the priest entered at the back door of his room, to administer the last sacrament.

When James II. succeded to the throne of England in 1685, he pledged his word to keep the laws and to protect the Church. It was the word of a king, but not of an honest man. He failed to observe either oaths or pledges. James attempted to seize the universities in order to place in them Roman Catholic professors. When he met with opposition, he sought to deprive of their offices those who appealed to the law against him. When the Bishop of London refused to suspend a vicar for preaching against Popery, he suspended the Bishop.

In 1687, James turned to the Nonconformists and made a *proclamation* which annulled all penal laws against Dissenters and Roman Catholics alike. The Dissenters understood James's *motive* too well to be flattered by so illegal a transaction. He ordered every clergyman in April, 1688, to read his Declaration in every church for two successive Sundays.

Sancroft the Archbishop, and six of his suffragans, signed a *protest* to the king, in which they declined to publish an illegal declaration. "It is a standard of rebellion," said James, as he looked at the protest. He ordered the ecclesiastical commissioners to deprive them of their sees. The commissioners shrunk from such an attempt. The Chancellor, Jeffreys, advised a prosecution for libel as an easier mode of punishment. The Bishops refused to give bail, and they were committed to the Tower.

On June 29, the Bishops appeared as criminals at the bar of the king's bench. No sooner were the words "not guilty" uttered by the foreman of the jury, than the glad plaudits of the multitude were heard on all sides. Had this assumption of authority attempted by James been admitted, the constitution in Church and State would have received its death-blow. The Bishops declared in their protest that it was from no want of loyalty to the king, nor from any want of tenderness to the *Dissenters*, but from the conviction that the declaration was absolutely illegal. The petition was signed by the Primate, by Lloyd, Bishop of St. Asaph, Turner, of Ely, Lake, of Chichester, Ken, of Bath and Wells,* White, of Peterborough, Trelawney, of Bristol.

The king's Declaration fell to the ground. The clergy were almost unanimous in refusing to read it. Louis XIV. sent word by the English embassador to the king of England that he was ready to give him every assistance needed. France was at this time the most powerful country in Europe. The days of James II., as a king, were numbered. The nation, disgusted with his tyranny and hypocrisy, determined to invite over William III., Prince of Orange, who had married Mary, daughter of James II., to be the joint sovereigns over the realm of England.

Mary was a Protestant in heart and education. She was the granddaughter of Hyde, Earl of Clarendon, the devoted friend of the Church of England. William was the cousin of Mary, as he was the grandson of Charles I., of England. In 1689, William III., by an express act of Parliament, relieved all Dissenters (except Socinians) from all penalties to which they were by law exposed.

Sancroft, Archbishop of Canterbury, and seven other Bishops, all men distinguished for their learning

---

* Ken was the author of the evening hymn "Glory to thee, my God, this night."

and for the purity of their morals, declared that they could not conscientiously take the oath of fidelity to the new king, William III., because in their view James II. was the legimate king of England.

Among those who chose to incur the penalty of deprivation, rather than transfer that allegiance which they believed to be indefeasible, were *five* of those seven to whose brave resistance the nation was mainly indebted for its deliverance from an arbitrary government and a persecuting religion. The Bishops who refused to take the oath were called Non-juring Bishops. "It must be admitted," says Mr. Southey, "that they judged erroneously, but never were men in error more entitled to respect." The government treated them with tenderness, and long put off the deprivation, which they were at length compelled to pronounce. The non-jurors died away long before the House of Stuart was extinct.

The Bishops who entered upon the sees of those who were displaced were Tillotson, Moore, Patrick, Fowler, Kidder and Cumberland. These men were among the brightest ornaments of the English Church.

We have spoken of emigration to, and colonization in, North America. As early as 1607 there was a Church of England settlement in Virginia, but the great mass of the emigrants to New England were Independents.

Maryland was settled by Roman Catholics, whose liberal laws gathered around them many other denominations. South Carolina was settled largely by Huguenots—French Presbyterians. The Dutch settled New York, but in a few years it became the possession of Englishmen. Georgia was colonized by General Oglethorpe with a hundred and twenty emigrants, together with a minister of the Church of England. Oglethorpe was a benevolent reformer.

The cause of religion must have suffered from the immoral sentiments and licentious living of Charles II. and James II. Yet there lived and labored during these reigns some of the brightest characters and most faithful men that adorn the "Annals of the Church." Mary, who succeeded her father, was a pious woman, as "simple concerning evil" as James was cunning and treacherous. Her husband, William, was a man of war, devoting but little time or thought to the arts of peace. Mary, however, was faithful in good works. The adoption of the Bill of Rights in 1688 gives honorable distinction to the reign of William III. Burnet was the chaplain of Mary. By his kindly intervention all disaffection was removed from William's mind as regarded the superior rights of his wife Mary to the throne of England.

The deadness of the religious sentiment in the eighteenth century has frequently been stated by religionists in writing of these times. Some have ascribed this indifferentism to the preaching of the Latitudinarians, who, it has been affirmed, preached merely moral essays. We believe this idea to be erroneous.

Such men as Jeremy Taylor, Chillingworth, South, and others, must have elevated rather than depressed the tone of true religion. They were opposed to dogma. They used enlightened reason as an interpreter of the word of God. These men were succeeded by Tillotson, Butler, and other learned, devout clergymen. But to whatever cause or causes the lukewarmness in religion is to be ascribed during the early part of the eighteenth century, we suppose the fact is indisputable.

After the termination of the social and political tyranny in religion of the Commonwealth, the *reaction* was terrible. The tone of Butler's Hudibras predominated in serious things. There was much iniquity in high places during the reign of Charles II., and the brief reign of James II.

England sent out large armies to war during the reigns of Mary and Anne. The demoralizing effects of war are easily understood. Bolingbroke and Horace Walpole, the Duke of Grafton and Lord Chesterfield, all exercised an immoral, irreligious influence upon the *higher circles* of English society. They were witty, worldly, wicked men.

Many of the statesmen of this time were unbelievers in any form of Christianity. The infidelity of Hobbes, and Hume, and Bolingbroke, in England, and the blasphemous wit of Voltaire in France, were shedding a baleful poison among all classes. But "at heart" England was religious. During the ministry of Walpole there were few new schools established, and few new churches built. But, in the rural districts there was family religion, and in the parish churches the grand old liturgy was still uttered by devout lips.

A great revival of religion, of which we will presently speak, was at hand. During the time of which we have just spoken—we mean the period of alleged indifferentism in religion—there was pulpit ability in the churches of London and vicinity.

Bishop Atterbury had not yet been banished from his native land for an imputed correspondence with the

Jacobites. (The adherents of the Stuarts, and the opponents of the accession of the House of Hanover, were called Jacobites.) This famous divine was accused of a correspondence with Charles Edward, grandson of James II. Atterbury was eloquent in the scriptures. He was the contemporary of the erudite Gibson, Bishop of London, also of Hoadly, Bishop of Bangor, in 1717, and much later, 1734, the Bishop of Winchester occupied a high place among the English clergy. He asserted in his sermon, "My kingdom is not of this world," that Christ was king in *his own* kingdom, and that he had not delegated this authority to any temporal power. William Law, the champion of authority, both in Church and State, was his opponent.

Law is the author of a book called "Law's Serious Call." The writer of these sketches read this book in her youth, and felt alarmed by its strict requirements. Secker and Warburton also lived at this time. Among the Presbyterians was Isaac Watts, who wrote so many beautiful spiritual hymns; and the devout writer of the "Rise and Progress of Religion in the Soul," Philip Doddridge. This is a book that the earnest seeker after truth reads with intense interest.

Surely "in these times of deadness and defection," there was no want of faithful, spiritual, intellectual men. In the literary world there were stars of the first magnitude. The glories of the age of Shakespeare, Milton, Newton, Boyle, still reflected a moral grandeur on the land. But there was indisputably much ignorance and vice among the masses. A new *phase* of religious fervor appeared in a knot of Oxford students. The earnest souls of these young men rebelled against the coldness so manifest both in professors and people. They began the work of inflaming their souls by a round of ascetic observances, and a methodical regularity of life which gained them the name of *Methodists*. Whitefield was one of these young men, and he soon attracted much attention by his fervid harangues. So extravagant was he in his declamation that some *time-serving* Episcopal clergymen closed the doors of the churches against him, and he began to preach in the fields. The vice chancellor of Oxford at this time seems to have been a godly man, as he shows great solicitude that the students should have excellent instruction. He had an edict posted in many of the college halls that, inasmuch as the prevalent news of infidelity had possibly affected some of the members of the university, the professors and teachers at Oxford should give double diligence to the explanation of the Articles of Religion and their Christian duty, and in recommending to them the careful and frequent reading of the scriptures.

A late biograper of Wesley, in order to give as dark a coloring as possible to the immorality of the times, quotes a sermon in 1724, of the Bishop of Litchfield, depicting the desecration of the Lord's day, and the drunkenness and sensuality of the times. Doubtless the times were very iniquitous, but such *testimony* as this biographer brings forward is extremely uncertain. If some of the sermons now preached in this nineteenth century, true pictures, too, of a large number,—if these sermons were published for a future century, the same views might be taken of our present time as our biographer would have us take of the eighteenth century; yet we believe the Church in every *branch* is increasing in power to overcome evil.

Whitefield and the Wesleys deeply loved the souls of men, and by the powerful principle of "love" they were mighty in overthrowing the citadels of sin wherever erected. The human heart, with its tenderest sympathies, not steeled and petrified by indulgence in evil habits, was aroused by the clarion call of these earnest preachers "to flee from the wrath to come." Mr. Whitefield's preaching was wonderful; his eloquence elicited admiration from the fastidious Walpole; it opened purses of gold in the pockets of those who had never before been moved by "melting charity." He (Whitefield) could look down at Kingwood upon the faces of twenty thousand colliers, begrimed with the coal dust of Bristol, and see, as he preached, the "tears making white channels down their blackened cheeks." All the phenomena of strong, spiritual excitement followed their preaching.

Charles Wesley was the poet of this Methodist movement. He wrote beautiful hymns, and sang them sweetly. The singing of hymns among the early Methodists was a source of much religious joy, as it has been ever since to all devout congregations. But John Wesley was the leading spirit, the great practical organizer of the body that became very numerous even before his death, and is now numbered by millions in England and America.

John Wesley lived from 1703 to 1791, nearly extended through the century. When Whitefield commenced to preach in the fields, Wesley "could not be reconciled to his strange ways." He struggled for a long time against the admission of laymen as preachers, until his great anxiety for the instruction of the ignorant and for the salvation of souls overcame his scruples. His father was an admirable man, and a regular clergyman in the Church of England; and had reared him with very strict and straight notions of clerical propriety. His mother, too, was a model wife and mother. She, like her sons, was very anxious to enlighten the ignorance of her humble neighbors. She would encourage them to assemble in her kitchen for prayer, and she would read short, stirring sermons to them, uniting with them in psalmody; these exercises she would have in the absence of her husband, who would be called from home on parochial duty. It seems *he* had some doubts of these *irregular* meetings. She, in writing to her husband on this subject, said, showing her great regard for her marriage vow, "If you do not approve of my work, *command* me to desist." The Wesleys had been nurtured in a pure and holy atmosphere, with great reverence for the traditions of their church, and no wish to violate any of the sanctities of their religious education, but their hearts were aglow with zeal for the benefit of their fellow men.

John Wesley clung to the last, passionately, to the Church of England, and looked on the members of the body he had formed as a lay society in full communion with it.* He censured the Moravians, who had been his early friends in the new movement, because he thought they endangered its safety by paying too little attention to forms. He also withdrew from Whitefield on account of his strong Calvinism.

It is said that when a young man he had been rebuked by the Bishops for his *too narrow* churchmanship. Of all Protestant churches, the Methodist Society, or

---
* Green's History of Wesley.

the Methodist Episcopal Church, is the most rigid in its organization, and most absolute in its government. The whole body is placed under the absolute government of a Conference of ministers. The members of this church are grouped into *classes;* they are gathered into love-feasts. So long as John Wesley lived he had the whole direction of the new religious society.

The Wesleys, John and Charles, seem to have been regarded with much kindness by Gibson, Bishop of London; also by Secker, afterwards Primate. The Wesleys did not quarrel with Church and State, but were only zealous to overcome sin and Satan. The action of the Methodists upon the Church was admirable. It aroused men from lethargy.. Poets like Cowper, and preachers like Cecil and John Newton, stirred the cathedrals, churches and chapels into life.*

The hymn "Jesus, Savior of my soul," written by John Wesley, and the hymn of Toplady, "Rock of Ages," are chanted by Protestants of every name, unmindful of the differing points of doctrine that animated a warm controversy between these two holy men. Toplady was an Evangelical minister of the Church of England, of Calvinistic tendencies. The beautiful hymns of the Presbyterian, Isaac Watts, were written about this time. Philip Doddridge, too, wrote his great work entitled "Rise and Progress of Religion in the Soul."

Near the close of the eighteenth century Robert Raikes, a regular attendant at Gloucester Cathedral, established Sunday-schools. He gathered in the chil-

---

* In Walpole's day, says Mr. Green, the English were idle and lifeless. In our time no body of religious ministers surpasses them in piety, in philanthropic energy, or in popular regard.

dren of the poor and neglected. He hired rooms for the schools in 1781, and employed poor women to teach them to read, at a shilling a day. This movement was very popular, and in a short time Sunday-schools were connected with all the churches in the large towns. Raikes was a man of liberal education and an earnest worker.

The labors of Hannah More, by her writings and by personal example, called the attention of the educated classes to the poverty, ignorance and crime that existed among the agricultural laborers. She journeyed from parish to parish to establish schools for the instruction of women and girls. She wrote religious tracts, that she might in some degree neutralize the effect of the *infidel* tracts that were constantly being sent over the channel from France, to be distributed among the masses. It was about this time that Clarkson and Wilberforce began a crusade against the slave-trade. And Cowper wrote:

> Slaves can not breathe in England,
> When they touch *our* shores their shackles fall;
> Then why abroad?

Among the many philanthropists of this time, John Howard stood foremost in his active sympathy for the most wretched of men. The felon in his cell attracted his Christian sympathy. He sought constantly to alleviate calamity in every form. For many years of his life he devoted himself to the cause of gaol and prison reform. He presented a bill to the House of Commons in 1774, containing a mass of information with regard to abuses in prisons. Parliament attended to his petitions, and passed bills for the better management of prisons, in adopting means for the health and comfort of the prisoners. The House of Commons thanked Howard for his humane zeal. He caused copies of the new improved prison laws, at his own expense, to be sent to every gaoler in the united kingdom. After examining all the principal penal establishments of England, he also visited those of France, Germany, Holland and Belgium. The result of his laborious researches was a *work* of profound interest "on the state of English prisons, and an account of some foreign prisons."

We will here quote from a speech of Burke, who eloquently sums up the public services of this good and great man. "He has visited all Europe, not to survey the sumptuousness of palaces, or the stateliness of temples; not to make measurements of the remains of ancient grandeur, nor to form a scale of the curiosity of modern art; not to collate medals nor to collect manuscripts; but to dive into the depths of dungeons; to plunge into the infections of hospitals; to survey the mansions of sorrow; to take the dimensions of misery, depression and contempt; to remember the forgotten; to visit the forsaken, and to compare and collate the distresses of men in all countries."

John Howard was an intelligent, scientific physician, and seems to have taken "the great Physician" as his model and exemplar in ministering to the bodies and souls of men. He died, at the age of sixty-four, from a fever contracted from a hospital patient in Kherson, on the Black Sea. Did Protestants *canonize* their saints, Howard, the Good, would be entered high upon the lists with those who have lived to bless and serve mankind. Man delights to record the names of the great and good on tablets of brass and marble; but these are perishable. The scroll of history perpetuates them from age to age; but when "time shall be no longer," the names of the saints of the Most High shall be found written in the "Lamb's Book of Life."

CHAPTER XLIV.

"WHAT SOUGHT THEY THUS AFAR?"

We must now cast our eyes upon our *American* shores, and ask what has the Church done here? What is the *present* state of the Church in our land? The numerous temples, whose spires point heavenward, from Maine to California, proclaim that we are a religious people. We must go back to the early establishment of Christian Churches throughout this land, but it must needs be a mere outline. Large bodies of Congregationalists, or Independents (as they were called in Cromwell's time), settled in New England in the seventeenth century. Their peculiar feature was a rejection of Episcopacy, of the Book of Common Prayer, and all the ritual of the Church of their mother country. Each congregation was united by a covenant, submitting themselves to a pastor of their own choice, and exercising discipline through certain ruling elders. Their doctrinal views were those of Calvin, but in *later* days their Calvinism has been much modified. They came to the New World, to the wilderness, "for freedom to worship God," and to effect a more perfect *reformation* than had been achieved in their native land. We believe there were many of these whose hearts were governed by strong, personal religion. Of their earnest piety there are abundant records, landmarks deep and broad.

But the consciences of these men, or of their *rulers*, seem to have been moulded more in the stern principles of the law than in the tender love of the gospel. Their self-will in matters religious was great. The lives and writings of their early governors and magistrates, are full of strong, personal religion. But they had not learned from their own persecutions lessons of toleration. Numerous sectaries soon pressed into the New England colonies. Baptists, Quakers, Church of England men, were all dealt with harshly. Quakers were treated with great severity. Banishment and imprisonment were the punishments most frequently resorted to. "For the security of the flock we pen up the wolf, but a door is left purposely open, whereby he who interferes with our religion may depart at his pleasure." The Puritans were at first too busy to occupy their thoughts with the instruction and conversion of the Indians. About 1634, John Elliot crossed the Atlantic to become the apostle of the Indians. Elliot was a man of primitive piety and zeal; he had been thoroughly educated at Cambridge, and he labored much in mastering the difficulties of the Indian language, of which there are many dialects. For the support of missions to the Indians a large fund had been collected in Cromwell's time. After the Restoration, this fund or trust was directed, through the influence of Clarendon, to the purpose for which it was intended.*

---

* NOTE ON UNITARIANISM.—Unitarianism has taken deep root, during the last century, in New England, especially in Boston. The creed of Unitarians is not easily defined, as they disavow the right to impose creeds. There are, therefore, many shades of faith in the Unitarian body. They all agree in the subordination of the Son to the Father. Arianism, in the early ages of the Church, was so much like Trinitarianism that it was not always easy to detect the difference. Modern

The honorable Robert Boyle, a distinguished philosopher and Christian, was placed at the head of this *trust* for the improvement of the Indians, the funds of which were mainly expended at this time in printing the Bible, and other religious books, of Elliot's translating, in the Indian tongue. His labor and example were not without fruit. About a century before this time, the venerable and admirable Las Casas, Bishop of the Roman Catholic Church, had labored in the wilds of Central America to Christianize and enlighten the Indian tribes of that region. So we see that when the love of Christ constrains us, Christians of every name will labor in His cause and suffer for His sake. "When Thou hadst overcome the sharpness of death, Thou didst open the kingdom of heaven to all believers."

At the close of the seventeenth century many well directed efforts were made for the propagation of the gospel among the heathen natives of New England. In the year 1685, the Bishop of London persuaded Dr. Blair to go as his Commissary to Virginia. For fifty-three years he zealously discharged its duties. By him the project of training for the ministry the English and Indian youth was revived, and through his labors brought at last to a successful issue in the establishment of the college of "William and Mary." Had Dr. Blair been made a *Bishop* instead of a Commissary,

---

Unitarianism is more outspoken. Dr. Priestley in the eighteenth century, and Socinus in the sixteenth, were distinguished teachers of a modified Unitarianism. Dr. Channing exercised much influence over his brethren in withdrawing them from controversial divinity. Dr. Channing was an eloquent sermonizer, and a devout, learned man. Theodore Parker, of Boston, and James Martineau, of England, have been leaders in what is called "A New School of Thought." Unitarians have been active in works of benevolence.

how different might have been the history of the Church Episcopal in the eighteenth century! It is probable that it was during the administration of Dr. Blair that the substantial brick churches were built in Virginia that still endure to attest the care of the mother-church for her colonial children. The writer of these lines has worshiped in a church with the date 1706 affixed to the walls. Dr. Bray was sent to Maryland as commissary soon after Dr. Blair. Dr. Bray was a man of rare devotion. He abandoned "the prospect of large English preferment, to nourish the infant church under many difficulties in the spiritual wastes of Maryland."

New Amsterdam, or New York, as it was called after its cession to the British, was finally given up to the English at the treaty of Breda, in 1667. The garrison chapel was now devoted to the use of the Church of England. "In 1696, another church was built called 'Trinity.' It was endowed by Gov. Fletcher temporarily, and in perpetuity by his successor Lord Combury." This then was the beginning of the famous Trinity of New York city, which has been enabled by her wealth and by God's blessing to plant so many branches from the parent tree. In 1679, a petition from a large body of people in the town of Boston was presented to Charles II., "that a church might be allowed in that city for the exercise of religion, according to the Church of England, bearing the name of the King's Chapel." It was found that throughout the populous district around Boston, there were but four clergymen who called themselves ministers of the Church of England. This being reported to the Church at home, several of the Bishops set to work to adopt some means to increase the number of missionaries and excite a zealous missionary spirit. A charter of incorporation was obtained as "The Society for the Propagation of the Gospel," in June, 1701, under the Archbishop of Canterbury as their president. Many great names in the English Church appear in the catalogue of their first and warmest supporters. Among these names were Beveridge, Wake, and Sharp, Gibson and Berkeley. The last mentioned Bishop, Berkeley, lived after this time in Newport, Rhode Island, two or three years. He came to America with the hope of carrying out a benevolent scheme he had formed of establishing a college in the Bermudas. Notwithstanding the efforts of his friends in England to aid him, they were all thwarted by Sir Robert Walpole, the premier, who was averse to strengthening the Church, and cared nothing for religion or morals.

In Trinity Church, Newport, Rhode Island, where Berkeley often preached, is to be seen the organ that he presented to this church after his return to the Old World. Through the influence of Queen Caroline, wife of George II., Berkeley was made Bishop of Cloyne, in Ireland. He gave to Yale College a library of 880 volumes. Atterbury said of Berkeley: "So much knowledge, so much piety, so much innocence and humility, I should have thought confined to angels, had I never known this gentleman." Berkeley was celebrated as a philosopher. He believed in and taught the strange theory of the non-existence of matter. Berkeley had an implicit trust in revelation, and never dreamed that his theories would be used as weapons of skepticism. Berkeley, until his death in 1763, never ceased to urge his countrymen to the discharge of their duty to the American colonies.

Bishops Butler, Sherlock and Gibson labored in vain with the court and ministry to send over a Bishop or Bishops to overlook and minister to the plantations in America.* But Walpole's government was dead to all appeals founded upon moral and religious principles. In Virginia, as in England, the Methodist Society had been formed in communion with the Church of England. Mr. Asbury, in America, a leader of the Methodists, had kept the young exhorters under his charge from assuming the power of ordained men. But after the American Revolution, Wesley, at the age of eighty-two, was persuaded (seeing that the mother-church had not yet sent a Bishop) to set apart Dr. Coke as a Bishop or Superintendent, and gave him authority to ordain Francis Asbury to the same office. Dr. Coke had been educated at Oxford, and was a Presbyter of the Church of England. In company with Asbury he traveled from one end of this country to the other, preaching and administering the sacraments. They then began to lay the foundations of the goodly structure which now occupies so large a place and portion in our land.

The first Wesleyan Conference was held in England in 1744. In this Conference, as in all subsequent Conferences, Wesley urged the importance of adhering to the established Church. Besides the two Wesleys, there were present † four ordained ministers of the Church of England and four lay preachers. He would say to his hearers: "Look all around you; you can not unite with the Presbyterians, Baptists, Quakers, or any

---

* Wilberforce. † At this first Conference.

others, unless you hold the same *opinions* with them; but the Methodists do not insist upon *this* or *that* opinion—they think and let think. This liberty of conscience is our glorying, and a glorying peculiar to us." Wesley, however, must have yielded *at the last* his opinion with regard to the necessity of ordination by a Bishop, or he would not as a Presbyter have assumed the power of ordination. He was doubtless betrayed into this irregularity by an ardent love for the souls of men, believing that with the *name* and authority of *Bishop*, an officer known from the earliest ages of the Church, more good could be effected. He was doubtless disgusted with the slowness and want of earnest zeal in the establishment, which delayed so long in sending an officer so necessary for godly discipline in the Episcopal Church.

Bishop Meade says, in speaking of the Episcopal Church of Virginia: "The authority of a Commissary was a very insufficient substitute for the superintendence of a faithful Bishop. For nearly two centuries did the Episcopal Church in Virginia try the experiment of a system whose constitution *required* such a head, but was actually without it. No such officer was there to watch over the conduct and punish the vices of the clergy." The Bishop of London was, of necessity, only the nominal bishop. It is evident that the Episcopal Church, without such an officer, is more likely to *suffer* than any other Christian Society, because our own church makes this office indispensable to some important parts of ecclesiastical government and discipline.

The Episcopal Church in Virginia commenced with the first settlement of the first colony. The code of laws of that colony was drawn up at a time when religion, as Bishop Taylor expresses it, "was painted upon banners divine, moral and *martial*," the laws being enforced sometimes in that day by civil pains and penalties, which we would fain forget. Oppression and arbitrary rule in this colony (we mean in its first history) is connected alone with *one* name, that of Argall, who in 1616 became governor for three years. He was removed by the Captain General Yeardley, and the wrongs of the colonists redressed.

So long as the heroic Smith remained with the colony, the hostilities of the Indians were restrained, and the injudicious acts of some members of the Council overruled. One of the first acts of Smith and his associates, after landing at Jamestown, was the erection of a rude church, made by fastening poles in the ground, with the sails of their vessels as a roof. Their first church, built of logs, was destroyed by fire; but as an evidence of their religious zeal, they soon erected another. A very erroneous idea of the first settlers at Jamestown, Virginia, has been adopted by some. We would not detract an iota from the pious faith that governed the Pilgrims of Plymouth in 1620; but if there is any truth in history, the little band that landed in Virginia in 1607 contained a large proportion of pious, noble souls. It was declared by some of them that their chief motive in crossing the sea was to instruct and convert the Indians. See the pious exercises of Rolfe, as related by Bancroft. In all the trials of Smith, in contending with the treachery and hostility of the Indians, he was supported by the zealous aid of the Rev. Mr. Hunt. There were three earnest ministers of Christ among the earliest settlers at Jamestown—Mr. Hunt, Mr. Bucke, who came over with Lord Delaware, and Mr. Whitaker. The name of Whitaker is connected with the romantic story of the first Indian convert, Pochahontas, whom he baptized into the Church of Christ.

"It was the great happiness of Virginia," says Wilberforce, in his History of the Church in Virginia, "that the company who managed her affairs looked *far beyond* commercial profit." The first care of Mr. Edward Sandys and Sir Nicholas Ferrar was to provide for a settled population by promoting female emigration and colonial marriages. They founded very early a college for both English and Indian youth. They set apart ten thousand acres of land for the support of this college." But though thus happy in the character of some of her early settlers, and especially in her early clergy, it must not be supposed that the infant church flourished, without many drawbacks and discouragements. That there was much sincere piety among those who incorporated the forms of the Episcopal Church in the colony of Virginia, I doubt not, says Bishop Meade, nor do I question the piety and fidelity of *some* of the pastors and people during their whole subsequent history; but it must be acknowledged that her spiritual condition was specially defective during a large part of the eighteenth century. Not more than one-half of the congregations were supplied with ministers, the rest of them being served by lay readers. There was at this time very defective preaching, and some of the clergy were addicted to all the fashionable vices of the day.

In the Church of Virginia there were few who made soul-stirring appeals to men "to flee from the wrath to come." The devoted Mr. Jarrett, and a few others, were faithful watchmen upon "the towers of Zion."

The war of the Revolution was approaching, and with it the partial eclipse of the *light* that had shone so brightly during the seventeenth century. The attachment of some of the clergy to the cause of the king subjected the Episcopal Church to suspicion, yet the great commander of the American armies was her devoted friend. The dispute about' church property came on; she was deprived of all the glebe lands that had been bestowed upon her by the mother-church of England. Many of her church buildings, erected in the early times, were occupied by the Baptists and other sects. The chief cause of the evils that came upon the Episcopal Church must have been the unfaithfulness of her clergy.

When the War of the Revolution began in 1775, Virginia had ninety-one clergymen officiating in one hundred and sixty-four churches and chapels; at its *close*, it is stated, that only twenty-eight ministers were found laboring in the best parishes of the State. The flame of devotion was kept burning in many excellent families by attention to the services of prayer in the prayer-book, by teaching the children regularly the catechism, and requiring them to commit to memory portions of scripture. Also, the morning and evening hymns of Bishop Ken, of Cowper and Wesley.

The morning service, when there was no public worship in the neighborhood, was read on Sunday in many households. Such families were effective auxiliaries in the resuscitation of the Church.

How often, says Bishop Meade, in looking at the present (1855) comparative prosperity of our Church, do we say, "Surely our Lord must have loved this branch of the holy Catholic Church, or he would not have borne so long with her unfaithfulness, or so readily have forgiven her sins."

CHAPTER XLV.

CONSECRATION OF BISHOPS OF THE P. E. CHURCH FOR THE UNITED STATES.

"Who shall ascend into the hill of the Lord, or who shall stand in his holy place? He that hath clean hands and a pure heart; who hath not lifted up his soul to vanity, nor sworn deceitfully." We come now to the successful efforts of the faithful in strengthening the things that seemed ready to perish. The Episcopal churches in America had felt, in consequence of their imperfect organization, that their beloved Church, "little by little, was drooping into decay." Candidates for orders were compelled to *cross the sea* for ordination, in order to obtain the episcopate.

Connecticut, New York, Pennsylvania, Virginia, now resolved to make an effort to obtain consecration for a Bishop from abroad. Dr. Griffith, a Presbyter of the church in Alexandria, Va., was selected for that diocese; but so depressed was the pecuniary condition of the friends of the Church in that vicinity (it was directly after the war), that suitable arrangements for his departure were not made until two years after his election. Meanwhile delicate health had supervened. Samuel Seabury, of Connecticut, who had suffered persecution in his own State for his devotion to Episcopacy, determined to cross the sea to obtain that which he and the whole Church, scattered and disjointed, as it was, so ardently coveted. Seabury received from three Scotch bishops—Petrie, Skinner and Kilgour—"a free, valid and purely ecclesiastical Episcopacy." His consecration took place in Aberdeen, 1784.

In 1787, Wm. White was consecrated Bishop of Pennsylvania, and Samuel Provoost, Bishop of New York, by the Archbishop of Canterbury, at Lambeth Palace. Dr. Madison, of Virginia, received consecration from the same prelate, at Lambeth, in 1790. Madison entered upon his duties with zeal. He admits that the depressed state of his church was chiefly due to the want of zeal in her clergy. Bishop Madison made an effort to bring back the followers of Wesley. It was too late. They had severed the tie.

After a few visitations of Bishop Madison through his diocese, he seemed to become discouraged with the languor of church affairs. The duties of the College of William and Mary, of which he was now President, absorbed much of his attention. At the Convention which met in 1805 he called for a suffragan or assistant Bishop. This call received no attention, and no convention met again until after Bishop Madison's death in 1812. During this interval, however, a young man was ordained to the Diaconate by Bishop Madison, who was called the Apostle of Virginia, and certainly won this title by his great ability, devotion and energy in the cause of Christ and his Church.

But Mr. Meade, the young man to whom I have alluded, may speak for himself, as I have near me a volume in which he recounts some of his early labors and struggles to resuscitate the Church of his fathers. "My earliest recollections of the Church are derived from my attendance at a stone chapel in Frederick county (then the backwoods of Virginia), whither I went either behind my father on horseback, or with my mother and the children in an English chariot. My father had lost, during the war of the Revolution, nearly all his property. In this war he had served as aid to General Washington. At the close of the war my father removed to the fertile and beautiful valley of Frederick, lying between the Blue Ridge and Allegheny Mountains. My father had taken an active part in the erection of this house of God.* It was about seven miles from our home. The clergyman was Mr. Balmaine. He had been a chaplain in the United States Army. He was very attentive to his clerical duties, and preached alternately at Winchester, where he lived, and in the chapel. The churches were about ten miles apart. When there was no service at the chapel, my father read the *prayers* at home in the assembled family; also a sermon. When a death occurred among the servants, he performed the burial service himself, and read Blair's Sermon on Death the following Sunday. "It was in the stone chapel that I officiated during the first twenty-five years of my ministry. At the age of seventeen I was sent to Princeton College, where, of course, I had no opportunities of acquiring any further knowledge of my own Church at that time, as there was then no Episcopal church at Princeton." He had been receiving, during his sojourn at Princeton, admirable letters from his mother and his elder sister, Mrs. Page, encouraging him to enter the ministry of the Episcopal Church, as they discovered from his letters the serious turn of his mind.

Before he left Princeton, when but nineteen years of age, the first *honors* were awarded to him, shared

---

* The stone chapel.

by two others, in a class of forty. While at college he says, "I had only one or two religious associates, and but few helps to advancement in the divine life. I took pleasure, however, in reading a few pious books, and was engaged in a warfare with my body." He speaks of some of the books that enlightened his mind at this time. These were the sermons and lectures of Bishop Porteus, Wilberforce's Practical View, and the works of Mrs. Hannah More. He thinks these books were largely instrumental in producing evangelical views among the influential families in Virginia. The books most in use before this time, at least among Mr. Meade's friends, were Blair's Sermons, The Whole Duty of Man, Sterne's Works, The Spectator, and sometimes Tillotson's Sermons, which were of the highest grade then in use. Of course we mean the religious works that were in popular use.

This was a very literary age, and some of the professors at Williamsburg were men of great erudition. But the pulpit needed much reform, for the sermons, for a long time, had been almost entirely moral essays, with the exception of the holy Mr. Jarrat's teaching, and a few others.

In February, 1811, Mr. Meade proceeded to Williamsburg, a distance of 200 miles, performing the journey on horseback. He went thither to receive ordination from Bishop Madison. He describes the church building at Williamsburg as in a desolate condition.

Bishop Madison was the President of William and Mary at this time. Though regarded as a pious and learned man, he seems to have been more engaged with the philosophical and literary studies of the professor's chair than with the sacred duties of the bishopric.

This institution at Williamsburg, of which we have spoken, was the *Alma Mater* of Jefferson, Madison, and many other noble sons, some of whom were very dear to the writer of these lines. Mr. Meade, after receiving his ordination to the Diaconate, proceeded to Richmond. He was much discouraged at the condition of the church buildings, as well as the low state of piety that he witnessed in both these cities. Less than a year after Mr. Meade's visit to Richmond, a large church was erected in Richmond called the Monumental Church, so called because it was built on the site of a theatre burned in December, 1811. It was considered as a monument to the loved and lost, as well as a temple for the worship of God. Mr. Meade commenced his ministry in the "stone chapel" in Frederick, but in a few months he took charge of Christ Church in Alexandria. He made salutary changes in the habits of the church people of Alexandria. Members of Congress came over from Washington to hear the young gifted preacher. Among these were John Randolph and James Milnor.

Mr. M. was a distinguished lawyer from Philadelphia. His connection with Meade began at a time when his religious character and new purposes of life were receiving their direction. He had now the privilege of such spiritual teaching as was rare in these days. How largely Mr. Milnor was indebted to this association with Mr. Meade, for those clear views which determined him to relinquish a profession which had secured to him honor and wealth, and to devote the rest of his life to the ministry of the gospel, is one of those disclosures reserved for the last day. Mr. Meade's pen, too, was often employed in preparing manuals of instruction for the young and prayers for families. His influence was so practical that "Family Prayer" became the general rule in congregations where he ministered.

In the spring of 1812 Bishop Madison died. The first voice that was raised to rouse and rally the supine members of the Church was that of the young Deacon that ministered in Alexandria. He, in conjunction with the Rev. W. H. Wilmer, wrote to the Rev. Dr. Buchanan, of Richmond, requesting him to call a Convention in May. Mr. Wilmer had come to Alexandria as pastor of St. Paul's Church.

When Mr. Meade was ordained to the priesthood, the ordaining was performed by Bishop Clagget, of Maryland, in Alexandria. The ordination sermon was preached by Mr. Wilmer. At the Convention in 1812 a professor in William and Mary College was nominated to the Episcopate. He received the majority of votes of the clergy, but the lay delegates, together with Mr. Wilmer, refused to vote, on some technical ground. Mr. Meade, with his accustomed moral courage, said with much pain that his refusal to vote was not from anything connected with the proceedings, but from an honest conviction of the unworthiness of the Bishop-elect. The professor, however, who had been elected, feeling perhaps his own unfitness for so responsible and so holy an office, sent in, soon after his appointment, his resignation, which was accepted. The honest conscientiousness of Mr. Meade and others, in their refusal to vote for Dr. Bracken, and his consequent resignation, opened the way for the entrance of the honored and beloved Richard Channing Moore. He came to Virginia from the diocese of New York. "He soon," says Mr. Meade, "became as one of us, and the people and clergy of Virginia loved him more and more unto his life's end."

In 1814, Dr. Moore was declared to be duly elected to the Episcopate of the Diocese of Virginia. With Mr. Moore's consecration, hope sprung in the hearts of many who had been hitherto despairing. The efforts of Bishop Moore were unremitting to build up "the waste places" of the Diocese committed to his care. He had many qualifications for the work of revival. His imposing, venerable presence,* his melodious voice, his fervid, eloquent preaching, his evangelical doctrine, his peace-loving temper, and above all, his warm love and zeal for the cause of the Master, and for the interests of his Church, contributed to make this servant of God eminently successful.

The Church greatly revived and increased under his ministrations. He exerted a hallowed influence over his clerical and lay associates. His parochial engagements with the Monumental Church in Richmond prevented him from crossing the Alleghany Mountains or visiting the more remote parts of the State.† He visited North Carolina when it was without a Bishop, after the death of Bishop Ravenscroft, in 1830. A large number of able, devoted men were now found among the clergy of Virginia.

---

*The life-like portraits of Bishop Moore attest his unusual personal advantages. The writer of these lines had in her youth the privilege of studying her Bible lessons with the daughters of Bishop M. in his well-furnished library.

† This section of the State, now separated and called West Virginia, has happily a diocese of her own. Under the energetic and zealous efforts of her present Bishop, the Rt. Rev. G. W. Peterkin, the Church, with the blessing of God, will be greatly strengthened and extended.

The Theological Seminary at Alexandria prospered. Dr. Keith, Dr. Wilmer and Mr. Norris, noble sons of learning and piety, were among her Professors. Mr. Meade was justly regarded as the father of the seminary at Alexandria. Though, as we have said, Bishop Moore was unable, from engagements and increasing infirmities, to visit West Virginia, yet he sent some excellent clergymen to that portion of the diocese at an early day.

We must now return to Mr. Meade, who was the assistant Bishop of Richard Channing Moore for the last twelve years of his life. After the erection of a church at Milwood, Clarke county, the stone chapel (of which we have spoken) was appropriated to the colored people. This example of providing church buildings for the slaves was followed in different parts of the State. Mr. Meade, many years before his death, liberated several families of his slaves and sent them to Pennsylvania. He was an active member of the Colonization Society.

Bishop Meade's sister, Mrs. Anne R. Page, of Clarke county, Va., was, it is believed, the first person in her native State who agitated the question of preparing slaves for freedom by suitable education. This lady devoted the best years of her life to the instruction of her own slaves. She afterwards sent them, fully provided with necessaries, to Liberia. An interesting memoir of this servant of God was written and published many years ago by the Rev. C. W. Andrews. "In a future world," says Gurley, in his Life of Ashman, when speaking of Mrs. Page and Mrs. Custis, "it may stand revealed that from the sacred retirement of a few devout ladies in Virginia, who, at the Savior's feet, had learned better lessons than this world can teach, emanated a zeal and charity in behalf of the *colored race*, which has widely spread, and has inspired ministers and statesmen with eloquence in their cause."

In 1829, Mr. Meade was made assistant Bishop of Virginia. On the death of the Rev. Channing Moore, in 1841, the *assistant* was made Bishop of Virginia, and in 1842, John Johns, of Maryland, was made assistant Bishop. Bishop Meade was engaged for thirteen years, during eight months in each year, in traveling over the State on horseback or in an open carriage. In after years, routes for traveling were easier, and the labor devolving upon the Bishop was performed in a shorter period.

The writer of these lines often heard the statement that Mr. Meade never received any compensation as Bishop for his varied and arduous services until Bishop Johns was associated with him. Then a change of circumstances occurred. We can appeal to his own written statement on this subject: "During the twenty-five years that I officiated in my parish in Frederick county, Va. (now Clarke), my salary did not exceed $250 or $300. I have been blamed for this; but in justice to my parish I must say that while I did not press my own claims, having a farm that yielded a sufficient support, I distinctly told my congregation of about thirty families that I should expect them to do more for other objects. According to my desire, my people for twenty-five years (at the end of which I gave up the charge) have annually sent out of the parish $1,000 for charitable purposes." This was a noble example of disinterested beneficence.

Mr. Meade was almost an ascetic in his way of living. He discouraged ostentation and luxury in every form. He lived in a refined, cultivated, hospitable neighborhood, but his household and belongings were marked by severe simplicity. His sermons on self-denial were very effective, because "he practiced what he preached."

We will close this long article on the Church in Virginia by quoting a few lines from Bishop Meade's writing in regard to his churchmanship: "I have frequently read over the arguments in favor of Episcopacy and concurred with entire satisfaction in the words of our consecration service. To those reading the Scriptures and the Holy Fathers, it evidently appears that from the Apostles' time there have been three orders of ministers. More than this our Church requires not even her Bishops to believe,* and he who would demand more may be conscientious, may be scriptural, but he has gone beyond the Church; he has departed from the spirit of the Episcopal Church of England or America. Whether God did positively ordain this form of church government as *essential* to the existence of a Church, what deviations from it would render ordination invalid, are points about which the most wise and learned and devoted Bishops have differed. I would that all embraced what I believe to

---

* Reply to a letter in Johns' Memoir of Meade.

NOTE.—Though the writer of these sketches has chiefly spoken of *the Bishops* of the P. E. Church, her heart turns with deep interest to noble Presbyters who have borne the burden and heat of the day. *In memoriam* is deeply engraven. May we mention C. W. Andrews, J. P. McGuire, James Chisholm, Dr. Sparrow—but their name is legion. Not only to these *known*, loved, honored, of *our communion*, but to all the true and faithful, though called by other names.

have been the Apostolic form. With none other would I be satisfied myself; but I dare not say God hath ever in this point rejected those whom he hath accepted and so highly blessed in others. I have the consolation of knowing that I herein agree with a noble company of Bishops and other ministers, whose labors in the gospel, and whose zealous attachment to the Church, I follow at a distance."

As an evidence of the enthusiasm of Bishop Meade's character, he states that when he read a work of Soame Jenyns on the "Atonement," he was so penetrated with the truth that Christ was indeed the sacrifice for the sins of the world, that he rose from his bed several times during the perusal, that he might praise God for enabling the author to testify so clearly and powerfully to so important a truth—the cornerstone of the Christian system.*

---

* Before we leave the subject of "the Bishops of Virginia," of whom perhaps *strangers* might say we have already said too much, we must testify to the matchless lightning-like eloquence of Bishop Johns. It *electrified* his hearers.

CHAPTER LXVI.

HOBART, GRISWOLD, EASTBURN, CHASE.

Bishop Hobart was the great energizing spirit that infused life and activity into the Episcopal Church in the State of New York. He was the head of the High Church party, but full of zeal for his Master's service. Bishop Hobart was specially active in founding a theological seminary in New York City. The result of his efforts is the General Theological Seminary. About the same time that Dr. Hobart was made bishop of New York, Alexander Viets Griswold was made bishop of what was then called the Eastern diocese, consisting of the States of Massachusetts, Rhode Island, New Hampshire and Vermont. They* were consecrated by Bishop White, of Pennsylvania, assisted by the bishops of New York and Connecticut. Mr. Griswold had labored as deacon and presbyter in three parishes in Massachusetts. Besides his clerical labors, in order to eke out a support for a large family, he was compelled to devote portions of his time to teaching and farming. "No ten years of my life," he said, "have been happier than the time passed in those three parishes."

In 1836 Griswold became the presiding bishop. The last act of Mr. Griswold was the consecration of Mr. Eastburn. Mr. Griswold was what is termed a

---

* Hobart and Griswold.

moderate churchman. He wrote * some valuable sermons. Bishop Griswold was the father-in-law of the distinguished Dr. Stephen Tyng, and the grandfather of Rev. Dudley A. Tyng and Stephen Tyng, Jun., so conspicuous for religious zeal and ability.

Philander Chase was the pioneer bishop of the West. He was a native of New Hampshire, and a Congregationalist in his religious views. After examining a prayer-book with great care, he was led to the conviction that he ought to enter the ministry of "the Church of the Book." He was ordained in St. George's Church, New York, in May, 1798. For some years he devoted himself to missionary labors in Western New York. He afterwards went South for his wife's health. While there he organized a church in New Orleans.

Mr. Chase came to Ohio in 1817. A diocese having been formed in Ohio, he was elected its bishop, and was consecrated in St. James' Church, Philadelphia, February 11, 1819. He now formed a design of founding a college and theological seminary in Ohio. With energetic perseverance he carried out his plan, though through much opposition and difficulty. He went to England in 1823, where he collected $30,000. He purchased 8,000 acres, giving he names of this benefactors, Lord Kenyon to the college, and Gambier to the site on which a village is built. Some troubles arising between the bishop and his clergy—some difference of opinion as to the disposition of funds—he resigned his jurisdiction in Ohio as bishop, and his administration of the affairs of the university in 1831. The General Convention gave their assent to this step.

* Published.

He was elected bishop of Illinois in 1835. Again he went to England in behalf of the education of the West, and collected money enough to enable him to found another institution of learning, which he called Jubilee College, in Peoria county, Ill. This college was opened in 1847. Bishop Chase spent the remainder of his life in Illinois.

As we have merely intended, in these Annals, to *sketch* the outlines of work and character of those bishops who laid the foundations of our church broadly and deeply in our beloved country, our task is almost done. We well remember the consecration of a bishop for Louisiana in 1838. It took place in Cincinnati. The service had commenced when we entered. The sweet and singularly sonorous voice of Meade, and the earnest impressive tones of Bishop Smith were heard above the rest. The refined and still youthful form of Leonidas Polk was the very symbol of purity. Bishop McIlvaine grandly preached the consecration sermon. The bishop-elect had been one of his converts, when McIlvaine was chaplain at West Point. We remember *he* said, "The church delights to call her servants from the most humble positions to fill the highest places in her gift." He said *this* in relation to the post Mr. Polk occupied when elected to the Episcopate. Mr. Polk was a young man of large wealth. After being in the ministry for a few years he went to Europe. On his return, finding himself without a parish, he went to Tennessee, his native State, where he had a large church erected * for the especial use of the colored people. He was the pastor of a congregation of negroes when called to take a bishop's place. The

---

* At his own expense.

sequel to his history is very sad. When the civil war commenced, as he had had a military education, he believed it to be his duty to lay aside his sacred robes and take up the sword. Fatal mistake! He soon perished, and his beautiful life was quenched in blood.

We can not dismiss this subject of the *early* bishops without speaking of Bishop Payne, who devoted the best years of his life to the most uninteresting of all mission fields, at least in a worldly point of view, the western shore of Africa. But in another aspect, exclusive of the claim that all souls have upon the Christian heart, the long service of her children in this country, ought to invoke a peculiar and strong interest. We make our extracts, with regard to Mr. Payne, from a letter written by himself to an old college friend, in 1874, a short period before his death, from his old home in Westmoreland county, Va.

"As we have never met," says Mr. Payne, to his correspondent, "since our separation at college, forty-one years ago, I will briefly relate my subsequent history. Leaving Williamsburg in 1833, thinking myself called to the ministry, I entered the theological seminary nearly Alexandria. After three years' residence there I was ordained. Believing that as a good soldier I should go where my services were most needed, I sought what I believed to be the most needy portion of the missionary field. In the spring of 1837 I sailed for Cape Palmas latitude 4° north in West Africa. I expected to live there about ten years. I remained thirty-three! After being in Africa fifteen years I was elected by the General Convention missionary bishop of Cape Palmas and the parts adjacent. Beginning at Cape Palmas with eight communicants, I, with other missionaries, gathered six hundred. I ordained about a dozen colored ministers. In 1869, my health so entirely failed that I returned to the United States, and in 1871 resigned my position. I am now living in my native county, Westmoreland, having in it Wakefield, the birthplace of the Father of his country. The parish Washington being vacant, I was invited to take charge of it. My wife, her sister, a nephew and niece constitute my family. I have a comfortable home in the upper part of this county. I have named my home 'Cavalla,' after the home in which I passed thirty happy years in Africa. Will you believe it?" Oct. 19, 1874.

One more little incident with regard to Bishop John Payne. He was frequently invited to preach after his return to his native county. On one occasion, when he was preaching at Yeocomico church, a gentleman, advanced in years, approached the chancel to partake of the Lord's Supper for the first time. This[*] gentleman was a man of exemplary Christian morals, and had much influence in his neighborhood. He had resisted until now the most eloquent appeals to partake of 'the Lord's Supper. The congregation were stilled by deep emotion when this beloved, honored man, so long known by them all, approached the chancel. This earnest old man from Africa could now add another leaf to the chaplet of immortelles he had gathered in the far-off land. There are many honored names in the episcopate, and also among our presbyters (some noble presbyters of blessed memory) that our limits will not permit us to mention, north and south, east and west. We have heard sermons from Presbyterians,

[*] Hon. Willoughby Newton, of Westmoreland county.

Methodists and Baptists that made our hearts to glow with thankfulness that God had raised up such witnesses to his truth.

We remember laymen of different ecclesiastical names who did much to recommend religion by their excellent conduct to all around them. Especially does memory dwell* on one beloved and exemplary layman,† who, for a series of years kept alive the flame of devotion among his neighbors (when no clergyman was at hand) by reading to them, in a "forest sanctuary," the prayers of the church and very admirable sermons. The missionary bishops of the Northwest have our most cordial sympathy. At the close of the civil war, the conciliation of Bishop Hopkins, of Vermont, must not be forgotten. He wrote brotherly Christian letters to Bishop Atkinson and other Southern Bishops. So potent is Christian love, that not a scar remains of the wounds made by differing political or sectional sentiment. Differing religious opinions, however, have presented some phases more *difficult* to treat.

About the year 1833, there was a movement at Oxford, England, called the Tractarian movement. Drs. Pusey and Newman, and others well known in England, began to publish a series of tracts connected with the faith and practice of the Church. These tractarians labored in their writings to bring the Church, as they said, more in accordance with the usages of the primitive ages of the Christian Church. The leaders of this movement lost their positions in the University of Ox-

---

* *Memoriæ prodere.*

* Col. Edward Colston, of Berkeley county, in the Valley of Virginia.

ford. Dr. Pusey continues in the communion of the English Church, but Newman, Manning and many others entered the Church of Rome. The Ritualistic movement, both in England and America, is the result of "Tractarianism." The Ritualists allege that they wish only to give impressiveness and beauty to the service by the introduction of more music and richer dresses. But it is believed that they symbolize in some of their innovations doctrines that are opposed to the standards of Protestantism and of the Episcopal Church. Some of the Ritualists believe that our presbyters are real priests, in the Jewish and Roman Catholic sense, and that when they offer the consecrated bread and wine, they offer real sacrifice. This view seems to Protestants to contradict our reason and common sense, as well as the plain, clear words of Scripture. The literal words of our Lord, but still more, the voice of priestly authority, induced many faithful souls to receive this view; yet all down the ages there have been voices lifted up in revolt against it. The delicate lines of distinction drawn by the Ritualists, between their views and the Romanists' view, are not easily grasped.

CHAPTER XLVII.

An adverse circumstance in the history of the Episcopal Church is to be found in the defection of Bishop Cummins. He was the assistant bishop in the diocese of Kentucky. Mr. Cummins was a preacher of remarkable eloquence, of pure morals and holy conduct. He became dissatisfied with some expressions in the prayer-book, connected with the baptismal service. Mr. Cummins became a schismatic and founded another church, which he called the Reformed Episcopal. This church retains the Book of Common Prayer, with few alterations.

Dr. Muhlénburg once proposed, we believe, to our General Convention to permit some alternating words in the baptismal service. Had the suggestions of this godly, liberal man been heeded, this schism perhaps might have been avoided. No church is infallible. There have been transient divisions in this country in nearly all the Protestant bodies. The Presbyterians, who, by their uncompromising principles for what they deem right, and by their pulpit ability, have drawn so many of the most intelligent classes into their churches, especially in Kentucky, separated forty years ago into what was called Old and New School. These differences were doctrinal. The breach is now healed and they commune together. The Methodists, too, have had their divisions. During the civil war they were divided into Northern and Southern Methodists. Their differences were political or sectional. The Methodists, through their zeal and wise church government, are very numerous. The writer of these lines remembers the thrilling eloquence of some of their preachers in the early days. The Baptists are very numerous; they include a large number of differing sects, but all agreeing in one point—in the mode of baptism and in the exclusion of infants as subjects of baptism. The sect of Baptists (called Christians) who embrace the tenets of the late Alexander Campbell, are very numerous in the West, particularly in the State of Kentucky. Some very distinguished men have been connected with this communion.

In 1792, when Kentucky separated from Virginia, there were some Episcopalians among her emigrants; but these "few sheep in the wilderness" had no pastor to gather them into their once loved fold. Marshall says in his History of Kentucky, in speaking of the Episcopal Church: "This church requires an educated ministry. Her form of worship is highly decorous, and her discipline calculated to make good citizens." This is but a cold commentary on a liturgy bought by the blood of the martyrs.

1798 Mr. Moore was admitted to Holy Orders by Bishop Madison. He ministered to a congregation in Lexington, Ky., and was made President of Transylvania University. The first minister of any name who offered prayer and praise to the living God in Kentucky was the Rev. Mr. Lythe, an Episcopal clergyman, who was chaplain to a proprietary legislature. This service was held under an elm tree. Mr. Lythe presented a bill to this legislature: "To prevent Sabbath breaking and profane swearing." This legislature met near Harrodsburg in 1795.

Yet, while Episcopalians, according to the historian, waited for educated men, the Baptists, with the New Testament in their hands, ignorant of what the Fathers taught, drew multitudes into their connection. For half a century the Baptists had the chief control in the spiritual vineyard of Kentucky. The first Episcopal Council of Kentucky assembled in Lexington in 1829. The parishes of Louisville and Danville were represented by three clergymen and nine zealous laymen.

Bishop Brownell, of Connecticut, and Ravenscroft, of North Carolina, visited the struggling church in 1829, and Meade of Virginia, in 1831, went through the State from Maysville to Hopkinsville, in the performance of church work.

In 1832 Kentucky claimed a bishop for herself. B. B. Smith, the rector at Lexington, was elected bishop at a Council in Hopkinsville. He was consecrated in New York, St. Paul's Chapel, October, 1832. In the summer of 1833 the cholera raged in Lexington. This scourge took away two of his presbyters, three candidates for Holy Orders, and fifty communicants from the episcopal diocese. Bishop Smith faced the pestilence with great bravery. His courage and devotion to *all* the people within his reach, at this trying crisis, were long remembered. Bishop Smith was very active in the cause of education. He lectured in many of the little towns in Kentucky to arouse the people to introduce common schools. We remember long years ago hearing his sonorous voice lifted in behalf of common schools, after he had driven some miles through cold and darkness.

Louisville is the stronghold of episcopacy in Kentucky. This city abounds in charitable institutions. "The

John N. Norton Memorial Infirmary" has been recently reared with funds left by this man of blessed memory, whose praise is in all the churches.

Bishop T. U. Dudley is now the bishop of the P. E. Church in Kentucky. He has made many friends for his church by his eloquent zeal in the pulpit, and by his pen in behalf of noble enterprises. While we believe in the sins of heresy and schism, yet it behooves all Christians to remember what our Lord said to his disciples when they complained that certain persons performed miracles in Jesus' name, still they *follow* not with us, and we forbade them. The Master said to them, "Forbid them not, for they who are not against us are on our part." In these words our Lord forbids compulsory measures for opinions' sake and casts a defense around liberty of heart and conscience. All bodies of Christians, with their leaders, who seek in Christ's name to *cast out* the demons of selfishness, dishonesty, impurity, intemperance and all vice to such the hand of Christian fellowship should be extended. They may not follow with *us*, but we must rejoice in the work of all who earnestly seek to elevate humanity.

Though the Episcopal Church has extended widely and prospered well in this nineteenth century, yet it is still a little flock in our country when compared with the Methodists, Baptists, Romanists and Presbyterians. England, as a great commercial nation, has become the agent of extended missionary operations. She has carried Christianity, and with it the Anglican Episcopal Church, to the four quarters of the globe. She has sent her missionary bishops to India, Africa, Australia and to her possessions in North America; even to New Zealand, so lately known to civilization. The English Episcopate was introduced by Bishop Selwyn into New Zealand.

"The churches of the United States," says Dr. Schaff, "send more men and money for the conversion of the heathen than any other nation, except the English." These two branches of the Anglo-Saxon race, as they have control over the seas and commercial intercourse of the world, are evidently intended by Providence to propagate Bible Christianity to the end of the earth. Of the immense sum sent last year by the American Missionary Society, the Presbyterians sent one-fourth.

There is at Rome a great college called the Propaganda, where every language of the world is taught, to qualify missionaries for their work. The Roman Church, with its seeming uniformity, embraces a great variety of sentiment and discipline in her monastic orders. In the many denominations of Christendom there is much seeming division, yet there are really many points of agreement. In the Greek, Roman, Anglican and in the American Episcopal Church, the same Creeds are used—the Apostles' Creed and the Nicene Creed. They are agreed in the ministry of three orders; also in the use of a liturgy.

Protestant churches agree substantially in points of doctrine with each other. This is proved in the work now carried on, with great harmony, since 1870. We mean the revision of our English Bible. "This revision," says Dr. Schaff, "will be a monument of the spiritual unity and exegetical consensus of English-speaking Christendom." The largest ecclesiastical establishments in the world are those of the Greek Church.

There are said to be sixty-five millions of members in the East. The Patriarchs, of Constantinople, Antioch, Alexandria, Moscow, rule over many Dioceses and Bishops. This Church is not represented in this country.

The Greek Church objects to one clause in the Nicene Creed—the procession of the Holy Ghost from the Son. There are three strange races in our land. These are not the descendants of Japheth. The negroes, the Indians and the Chinese have presented difficult problems, not only to the government of the United States, but to the Church. Who could have foreseen that the wicked slave trade, which brought to these shores, and to the Islands, so many thousands of Africans would ever exemplify the paradox of the Psalmist, "The wrath of man shall praise thee." Enslaved millions have been civilized and Christianized, who would not have been reached in their own country.

This is no defense for slavery. No, no! but it is a side of the diagram that ought not to be overlooked. It proves that God, who sees the end from the beginning, can overrule the sin and cupidity of one race to the benefit of another. The civilization and Christianity of these poor people may be very imperfect, but is far, very far, above the degrading heathenism of their ancestors.

For a long course of years missionaries have been sent to China; the Jesuits have been particularly active in this field. Since the opening of the ports many years since, missionaries from every Protestant Church have found a place in that vast empire. Missions have been established in Japan with much success. Now a door is opened wide for Christianizing the Chinese within our own borders. How wonderful are the ways of God! Let the earth rejoice! The Lord reigneth! May our people professing to be Christian improve the opportunities thus presented. May no narrow, national policy hinder the good work; but, alas, race prejudice is an obstacle hard to surmount.

"Spiritual light," says Bishop Lee, "is dawning upon Mexico. Within ten or twelve years a Reformad Church, called the 'Church of Jesus,' has been opened in the city of Mexico." This movement claims sympathy from all who love pure primitive Christianity. This church in Mexico* has received Episcopal orders from our Protestant Episcopal Bishops.

NOTE ON JAPAN.—A late writer, an Englishwoman, gives us some facts as to the work of Christian missionaries in Japan. She speaks of the intelligent zeal of the C. M. S.; also of American missionaries. The mission stations of Osaka, Hioga and Sunda have all been opened by direct medical missionary effort. The writer complains of the small mission force sent to Japan. "Did our Father," she asks, "make the salvation of millions depend upon a church selfish, tardy and niggard in men and money?" Will we not be excused in giving a sketch of a Japanese convert? "Neesima, an intelligent Japanese, educated as a Sun Worshiper, saw at Tokio some Christian tracts in the Chinese tongue. He read them with interest, and at once received the belief of a Creator who had claims upon all his creatures. He had a strong sense of filial duty, but he now felt that the Christians' God required him to leave his parents and country. He went to Yedo, and went on board of a ship, hoping to learn from the American captain more of the new religion. The trade of Neesima was shipbuilding. He soon found that the captain knew little of religion. He, however, set out with him for Boston, studying English in the New Testament on his way thither. He was associated with Christians, in whom Christianity was a life as well as a creed. He gave up his trade and determined to devote himself to his countrymen, in teaching them the truths of the New Testament. He studied both at Andover and Amherst, and is now striving to elevate his Japanese countrymen."

---

*Since these lines were written about Mexico, some adverse circumstances have shadowed the advance of the "Church of Jesus" in Mexico.

Lo, the poor Indian! It is frequently said that the Indian race, the original lords of our wide domain, are fast dying out. It is said in some late reports that the number of Indians (exclusive of Alaska) in the United States is but 251,000.

There was much interest manifested in the early settlement of this country by the English for the conversion of the Indians, but this strange people, through all their tribes, seem to have been singularly inaccessible to changes in their condition. From the little log church at Jamestown, Va., where the baptism of Pocahontas, 275 years ago, was performed by the Rev. Mr. Whitaker, to the present time, the number of converts might almost be counted, so small has been the remnant embraced in the Christian fold. We suppose that Bishop Whipple, within a few years past, has done more for this people in these States than any other individual since the days of John Elliott. Archdeacon Kirby has ministered to the Indians for twenty-nine years past in British North America. He supposes there are 10,000 Christians in that desolate land. We must not forget, in this summary, the efforts made by French Roman Catholics to Christianize the Indians.

After the settlement of Canada by the French, missionary stations were established among different tribes by devoted, earnest men. Before the Pilgrims anchored at Cape Cod, Jesuit priests had penetrated in Eastern Maine. Marquette, Joliet and La Salle had erected the cross on the great rivers of the West. Commercial enterprise was connected with these missions; but of the noble Champlain it is said that he esteemed the saving of a soul more than the conquest of an empire. The Christianity of the Indians in Canada, and also in

Mexico is, we presume, the result of the early French and Spanish missions. It is mixed with much ignorance and superstition, but we can safely trust these wandering children, if they live up to the light they have, to the Great Spirit who will have compassion upon them in the days of their ignorance. The light of Christianity, as we have seen, has fitfully gleamed on the path of the red man at different periods. Their savagery, however, when let alone by Christianity or civilization, is terrible. Dr. Whately says there is no instance of a self-raised nation from savage life. Is not this fact an argument for the primeval civilization of man? Sin degraded man to savagery. Mighty efforts are now being made to convert the nations.

"Many," says the language of prophecy, "shall run to and fro, and knowledge shall be increased." But amid much hope there are some substantial fears. One writer tells us that from the great influx of Roman Catholics in this land, they must ultimately triumph, whereby civil and religious liberty will be endangered, if not destroyed. So far as civil liberty is concerned, we believe Roman Catholics appreciate political rights as much as Protestants. The Roman Church teaches many errors, mixed up with the truth; but we trust there are many within her fold who look above and beyond the vanities connected with her worship "to the Lamb of God that taketh away the sin of the world."

The church of Xavier and Fenelon must contain good Christians, though some of her Popes, deeming themselves infallible, have added to her faith doctrines not taught in the Scriptures and unknown in the purer and earlier ages of the Church. Far more to be dreaded than Romanism is the spirit of skepticism, that would question and explain away all the mysteries that our finite minds can not fully comprehend. Some foretell the approach of an age of unbelief. They inquire, are not points of doctrinal faith yielded now that were once held dear? To this position it may be replied that Biblical criticism is much better understood in the nineteenth century than in the sixteenth century. Some of the leaders that dominated religious thought in the early part of the Reformation, especially Calvin, who systematized and attempted to fit in the doctrines of the Bible to suit a preconceived system. Calvin was a grand logician and metaphysician, but, like the great Augustine in the fourth century, his theory seemed, to common minds, to sacrifice God's mercy or love to his sovereignty. The Christian of to-day thinks more for himself, and humbly trusts to his private judgment in studying the sacred oracles. He knows that all men are finite. He is willing to leave these hard questions to God, knowing that He alone is the great Artist and Metaphysician who can reconcile and solve the problems of God's sovereignty and man's free will. "Canst thou, by searching, find out God?" cries the Patriarch. "Canst thou find out the Almighty to perfection?" The scientist may explore at will the secrets of the material universe, but he can not explain the spiritual side of man's nature.

We know that our Father in heaven is a God of Love, and that in the name of Jesus Christ all blessings that are promised will be freely vouchsafed to those "who do justly love mercy and walk humbly with their God." From the time that our Lord said to his disciples on the mount, "Ye are my witnesses to the uttermost parts of the earth; go teach all nations, baptizing them in the name of the Father, Son and Holy Ghost," this work has gone forward. For three centuries it was a grand and glorious light to the nations of the world.

In the days of Constantine there was a partial eclipse of this glory. This was caused by "the friendship of the world." Desolating wars and the inroads of savage hordes, threatened civilization and Christianity with extinction. But this could not be. The promise of our Lord could not fail. The Church breasted the waves of the turbid waters, and now it securely rests upon the Rock of Ages. The earth shall be filled with the knowledge of the Lord, as the waters cover the sea.

> "Let all the saints terrestial sing
> With those to glory gone,
> For all the servants of our King
> In earth and heaven are one."

ALPHABETICAL INDEX.

Aramaic, or Syriac Language, 57.
African Martyrdoms.
Arius, 113. Nicene Council, 107, 108.
Alexander Severus, 84, 85.
Ambrose, Bishop of Milan, 137, 138, 139.
Alexander VI. (Borgia), 268.
Augustine, St, Bishop of Hippo in Africa, 146, 148.
Arianism Settled by Theodosius, A. D. 380, 163.
Augustin, Missionary to the Saxons in England, 175, 176.
Anselm of Canterbury, 216. Ammianus, 119.
Apocalypse, 63. Andalusia, 183. Apostles, 56.
Avignon, captivity of Boniface VIII., 283. Alcuin, 180.
Abbeys of the Middle Ages, 157, 158.
Athanasius, 116.
Anthony, 153. Alban, British Martyr, 97. Abelard, 217.
Articles of Lambeth, 403. Armenia, 96.
Alexandria, 57. Antioch, 30, 31, 57.
Adrian, Emperor, 64, 68.
Adrian's Dying Words, 69. (Note) Alaric, 150. Agrippa, 28-95, 449.
Atterbury, 436. Asbury, 450. Abbott, 419. Aurelius, 71. Aurelian, 79.
Aquinas, 280. Alhambra, 283. Albigenses, 201.

Bernard, St., 217. His hymn, 218. Berengarius, 260 (note).
Bancroft, 410. Beranger. Baptists, 362. Bishops U. S., 456.
Barret, 403. What is Reprobation?
Bacon, Francis, 380. Burleigh, 390. Burgundy, 414.
Beni, 414. Basis, 133. Benedict, 160.
Bede, 179, 180.
Bishops of Antioch, 91. Belisarius, 189.
Bertha, 173. Britons, 175.
Boniface, Missionary to the Germans, 184. Boniface VIII. (Pope), 248.
Becket, 239. Basil, 59, 117. Butler, 450.
Berkeley, 449. Bray, Blair, were Commissaries, 447.
Brick Churches (built by the Mother Church), 448, 450. Byzantine Temples, 180.
Besa, 356.

Cyprian, 87. Cyril of Jerusalem, 118, (valuable historian). Cyril of Alexandria, (fierce persecutor).
Chrysostom (the golden mouthed), 41, 67. Cid, 280. Caliphs, 284.
Circus of Nero, 48. Clement, Bishop of Rome, 62 A. D., 102. Constantine, 105, 109, 113.
Constantinople built by Constantine, 110, 111, 280. Charlemagne, 182.
Confessional, 287. Crusades, 221.
Council of Constance, 266. Chaucer,

260. Cromwell, Thomas, 330. Cromwell, Oliver, 430. Corpus Christi, 249.
Chivalry, 287. Christianity a Greek religion for three centuries, 145. Christianity Latin from St. Augustine's time, 148, 149. City of God, Augustine's work, 149-156.
Chillingworth, "Take away this persecution," 431.
Calvin, 400. Colet, 282. Cowper, 460. Cranmer, 399. Cartwright, 331.
Controversy on the ministry, 331. Cartwright and Whitgrift, Church buildings, 71. Colonization Society, 463.
Commissary, 447.
Corinthus, 52. Chase, 460. McIlvaine, successor to Chase in Ohio, and the eloquent Bedell, and the gifted, devout Jaggar, Bishop of Southern Ohio, now the Bishop of Northern Ohio—Cummins, 474.
Chapter 46th, Church in Ohio; 47th. Church in Kentucky.
Christianity (in Japan), Chinese, Indians, 480. Skepticism, 483.
Civilization primeval (according to Whately), Sin makes Savagery, 482.

Donatists, 102, 104. Diocletian, 54, 91.
Dante, 281. Decretals false, 181 (ninth century). Death of Julian, 130. Dunstan, 209. Dominic, 203. Decius, 85, 89.

Elizabeth, Queen of England, 380. Edict of Milan, 100 A D., 376.
Eneas Sylvius, 278 (afterwards Pius II.) Ephraim, 117.
Erasmus, 318, 320 Eusebius, 212. Ethelbert, 173. Eucharist, 247.
Episcepacy (Milman's view), 374, 362, 363. Erastus, 320.
Elagatalus, 83. Elders at Ephesus, 52. John Elliot, 446 (crossed the sea in 1634 to teach the Indians).

Felix, 42. Festus, 43. Fratricelli, 281. St. Francis, 203.
Funerals, 250. Fabiola, 250. Fenelon, 411. Falkland, 414.
Frederick Barbarossa, 205. Ferdinand and Isabella, 287.

Gregory I., 172, 175. Gregory VII., (Hildebrand), 198, 211, 212.
Gregory X., 237 Gregory Nyssa, 117. Gregory Nananzen, 139.
Gelerius, 95. Greek Church, 480. Genseric, 169. Gnostics, 53, 52.
Gratian, 133. Gibbon, 101. Griswold, 472, 471. Grindal, 389, (noble man!)
Garrison❦Chapel, 448, was given to the English for worship by the Dutch after the treaty of Breda.
Guyon, Madame, 411, 418. Godfrey Bouillon, 229. Gladiators, 114.

ALPHABETICAL INDEX.

Helena, mother of Constantine, 108. Hosius of Spain, 109, (presides at the Council of Nice). Huss, Martyr of Bohemia, 265. Hooker, 383. Howard, 443. Hymns of Ken, Cowper, Wesley, 454. Hymn of St. Bernard, 217.
Homoousious, 196. Hypatia Greek, 163. Henry IV:, German Emperor, 210.
Henry II. of England, 239. Hallam, 267. Hilda Abbess, 177.

Innocent I., 162. Irenæus, Martyr Bishop of Lyons, 49, 70. Ignatius, Martyr Bishop of Antioch, 68. Indians, 481. Inquisition, 286.
Indulgencies, 296. Iconoclasm, 188. Isabella, 236. Iona, 177. Independents, 445.

Japan, 480. Julius, Bishop of Rome, not at the Nicene Council, 109. Jamestown, 445, (three good clergymen at the settlement in 1607).
Jerome of Prague, 267. Jerome, 152, (translator of the Vulgate) in a cell at Bethlehem.
Josephus, 28. Jews, 63. Justin, Martyr, 72. Jansenists, 412.
Jewel, 382. James I., vain and vacillating, 408.

Knox, 375. Koran, 237. Knights Templar, 205. Knights Teutonic, 206. Knights Malta, Thomas à Kempis, 281.

Lanfranc, 215. Leo I, Pope, 166, 168. Leo, Emperor, Leo X. Pope, 296.
Luther, 296, 297. Louis IX. (the good king of France), 236, 237.
Louis XIV., 419. Latimer, 343. Loyola, 430 St. Lawrence, 90.
Laud, 390. Labarum (Constantine's), 99. Laterans, 243.
Letter of Clement, Bishop of Rome. 62. Latin Church (lost its unity), 279.
Leicester (opposed to the Church of England, 392. Grindal's Letter to the Queen, 392. Lombards, 192. (Charlemagne overturns the power of the Lombards and makes Pope Hadrian king, 192) A. D. 774.

Matilda, 216 (niece of Edgar Atheling). Monachism, 154. St. Martin, 144, 145.
Monica, mother of St. Augustine, 146
Mystics, 281. St. Maur. 260 (preserver of literature). Madison (Bishop), 460, 461. Bishop Moore. 462 (he built up the waste places). Meade, 460 461, 462.
Melchiades, 98. Magnentius, 98. Mother of Churches, 61 (Jerusalem).
Magyars, Martin V, 265. Moravians, 400.
Melanchthon, 236. Moors, 283. Monks (the word "monk" first appears in the fourth century), 154.

Nicholas V., 295. Nero, 48. Nicholas I., 81. Nestorius, 163. Nicomedia, 91.

Nominalists, 244. Newman, 465. Narses, 169.

Odoncer, 188. Omar, 125. Origen, 80. Orders, 1, 2, 3, 60.
Oldcastle or Lord Cotham, 260 (martyr).

Peter the Hermit, 224. St. Paul, 24. St. Peter, 25.
Pliny's Letter to Trajan, 66. Pragmatic Sanction, 239.
Petrarch, 281. Parker, 380. Polycarp, 74, 76. Parthian War, 76.
Pelagius, 164. St Patrick, 178. Pepin, 192. Ponthinus, 98.
Port Royal, 419. Port Royal Authors, 420. G. W. Peterkin, 462 (note). Memoir of Mrs. Poge, by C. W. Andrews, 463. Propaganda, 475. Prophesyings, 399.
Puritan, 391, 390. Priscillian, 144. Parliament of Paris, Polk, 465, 467. Payne, 467, 468. Pauline, Petrine, Apolline parties.

Quakers, 443, Fox, Barclay, Penn, leaders.

Rome, 62. Rienzi, 271. Raymond of Toulouse, 272. Rudolph, 213.
Radagaisus, 149. Raikes, 418. Ritualism, 470.

Servetus (martyr), 370. Sybilline Books, Silas, 36. Segismund, 264.
Savonorola, 268. Sclaves, 187. Sermons of Leo I., 168. Sylvester, 98.
See of Rome, Stilicho, 150. Saladin, 232. Sherlock, 412.

Temple of Jerusalem, 124. Teutonic Nations, 187. Theodosius, 142.
Tenth Persecution, 75. Tertullian, 61, 58. Te'zel, 296. Titus, 50. Theodosian Code, 116.
Talavera, 293. Torquemada, 289. Three Questions, 62. Toplady, 450, author of the hymn, "Rock of Ages." Tomb of Beckett (note), 241. *Theories* of the Visions of Constantine, 99. Trajan's Persecution, 64. True Church, 129.

Ulphilas, 135. Ulphilas Bible, 136. Universal Bishop, 170. Usher.

Valentinian I., 131. Valentinian II. 133. Valens, 133. Vatican, 48, 296. Valerian, 87.

Whipple, 476. Wesleys, John and Charles, Whitfield, 450, 460. Wickliffe, 263, 255. Wesselius, 282.

Ximenes, 236.

Zenobia, 90. Zuinglius, 297. Ziska, a famous Bohemian captain, 275. Zozimus, 101.

www.ingramcontent.com/pod-product-compliance
Lightning Source LLC
Chambersburg PA
CBHW051233300426
44114CB00011B/717